AF513018

The People and Culture of
Jammu-Kashmir-Ladakh

Attention Authors

Manas Publications is fighting a war to tell the world that India can win the battle not only by the bullet but also by pen. We are converting fighters into writers. There is no dearth of intellectuals in our country. However, their knowledge is confined to them only. No sincere effort has been made by any other publisher to channelise their knowledge. That is why the talent of every intellectual remains latent. An author always presents the raw material in the shape of a manuscript and it is the job of the publisher to convert it into a completely finished book. Manas has been motivating intellectuals continually and publishing their manuscripts for more than three decades and would like to publish your manuscript too. If you or your colleagues have a manuscript ready for publication or are working on it, contact us with a detailed synopsis and list of contents. Manas can also suggest you a suitable title for writing related to your area of expertise. Manas is known for its publishing quality. We take utmost care in production and give wide publicity to the book and its author through our national and international distribution network.

The People and Culture of Jammu-Kashmir-Ladakh

Parvéz Dewân, IAS

Manas Publications
(We Convert Fighters into Writers)
New Delhi-110002 (INDIA)

MANAS PUBLICATIONS
(Publishers, Library Suppliers, Importers & Exporters)
4402/5-A, Ansari Road (Opp. HDFC Bank)
Darya Ganj, New Delhi-110 002 (INDIA)
Off. ✆ 23260783, 23265523, Res. ✆ 23842660
Fax: 011-23272766
E-mail: manaspublications@vsnl.com
manaspublications@yahoo.com

© Parvez Dewan and
The Parvez Dewan Foundation
2011

ISBN 978-81-7049-343-3
Rs 995/-

No part of this book can be reproduced, stored in a retrieval system, or transmitted in any form, by any means, including mechanical, electronic, photocopying, recording, or otherwise, without prior written permission of the publisher.

The views expressed in this book are those of the author and not at all of the publisher. The publisher is not responsible for the views of the author and authenticity of the data, in any way whatsoever.

Designed at
Manas Publications

Printed in India at
IYN Graphics, Delhi
and published by Mrs Suman Lata for
Manas Publications, 4402/5-A, Ansari Road
(Opp. HDFC Bank),
Darya Ganj, New Delhi-110 002 (INDIA)

For the Seths

Sudershan, Kamlesh, Devinder, Pratima,

Ashwani, Nidhi, Akshit and Arnav

Some of the important books written by Parvéz Dewan, are:

A History of Jammu

A History of Kashmir

A History of Ladakh

Parvez Dewan's Jammu–Kashmir–Ladakh: Jammu

Parvez Dewan's Jammu–Kashmir–Ladakh: Kashmir

Parvez Dewan's Jammu–Kashmir–Ladakh: Ladakh

The Other Kashmir: Almost Everything About
Aksai Chin, Baltistan, Gilgit, Hunza, Mirpur, Muzaffarabad

Contents

Inside a Buddhist monastery, Ladakh

Winter in Gulmarg, Kashmir

Girl in Kashmiri costume and jewellery

A traditional, non-touristy boat on the Dal Lake, Srinagar, Kashmir

At the main entrance of an exquisite Muslim shrine, Kashmir

Floating vegetable market on the Dal Lake, Srinagar, Kashmir

Inside an intricately detailed Muslim shrine, Kashmir

Bakerwal (Muslim shepherd) children, Jammu and Kashmir

Tribal (Muslim) women, Kashmir

Picking flowers, Kashmir

Bakerwal (Muslim shepherd), Jammu and Kashmir

Houseboat on lake, Srinagar, Kashmir

Craftsmen, Kashmir

Pherans (cloaks) for women, Kashmir

Buddhist in prayer, Ladakh

Prayer flag in
hill temple, Jammu

Buddhist monastery, Ladakh. Two rows of low tables facing each other have been arranged for monks to keep books and food on. They will sit on carpets.

Pronunciation

This book has used diacritical marks to double the value of three vowels: a, i and u. Therefore

'a' is as in 'c*a*thedral'
'â' is as in 'f*â*ther'
'e' is as in 'g*e*t'
'é' is as in 'caf*é*'
'i' is as in '*i*t'
'î' is as in '*e*at'
'ñ' is a brief, almost silent 'n,' much as in 'mo*n*k.'
'o' is always as in 'g*o*'
'u' is as in 'p*u*t'
'û' is as in 'f*oo*d'

'ts' is much like the 'z' in 'Mo*z*art'. Most Hindi, Urdu and English-speaking people settle for the 'ch' sound. They thus turn 'Tséwâñg' into 'Chéwâñg,' which the people of Ladâkh find quite acceptable.

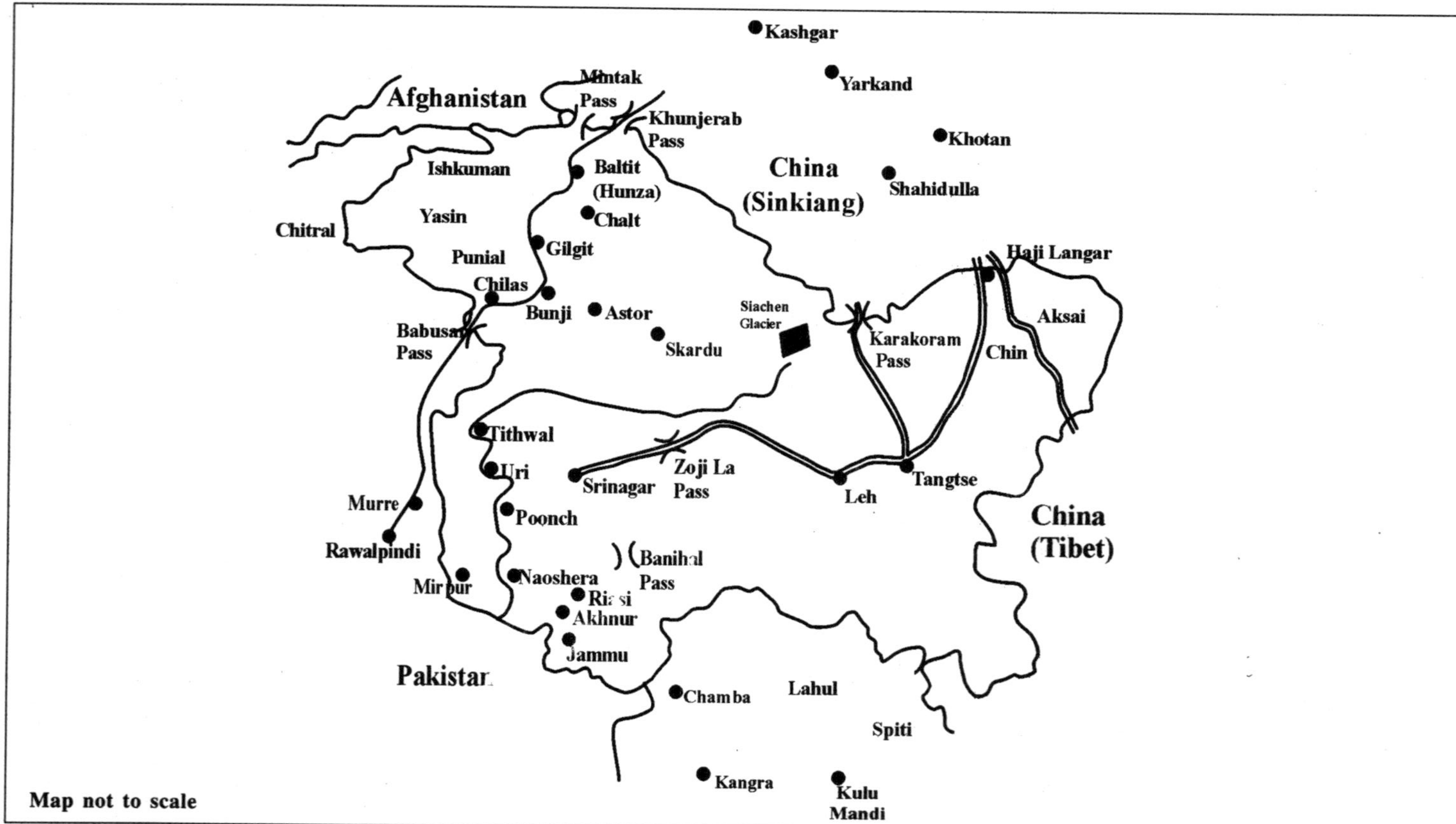

Jammu & Kashmir (including Ladakh)

Preface

The essential unity of Jammû, Kashmîr and Ladâkh

Was the state of Jammû & Kashmîr, as it existed in August 1947, an artificial construct put together in the 19th century by the Dogra maharajas—mainly Maharaja Gulab Singh and his legendary general Zorawar Singh? Many writers believe it to be so, given that the people of the different regions of the state speak different languages—each incomprehensible to the other, wear totally different kinds of clothes, have dissimilar cuisines and customs, and belong to different religions and different sects within the same religion.

The Muslims of the Valley of Kashmîr are mainly Sunni, those in Kargil-Baltistan and parts of Leh mainly Shia (Shiite), in Hunza they are Aga Khani and in Turtuk (Ladâkh) primarily Nûr Bakhshi. The Pandits of Kashmîr are Shaivite, while the Hindus of Jammû either believe in Shakti or are Vaishnavite. Besides, there are huge, almost insurmountable, mountains between Kashmîr and Ladâkh in the north, between Kashmîr and Jammû in the south and between Jammû's Kishtwar district and Ladâkh's Kargil district in the east.

And yet none of this has prevented the people of the state from forging deep bonds in the last two thousand years of recorded history.

Ruling over and being ruled by each other: The Dogras did create a great empire out of the many tiny princely states in the region, but they were not the first to rule over the entire state.

Kashmîr has been ruled by the Lohara dynasty (AD 948 to 1339, with interruptions) that originated in Jammû's Poonch district, by Rinchen/ Sadr ud Din (1320-23) a prince who came over from Ladâkh, by the Chaks (1561-1589) whose ancestors had migrated from Dardistan (Gilgit-Astor, now in Pakistan occupied Kashmîr) and by the Dogrâs of Jammû (1846-1947).

Kings from Kashmîr, in turn, have ruled or exercised suzerainty over many parts of Jammû province and Ladâkh-Baltistan. Abhimanyu I was the king of Kashmîr around the second century. He used to spend his winters in Darvabhisara (Rajouri-Poonch). Obviously this region in western Jammû was part of the kingdom of Kashmîr as early as that. More interestingly, the system of having a winter capital in the warmer Jammû province is as old as that.

The empire of Lalitaditya- Muktapida (AD 725- 753 or 724-761) included Baltistan, Dardistan and Jammû. From the Chamba copper- plates of around AD 1050- 66 we learn that at some stage between AD 910 and 930 'the lord of Durgara and the Saumataka' were among the kings who assisted the Kiras (presumably, the Kashmîris) in their invasion of Chamba (now in neighbouring Himachal Pradesh). Saumâtâ (Sâmbârta) was perhaps the capital of Vallapura (present Billawar). This could be the incident mentioned in the *Rajatarangini* but dated at AD 1028-63, when Raja Anant Dev of Kashmîr is said to have defeated the king of Chamba and replaced him with his own nominee. What is clear from both is that Kashmîr enjoyed suzerainty over Durgara, as well as some other hill States.

This conclusion is reinforced by the fact that eight hill chiefs including Kirti Dhar, king of Babbapura (c. AD 1070-90), and Raja Sangram Pal of Rajouri went over to Kashmîr in 1087-8 to pay homage to King Kalash of Kashmîr.

Shihab ud Din, Sultan of Kashmîr (1354-73), conquered Ladâkh, Gilgit, Dardistan, Baltistan, Kishtwar and Jammû. His Shahmiri dynasty continued to be suzerain over most of these areas for more than a hundred years. The Chak sultans of Kashmîr (1561-1589, with interruptions) fought their battles with the Mughals in the Rajouri-Poonch area. That, obviously, was the frontier of their kingdom.

Zain ul Abedin, as we have seen, had a kingdom that included all of undivided Punjâb. It stopped just short of Delhi. Much of Western Tibet and the Buddhist areas of Himachal Pradesh, too, were part of his kingdom.

The people of the different regions always helped each other. In 1679 and 1680 the Dalai Lâmâ sent his army to subdue Leh. The Tibetan army overran Guge and all of Ladâkh's western territories till it was stopped at Basgo. The Tibetans laid siege to Basgo for three years. Deldan Namgyal, king of Leh, requested the government of Kashmîr, then under a Mughal governor, to help him. It was they who pushed the Tibetans back. (That, incidentally, is when the people of Kashmîr were granted a monopoly on the purchase of pashmina wool.)

Sects: Doctrinal differences between the Shias and Sunnis are minor, while the Nûr Bakhshi movement arose to bridge such divergences as there were. The war between the Chaks, who were Shiite, and the Mughals, who were Sunni, is seen as one between the Shias and Sunnis. But the Chak government and army consisted of Sunni nobles like Ibrahim Khân and the Baihaqi scion Abul Mâli. Their main detractors within Kashmîr, who invited the Mughals to take over the administration of Kashmîr, were the Sunni saints Bâbâ Daood Khaki and Sheikh Yaqoub Sarfi, who were united on this with Bâbâ Khalilullah, the leading Shia saint of the time. There was, thus, no sectarian angle to the conflict.

The Dogras of Jammû are mainly Shaktaists who have willingly absorbed the Vaishnavism of their last ruling dynasty. *Shakti* is the divine wife of Lord Shiv. Therefore, Shaktaism is merely another form, or offshoot, of *Shaivism*. The Shaktaists of Jammû know that Sri Mata Vaishno Devi was a devotee of Sri Ram, the main Vaishnavite deity. Kheer Bhavani at Tulmula (in Kashmîr) is the most important shrine of the Kashmîri Pandits. This temple of the deity Ragnya Dévî was originally located in Lanka. After Srî Ram defeated Râvan, the demon king, he asked his lieutenant, Srî Hanumân, to shift the temple to Kashmîr.

Matrimonial links: Neither religion, race, region or sect prevented intermarriage. The Shiite Chaks gave their daughters in marriage to Sunnis, notably the Baihaqi Syeds.

Twice when Chak princes (Yusuf and Yaqub) from Kashmîr got into trouble in the Valley, they ran across the mountains to Kishtwar (in Jammû province), because their (certainly Yaqub's) wives were from there. In 1572 Yaqub Shah Chak, the last independent ruler of Kashmîr, married Shankar Devi (later Fath Khatun) the sister of Bahadur Singh, king of Kishtwar. Later, when Yaqub came under pressure from the forces of the Mughal emperor Akbar, he fled to Kishtwar where he died and was buried.

Matrimonial links between the royal families of Kashmîr and Jammû have almost always been there.

King Sunder Sen of Rajouri, sent his daughter Rajya Devi in a palanquin to Kashmîr for Sultan Zain ul Abedin @Budshah (1420-70) to marry, without informing him in advance. Budshah did not see the veiled princess and referred to her by the honorific 'mother' instead. Therefore, he could no longer marry her. (She stayed on in Kashmîr, converted to Islâm and later got built the bridge now known as Rajouri Kadal.)

Sunder Sen persisted. He then sent his second daughter, Sundara Devi, to the sultan. This time Budshah agreed to marry her. She bore him a son, Âdam Khân, the Wali (heir apparent). The people called her Sunderma-jî.

Budshah's brother, Sultan Ali Shâh (1413-20), was married to the daughter of the king of Jammû. In her dower came a retinue of people from Jammû to keep her company. They settled in an area that came to be known as Jamalatta, pron. ja-mâl-aT-Tâ. Its name means Jamwâl-hatta, or the 'marketplace set up by people from Jammû.'

Migration: There have always been very substantial Kashmîri communities—Muslim as well as Pandit—in Kishtwar, Banihal, Rajouri and Poonch, and later in Doda, Bhaderwah, Banni, parts of Udhampur, Reasi, Basohli town and even Chamba. The great shawl weavers of Basohli and Ramnagar towns were ethnic Kashmîri Muslims, as were the people who controlled the pashmina trade in Leh. Bureaucrats in the court of the Buddhist king of Padam (Zanskar) were Kashmîri Muslims from Kishtwar. They went on to form a considerable Sunni community in Zanskar.

The traffic was two-way. The Mian Rajputs of Kashmîr were perhaps the biggest group of Jammûites settled in rural Kashmîr. A very substantial portion of the population of cosmopolitan Srinagar was, till 1947, from Jammû province, including Bhaderwahi Hindus.

The Buddhist community of Padar (Kishtwar) is the most significant Ladâkhi presence in Jammû province. However, a small clan of Balti Shiites has been living in Jammû proper since the early 1900s. Both have had a profound impact on the culture of the region, well beyond the town that they are in. The chaugan (polo ground) of Kishtwar town as well as the rope-bridges of that district are of definite Ladâkhi origin.

And as for different languages, customs and food habits, neither the French nor the Spanish can understand a sentence of Euskara/ el vasco, the language of the considerable Basque community. The English are totally at sea when Cymraeg or y Gymraeg (the Welsh Language) is spoken. Tiny communities in the mountains of Italy and in Germany are like their counterparts in Ladâkh and Nagaland: each has an absolutely distinct language. The Scotts wear kilts and eat Haggis which other Britons do not.

That has never prevented them from becoming one people. Then why should eating rajma, goshtaba and thukpa or wearing the pheran, goncha and suthan?

Glossary

'AJK': 'Âzâd' Jammû and Kashmîr. Pâkistân has illegally occupied a large part of the state of Jammû and Kashmîr. It has divided POK (Pâkistân Occupied Kashmîr) into three board entities: i) the so-called 'AJK' (which is mainly occupied Jammû plus the Muzaffarâbâd area/ Kishen Gañgâ valley of occupied Kashmîr); ii) the so-called Northern Areas (which consist of occupied Ladâkh-Gilgit), and iii) Shaksgam (which Pâkistân has ceded to China). People wrongly assume that 'AJK' and POK are synonyms. 'AJK' is only one part—and a very small part, at that—of POK. The quotation marks around the word Âzâd (meaning 'free' or 'independent') and around the acronym AJK draw attention to the fact that 'AJK' is not an independent political entity but is an occupied territory.

AJKMC: 'AJK' Muslim Conference

ashtamî: The eighth day

chowk: Crossroads. The point where roads meet. Also, sometimes, the village or town square.

galî, gallâ, lâ: These are, respectively, the Urdû, Dogri and Ladâkhi words for 'mountain pass.'

gurudwârâ: Sikh temple.

havan: Classical Vedic prayer before a sacred fire.

HP: Himâchal Pradésh, the state on the eastern boundaries of the Jammû and Ladâkh regions of J&K.

ISI: Pâkistân's Inter-Services Intelligence

J&K: Jammû and Kashmîr, the name of the state that Jammû is a part of.

jâgîrdâr: A *jâgîrdâr* was a person whom the king (all right, the state) had given a *jâgîr*. In turn, a *jâgîr* was a large tract of land, normally consisting of one or more villages. The *jâgîrdâr* was much more than a headman. He collected land revenue (and, sometimes, other taxes) on behalf of the state, was responsible for law and order and maintained a number of soldiers—cavalrymen as well as foot soldiers—for the army of his state.

jeepable road: A track on which only rugged sports-utility vehicles can ply.

kol, kuhl: Water channel.

ling/ lingam: A stone shaped like a thimble, found in most Shiv temples.

LoC: Pâkistân has illegally occupied 35.15 per cent of the state of Jammû and Kashmîr. India actually administers 45.62 per cent of the state. (China is in the illegal occupation of the rest.) A 'Line of Control' separates the portion where the Indian tricolour flies from the portion illegally occupied by Pâkistân. It is not an 'international border' (IB) because neither side accepts it as that. It serves the same purpose as a border but lacks the legal status of one.

mañdir: Hiñdû temple.

masjid: Mosque.

MC: Muslim Conference

mohallâ: A traditional urban Indian neighbourhood.

motorable road: 'Motorable' means that in theory a car (or bus) can drive on that road. In practice most 'motorable' roads are only 'jeepable.' A 'motorable stretch' (or motorable distance) is one on which you can travel in a vehicle. You don't have to walk on that stretch, except for exercise.

muñdan: Ritual shaving of the head of a male child.

nâllâh: Stream.

navmî: Ninth day.

pass(es)/ mountain passes: What is a pass? A pass, more precisely a mountain pass, is a gap between two mountain peaks. It the highest point on a segment of a mountain road. There might be more than one pass on a road, and the next pass might be higher still. There always are mountains on the right and left of a pass. These mountains are much higher than the pass. The job of a pass is to help you cross from the place behind you to the place in front, without having to climb all the way to the top of the mountain. A pass is called a *gallî* in Urdu/ Kashmîrî, a *gallâ* in Dogri and *lâ* in Ladâkhî.

POK (Pâkistân Occupied Kashmîr): These are areas of Jammû & Kashmîr that are under Pâkistân's illegal occupation.

PPP: People's Party of Pâkistân

roadhead: This is the place to which one can travel in an automobile. In Indian English, it is the point till which there is a 'motorable' road. After this place one has to walk (or ride a pony) to get to the final destination. Conversely, on the return journey, this is the point where the trek ends and the 'motorable' road begins.

sâdhu: A Hindû ascetic, who normally lives a very frugal life.

samâdhi: This is a Hindû tradition in which a saint enters (or a group of saints enter) a cave or temple or a pit in the ground. They lock themselves in there, without food or water, and let themselves die. In Kashmîr, both Hindû and Muslim saints are known to have done this. Hindus everywhere (and in Kashmîr the Muslims, too) glorify such acts as a form of martyrdom.

The act is called 'performing/ obtaining/ taking *samâdhî.'* The place where they commit this act is called a '*samâdhî.'* Thus the word is both an act and a shrine.

saptamî: The seventh day

-sar: The Hindi-Sanskrit-Dogri word for 'lake'.

sarai/ serai: A rest house, as in caravanserai.

satsañg: Congregation of devotees

TRC is an important abbreviation to remember. It stands for 'Tourist Reception Centre.' Jammû has a fairly elaborate TRC and is supposed to offer every facility needed by a tourist, including reasonably priced accommodation. Katrâ, too, has a TRC though not as elaborate.

trekker: Indian English. A trekker is someone who treks.

urs: This is something like a Catholic Saint's Day. It is a religious occasion held at shrines, and is marked by prayer. At most shrines the *urs* is held once a year:, often on the death anniversary of the saint. At some shrines (notably that of Khwaja Moinuddin Chisti at Ajmer Sharief, Râjasthân) it is held twice in a year. The Islâmic calender (Hijri) is lunar. Therefore, the dates of annual events shift every year.

However, in many parts of South Asia (including Kashmîr) *urses* are observed according to solar calendars, normally the one used by the local Hindu community as well. *Urs*, incidentally, is a singular. The plural would be *urses.*

yagya: Classical Védic prayer ceremony

yâtrâ: a Hindu pilgrimage; a journey towards a sacred shrine. 'Yâtrâ' literally means 'trip' or 'journey.' There are several important Hindu shrines in the Himalayas, especially in J&K, HP and the UP hills. Devotees normally trek up to the shrine once a year on a designated day (or set of days). These yâtrâs normally take place in summer, because in winter it would be difficult to reach the concerned shrine because of the snow. In a religious context, *yâtrâ* means 'pilgrimage.

These *yâtrâs* have a fixed starting point, normally a temple at the bottom of that hill. Devotees gather there and then trek up to the shrine in a longish procession. Most yâtrâs terminate at the hilltop shrine where, often, a colourful fair is held. Yatris (pilgrims) return to their homes in the plains or foothills not in a procession but when they please.

Pilgrimages in the hills are normally connected with Lord Shiv or the Mother Goddess Durgâ (in one of her several manifestations). Lord Shiv's wife, the goddess Pârvati, is one of Durgâ Mâtâ's best-known incarnations. Yet, some of the Mâtâ's major forms (especially that of Srî Mâtâ Vaishno Dévî jî and Ragnya Dévî) are connected with the story of Srî Râm.

yâtrî: Hiñdî for 'pilgrim'; the Dogri word for 'pilgrim' is *yâtrû.*

JAMMÛ

Undivided Jammû (Important Towns)

1

The Population of Jammû Province

The undivided Jammû province: In 1947, Jammû province was divided into five districts, each under a Wazîr é Wazârat. The districts, along with their tehsils (in brackets) and, in the case of Réâsî, niabats, were:

Jammû (Jammû, Sâmbâ and Akhnoor); Mirpur (Mirpur, Nausherâ, Bhimber and Kotlî); Udhampur (Udhampur, Râmban, Râmnagar, Bhaderwâh and Kishtwâr); Réâsî (Réâsî and Rajourî. Niabat: Gulabgarh) and Kathua (Kathuâ, Jasmérgarh and Basohli).

Jammû had an area of 12,401 sq. miles (approx. 32,200 sq.km.). In 1941, according to Daya Sagar, its population was 20,01,557 (i.e. 2 million). He is marginally off the mark. Journalist-historian B.P. Sharma has a slightly different figure for the population of Jammû province. Based on census figures, he puts it at 19,81,433.[1] Either way, the Muslims, with a population of 12,15,676 in 1941, were in an overwhelming, 61.53%[i] majority in Jammû province.

1. My figure, also based on the census, differs by 12. That's because my sub-totals are slightly different.

1941: The population of undivided Jammû province ***(actual numbers)***[ii]

District of district	Total Scheduled Caste	Hindus/ Others	Hiñdus/	Muslims	Christians	Sikhs	Buddhists	Jains	Others	Pârsîs	Tribes
Jammû	431362	51120	197053	170789	2297	1519	2	895	3	23	29
Kathuâ	177672	18949	112974	45214	204	431	0	0	0	0	0
Udhampur[2]	294217	21646	143175	128327	98	445	520[3]	6	1	0	0
Réâsî[4]	257903	15720	65005	175539	98	1541	0	0	0	0	0
Mîrpur	386655	3008	60568	310880	88	12111	0	0	0	0	0
Chenainî jâgîr[5]	11796	2670	6911	2205	0	10	0	0	0	0	0
Pooñch jâgîr	421828	410	23727	382722	3	14	0	0	0	0	0
Total	19,81,445	1,13,523	6,09,413	12,15,676	2,788	38,566	522	901	4	23	29

There were no Jews in Jammû province.

2. Includes present Dodâ but not Réâsî or Chenainî.
3. Presumably, mainly in Pâdar (now in Dodâ).
4. Includes almost all of present Rajourî district.
5. Now a part of Udhampur.

1941: The population of the present Jammû province *(percentages)*

District[iii]	Hindus	Muslims	Christians	Sikhs	Buddhists	Jains	Others
Dodâ	42.22	57.35	N	0.15	0.26	N	0.02
Udhampur	66.53	33.17	0.03	0.22	N	N	0.08
Jammû	59.44	37.36	0.34	2.45	N	0.16	0.75
Kathuâ	74.19	25.45	0.1	0.24	-	-	0.12
Pooñch	13.25	85.59	0.01	1.15	-	-	0.01

1941: The population of undivided Jammû province *(percentages)*

Year 1941[iv]	Hiñdus	Muslims	Sikhs	Buddhists	Others
Jammû	57.53	39.6	2.12	-	0.75
Kathuâ: Jasmérgarh[6] and Kathuâ tehsils	68.49	30.99	0.39		0.13
Mîrpur: Mîrpur and Bhimber tehsîls	20.03	76.06	3.88		0.03
Basohli tehsîl **(Kathuâ)**	82.85	17.07	0.02		0.06
Kotlî tehsîl **(Mîrpur)**	7.55	91.17	1.28		
Udhampur	56.02	43.62	0.15	0.18	0.03
Réâsî	31.30	68.06	0.60		0.04
Chenainî Jâgîr	81.22	18.70	0.08		
Pooñch Jâgîr	5.72	90.73	3.53		0.02
Total	**36.48**	**61.34**	**1.95**	**0.03**	**0.20**

1961:[v] The population of the present Jammû province *(actual numbers)*

District	Buddhist	Christians	Hiñdus	Jains	Muslims	Sikhs	Religion not stated	Total
Dodâ	612	13	92797	0	174499	480	9	268410
Udhampur	0	0	165506	0	86059	2259	2	253826
Jammû	29	2010	428835	1418	51847	32788	0	516927
Kathuâ	0	0	177666	4	27005	2553	5	207233
Pooñch	0	0	58712	0	259082	8193	2	325989
Jammû Province	641	2023	9,23,516	1422	5,98,492	46,273	18	15,72,385

6. Hîrânagar.

1961: The population of the present Jammû province *(percentages)*

Districts[vi]	Hindus	Muslims	Christians	Sikhs	Buddhists	Jains	Others
Dodâ	34.57	65.01	0.01	0.18	0.23	N	N
Udhampur	65.15	33.87	0.09	0.89	N	N	-
Jammû	82.96	10.03	0.39	6.34	0.01	0.27	N
Kathuâ	85.65	13.02	0.1	1.23	-	N	-
Pooñch	18.01	79.46	0.02	2.51	-	-	N

N = negligible.

Note: The tables on page 237 of the census report have very obviously interchanged the Sikh, Buddhist and Jain populations of Jammû with those of Udhampur. (All rows that begin on page 236 with the name of a certain district end on page 237 with the name of the same district. Only in the case of Jammû and Udhampur has the order been interchanged on page 237.) I have taken the liberty of transferring these figures back to where I think they should belong.

The census authorities' note: 'The break-up of Christians and Jains is not available separately in the Village Tables of [the] 1941 Census. The figures of these religions have, therefore been included in "Others"[vii]

1981: The population of the present Jammû province *(actual numbers)*

District	Total	Hindus	Muslims	Sikhs	Christians	Buddhists
Dodâ	425,262	179,538		243,666	847	1,113
Jammû	943,395	824,209	40,309	72,034	5,413	
Kathuâ	369,123	336,503	25,699	6,082	N/a	
Pooñch	224,197	16,339	199,674	8,134		
Râjourî	302,500	118,705	176,302	7,325		
Udhampur	453,636	327,538	118,987	5,741	N/a	
Total	27,18,113	18,02,832	8,04,637	1,00,163	6,260	1,113
%		66.30	29.58	3.68		

2001: The population of the present Jammû province *(actual numbers)*

District	Total	Hindus	Muslims	Sikhs	Christians	Buddhists	Jains
Dodâ	691929	286849	400765	1942	439	1866	26
Jammû	1588772	1366711	90272	117490	11115	1155	1899
Kathuâ	550084	493966	44793	9152	1458	138	25
Pooñch	372613	19391	342512	10297	283	108	0
Râjourî	483284	180162	291067	11601	206	94	7
Udhampur	743509	542593	190112	7723	2632	211	57
Total	44,30,191	28,89,672	13,59,521	1,58,205	16,133	3,572	2,014
%		65.22	30.68	3.57	0.36	0.08	0.045

Literacy

Distt	Popn	Lit2001	R2001	M	F	Lit1981	R1981	Growth	Gender
J&K	98,86,585	53.57		64.6	41.61	32.68	3.41	900	
Dodâ	6,81,152	46.08	10	62.49	28.30	18.5	13		
Udhampur	7,10,493	52.15	7	64.02	39.08	23.52	7		
Pooñch	3,68,544	50.60	8	64.81	35.28	34.79	2		
Rajourî	4,70,968	56.85	6	68.56	44.11	24.73	5		
Jammû	15,14,468	76.54	1	84.13	68.38	42.86	1		
Kathuâ	5,43,266	65.22	2	75.64	53.92	31.90	4		
Jammû province	42,90,871	63.07						3.09	890

Popn.= Total population (of the district, province or state mentioned); Lit2001= The percentage of the total population that was literate in the year 2001; M= the percentage of men who were literate in 2001; F= the percentage of women who were literate in 2001; Lit1981= The percentage of the total population which was literate in the year 1981; Growth= the average annual percent rate of growth of the population between 1981 and 2001; Gender= the number of women for every 1,000 men. R1981: 'Rank in 1981' or how the district ranked in 1981 in terms of literacy among the 14 districts of the state. R2001: 'Rank in 2001' or the district's rank in 2001 in terms of literacy among the 14 districts of the state.

Literacy and the peace dividend: Kathuâ is generally considered a nondescript district that has nothing to commend it other than its tradition of being the most peaceful district in Jammû and, perhaps, the state. (Budgâm has a similar peaceful reputation in Kashmîr and Kargil in Ladâkh.) Kathuâ carried this tradition forward into the 1990s when some other districts got involved with senseless, suicidal militancy. Kathuâ, along with Muslim-majority Kargil and Buddhist-majority Leh, stayed totally aloof from militancy.

The dividend was immediate. 'Colourless' Kathuâ suddenly became the 2nd most literate district in the state. (Leh and Kargil reaped similar benefits. And Jammû bettered its traditional no.1 status by becoming the educational capital of the state—as well as of the neighbouring districts of the Punjãb and Himâchal Pradésh.)

Considering that Jammû province as a whole reaped the peace dividend, why did Pooñch plummet from no. 2 to no. 8? Perhaps Pakistan-inspired troubles in the Surankot area made it drop to Pakistani levels of literacy. Neighbouring Rajourî dropped by only one rank, but drop it did, again because it had some problems, though insignificant compared to what happened in parts of Surankot (Pooñch). Dodâ, which, too, has had some troubles, *seems* to have climbed from rank no.13 to no.10. However, if you look at the percentage of literacy there, it is the worst in Jammû—and by a very large margin. It improved its rank only at the expense of Kashmîr, where the troubles were much worse.

Pooñch, Dodâ and Rajourî might have lost their relative ranks but, as in the rest of the province, the percentage of literacy in all six districts of Jammû improved, and noticeably.

References

i And not 66% as I had stated in the 'Kashmîr' volume.

ii Census of India, 1941, Vol. XXII Jammû & Kashmîr, Parts I and II, Essay and Tables, by Capt. R.G. Wreford, Census Commissioner, Jammû and Kashmîr State, Jammû (1943) pages 341-343.

iii Census of India, 1961, Vol. VI Jammû & Kashmîr, Part 1-A (iii), General Report; MH Kamili, Superintendent of Census Operations, pages 236-237.

iv Census of India, 1941, Vol. XXII Jammû & Kashmîr, Parts I and II, Essay and Tables, by Capt. R.G. Wreford, Census Commissioner, Jammû and Kashmîr State, Jammû (1943) pages 346-347.

v Adapted from the Census of India, 1961, Vol. VI Jammû & Kashmîr, Part II-C Cultural and Migration Tables; MH Kamili, Superintendent of Census Operations, pages 272-273. Irritatingly, the total population of districts has not been given. Instead we have been told how many men and how many women were there in each district. We are left to add the two figures together to get the total and sub-totals.

vi Census of India, 1961, Jammû & Kashmîr, Vol. VI Jammû & Kashmîr, Part 1-A (iii), General Report; MH Kamili, Superintendent of Census Operations, pages 236-237.

vii Census of India, 1961, Jammû & Kashmîr, Vol. VI Jammû & Kashmîr, Part 1-A (iii), General Report; MH Kamili, Superintendent of Census Operations, page 236.

2

Jammû: 1885-1947

A Composite Culture

'There was a lot of poverty but there was a contentment and a glow on the faces of people.' [i]

-Malkâ Pukhrâj, *Song Sung True*.

'It was a time of happiness and contentment.'

-Khâlid Hasan, *Memory Lane to Jammû*.

In the early 20th century, Hamîrpur Siddhar, a village in Jammû district, had a saint called Bâbâ Roti Râm. 'No one knew…whether he was a Hiñdu, a Mussalmân, a Sikh or a Christian,' the legendary classical singer Malkâ Pukhrâj writes.[ii] And, as we shall see, it didn't matter. The Râm in his name would suggest that he was a Hiñdu. However, it was the people of the village—Hiñdus and Muslims together—who had given him that name. Bâbâ, on the other hand, is an Arabic word, normally used for Muslim divines.

The Bâbâ was a follower of Kabîr, the great 15th century Central Indian bridge between Hiñduism and Islâm. Many of the religious symbols that Roti Râm used were Hiñdu-Sikh. He would call men—including Muslim men—Gobiñdâ, and women—Hiñdu as well as Muslim—by the name Pârvati. This would not only not offend the Muslims, they saw it as a form of endearment. They would take their newborn babies to the Bâbâ for his blessings. The Bâbâ would then give elegant, purely Persian-Arabic names to the Muslim children.

This, too, is a cherished Indian tradition. Ali Shér Khân Añchan, the great 15th century emperor of much of Baltistân-Ladâkh, gave a pristine Buddhist name to his grandson, because the child's father was a Buddhist. And the name that he gave the future Emperor of Leh—Sengge Namgyâl ('the lion' + 'king')—was as carefully chosen as the one that the Bâbâ would, five centuries later, give the greatest known singer in the history of Jammû, Malkâ Pukhrâj ('the empress' + 'topaz').

Malkâ Pukhrâj was born during the reign of Mahârâjâ Pratâp Singh (1885-1925). Even before she entered her teens, she was employed as a singer by Mahârâjâ Hari Siñgh (1925-1947). In the 1940s Pukhrâj shifted base to Lahore, which later became a part of Pâkistân. Her fascinating memoirs, ably translated as *Song Sung True* by Saleem Kidwai, conjure up a Jammû where the Hiñdus and Muslims lived in harmony and where people were content despite their poverty. Her memoirs are an invaluable source of history. I have culled information from this remarkable book to put together a social history of Jammû from roughly 1885 to 1947.

Mahârâjâ Pratâp Singh embodied the composite religious identity of Jammû. He also personified the contradiction that many well meaning, God-fearing Hiñdus of his era suffered from. On the one hand, he allowed himself to believe that if he saw a Muslim before breakfast the purity of his piety would be compromised.

On the other, as Pukhrâj reminds us, he was as generous in his charity towards the Muslims as with his Hiñdu subjects.[iii] Miyâñ Lâl Dîn, a high-ranking Muslim official, was one of Pratâp Siñgh's closest advisors. Besides, the Maharaja 'had great faith in holy men of all types.'[iv]

So did the people of Jammû.

For instance, when the women of Pukhrâj's family wanted to travel from distant Jammû city to Hamîrpur Siddhar village (it was a full day's journey by horse) to pay respects to the Bâbâ, a Hiñdu and a Muslim insisted on escorting them—partly to protect the women and partly in the hope of receiving the Bâbâ's blessings for themselves.[1]

Bâbâ Roti Râm predicted that some deadly epidemic would strike Jammû city. Hiñdus and Muslims alike believed him. His prophecy came true. A terrible plague swept through Jammû city. Both communities started seeking the help of Dr Râdhâ Krishan and both blessed him for helping them without charging a high fee.[v]

Bâbâ Charas (marijuana) Sâheb was the other important religion-indeterminate saint of that era. Not everyone in Jammû had faith in medical doctors. To this day, rural Jammû often prefers the local medicine man. Pukhrâj's father did not like doctors either. Like many Jammûites of both communities, he relied on the blessings of Bâbâ Charas to see him through that plague. At least in his case it worked.

---

1. In some parts of the world this craving for the blessings of a saint of another religion (or of no particular religion) might seem strange. However, in Jammû this has continued into the 21st century. Tens of thousands of Jammû Hiñdus would similarly travel great distances to pay their respects to Darvésh Ishâq Sâheb of Kishtwâr, till he died at the turn of the century (circa 1996). Similarly, till their migration in 1990, the Puñjâbi and Kashmîrì Hiñdus of Srînagar would not think twice before going to the fields near the entrance to Makhdoom Sâheb to sit at the feet of the (Muslim) Goph Peer ('the saint who lives in a cave').

The royal succession

Mahârâjâ Pratâp Siñgh's queen was called Mahârânî Chârak, after her maiden name. The royal couple did not have any children. Mahârâjâ Pratâp wanted his nephew, Hari Siñgh, to succeed him. The queen, instead, was in favour of the prince of Pooñch, whom she had adopted. Pratâp Siñgh was a drug addict and mostly oblivious to the world. His ambitious wife, therefore, wielded more power than a queen consort would normally have. She saw to it that Hari Siñgh never got to speak to his uncle except in her presence.

The loyalties of the palace staff were with the queen. She also had the British Resident on her side. This was important because the British often decided who would succeed kings who died without any children.

Hari Siñgh was married to Rânî Billaurâñ and loved her deeply. When the Rânî was with child, Mahârânî Chârak got an order passed that Hari Siñgh should not be allowed to meet the Rânî till the child was born. Hari Siñgh decided to spend those months of separation in England. The Rânî died during labour. Hari Siñgh, who later became the Mahârâjâ, always believed that Mahârânî Chârak had poisoned his wife.[vi]

Mahârâjâ Hari Siñgh then married the princess of Dharamkot. He was the first of his dynasty 'to marry the daughter of a Mahârâjâ.'[vii] His predecessors would take as wives the daughters of the nobles of Jammû.

The royal administration: The Diwâns of Jammû and Kashmîr (no relations of this author) apparently received a very substantial share (12.5 per cent) of the revenues of the state. (Don't I wish we'd been related?) Mahârâjâ Hari Siñgh put an end to this custom. He also outlawed untouchability. The so-called untouchables were allowed to enter any temple that they chose to.

Once every year, on the day after his birthday, the Mahârâjâ would invite the Râjpûts—rich as well as poor—to dinner at the palace.[viii]

Today, we think of corruption as a modern disease. However, the money that Mahârâjâ Pratâp Siñgh had kept apart for the poor and infirm—Rs.200 a day—was often pocketed by his courtiers instead. They would take advantage of the illiteracy of the people for whom the Mahârâjâ had sanctioned grants. These courtiers would give the beneficiary only a fraction of what had been authorised, but would make them sign a receipt for the full amount, pilfering the rest.

Religious rituals

Baisâkhî used to be a religion-neutral festival. These days corporations (and rich doctors and dentists who have flourishing practices) send gifts to important clients for the (Christian) New Year. In the Dogrâ era—and, perhaps, in the preceding centuries, too—rural midwives (irrespective of religion) would send garlands of dry fruits beaded together to all the children (again, regardless of religion) that they had delivered.[ix] (I often wonder how those impoverished midwives could afford to do this.)

Urban Jammû was equally liberal. It had a Séwâ Samiti ('a committee of the servants of the society'), a government-backed organisation, which had eight members—an equal number of Hiñdus and Muslims. (Some might argue that the Muslims should have had greater representation, because the kingdom was overwhelmingly Muslim. Others would say that the Samiti was meant only for Jammû town, which was mainly Hiñdu—as were the districts to the immediate north and south of Jammû. Therefore, the Hiñdus should have had more members. In the event exact parity seems to have satisfied both.)

One of the main tasks of the members was to arrange for the cremation or burial of the unclaimed bodies of members of their community. The hospital where the bodies were kept would give four rupees to the member—again regardless of religion—who took on this task. At the time, the sum was more than adequate for the last rites.[x]

For Eid, Mahârâjâ Hari Siñgh would go to the mosque where the biggest congregation offered prayers. He would take the Nawâb of Pâlampur along to the mosque, where the Nawâb would join the Muslims of Jammû in prayer. Hari Siñgh would stand respectfully for two hours[2] while prayers were being offered—a gesture greatly resented[3] by some non-Muslims.[xi] When the Eid prayers were over, the Mahârâjâ would give the Imâm (the leader of the congregation) an expensive *pashminâ* (cashmere) robe and a cash grant.[xii]

All this affection for the Muslims came at a price. A rumour, obviously spread by hardliners, swept Jammû that Hari Siñgh had converted to Islâm but was keeping that a secret lest he be deposed from his throne.

The Mahârâjâ had shifted his palace from the ornate and huge Mubârak Mañdî complex to the infinitely smaller Râmnagar palace, later known as Hari Niwâs, because he shunned ostentation. However, certain fanatics alleged that he had done so because he did not want to hear the bells that rang in the Mañdî's temple.[xiii] Incidentally, the Hiñdu Dogrâs chose the Arabic—even Islâmic—name 'Mubârak Mañdî' for their main palace.

As a child Pukhrâj was trained, by Muslim *ustâds* (maestri), to sing *bhajans* (sacred Hiñdu songs). At the Mahârâjâ's court she sang '*Arey Râm, kaisey paar utaariye*?', "O Râm! How will you take me across to the other (river) bank?" which Mamman Khân of Delhi had taught her. She recalled this without hesitation in her old age in Pâkistân. Like countless Muslim singers throughout South Asia, her favourite râgs (Jaijaiwañti and Shañkarâ) had a 'Hiñdu origin.' She also sang *holîs* (traditional songs connected with the Hiñdu festival, Holî).[xiv]

---

2. The two hour figure is from Pukhrâj, op. cit., p. 94.
3. The right always asks two questions—and does so with venom—to justify its resentment: Does the other community reciprocate during our festivals? Do these bleeding hearts from our community do as much for their own festivals as they do for the festivals of the other community?
   I have tried to answer both questions in this chapter.

When she entered her teens, every morning Pukhrâj would sing bhajans at the temple in Mubârak Mañdî. She did not consider this odd. On the contrary, she would later write, 'Singing bhajans there was considered a great honour.'[xv] Nor did any Hiñdu feel that the temple (or the purity of the bhajans) had been compromised because of a Muslim. Indeed, the temple priests would chant prayers, blow into the sacred fire and ring the temple bells while Pukhrâj recited bhajans.[xvi]

Sorayyâ Khurshîd, who proudly recalls that Jammû was 'called the city of temples,' was one of the countless Muslims of that era who would 'every morning hear the sweet sound of temple bells which would be rung all together. The great temple of Raghunâth was surrounded by other temples. I can still [in 2002, 55 years after I left Jammû] hear those bells, and their music reverberates in my ears.' Hâshmî reminds us that the street of this famous group of temples was then called Mañdarâñ Wâlâ Bâzar ('the market where the temples are'). Râd fondly adds, 'We recall the high golden steeples of the temples.'

Similarly, even in the early 21st century, the Hiñdus of Ustâd Mohallâ are proud of how 'their' mosque has become grander over the years. They fondly recall the voices of the better muezzins of their mosque.

Every morning before dawn during the holy month of Ramzân, an expert trumpeter would go to the roof of the Mastgarh mosque—which has been built on an elevation—and blow the trumpet loud. It could be heard for miles. (Today, Muslim youths go through all streets with a significant Muslim population playing a drum. The idea in both cases is to wake the devout up.)

Pukhrâj writes that when the people saw her, then a nine-year-old, decked in jewellery (given to her by the Mahârâjâ), 'they were convinced that [she was] a goddess.'[xvii] They did not consider it strange to think of a Muslim child as a little goddess, nor did she that they regarded her so.

Clothes, books: On occasion Pukhrâj would wear sâris, a dress that the Pâkistânî establishment would, in the 1980s, decree a 'Hiñdu dress' and therefore, not to be worn by Muslims. (Never mind that all Bâñglâdéshî Muslim women—including their Prime Ministers—wear saris.) The sari should really be associated with the region (which stretches from Central and East India to Srî Lañkâ), and not a religion. If the sari is a Hiñdu dress, then Pukhrâj was more Hiñdu than the Hiñdu women of Jammû, who still mainly wear the *shalwâr qamîz* (which the Pâkistânis and some Indians wrongly think is Islâmic) because that is the dress of the Punjãb-Jammû belt.

Reading habits, too, were eclectic. The Hiñdus were diehard fans of Iqbâl, the poet, and the Muslims avidly read the 'four large, thick volumes of *Fasânâ é Âzâd* by Rattan Nâth Sarshar'—a Hiñdu who had given himself a Persian ('Muslim') last name. Everyone in Pukhrâj's family wanted to read the series. She reminisces, 'Rarely has the Urdu idiom been used better than in this book. My world changed after I read [it]. The description of Eid is so real that it seemed I was part of the festivities of that time.'[xviii]

But things began to change. For instance, in contemporary Delhi, by the early decades of the 20th century, 'you could [no longer] make out a Hiñdu from a Muslim.'[xix] That's because everyone was wearing the same Western-style clothes. Ironically, so long as people of different communities wore clothes that proclaimed their ethnic identity, there was no tension between them, and very little (if any) prejudice. It was only after external marks started disappearing that stereotypes and generalisations about other communities—and, thus, hatred—started creeping in.

Today, perhaps the Gujjars and Bakerwâls alone can be identified by their clothes, beards and jewellery. And these are the two most integrated communities of the state. They hate no ethnic group, and no one dislikes them.

Jammû town before 1947

Till 1947 the Gumat Gate—very ornate even today, though illegal shops have obscured its old elegance—was where the town began and was its lowest end. The palace complex in the Râmnagar Rakh was the highest point and the northern extremity. All visitors from the plains in the south would enter through the Gumat Gate and start climbing up its steep stone steps.

The bridge on the Tawi was built in the early 20th century. Before that people would cross the river by boat when its waters were substantial and wade through it during the rest of the year.

To this day many villages in the *kañdi* (semi-arid) belt—Gurhâ Salâthiâ, for example—have ponds (*tâlâbs*) where they store rain- and spring-water, to drink and to wash with. Jammû's famous tâlâbs—Puccâ Tâlâb, Rânî dâ Tâlâb, Tâlâb Khatîkâñ and Tâlâb Tillo—have, like the *bâghs* (gardens and orchards) of Srînagar, since been built over and been converted into residential districts.

According to an estimate, in 1941 Jammû city had a population of around 50,000, of which roughly 16,000 were Muslims.

Sorayyâ Khurshîd's otherwise unprejudiced account very gently hints that old Jammû was ghettoised. She writes, 'Jammû city was divided into two parts, the upper and the lower. While one did not understand as a child why the city was laid out like that, years later I found many Italian cities similarly laid out. In Jammû the upper or the elevated part of the city was mostly peopled by Hiñdus—though there was a Pathân mohallâ right in the middle of it.'

This is an incredible statement. Obviously five decades of separation have blurred that gracious lady's memory, for the uppermost mohallâ in town, the one closest to the royal palace, was the overwhelmingly Muslim Ustâd Mohallâ. Forest lessee Sheikh Amîn's tony mansion—the only one with Italian marble—was also close to the palace and was perched atop a similar elevation.

On the other hand, some very rich Hiñdus—notably shopkeepers and jewellers—lived in the southern half.

The Ustâd Mohallâ: Ustâd Ghaus Muhammad Khân, who belonged to Râmpur (Uttar Pradésh), was known for his expertise with horses, bows and arrows. The Mahârâjâ of Jammû and Kashmîr, Pratap Singh, invited the *ustâd* (maestro) to the state to teach his brother, Râjâ Ram Singh, and him, as well as other royals, these arts.

The Mahârâjâ granted his tutor an enormous estate close to the palace. Râjâ Ram Singh got a grand mansion, which is still intact, built for his *ustâd*. According to Prof. Suneethi Bakshi, the raja personally supervised the construction of this *havéli* (mansion) and ensured that its ground floor was built of the same materials as the Mahârâjâ's palace, which was then being constructed. And when Râjâ Ram Singh added an upper floor to his own house, he got a similar floor made for his tutor.

(References to Prof. Suneethi Bakshi are for her article 'Mute witness to a bygone idyllic and historic time,' *The Kashmîr Times,* 23 and 30 October, 2005.)

Ghaus Muhammad—whom the Mahârâjâ gave the title Sardâr—was some kind of a modern day Arjun. Apparently, the *ustâd* could, with his arrows, shoot down birds flying above him without looking at them. He only needed to see their reflections in a tub of water.

The *ustâd* founded a very illustrious line. He married Bégum Jân, whose father General Samad Khân was the landlord of Balliâñ, a village near Udhampur. The legendary Col. Peer Muhammad was their eldest son. (The colonel was, for a while, the state president of the Hiñdu nationalist Bhâratiya Jan Sañgh—the precursor of the Bhâratiya Janatâ Party. And when Pâkistân gifted armed militancy to the state in the 1990s, Farooq Khân of the Indian Police Service—who is the colonel's grandson and the *ustâd's* great-grandson—became one of the foremost militancy-fighters of the state.)

Upon Bégum Jân's death, Râjâ Ram Singh persuaded the *ustâd* to marry again. Each time that a child was born to the *ustâd*—and he had five children—the royal queens would come over with gifts of gems and robes embroidered with gold.

All this royal attention encouraged other elite Muslims to build houses on the *ustâd's* estate—which came to be called the Ustâd Mohallâ.

A widow of Mîr Mânu, the Mughals' Viceroy of Lahore, had, in the 1770s, built the substantial Wazîrni mosque at the point where the mohallâ meets Palace Road. She also built a *havéli*—the Bégum ki Havéli—for herself.

Râjâ (General) Râo Firmân Ali Khân, another illustrious resident of the mohallâ, too, had a spacious *havéli*. If Brig. U.C. Bakshî's Edwardian house was the biggest of them all—with a row of stables and garages, lawns that stretched over half an acre and three large western-style 'halls'—it was because he had the Anglicised need for lawns and the advantage of being a late comer to the mohallâ.

After the unfortunate exodus of 1947, Râo Firmân Ali Khân's mansion was, for a few years, converted into a refugee camp.

Ghaus Muhammad Khân was a gourmand, and his *havéli* was known for its colourful soirees. The best dancing girls and female singers of the day—

notably Iqub alias Ballo of the Urdû Bâzâr—would enliven things for guests, who often included the Mahârâjâ's brother.

The Urdû Bâzâr: Jammû's Urdû Bâzâr (later renamed Râjinder Bâzâr after the great military martyr of 1947) used to have a major Muslim presence. Its southern end was called Pîpalwâlâ Chowk. (The pîpal tree is still there but the square has been renamed Shahîdî Chowk.)

Urdû Bâzâr had the town's most successful bakeries, both owned by Jammû Muslims—Ghulâm Muhammad and Sâdiq—and, later, another two owned by the biggest names from Srînagar—Âhdoo and Lâlâ Sheikh. This bazar was where people went for kebabs and perfumes. (Perfumes made in Kannauj, U.P., are still sold there.)

The Tâj Hotel, owned by Dogrified Muslims from Baltistân, had already made a name for itself. It has gone to greater heights and vastly expanded since.

Indeed, only Muslim chefs made certain kinds of delicacies. Omar was known for the kebab, Masood Billâ for several kinds of sherbet, Miañ Latîf for pickles, Châcha Shammâ for the Kashmîri *tsachéroo* bagel, Qutubi for the *katlammâ* and Laloo Billâ for the *bâqar-khâni*.

The Bâzâr was best known for its sex artistes. (Sex artistes are women who, in Hindi-Urdû films, sanctimoniously proclaim, 'We sell our art [classical singing and/ or Kathak dancing], not our bodies.' And yet the world—Râd, for instance—associates them mainly with 'the world's oldest profession.)

Only Malkâ Pukhrâj, who lived for a few years on that street of talent and pleasure, was able to establish herself in Pâkistân after the maelstrom of 1947. But then she had shifted to what later became Pâkistân much before partition—and was already a superstar.

The Muslim elite—and middle class

Incidentally, how big was the Muslim elite—and middle class—of Jammû? Different writers have offered various estimates. Pukhrâj was under the impression that the Muslims did not own shops or get government jobs in the same proportion as their share of the population. I have tried to crosscheck that noble lady's gut feeling. In this book, I have listed the Muslim elite, without expressing its number as a percentage. I have also tracked down the better-known Muslim entrepreneurs and shopkeepers of that era.

Prof. Suneethi Bakshi writes, 'By 1947, there were 167 Muslim families in the [Ustâd] mohallâ of whom barely 12 per cent in all were in the upper elitist bracket.' The percentage would have been no different among Hiñdus in similar mohallâs.

For Jammû province—and, indeed, the state as a whole—there is another indicator. 71,667 soldiers and officers from the state served in the British Indian Army during the Second World War. Of them 60,402 (or 84.28 per cent) were Muslims. (In 1941, 77.11 per cent of the people of the state were Muslim.)

The state had a very tiny organised private sector at the time and it consisted mainly of the production of and trade in handicrafts and fruits. Forest lessees were among the richest people in the state. The civil service was small. Service in the army accounted for the biggest chunk of salaried employment. Therefore, soldiers, even the ones at the bottom of the army's food chain, constituted the bulk of the middle class. Brigadiers, on the other hand, formed the rung just below royalty.

Perceptions—of the self and of others

In South Asia the various communities began to think of themselves as belonging to the majority community or to a minority only after 1881. That was when British-administered censuses started informing Indians which community formed what part of the population in which city or state or the country as a whole. Till then people went by general impressions. That's the feeling I get from all pre-1880 Indian literature, which normally seems to assume that the Hiñdus and Muslims were roughly equal in numbers. (In fact, the ratio was almost 3:1.)

Even afterwards, only educated and politically aware sections of the population knew the exact figures—and cast aspersions on the accuracy of figures that did not suit them.

Pukhrâj's is a classic example. In order to justify the reaction of some Hiñdu fanatics against the Mahârâjâ because of his concern for the Muslims, she writes, 'There were more Hiñdus than Muslims in the kingdom'.[xx] Please consider this: a Pâkistânî Muslim, writing in her old age, for a readership that was entirely Muslim and Pâkistânî, was making excuses for the Hiñdu right, based on figures (and reasoning) that were widely off the mark. But why did she get this impression? Perhaps because in the belt that she lived in (the districts now called Jammû, Kathuâ and Udhampur) the Muslims were in a minority. (In Jammû province, as well as the state as a whole, the Muslims were overwhelmingly in the majority.)

The impetus arrives from the cities: Till India was partitioned along religious lines in 1947, the common man was not much concerned about religion. To a great extent things are much the same to this day in the remoter villages of all South Asian countries—villages not yet polluted by fanatics from the cities. The same is true of the urban poor.

Pukhrâj tells us that the rural Muslims of Jammû rarely knew the *kalimâ*—the two-phrase fundament of Islâm. (I get the same impression about the rural Pâkistânî Punjãbî Muslims of the 1940s from the liberal Pâkistânî literature of that era.[4]) She says that there were no mosques—or schools—in these Muslim villages. (There were countless Muslim shrines, though, and these continue to be venerated by the Hiñdus and Sikhs after the unfortunate exodus of the Muslims.)

---

4. Sabîhâ Sûmar's classic film, *Khâmosh Pânî* (Silent Waters, 2004), brings this point out very powerfully.

Sâîñ Rahîmâ, a *faquîr* (Muslim mendicant) took it upon himself to correct some of this. He started reading the *azân* (call to prayer) but initially the entire rural Muslim population ignored his call. Later, Pukhrâj's grandfather and one other Muslim began to respond to it. The Sâîñ then tried to teach the *kalimâ* to rural Muslims but only a few bothered to learn from him. Most rural Muslims considered religious rituals 'useless.'[xxi]

However, because of the constant efforts of outsiders like the Sâîñ (and his Hiñdu counterparts) a thitherto indifferent rural population gradually began to become religious.[xxii] That is one reason why a people who had lived with each other like brothers for centuries slowly started drifting into two implacably hostile nations.

Contentment: From the time that it was founded, Jammû had the reputation of being a very clean city. Because it is built on the slopes of a hill, all it took to wipe the city clean was one rainfall—and stone-lined streets and a good drainage system. Every visitor—and visiting writer—has commented on this. 'Modern' engineering has interfered with the drainage somewhat, and the streets are now made of cement or asphalt.

The Mahârâjâs' Jammû was also a particularly inexpensive place to live in—especially when compared with neighbouring Puñjâb. *Ghee* (melted butter), for instance, was almost forty per cent cheaper than in Lahore. This was mainly because the Mahârâjâ had banned the export of a very large number of local products.[5] As a result prices were kept down. Pukhrâj writes, 'This might have been the reason that people, in spite of being poor, felt content.'[xxiii]

Ustâd Khân Sâheb Ali Baksh was one such person. His musical talents—singing, as well as playing the tânpurâ—won him acclaim in Lahore and Sindh. He was supposed to be the best Hiñdustanî music singer in undivided India—a talent that was never recognised formally. (That of his son, the legendary Badé Ghulam Alî Khân, was—by fans, by the market and by the Indian State.) The Ustâd would have earned at least a living wage (if not much more) had he migrated from Jammû to where the real market for his music was. But he chose not to. Pukhrâj comments, "Lord knows what attractions, what magic, Jammû had that he did not want to leave even though he was on the verge of starvation."[xxiv]

And he was not the only Muslim who loved Jammû so intensely. Pukhrâj writes that the Hindus and Muslims would alike 'pray for their Mahârâjâ. They sincerely believed that since Allah had appointed the rulers, it was their duty to love and respect them. They loved their land so much that they did not think of moving to another city."[xxv]

In turn, when Pukhrâj was a child and unknown in the world of singing, the Jammû elite encouraged her because she was a fellow Jammûite. They did not see her as a Muslim. Thâkur Kartâr Siñgh was one such noble.[xxvi]

5. The ban on the 'export' of *râjmâ* [red beans] and Jammû's famous basmati rice to the rest of India remained in place till the mid-1990s.

On his coronation, Mahârâjâ Hari Siñgh sent every family in his kingdom—Hiñdu as well as Muslim—two seers (roughly one kilogram) of sweets. Both communities were equally excited about his ascension to the throne. The Mahârânî of Jammû was a style icon even for Muslims like Pukhrâj.[xxvii]

Muslims at the royal court—and in the arts

Ustâd Ali Baksh and his first cousin, Allâh Baksh, were the great singing geniuses that Jammû city produced in the early 20th century. Unfortunately, some mental illness overwhelmed Allâh Baksh.

There was a very large number of Muslim musicians in the Mahârâjâ's court. The king always made sure that all the best musicians were invited. Therefore, there was no discrimination. The Mahârâjâ was so impressed by Ustad Mamman Khân's singing that he gave the Ustad his own emerald necklace. The other top classical singers of his era included Miyâñ Maulâ Bakhsh Talwañdîwâlé.

When the Mahârâjâ decided that Malkâ Pukhrâj ought to go in for advanced training in music, he specified that a good 'Khân Sâheb' should train her, when he could as well have sent her to a Pannñdit jî. Maulâ Bakhsh was the best available, so Hari Siñgh got his government to employ him.[xxviii]

The Mahârâjâ had a number of Muslims in his employ. Many of them were in senior positions. Among the ones mentioned by Pukhrâj are his secretary, Abdul Qayyûm Khân and Nawâb Khusrau Jung.[xxix] Pukhrâj talks about several Muslim ministers at Mahârâjâ Hari Siñgh's court. These included a poet. His name was 'Khushi Muhammad or perhaps Nazîr Ahmed,' she recalls.[xxx] (Actually, his name was both. Khushi Muhammad Nâzir was the greatest Urdu poet of undivided India at the turn of the 19th/ 20th centuries.)

Muhammad Abdullah of Chamkor Saheb (Ropar, Punjab), who graduated from the Aligarh Muslim University in the 1890s and was thus one of the few Indians with a BA at the time, joined the highest rungs of the Mahârâjâ's civil service. His son, Qudratullâh Shahâb, of the Indian Civil Service, became a great Urdu writer. Shahâb would later recall that while preparing for the ICS examination, whenever he needed pin money he would go to the Pañj Pîr shrine in Ramnagar Rakh, and pocket some of the coins placed there by devotees. He kept a meticulous account of all the money he had taken. After he got into the ICS he returned every penny.

Moulvi Hashmat Ullah Khan was another ranking civil servant who, like Muhammad Abdullah, held the highest office in Gilgit. Incidentally, the Flagstaff House in Gilgit is still called Samad House after the aforementioned Gen. Samad Khan, who had led the Gilgit Campaign on behalf of the Mahârâjâ.

Dr Noor Hussain was the Mahârâjâ's personal physician and was appointed the Director (Health Services) for the entire state in 1947. The government gave him a large, Victorian bungalow on Jammû's elite Residency Road. He 'was looked upon with favour by Mahârâni Târâ Devi,' his son, Khâlid Hasan, recalls.

Other leading doctors of the era were Dr Abdul Karîm, Dr Azîz Kash, Dr Rehmatullâh and Dr Wazîr Ahmed Qureshi.

The highest ranking Puñjâbi/ Dogri/ Pahârhi-speaking Muslim officers who stayed on after 1947 were Chaudhary Niâz Ahmed, Chief Secretary (the highest ranking government servant in the state), Malik Muhammad Maqbool, who was the Registrar (Cooperatives), Syed Nisâr Hussain Shâh, Food Controller, and Wazîr Muhammad Khân, Senior Superintendent of Police.

Chaudhari Fazl e Haq was the deputy inspector of customs. Abdul Hai, too, was in the customs department. Malik Fazal Haq was the inspector of schools.

Though the Muslims—like the Mohyâl Brahmins—were not proportionately represented in the civil services and shop keeping, they did quite well in the army, the police and professions that required specialisation—again, like the Mohyâl Brahmins.

After the state army came under the British Indian Army and was given parity of rank, Brigadier was the highest rank that an Indian could hope to rise to. There were two Brigadiers in the state at any given time: one each in Kashmîr and Jammû. In 1947, Brig. Khudâ Baksh headed the army in Jammû province. He then became the head of the state army, first as a Brigadier and then as a Major General. (Pooñch was later put under a Brigadier.)

Earlier, the state army had several Muslim generals—notably Gen. Samunder Khân and Gen. Farmân Ali Khân. Brig. Bashîr Ahmed and Col. Jamshed were among the other ranking officers.

During the troubles of October 1947 the head of the Jammu Sadr [central] Thâna [police station], which controlled the entire town and some adjacent villages, was Râjâ Sohbat Ali, sub-inspector. (Throughout South Asia, the Thâna Sadr of the state capital is the posting most sought after by policemen of the appropriate rank.)

The Superintendent of Police [SP] of Udhampur, the highest ranking police officer of that district, was Sheikh Muhammad Salîm. Muhammad Yâhyâ Qureshi was the SP of Mîrpur. Miâñ Abdul Rashîd, the Inspector General of Police, was the head of the state police. [Yusuf Saraf says that Rashîd was the SP of Jammû. According to Hasan he was the IGP.] Miâñ Saîd Ali was the district inspector of police.

Other ranking members of the tiny corps of police officers were Syed Sultân Ali Shâh, Sheikh Fazal Âlam and Durrâni.

Chaudhary Feroz Dîn Salâria was the Divisional Forest Officer. Malik Âftâb Ahmed was an engineer, Bâbu Roshan Dîn was in charge of the water works in Udhampur and Bâboo Abdul Hamîd was an overseer.

The arts: Gâmâ made the best sitars in the state, and among the best in undivided India. People from Bengal and Bombay would travel to Jammû to buy his fabled sitars.

From all accounts, Jammûites of the pre-1947 era had a very advanced knowledge of classical music. And this was not confined to the elite. Street singers would sing classical songs and teenagers would be able to identify the râg that the songs had been set in. Kashmîr and Jammû were not as insular as they later became. Most of the songs were in the Awadhi language of Eastern Uttar Pradésh. Zubaidâ, a teenaged singer from Tâlâb Khatîkâñ, would sing in the Benâres style.

Râd informs us that on winter evenings at the Peer Mitthâ Chowk, Muhammad Dîn Mirâsi would often be found playing Râg Gujri Todi on the clarinet, with the legendary Allâh Rakhâ Mirâsi accompanying him on the drum. (Allâh Rakhâ went on to become India's best known and highest paid tablâ player. His grandson, a trendy tabla player and sometime film star, is better known for hawking tea on television.)

Ustâd Âshiq Ali Khân of Patiala, another music luminary of that era, would camp at Sâîñ Samiullâh's Ahâtâ (courtyard) and perform at the Kashmîr Soap Factory on Residency Road.

The Khudâ Bux Band operated at a different level. But as the city's only [military-style] 'band' it was in great demand at all weddings—and at the funerals of very old Hiñdus. Later, Bairo Sâheb, too, started a band. Ooyi Allâh, Ferojâ Mirâsi and Jânâ were the leading clowns of the era.

Ghulâm Pehelwân ran a successful wrestling pit. Hakîm Barkat Ali owned the famous Râz é Hayât Clinic. Habîb Kaifvi's shop, Hobsons, sold furniture and rented tents and other accessories for weddings and other feasts. His shop also doubled as a literary salon for all communities.

Mirzâ Jâfar Ali Khân Asar and the great litterateur Maulvi Abdul Haq were among the state's elite.

Urdû remains the official language of Jammû to this day. Till the 1950s it was the only Indian language that most Hiñdu, Sikh and Jain men knew. It was also the language of their choice. Jammû was known for its mushâirâs (soirees, where Urdu poetry is recited), Sorayyâ Khurshîd notes.

Qais Sherwâni permanently headed the Bazm e Urdû. He was also its founder. Sherwâni later joined the Mahârâjâ's civil service.

Col. Adâlat Khân had served as the Mahârâjâ's ADC.

Just before partition, two of the Mahârâjâ's *aides de camp* (ADCs)—Sâhebzâdâ Nûr Muhammad and Malik—were Muslim, as were his head chef, head-waiter and several orderlies. (Fundamentalist Indians, especially before 1947, would rather appoint people of the other community as Prime Ministers than eat food cooked by them or have them in the immediate household staff.)

Under Hari Siñgh the royal kitchens cooked only *halâl* (kosher) meat, because his Muslim officials and other subjects would eat no other. The Hiñdus of Punjãb-Jammû—including Hari Siñgh's own clan, the Râjpûts—on the other hand, did not eat *halâl* meat. Forced to choose between the two, Hari Siñgh went with the majority community of his state.[xxxi]

Then why the impression in Kashmîr that the Dogrâ Mahârâjâs did not employ Muslims? Perhaps what is meant is that they were not employed in proportion to their share of the population. Some of the Muslims in the Dogrâ Mahârâjâs' government were from outside the state. Khusrau Jung, for instance, was Hyderâbâdî royalty.

However, when one reads about the Mahârâjâ's army — one cannot fail to note the preponderance of Muslim names, among officers as well as soldiers.[6] Perhaps they were mostly from old Pooñch-Rajourî.

Patronising Kashmîrî crafts: The Dogrâ Mahârâjâs used the culture of Kashmîr to represent not just the Valley but also the state as a whole. The Mubârak Mañdî of Jammû, for instance, 'was a brilliant example of Kashmîrî craftsmanship.'[xxxii] In particular, the doors of the large hall in that royal campus showcased the best of Kashmîrî art.[xxxiii]

The hallmark of the architecture of the Dogrâ Mahârâjâs—especially Hari Siñgh—was elegance in simplicity. The quality of construction was uniformly good. The location of the Dogrâ palaces—whether in Jammû, Udhampur, Srînagar or Gulmarg—was always outstanding. These palaces were built overlooking the best views in town.

Simplicity pervaded every aspect of Hari Siñgh's character. His palaces had none of the ornate curves and flourishes of, say, Râjasthânî palaces. Hari Siñgh would often say that he felt 'uneasy with the priceless things around [him].' He preferred rooms with 'plain walls and ceilings, which had no embellishments on them.'[xxxiv]

So, he left the elaborate Mubârak Mañdî palace and shifted to spartan Râmnagar (where his descendants now stay and also run a hotel). His advisors tried to dissuade him on the ground that a mahârâjâ ought to live in a palace that befitted his status. However, Hari Siñgh persisted with his decision. While this saved the contemporary taxpayer some money, the maintenance of the Mubârak Mañdî palace suffered. So much so that most Jammûites born after 1947 do not realise that the Mubârak Mañdî was once a palace.

One Kashmîrî craft that grew further during the Dogrâ era was that of building houseboats. Some three- and four-storey houseboats would be anchored near the Srînagar palace that now houses the state legislature. Considering that the traditional houseboat has only one floor, these were greatly admired by spectators.[xxxv]

In order to promote Kashmîrî handicrafts, Mahârâjâ Hari Siñgh got an exhibition ground—with permanent stalls—constructed in Srînagar. Private dealers could display their goods there. This triggered off a wave of creativity.[xxxvi] Kashmîrî craftsmen started thinking up new designs and

6. For instance, the 6th Jammû and Kashmîr Infantry Battalion, posted at Bunji (old Gilgit-Ladâkh), consisted of two companies of Pooñch Muslims, one Dogrâ Hiñdu company and one Sikh company.

products now that they, for the first time in history, had rival shops next to each other, each exhibiting its products. (The traditional way of selling goods—which continues to this day—is from the workshop or factory itself. Displaying goods in a show window is a western concept that dates, in J&K, to the 1930s and was perhaps introduced to Kashmîr by this exhibition.)

Travelling to Kashmîr: Before the era of automobiles, travelling from Jammû to Kashmîr (or back) was a hazardous and time-consuming affair. Those who could afford to hire a horse or mule would do so. Others took almost a fortnight on foot. The Jawâhar Tunnel at Banihâl was built only in the 1960s. Before that whether on foot or in a car, people had to go all the way up to the Banihâl Pass, which received snowfall in spring and autumn as well. People would freeze to death there. Which is why those who were about to embark on that journey would first go to all their friends and relatives and ask them to forgive them their trespasses. (This custom probably has its origin in the Islâmic Haj. People seek to be forgiven for fear that they might not come back alive.)

The Mahârâjâ of Kashmîr, like his Mughal precursors, would be carried in a palanquin. A staff of around twelve hundred people of varying ranks accompanied him. Their first halt in Kashmîr would be at an elegant rest house in Qâzigund which was burnt down by militants in the early 1990s.

Friends and counsellors: The first prince to arrive in Jammû for Hari Siñgh's coronation as mahârâjâ was the Nawâb of Pâlampur, a Muslim. He was, arguably, Hari Siñgh's closest friend. 'They behaved as if they were brothers.'[xxxvii] Such was the depth of their friendship that the Mahârâjâ got a palace called Tâleh Mañzil in Urdu (and Karan Mahal in Hiñdî) specially built for him near his own palace in Srînagar. He wanted to ensure that the Nawâb had a place appropriate to his status to stay in when he came visiting in the summer. This honour was extended to no other visitor.

Tâleh Mañzil was built at the highest point of Gupkâr Road, where the Mahârâjâ's nobility lived. I used to, half a century later, stay at the bottom of the road. Except for the house allotted to me, which was built as the official residence of the Governor of Kashmîr, and perhaps two other houses, all the vast mansions on Gupkâr (with names like Effendi Villa) housed Muslim nobles. Almost all of them migrated to Pâkistân after 1947, because they did not hail from the state.

Another regular and favourite guest was Maulânâ Sâheb. He belonged to central Indian royalty and lived in Lucknow. Whenever he came to the state the Mahârâjâ would insist on the Maulânâ spending at least two or three months with him. Even though other Muslims would (unfairly, as it turned out) warn the Mahârâjâ that the Maulânâ was not the good-natured simpleton that he appeared to be, Hari Siñgh always stood by his guest.[xxxviii]

The rulers and the ruled—an informal relationship: The Mahârâjâ does not seem to have been the 'oriental despot' of Western imagination. His employees and subjects—including Muslims—felt free to take certain liberties without being victimised. When the Mahârâjâ's secretary, Abdul Qayyûm Khân, came to summon Pukhrâj, then a child, to the court, she was asleep. Her mother refused to wake her up, saying, "If they want to listen to her singing they can send the car tomorrow."[xxxix] There seems to have been no fear of the Mahârâjâ's wrath.

In nearby Chenainî, relations with the king (who was subordinate to Jammû) were even more informal. If a person (accused, normally, of a minor crime) was summoned to the court of the king (who doubled as a judge), and if it was not convenient for him to attend the king's court that day, the accused would say so to the king. The king of Chenainî would then fix the next hearing according to the pleasure of the accused.

And if the person was found guilty and imprisoned, he could still move about freely during the day—he could till his fields, tend his flock or keep shop. He was required to report to the jail only in the evening, to spend the night there. This idyllic state of affairs continued in Chenainî till 1947. Malkâ Pukhrâj comments, 'There were no restrictions on them, and therefore the prisoners broke no rules.'[xl]

Crime was virtually unknown in the hills of Jammû—as it is to this day in Leh, Kargil and the 'Northern Areas' of occupied Kashmîr. People in these areas are simple and content with their lot—and their isolation from the world of the plains.

Jammû and Kashmîr—especially the 'Northern Areas'—was an exceptionally peaceful place at the time. (Unlike, say, the Punjâb or UP, which were not.) The Mahârâjâ of Jammû and Kashmîr would move around in his state without any bodyguards or other security—and so would visiting kings, while in the state. Nor would the mahârâjâ keep guards around his chambers at night when he went to sleep.[xli] Murder and violent attacks on people continued to be rare—till, in 1989, a generous neighbour changed all that, and exported its own culture (and weapons) to this uniquely serene state.

References

i Pukhraj, Malka, *Song Sung True*, trans. and ed. by Saleem Kidwai (2002), Zubaan, Kali for Women, Hauz Khas Enclave, New Delhi 110016, page 154.

ii Ibid, page 1.

iii Ibid, page 88.

iv Ibid, page 2.

v Ibid, page 37.

vi Ibid, pp. 191-194.

vii Ibid, page 113.

viii Ibid, page 211.

ix Ibid, page 3.

x Ibid, page 21.

xi Ibid, page 94.

xii Ibid, page 93.

xiii Ibid, page 94.

xiv Ibid, page 136.

xv Ibid, page 76.
xvi Ibid, page 87.
xvii Ibid, page 84.
xviii Ibid, page 42.
xix Ibid, page 48.
xx Ibid, page 94.
xxi Ibid, page 95.
xxii Ibid, page 96.
xxiii Ibid, page 19.
xxiv Ibid, page 25.
xxv Ibid, page 66.
xxvi Ibid, page 62.
xxvii Ibid, page 140.
xxviii Ibid, page 131.
xxix Ibid, page 92.
xxx Ibid, page 83.
xxxi Ibid, page 89.
xxxii Ibid, page 67.
xxxiii Ibid, page 90.
xxxiv Ibid, page 78.
xxxv Ibid, page 115.
xxxvi Ibid, pages 146-7.
xxxvii Ibid, page 70.
xxxviii Ibid, page 133.
xxxix Ibid, page 62.
xl Ibid, page 81.
xli Ibid, page 77.

3

Did the Gujjars come from Georgia?

The Gujjars are a six million strong community of cowherds who later became farmers and soldiers as well. They live in north and west India, Pâkistân and Afghanistan. Some educated, middle-class Gujjars claim that their ancestors had migrated to India from a land called Gurjria or Gurjistan.

There was a very powerful, and very sizeable, Gujjar kingdom in ancient India. In modern times people from this community have held high positions in India and Pâkistân—including India's first (and most powerful yet) Home Minister and a Prime Minister of Pâkistân. However, a substantial number of Gujjars still live as cowherds, albeit fairly prosperous ones. Some Gujjars are nomads.

The Gujjars are Hiñdus in the Indian plains and Muslims in the Indian Himalayas and Pâkistân. There are some Sikh Gujjars, too.

In India the Muslim Gujjars mainly live in Jammû, Kashmîr, Himachal Pradesh, the northern tip of Indian Punjâb (Deena Nagar) and Uttarakhand.

'The Gujjars came to India from Central Asia or Europe'

There are two broad views about the origin of the Gujjars.

Nationalist historians believe that they are indigenous to India.[1] The evidence that they offer is convincing—especially that the language that the Gujjars speak is very Indo-Aryan, whether in Indian Râjasthân or in Pâkistâni Swât. What the nationalists have not been able to explain is the presence

1. These nationalist historians include Hiñdus as well as Muslims. They believe that the Gujjars have been in India since at least the first century AD (if not, as we shall see, 200 BC.) If they accept the 'Gujjars are Khazars from Georgia' theory then they will have to push the Gujjar period forward by at least four hundred years, because the Georgians/ Khazars could not have come to India before the 5th century AD. Contd...

of Gujjars right up to Afghânistân, and perhaps beyond as well, in the direction of Central Asia.

Those who say that the Gujjars came from Central Asia point to the presence to this day of Gujjar communities all along a trail that definitely leads from India to Central Asia—to Georgia in particular. This school feels that the Gujjars came to India around the 5th century AD[i] (A tiny minority of scholars puts the date at the 2nd or 3rd century AD.) In either case the community has been in India long enough to have become totally indigenised.

W. Crooke, *Castes and Tribes of North Western India*, Vol. 2, is among the votaries of the Central Asian origin of the Gujjars. Vincent A. Smith wrote that the Gujjars were perhaps "allied in blood" to the Huns.[ii]

Others believe that the Gujjars have descended from the Central Asian or Indo-Iranian Scythian (Sacae or Saka) community[iii] West, S "Scythians" in: Egbert Bakker, Irene de Jong and Hans van Wees (eds.), *Brill's Companion to Herodotus* (Leiden: 2002) 437-456 which came to India in the 1st century BC or the Central Asian Yue-Chi/ Yachi (Kushân)[iv] community that migrated to India in the 1st century AD. The Yachi/ Kushân peoples are said to be clans from the Eastern Tartars (erstwhile USSR).

These new warrior migrants (whatever be their name and origin) were incorporated into Hiñdu society, mostly into the elite Kshatriya/ Râjpût caste of kings, farmers and soldiers.[v]

One theory that should be rejected outright is that the Gujjars were some kind of Hiñdu Rajputs who entered into an agreement with the 17th century Mughal Emperor Aurangzeb to the effect that if they lost to the Mughals in a war, some of them would convert to Islam. They lost and the group that converted came to be called the Gujjars. (The present Muslim Gujjars' ancestors were Muslims before Aurangzeb's 15th century ancestor, Babar, came to India. Secondly there is no historical mention of this incident. Above all there have been Hiñdu Gujjars for at least twelve hundred years before Aurangzeb.)

Contd...

This 'indigenous origin' vs. 'foreign origin' debate is present throughout India. Some people believe that the Kashmîris are the descendants of Jews. Nationalist historians ridicule this claim. (My own view is that most Kashmîris are of indigenous origin. However, a few Jews migrated to Kashmîr and got assimilated into Kashmîri society.)

Most North (and some South) Indians are said to be the descendants of 'Aryans' who migrated to India from the Caucasus. The nationalists believe that the Aryans originated in India, from where they fanned out to Europe and Central Asia.

So, are at least the 'Dravidians' of South India (and some parts of the North) indigenous, as South Indian nationalists claim? No, say people,\who have gathered evidence to the effect that the 'Dravidians' are really a Mediterranean people

Where within Georgia did the Gujjars come from?

Among those who believe that the Gujjars migrated from Central Asia to India, the majority agrees that they came from Georgia in particular. Is this belief based on the mere philological similarity between the words Georgia and Gujjar/ Gujarât?

Certainly not. And this is not a 19th or 20th century belief either. The Persians have, since at least mediæval times, called neighbouring Georgia by the name Gurjistân[vi] ('the land of Gurj' or 'the land of the Gurj community'). Georgia has also been called Gurjia. In ancient Indian texts (and in Sañskrit to this day) the Gujjars are called 'Gurjar.'

The Arabs knew Georgia by the name Gurz. They tend to use the 'j' sound interchangeably with 'g'. Suleimân, an Arab merchant, called the ninth century Gurjar dynasty of Méwâr (Râjasthân, India) by the name Jozr. James M.C. Campbell, the renowned British Râj authority on the Gujjars, felt that 'Gurz... corresponds so closely with Jozr... that in AD. 1860 the derivation was viewed with favour both by Dr Glasgow and by Dr Bhâu Dâjî.'[vii]

Apparently, the fourth class of Ossetes of the Caucasus are known as the Gurjaks. They are the descendants of Georgian prisoners of war.

Within Georgia the Gujjars' original habitat was *between* the Black Sea and the Caspian Sea.[viii] Persian speaking people call the Caspian Sea by the name Behr-é-Khizar. Communities from the Caspian Sea area are said to be called by the names Khizar, Guzar, Gurjar, Gurjara and Gujjar. Indeed, many scholars believe that the Gujjar community is the same as the Khizar or Khazar nation. Once again, as we shall see, the evidence goes much beyond mere philological similarities.

Who were the Khazars?

The Khazars were perhaps of Scythian stock. Little is known about their history before the sixth century AD.

The Khazars are closely related to the Huns. The clans of the Khazar community are similar to the various Turkic tribes that used to live within the Khazarian Empire, between the Black and Caspian Seas. (This area is today divided between Georgia. Armenia and Azerbaijan.) The Khazars were probably a Caucasian people who became part of the Scythian and, later, Turkic peoples.[2] Most scholars agree that the Khazars were perhaps Georgians and Armenians.

From around 550 to 630 AD the Khazars were subordinate to the Kök Turks. That empire disintegrated and the Khazars became independent. The Khazars went on to found a powerful empire in Southern Russia that stretched to the Aral Sea (which straddles present-day Uzbekistân and Kazakhstan) in the east.

---

2. Thus the Gujjars can be Georgian, Scythian, Turkic and Hun at the same time.

It was a flourishing kingdom. Some (but not all) Khazars accepted the Jewish religion, Judaism. Khazarian royalty was among those who converted to Judaism. These kings were an extremely tolerant lot—before as well as after their conversion. Besides, theirs was a very prosperous kingdom, called Khazaria. This attracted Jews, as well as others, from many parts of Central Asia and Europe (mainly Eastern) to migrate to their land.

Around 720 AD the Khazars established their capital at Samandar (which means 'the sea' in Indo-Aryan languages), near the Caspian Sea. When the Khazar Empire fell, the Kievan Rus took over most of its lands.

Nothing seems to be left of Khazar culture. There is no trace of the Khazarian language among Jews. None of the places that they ruled over in Europe points to a Khazar origin. None of their European descendants has a Khazar surname. Nor have their customs survived in Europe.

It is only because of a few references in Arabic, Persian and other sources that the world knows about the Khazars at all. In other words, in the later Islamised East alone are any memories of this great empire-building community left.

But if they are the same as the Gujjars then the East is full of places named after them and people with surnames derived from this clan. Their customs, too, have survived if they are the same people. But not their language.

The word 'Khazar' is much like 'Gujjar.' The Indo-Aryan languages do not have the "kh" and "z" sounds. So, 'kh' got converted to "g" and 'z' to "j". This, incidentally, is not a guess. This is the standard rule of phonetic change from any language into an Indo-Aryan language.

In any case, north of the sea of Asof this community is called Gazar. The Lesghians of the Caucasus knew them as Ghysar.

Abul Faraj (AD 1243), an Arab writer, has categorically stated that the Georgians (or Gurges) were the same people as the Khazars or Khozars.

Apart from the philological similarity, both the Gujjars and the Khazars are said to have lived in Georgia and both have Scythian and Hun blood in their veins. And both started founding empires at around the same time: the Gujjars in the 5th century AD in India and the Khazars a century later in Central Asia.

The Gujjars of undivided India are quite dark skinned. Considering that they spend most of the time in the sun, they could have got tanned. However, even stay-at-home types in this community are normally darker than, say, their Kashmîri or Punjabi neighbours.

Then how could the Gujjars possibly be of Georgian descent? Even fifteen hundred years in India could not have changed the colour of hair, eyes or unexposed skin.

The explanation lies in the Khazars themselves. They were divided into two communities: the fair Ak-Khazar and the dark skinned Kara Khazar.

(Kara is the ancient Indian word for 'dark.' It is interesting that even the Khazars used this word.) Campbell[ix] writes, 'The Kara Khazar was short, ugly and black as an Indian.[3] He was the Ugrian nomad of the steppes who formed the rank and file of the army.'

Some Ak-Khazars, too, must have come to India. There is a small Gujjar clan in the Punjâb called the Javlas or Jhawlas. They are the descendants of the White Huns.[4]

Why did the Georgians go to India?

The great King Vakhtang (AD 469-500) is the founder of 'Tiflis' (Tbilisi), the present capital of Georgia. He is also known as Gourgasal[5] or wolf-lion. He defeated the Ossetes, Abkhasians and Armenians. He then entered into a treaty with Persia. According to a Georgian legend, he then invaded India.[x]

Indian histories of that period do not mention either Vakhtang or Georgia or even Khazar. However, there definitely were invasions from Central Asia around that time. Also, this was the precise period when the first known Gujjar kingdom came up in India. To top it all, the invading king had a 'gourg' in his name.

It is difficult to dismiss all this as a set of coincidences.

Campbell feels that the story of Gourgasa's invasion is really a dramatisation of the actual movement of the Khazars of South Armenia and north Media towards India. He writes that the Khazars joined their relations, the White Huns of Badeghiz, at Herat. The two groups then invaded India together.[xi]

The Gujjars' route from Georgia to India

When the Gujjars left Georgia, they are believed to have travelled slowly through Central Asia, Iraq, Iran and Afghanistan. They entered India through Baluchistan finally reached Gujarât around the 5th century AD. They founded settlements all along this route, which is the ultimate proof of a 'Gujjar corridor' that stretches from Indian Gujarât to the Behr-é-Khizar (the Caspian Sea).

In Iran, Afghanistan, Turkmenia, Pakistan and India there are places called Gujar (Central Asia), Juzrs (Gurjara), Gujrabad, Gujru/ Guzru, Gujar Khasi, Chusak Gujar, Gurjistan, Gujrabas, Gujdar-Kotta, Gujar-Garh,

3. Being an Indian I won't comment on what he has said about Indians. However, I can safely assert that the nomadic Gujjars of the Himalayas are tall by any international yardstick. The men, typically, are six feet tall and the women 5'6" or more.
4. This factoid is from Cambell, *The Gujjars-IV*. reprinted in *Âwâz-é-Gurjar*, Sep. '96, page 14. However, Sir Campbell feels that this 'trace of Javla remains among Gujjars [does not prove that] they at first belonged to the Khazar tribe.'
5. Scholars like Campbell feel that if Gujjar is a Central Asian word, then it is probably derived from the Persian word *gurg* (wolf).

Gujarkhan and Gujranwala. Apart from the Western Indian state of Gujarât, there is a place called Gujrât in West Punjâb which has a substantial Gujjar population. There is a third Gujrât in Saharanpur.[xii] Even Gujarghar (Gwalior, Central India) is said to be named after this great community.

The first mention of Gujjars in Indian history

Poet Bân Bhatt's *Harsh-charit* (6th century AD.) is the oldest extant record that mentions the Gujjars. Hieun Tsâng, the Chinese traveller, was the next to write about them.

However, if we accept the theory that the Gujjars entered India with the Kushâns or Yu-che, then they probably came over in the first century BC.

The *Pañch-tañtr* is India's equivalent of Æsop's *Fables*. It mentions Gurjar Désh, the land of the Gujjars. It is generally believed to have been written around the 5th or 6th century AD A 20th century Indian novelist, Ruskin Bond, wrote that the *Pañch-tañtr* dates to 200 BC. Ever since several articles have appeared citing Mr. Bond and claiming that the Gujjars have been in India since at least 200 BC. But Mr. Bond is a novelist, not a historian.

Gujjar kingdoms in India

The first Gujjar kingdom that there is evidence of existed around the fifth century AD. This was in Rajasthan, on the borders of present day Gujarât. Bhinmal (Shrîmâla), near Mount Abu, was its capital.

Perhaps around the same time some Gujjars migrated to the foothills of the Himalayas. The area in which they live ranges from Jammû in the west to Uttarakhand in the east.

Some Gujjar leaders[xiii] believe that their ancestors migrated to the Kutch district of Gujarât in the 7th century in order to protect the 'motherland' of Gujarât from invaders from 'the Middle East'. This belief is based on ancient records maintained by Bhat priests. It does not say where the Gujjars came from. Since this was before the advent of Islam, the invaders were not Muslim but one of the groups referred to above. In India, to this day, all except academics and specialists regard the Middle East and Central Asia as the same region. Clearly, the Gujjars' migration to India has a 'Middle Eastern' angle to it. Perhaps they had to flee a better-armed Central Asian clan.

These Gujjar leaders say that the Gujjars fanned out from Kutch to other parts of India (and present day Pâkistân). Well, Gujjars all over India and Pâkistân do speak the same language. But did they fan out from Kutch to Swât (Pâkistân) and Afghânistân, both of which are between Gujarât and, say, Georgia, or did some of them stay behind in Afghânistân and Swât on the way from some 'Middle Eastern' country (say, Georgia) on their way to Gujarât?

The Gujjars had a major presence in Tughlaqâbâd, a suburb of Delhi. We know this because of a curse said to have been placed on Delhi by the 12th century Muslim mystic, Hazrat Nizamuddin Auliyâ, *Yâñ rahé Gujjar, Yâñ rahé Ujjar* ('Either Gujjars will live [in Delhi] or a wasteland will.' In other words, 'If Gujjars cease to live [in Delhi], the place will become a wasteland.').

This indicates that i) the Gujjars were an important factor in Delhi by the 12th century; ii) someone (reportedly, the Sultan of Delhi) was preventing them from living in Delhi; and iii) the great Hazrat Nizamuddin felt strongly enough about his Gujjar friends to take on the might of that someone (the Sultan, perhaps) on their behalf.

At that stage the Gujjars were probably Hiñdus. That Hazrat Nizamuddin supported them is a fact. Could it be that some of them converted to Islam under his influence? This is a pure guess based on the fact that by the 14th century the present-day Muslim Gujjar community had been established.

In the 15th century there was a beautiful Gujjar princess called Mrignayani. Raja Mân Singh Tomar, the king of Gwalior, married her and got a palace-fort complex built for her. It is generally known as the Gujjari Mahal ('the Palace of the Gujjar lady').

We next hear of a Gujjar chieftain called Jamâtullâ. Bhai Sahib Singh (1669-1705) killed him in a battle at Anandpur (Punjab).[xiv] The Bhai is one of 'the Five [Most] Beloved' people in Sikh history. Jamâtullâ was obviously a Muslim. This indicates that some Muslim Gujjar communities had struck deep roots in the Punjab by the seventeenth century.

...and then reverse migration?

All over Europe there are brown-skinned, Indian-looking gypsies of the Români community. The language that they speak is halfway between Gojri (the language of the Gujjars) and Punjâbi, with a fair sprinkling of European words. The Gujjars of the Indian sub-continent are divided into eighty-four clans. The Românis claim to belong to the exalted Bad-gujjar clan and worship a devî (female deity) called Satsara.

The Gujjars of India accept them as one of their own. The Gojri Research Institute is of the opinion that the 'Românis are in fact Gujjars who resemble their counterparts in the sub-continent in physique, appearance and stature.'[xv]

If this is true then my theory is that after a few centuries in India, the pull of atavism took the Români clan of Gujjars back to Central Asia and Eastern Europe.

The spread of Gujjars in India

There were around 2,038,692 Gujjars in undivided India in 1931. That was when the last census was conducted that enumerated clans such as the Gujjars separately. This was a major increase over the 1,416,837 Gujjars counted in the 1881 census.

In 1931 the Gujjars were found to live in eight Indian provinces in particular: Delhi, Jammû & Kashmir, undivided Punjab, the North-West Frontier Province (NWFP, now in Pakistan), and the Indian states now called Uttaranchal and Himachal Pradesh. They also live in North-Western India.

The 1881 break-up was: 627,304 Gujjars in undivided Punjab, 402,709 in Râjputânâ, 337,466 in Central India, 308,909 in the NWFP, 64,609 in the Bombay presidency, 32,690 in Ajmér, 967 in Bérâr, 562 in Hyderâbâd and 41 in Bengal. The regions mentioned in the 1881 census have since been reorganised into the eight provinces mentioned above.

If the Gujjar population has increased at the same rate as the rest of India, there should be around six million Gujjars in the Indian sub-continent today.

On the 1st May 1960 the Gujjars got a state of their own, Gujarât, which was carved out of the erstwhile Bombay Presidency. Gujarât is short for 'Gujjar Râtra', the land of the Gujjars.

Thus, if the Gujjars have indeed come from Georgia, it can be said that ethnic Georgians now have an entire Indian state to themselves (a state that is almost as big as Georgia itself). In addition they are spread over seven other regions in the Indian sub-continent.

Gujarât is India's fourth richest state and routinely produces eminent industrialists and businessmen. The Indian diaspora in East Africa is mainly from Gujarat.

Similar customs

Marco Polo noted that the Georgians cut their hair short, like churchmen. So did the White Huns and the Khazars. And so did the Shrîmâlîs of South Kâthiâwâr (Gujarât).

A few scholars have noticed some Jewish customs among the Gujjars. The Khazar connection would explain that.

A writer, identified only as Qaisar,[xvi] feels that the Gujjars' 'way of life closely resembles [that of] Central Asian people.' He claims that even the names of household goods and sub-castes are the same. This is a very serious assertion and, if correct, will conclusively prove the Central Asian origin of the Gujjars. However, Mr. Qaisar has not given any further details. My own fieldwork suggests that whatever other similarities the Gujjars might have with Central Asian people, their language and system of *gotr* (sub-caste) is entirely Indian.

Qaisar does mention that 'the hairstyle of the womenfolk is exactly the same without even [the] slightest change.' This is correct. Gujjar-Bakerwâl women braid their hair in a manner resembling North African dreadlocks.

The nomadic lifestyle of the Gujjars does have some Central Asian features. However, we need to compare the two more minutely before jumping to conclusions. After all, the lives of nomads everywhere would have some similarities.

Mr. Qaisar says that both the Gujjars and Central Asian people have the 'same caravans, with pack ponies, watchdogs, [similar] utensils, mobile hearth, [a holder called trangrhi to pack] luggage [in] and wooden spoon...The same kind of jewellery, clothes and lifestyle...[And women of both communities cover their heads with a] triangular head-covering called kasâwâ or kajâvâ...'

These perceived similarities certainly need to be compared. So do Gujjar footwear (which are doubtless of Central Asian origin) and waistcoats. However, I am not sure if Gujjar 'caravans' are anything like their Central Asian counterparts, because most Gujjars migrate from the plains to the hills and back on foot—and not in wagons or on horses or camels. What is certain that both communities travel hundreds of miles with their herds.

Also, the Bakerwâls' dogs (and the horses of Kâthiâwâr) are certainly of non-Indian origin. Qaisar believes that the Gujjars' 'goats, sheep, ponies [and] mules...are also [of] Central Asian Breed.'

The view in Georgia

Prof. Chogoshvili of the Georgian Academy of Sciences conducted an ethnological study of the Gujjars in the 1960s. In 1967 he concluded that there were 'remarkable similarities' between the Georgians and the Gujjars. Prof. Levan Maruahvili of the Georgian Institute of Geography wrote 'there is enough evidence to sustain a case for a thorough study to find out when the Georgians started moving to India.'[xvii]

What really needs to be studied

This author feels that what needs to be investigated first is whether the jewellery, dreadlocks, utensils, headscarves and other things mentioned by Qaisar are indeed the same among the Gujjars and Central Asians. Are the sheepdogs of the Gujjar-Bakerwâls of a Central Asian breed? And the ponies of Kâthiâwâr?

I do not believe that the language of the communities is likely to be the same, except to the extent that both might be Indo-Aryan languages. The Gujjars' language took ages to evolve in India and for centuries was a spoken, rather than written, language. This fits perfectly with the Georgian-origin theory because the Georgian alphabet was invented only in the 3rd century BC by the King of Iberia, Farnavaz I. So, in the fourth or fifth century AD the visitors from Georgia must have mostly been an unlettered lot.

Similarly, we are unlikely to find similarities in architecture. The oldest extant Georgian monument is the 4th century Georgian Church in Bethlehem. If Georgian high architecture was developed as close to the supposed date of the Gujjars' migration to India as that, the migrants are not likely to have taken any major architectural skills with them. In India, the Gurjars built great monuments (around the 8th century AD) but to this day the nomadic Gujjars live in makeshift shelters during the six warm months and in unprepossessing houses in winter.

I took some Gujjar jewellery to Geergia. Nothing similar exists in the Caucasus.

What intrigues me is that the currency issued by the Gurjar kings of India was called the dramma.[xviii] It certainly was in the 9th century, but perhaps also in the 7th century AD. It is claimed that dramma is the Indian name of the Greek drachma. Now, obviously the Gujjars are not of Greek origin. But did Georgia ever use the drachma? I have scanned several dozen websites for a clue, but without success. If any part of Georgia-Armenia had ever used the drachma in ancient times, it would be proof of a very high order of the Gujjars' links with Georgia.

I found no such proof during my visit to the Caucasus in 2004. I returned from Georgia to Yerevan in neighbouring Armenia, from where I was to fly back to India. Dram, I noticed in a Eureka moment, was the currency of Armenia even in the 21st century. And, what is more, in the famous Vernissage Sunday-market I found hawkers pronouncing the word *dram-uh*.

Three years later, in 2007, I was back in Tbilisi, Georgia. We made the obligatory pilgrimage to McDonald's, this one being in the Marjanishvili district, where the Agmashebeli Street meets the Tamar Mephe Street. As we climbed up the stairs we saw on the walls many sepia monochrome photographs, presumably taken in the early 1900s. One of them showed a Georgian family in traditional clothes, the women sitting on a horse, with grand mediæval architecture behind them. Except that the horse is very tall, from their clothes, cap and hairstyle, these could easily have been nomadic Gujjars or Bakerwals from the Jammû and Kashmîr of 2011, commencing their twice-a-year trek.

So, perhaps there is something to the theory, after all.

References

i, Pemble, J., *The Raj, the Indian Mutiny, and the Kingdom of Oudh, 1801-1859* (Sussex: The Harvester Press Limited 1977), 122

ii. *The Early History of India* (Oxford: OUP 1962)

iii. West, S. "Scythians" in: Egbert Bakker, Irene de Jong and Hans van Wees (eds.), *Brill's Companion to Herodotus* (Leiden: 2002) 437-456
M Chauhan *Scythic Origin of the Rajput Race* (Ujjain: Rajputana Liberation Front, 1999)

vi. General Cunningham

v. Sharma, JC, *Gojri and its Relationship with Rajasthani* cited by Dr David Emmanuel Singh, OCMS, Oxford, UK *Muslim Van Gujjars of Rajaji National Park in Uttaranchal, India* (available on the internet).

vi. See, for instance, Rawlinson, Trans. Royal Geographic Society, IX 51; and Bibliotheque Orientale II.158.

vii. Sir J. Campbell's masterpiece *The Gujjar*, written perhaps in the 1890s, has been serialised in *Âwâz-é-Gurjar* March-April, 1996, May 1996, August 1996 and September 1996. This work was first published in the *Bombay Gazetteer, Hiñdus of Gujarat*, Appendix B The Gujjars.

viii, Husain, Majid, *Geography of Jammû & Kashmir State* is one of the many writers who have recorded this belief.

ix. *Âwâz-é-Gurjar* March-April, 1996, page 23.

x. This legend was recorded in late 19th century/ early 20th century editions of the Encyclopædia Britannica (in the article about Georgia) X.432.

xi. Reprinted in *Âwâz-é-Gurjar* March-April, 1996, pages 19 and 20.

xii. See, for instance, '*The Gujjars,*' a magazine published by the Gurjardesh Charitable Trust, Jammû. Page 23. (Year not stated; perhaps 1994.)

xiii. The Shri Kutch Gurjar Kshatriya Mahâ sabhâ is a federation that represents the Gujjars of Kutch and Gujarât in particular and western, central and south central India in general. Happily, it speaks for Hiñdu as well Muslim Gujjars. The leaders referred to represent this organisation. From http://www.chawra.com/kgk/main.htm cited by Dr David Emmanuel Singh, OCMS, Oxford, UK *Muslim Van Gujjars of Rajaji National Park in Uttaranchal, India* (available on the internet).

xiv From the *Encyclopedia of Sikhism*, ed. Harbans Singh Ji at http://www.sikh-history.com/sikhhist/gurus/psahibs.html cited by Dr David Emmanuel Singh, OCMS, Oxford, UK *Muslim Van Gujjars of Rajaji National Park in Uttaranchal, India* (available on the internet).

xv. 'Romanis and Gujars, *Awaz-e-Gurjar*, Dec. '96, page 5.

xvi. 'Gujjars in historical perspective,' *Awaz-e-Gurjar*, Jammû, Vol.1, Issue 7, Dec. 1995. pages 7-9.

xvii. Both quotes are from Saraf, Suraj, 'Between Hills and Plains' *Awaz-e-Gurjar*, Jammû , Vol.1, Issue 7, Dec. 1995.

xviii. 'Gujar Coins, *Awaz-e-Gurjar*, Oct. '96, page 9.

4

The Hiñdu-Sikh Clans and Sub-castes of Jammû[1]

Caste can be a divisive—and, in the case of the oppressed people, iniquitous—concept. For that reason, censuses conducted by the government of independent India (including castes of which some members are Muslim) discouraged listing communities by caste. The 1931 census was the last to do so in J & K. And yet, not only anthropologists but also lay teenagers always want to know about the history of their own caste—and that of their friends.[i]

In the 20th century, historians from (as well as community associations that claim to represent) almost all the castes and sub-castes of India brought out books about the glorious past of their community. 'Once we were kings.' That kind of stuff. And this is true not only of the so-called 'upper' castes.

The stranglehold that caste has on the imagination of all Indians can be seen from the fact that in the census of 1931 only a little more than 3% of the Hiñdus of the state (plus just under 3 per cent of the Jains, around 6% of the Buddhists and just over 4 per cent of the Muslims) did not indicate their 'caste.' Only in the tiny Sikh community of the state did as many as 44 per cent not do this. And most of these seemingly 'casteless' people—regardless of religion—actually belonged to castes that had so few members that the census records did not list their castes. So, the actual number of people who refused to slot themselves as a matter of principle—people like this author—was smaller still.

---

1. In this chapter we have used the words clan, sect, sub-caste and community interchangeably, mainly in order to avoid the monotony of repeated words. Only when used for the Muslims does the word 'sect' have an assigned meaning—the Shias and Sunnis belong to the two main sects of Islâm.

   A 'got' or 'gotr' is a bloodline.

Jammû is unique in that the proportion of the *scheduled castes* is almost twice the national average. More important, the 'scheduled castes' live in the fertile and prosperous plains, while the ruling Râjpût community—like the Brâhmins—has traditionally dwelt in the arid, poverty-stricken hills.

Thus, the 'scheduled castes' of Jammû (as in the neighbouring Punjãb) have traditionally been well to do and educated.

Untouchability was outlawed in the state in 1930. The Mahârâjâ of Jammû and Kashmîr, Hari Siñgh, made sure that the members of the 'scheduled castes' were allowed access to all wells (unlike many parts of India where they could not drink water from the same wells as the 'caste Hiñdus'), temples, schools and government employment. Indeed, he sanctioned special scholarships for children from the 'scheduled castes.'

Champa Sharma adds, 'Folk ballads certify that the Dogrâ Brâhmins had fraternal relations... with the people of the fourth *varna*. Eso (a Scheduled Caste) was a close friend of the [late mediæval, revolutionary peasant leader] Brâhmin Bava Jitto.'[ii]

The British Râj had branded certain clans as *criminal tribes*. During that era, the Mahârâjâs' Jammû and Kashmîr was mostly free of crime. There were all of 42 members of the Pernâ tribe and 134 Sâñsî tribals in the state in 1931.

For a while the Bakerwâl tribe had been classified as criminal. But, in the 1920s, the ban on them was removed 'as a temporary measure subject to their good behaviour in future.' It was never imposed again.

Independent India found it offensive to brand entire communities as criminal because of the actions of a few members. This category was done away with after the 1950s. Indeed, as part of affirmative action, people from the so-called criminal tribes of yore (along with other, non-criminal 'scheduled' tribes) receive preferential treatment in matters of employment under the government.

The biggest communities of the *state* as it stood in 1931, in the descending order of their size, were the Kashmîrî Muslims (37.1 per cent of the population), the Gujjars (11 per cent), the Râjpûts—Hiñdu as well as Muslim (9.7 per cent), the Brâhmins (5.5 per cent; not counting the Kashmîrî Pañdits, who accounted for another 1.7 per cent of the population) and the Jâts—who were mainly Muslim (just under 4 per cent).

23.2 per cent of the *Hiñdu* population of the state consisted of the 'scheduled castes' in 1931. The Méghs were the most numerous among the scheduled castes, followed by the Cham(i)âr and Dûm communities. In terms of numbers, the next ranking 'scheduled castes' were the Basîth community of Réâsî and Mîrpur; the Batwâl clan of Jammû district; the Barwâlâ clan; the Dhyâr clan (of Réâsî), the Saryârâ clan (spread over much of the province) and the Chûhrâ sub-caste (mainly of Pooñch). The Rattal (based in Udhampur-Réâsî), Gar-di and Hiñdu Julâhâ communities came next but their populations were and are limited to a few families each. This distribution of the population prevailed till 1947.

The 1931 census mentioned two 'alien' (i.e. non-indigenous) castes among the Hiñdus: the 1,073-member strong Gurkhâ community and all of 43 people who belonged to the Kâyasth caste of central India. Among Muslims there were four 'alien' communities: Syed, Mughal, Pathân and Turk. All four were fairly substantial in number.

People from the neighbouring states of Punjãb and Himâchal Pradésh were obviously not considered aliens.

We have mentioned below all communities with a sizeable presence in Jammû province. Their shares in the 1931 population of the *undivided state* have been mentioned in brackets towards the end of the relevant entries. In many cases the actual population of the community as in 1981 has also been given. In 1981 Jammû province (the portion actually under the Indian flag) had a population of 27,18,213 (2.7 million) or 45.39 per cent of the population of the state not under Pâkistâni or Chinese occupation.

Birâdarî congregations: Birâdarî is a Persian word that means 'brotherhood' or 'fraternity.'[2] The word was brought to India by the Muslims. Interestingly, this is the word used by the Hiñdus of Jammû (and the Punjãb) for 'clan,' 'community' and 'sub-caste.' Each birâdarî has a presiding deity (who might also be the presiding deity of birâdarîs elsewhere in India) and a community temple (which would be used by all other people, especially those who live in that village, for the other 364 days of the year).

Once every year members of that birâdarî, who would be scattered all over Jammû province (or North India or even the world) gather at that temple (called *dév sthal*, lit. 'the place of the deity')—ostensibly to pray (*pûjâ*) together around a scared fire (*havan*).

This system has also been devised to ensure that members of the clan meet each other at least once every year: like a class reunion. They renew friendships and, often, explore matrimonial alliances, on that day. A vegetarian lunch (*prîti bhoj,* lit. 'affection food') is served. Because of modernisation, birâdarîs have started issuing notices through the Jammû press to inform readers where, and at what time, they should gather if they want to board the buses chartered by that birâdarî.

In theory each birâdarî has its own annual day—normally a day considered auspicious by other Hiñdus, Sikhs and Jains as well. In actual practice there are only half a dozen or so such days in a year. Therefore, you will find dozens of birâdarîs celebrating their annual ritual on the same day. For instance, more than a dozen and a half clans informed the press[iii] that their annual congregation would be held on Friday the 26th November, 2004 (which was also the anniversary of Guru Nânak, the founder of the Sikh religion). There must have been many more that did not tell the press.

---

2. *Birâdar* means exactly the same as the English 'brother' and the Sañskrit *bhrâtri.* The three words sound almost the same. This is one of the many proofs of the common ancestry of the Indo-Aryan group of languages.

Shared caste-names: The reader will notice that the same surname (e.g. Malhotrâ) is sometimes used by people of more than one caste—in fact by members of absolutely dissimilar castes. Often when an underprivileged caste has the same name as a so-called upper caste, some observers snigger. They should not. This is not a recent trend. Nor is it a 'lower' caste conspiracy to appropriate 'upper' caste names. This trend was very much in evidence in the 19th century—and almost certainly in several preceding centuries as well. As Ibbetson points out, 'many of these tribal names are merely taken from the dominant race in whose service the tribe was formed.'[iv] There was a similar trend of adopting employers' surnames in 19th century Southern USA.

Sculptors, craftsmen and specialists

Every traditional neighbourhood (*mohallâ*) of the older towns of India—including Jammû—would have a name that said something about its origins. Many Jammû neighbourhoods were obviously founded by castes of talented craftsmen. Thus we have the weavers' *Julâhâ kâ mohallâ*, the barbers' *Dhakki Nâîyâñ*, the funeral-priests' *Dhakki Chârjî-yâñ* ...

As almost everywhere in India, the majority of craftsmen were Muslim. The violence of 1947 caused the unfortunate migration of Muslims to Pâkistân. The neighbourhoods that they had founded (with one or two exceptions) still retain their names, though the *mohallâs* of Jammû are no longer associated with specific professions.

The castes of *craftsmen and artisans* in Jammû are more or less as follows: The Thathiyârâ clan makes utensils; murals are painted by the Salehr(h)â clan—especially the women of this sub-caste; and the Mégh clan, inter alia, weaves baskets.

Clans of musicians include Bañjtarî, Gâr-rhî (or Gâr-dî), Darés and Yogî (or Jogî). The Darés clan of Muslim singers was an integral part of the composite culture of the land. They specialised in singing ballads in praise of Râjpût kings, chiefs and warriors, who, in Jammû-Kathuâ-Udhampur, happened to be Hiñdu. The better-off Râjpûts would always invite Darés singers to their weddings, so that the guests could be informed about the brave and powerful ancestors of the hosts.

The Hiñdu-Sikh clans and sub-castes of Jammû province are:

Barwâlâ is a sub-caste of Dûm. Traditionally the Barwâlâs skinned dead animals and sold their hides. With prosperity they have switched over almost entirely to agriculture. Many of them were bonded labour. Their traditional homes are in Chenainî, Nausherâ, Réâsî, RS Purâ and the areas now in Pâkistân occupied Kashmîr. There were 18,882 Barwâlâs in Jammû province in the 1981 census. The clan is known as Batwâl in Kâñgrâ and Chambâ (both in Himâchal Pradésh). In some parts of the Dogrâ hills, especially Kâñgrâ, they worked as coolies (Kirâwak or Kirauk). Since at least the 19th century they have claimed to be Râjpûts. Indeed, two of their sub-castes are called Manhâs and Janjûâ. The majority of the community in the plains converted to Islâm, obviously to escape the caste system that had given them what Ibbetson called "the lowest or almost lowest standing as a caste, apparently hardly if at all above the Dúmna [Dûm]."[v]

Réâsî and Mîrpur are the original homes of the **Basîth** community. They believe that they migrated from Chambâ (Himâchal Pradésh) to these two Jammû areas in the late eighteenth century. Today they mainly live in Pooñch. Many of them claim to be descendants of the Vashisth or Bashisth Râjpût clan. During the 1965 war they displayed exceptional valour in defending the country. 1981 population: 9,962.

Batehrâ is a sub-caste of the Râj (mason) community (which, in turn, is a Tarkhân clan). The Batehrâ group consists of stone-workers and old-style sculptors. Among other things, they sculpt idols, including the ones mentioned in the chapter about Wellside Sculpture. The Batehrâs also live in Himâchal Pradésh and have a miniscule presence in Jâlañdhar and Amritsar. In Kulu (HP) they belong to the Koli (Dagi) clan and work with slate.[vi]

Sub-castes of the **Batwâl** clan include Dhaggâ, Jhañjotrâ, Kaiñth, Lakhotrâ and Sargotrâ. They have organised themselves into the Nakodar *gotr,* the Kasim *gotr* and the Motem *gotr.* Jammû district (Bâhu Fort, Chhannî Bîjâ, Bishnâh and Sâmbâ) is their main home. However, they also live in Udhampur and Kathuâ. Traditionally the Batwâls have been landless agricultural labourers. They rank 'slightly higher'[vii] than their Barwâlâ cousins. With prosperity, they have set up small hotels and textile shops. Some of them claim descent from the Bat Râjpûts. 1981 population: 26,693.

Bâzîgar (or Madârî): This is a nomadic community of acrobats and sorcerers. They claim that their ancestors came from Méwâr in Râjasthân. This might be true because the Bâzîgars are darker skinned than the indigenous population. As they migrated north some of them settled in the Punjãb, in the districts that are now on the Indo-Pâkistân border. In Jammû and Kashmîr they are found mostly in Jammû district and within it in Akhnoor, Bâjîpur, Misrîwâlâ and the Bâgh-é-Bâhu. Most Bâzîgars are Hiñdus. Because their lifestyle is vaguely similar to that of the Gujjars, the Muslim Bâzîgars have been trying to get clubbed with that powerful community, especially since the 1990s when the Gujjars became eligible for affirmative action. They speak Punjãbî, Dogrî and Hiñdî. The community is spread over most of north India.

Bhagat (Kabîr-pañthî): This numerically significant community is often accepted as a branch of the even more important Mégh sub-caste. However, many Bhagats reject all theories which suggest that they are of a Mégh origin. Some Bhagats claim descent from Kshatriyas who took to weaving and migrated from Vârânasi to Jammû.. The mediæval central Indian Saint Kabîr was a weaver. Because the Bhagats are his followers, they are also called Kabîr-pañthîs.

Yet other Bhagats believe that their ancestors were Brâhmins who were thrown out of their community because they personally disposed of the carcass of a dead cow, instead of getting a subaltern to do that 'unclean' job. Deprived of their ancestral calling, members of this family became weavers.

After the community migrated to the state, it is said that people from the Thakkar community of Pañjgrâîñ (in Râmnagar, Udhampur) were so impressed by the teachings of Saint Kabîr that they joined this sect.

Not all Bhagats claim a Vârânasi/ central Indian origin. Some, especially those from Kathuâ, believe that their ancestors were the rulers of that area. Many of them say that they were the original inhabitants of Jammû.

Today, most Bhagats are farmers and agricultural labour. Many are in the civil services. They mostly live in the prosperous plains of Jammû and Kathuâ and are concentrated in the RS Purâ area of Jammû district.

1981 population: 1,30,800 or 16 per cent of the present Jammû province. (I think this figure includes most of the scheduled caste population of the province.)

The **Chârjî** [Achâri] group of Brâhmins conducts funeral ceremonies. Theirs is a noble, if sombre, profession. 'After the cremation [the Chârjî] is seated on the dead man's bedstead and the sons lift him up, bedstead and all, and make obeisance to him,' Ibbetson noted.[viii]

Traditionally the Chârjîs referred to themselves as Âchârya and Mahâ-Brâhmin but have, since the twentieth century, started taking on the generic Brâhmin surname, Sharmâ. 'They call themselves Mahâ-Brâhmin, Mahâ-Pañdit and Mahâ-Patra,' writes Archna Kesar. 'In justification, they say that [the] *antdân* [the donation made at death ceremonies] [has such a powerful spiritual quality] that it cannot be digested easily. Only Shudh [pure] and Prabudh Âchâryas have the power to accept and digest this type of [a donation].'[ix]

The Chârjîs routinely inter-marry with their counterparts in the neighbouring states. This has influenced their customs as also the language that they speak.

Their *gotrs* include Atrî, Bhârgav, Gautam, Kashyap, Kaushal, Mudgal and Vashisth. Their sub-castes are Chûrâmani (in Jasrotâ), Gaur, Tamnot and Jamwâl (in Udhampur-Katrâ), Ratanpâl (in Chenainî) and Mudgal (in Basohli).

Kesar adds, 'There are some surnames which indicate the [name of the place where that clan originally lived] such as Charprar (now in Pâkistân), Ghagwâlié, Hîrânagarié, Marin, Khaoorié, Bhedhué etc.'

The good looking, fair-skinned[3] Charmkâr ('those who work with leather') community (the name is normally shortened to Chamiâr or

3. In the Punjãb, apparently, the Chamârs are dark-skinned, or so Ibbetson noted. (Page 297.) So much so that the British scholar even recorded a proverb which claimed that fair-skinned Chamârs were as unusual as dark Brâhmins and that such exceptions from both communities were inauspicious companions to have while travelling in a boat. However, even Sir Ibbetson agreed that Chamâr women were so good looking that 'higher' caste men often lost caste because of their 'great partiality for a Chamârni.'

Chamâr) makes and tans leather goods and has traditionally been quite well to do. Some members of the community once claimed that they were Chañdr-bansî Râjpûts. This was not accepted by the British census authorities.[x]

In Jammû, and even more so in Indian (East) Punjãb, there are Sikh Chamârs, too. A substantial section of the community follows the teachings of the mediæval saint Râmdâs (aka Râé-dâs). The Râmdâsi sect gave up its ancestral association with leather, stopped eating carrion, became weavers and rose in the social hierarchy. Today the Chamârs are doing extremely well in the civil services (as generalists as well as technical professionals) and politics. The Khatîk clan (after whom Jammû's famous Khatîkâñ Tâlâb is named) was left to tan and craft leather.

British census authorities were careful not to confuse the mainly Sikh Râmdâsi Chamârs with the Râidâsi/ Râbdâsi Chamârs. The 'latter are Hiñdus, or if Sikhs, only Nânakpañthi Sikhs and do not take the *páhul*,[xi] The founder of the Râidâsi sect was Bhagat Rav [Rab] Dâs, who belonged to the community and lived in the 15th/ 16th century. Like his contemporary, the great Kabîr, he was a follower of Râmânañd.

The important Hiñdu-Sikh clans of Jammû-Punjãb-Haryânâ that belong to the larger Chamâr-Mochî community are: Jâtiâ, Râidâsi, Chãñdar, Chauhân, Chamâr, Goliâ, Bhattî, Mahmî, Phuñdwâl, Jâl, Batoi, Badhan, Siñdhu, Hîr, Bains, Ghamérî, Râmdâsiâ, Bhûtî and Kathânâ. These nineteen clans have been listed in the order of their geographical spread (starting from Haryânâ and going northwards to Jammû). They do not intermarry.

Muslim Chamârs were, even before 1947, concentrated in what is now the Pâkistânî state of (West) Punjãb.

While the community mainly lives in Jammû district, it is found in almost all the other districts as well. 1.1 per cent of the population of the undivided state, as it stood in 1931, belonged to the Chamâr community, an offshoot of which is called Mochî (see below).

Chib: There are Hiñdu as well as Muslim Chibs. The latter now mostly live in the areas illegally occupied by Pâkistân. (See 'Chibali' under 'Muslim castes.') The ancient Greeks wrote about the Sibæ clan. It is possible that they were talking about the Chibs. Till the 18th century the Chibs were too well off to touch the plough. However, they lost much of their power after the rise of the Sikh empire (18th-19th centuries) and began to cultivate their own fields.

Many Chibs claim that they are a breakaway faction of the Katoch Râjpût community, whose leader Chib Chañd migrated from Kâñgrâ (Himâchal Pradésh) to Maghlorâ (Bhimber, Jammû province) around the 5th or 6th century AD.

Some Chibs modify this claim by claiming to be Katoch only from the 'maternal' side. They say that the Chibs came from Persia. Gauhar Shâh, the prince of Khorâsâñ (Persia) went to the Indian Deccan and married the daughter of King Nâhir (or Nâhar) Chañd. Their son, Abdar Chañd, was brought up as a Hiñdu. He went on to found the Kâñgrâ line.

Chib Chañd is said to have married the daughter of King Srîpat of Bhimber. He then murdered his father-in-law, as well as many of Srîpat's Thakiyâl clansmen 'by treachery.'[xii] He thus grabbed the Bhimber kingdom and established the Chib dynasty, which spread to the neighbouring parts of the Punjãb—notably Gujrât—as well.

Critics dismiss this as a 'wonderful story.'[xiii] They reject any kind of a Katoch origin, and suggest that the Chibs might be an offshoot of the Punwâr clan.

Serious historians like SDS Charak believe that Prince Pratâp Chañd, a Katoch from Kâñgrâ, was the one who, together with some clansmen, migrated to Bhimber around AD 1400, and founded the Chib clan. Pratâp was the youngest of the four sons of King Mégh Chañd (AD 1390-1405).

The area of the Chibs' original influence is known as Jhibhal (Chibhal). In present times they live in Akhnoor, Jammû, Nausherâ, Rajourî and RS Purâ. In the Punjãb they have, for centuries, lived in the northern part of Gujrât district (now in Pâkistân).

Sûr Sadi, a contemporary of Aurañgzéb, was the first Chib to convert to Islâm. The Muslim Chibs consider him a spiritual leader and martyr (for he died during a fight). Muslim Chib boys—like their Hiñdu cousins—must get their heads shaved completely once, at age three or four. The difference is that their hair are then placed in Sûr Sadi's tomb. Only after this is done can the boy claim to be a real Chib and his mother can start eating meat again.

The clans of the Muslim Chibs are Mañdiâl, Srâhiâl and Dhériâl. The Ghaniâl people, too, are Chibs. Ghani Chañd was the first Chib *ruler* who converted to Islâm. Billawaria writes that he did so when 'the ruler of Delhi gave [him] the Bhimber' kingdom.[xiv]

Hiñdu Chibs use the titles Miyâñ and Thâkur. Muslim Chibs were also given the title Râjâ. Within the Muslim community the Chibs have an elevated status. The Syed and Gakkhar communities have traditionally married Chib girls.

Chhîmbâ: In Jammû province this is a tiny Hiñdu community of dyers and cloth-printers. It inter-marries with its Sikh counterparts in the Punjãb. This talented clan of craftsmen and calico-printers insists that the correct name of the community is Tâk Kshatriya. Traditionally they would carve elegant patterns on blocks of wood and then smear a dye (almost invariably of the 'madder'—reddish purple—colour) on the block (or stencil). They would thus make prints on cotton—and, sometimes, paper.

The Chhîmbâ clan is akin to the Dhobî (washerman) and Darzî (tailor) communities. In many parts of undivided Punjãb the three sub-castes are really the same. Some members of the community call themselves Chhâpégar, while others use the name Chhapérâ. Variations of the main community name include Chhaimpâ, Chhîpi and Chhîmpi.[xv]

The **Chhâpégar** (printer) sub-caste specialised in decorating calico with designs in tinsel and foil alone.

'Because of various reasons, the community hide[s] its identity and has adopted [the] surnames...Chauhân, Arorâ and Khatrî,' writes Bageshwar Siñgh. 'Recently, the Chhîmbâ, have become the followers of Srî Namdeo.'[xvi]

Chhîmbâ *gotr* names include Kumbho, Tagad, Teji, Pradhân and Purvâ. Sippal, Bhatti and Khokhar, too, are Chhîmbâ names.

In Jammû province, many of this urban community are migrants from Mîrpur. Some have taken to trade and selling Indian sweets. They live mostly in Jammû, Kathuâ, Sâmbâ and Udhampur.

2001 population: around 2,000.

The word **Chûhrâ** is offensive and no longer used. The community hailed mainly from Pooñch. (0.1 per cent of the population of the undivided state, as it stood in 1931, belonged to this community.)

Dholwâlâ: This is a community of drummers. Their Jogî sub-sect performs on secular as well as religious occasions. However, the Gardwachi clan restricts itself to religious rituals. All rituals in honour of Lord Shiv must have at least one Gardwachi drummer in attendance.

The community is found all over Jammû province but especially in Bhaderwâh, Jammû city, Katrâ, Nausherâ, Rajourî and Udhampur.

Dhuñd: This community mainly lives in Pooñch and Muzaffarâbâd. (0.4 per cent of the population of the undivided state, as it stood in 1931, belonged to this community.)

The **Dhyâr** clan of miners used to live mainly in the coal-rich Sañghar-Kalakote region of old Réâsî. Not only do the Dhyars believe that they are Râjpûts, this is one of the very few communities in India that is prepared to forego the benefits of affirmative action ('reservation') in support of its belief. The Dhyars have petitioned the state government to remove them from the list of scheduled castes.

The Dhyârs used to mine iron ore They used the 'open pit' method. Animals, especially cows, which are particularly sacred to the Hiñdus, used to fall into these pits and die. This, naturally, got the Dhyârs a terrible reputation among the Hiñdus, who started calling them *hatyâré* (murderers). In Hiñduism killing a cow is as bad a crime as killing a human. Dhyâr is the Dogrified version of the word *hatyâré.*

The Dhyârs believe that this was what led to their expulsion from the Râjpût fold. Now that they have more or less given up mining and have started living in Budhal, Mohér, Rajourî, Rausu and Teot as well, they want to be accepted as Râjpûts once again. They are mainly farmers and traders now.

Their sub-castes include Jhakhar, Katiyâr, Nâg, Nagoti and Sangarh.

1981 population: 4,797.

Dosâli: This small clan of the Jammû and Sâmbâ tehsils is said to have once been Râjpût but was excommunicated from the main Râjpût fold at some stage in history. Such ousted people are known as *doswâlé*, which word probably later contracted to Dosâli. Ever since the clan has earned a living by making cups and saucers with green leaves. Such ecologically-correct 'crockery' was used during ritual feasts till the 1980s when plastic plates replaced them.

The Dosâlis, too, have moved with the times and have started doing other things like trade and running buses and trucks.

According to another theory the name of this clan derives from *dúsa*, a straw used to sew one leaf with another.

Ibbetson[xvii] wrote, 'They are a very low [hill] caste...of superior standing to the Chamâr.' Parmanand Lal adds, 'The Dosalis are considered to be an impure caste...deemed higher than the Sarera [Saryârâ?] or the Banjara but below the Bahti or Girth and nearer to the Chimba.'[xviii]

Many subaltern communities claim a Râjpût origin but in this case the Râjpût Sabhâ of Jammû officially accepted them as one of their own in 1984. It is possible that their ancestors came from Râjasthân. They continue to have a bittersweet relationship with the Râjpûts who consider them so 'inferior' that they refuse to marry Dosâli women.

This provoked some Dosalis to request Bakhshi Ghulâm Muhammad, the Prime Minister of Jammû and Kashmîr in the late 1950s, to declare them a backward community. However, less than one eighth of the community opted for this status, which had made them eligible for affirmative action (especially employment under the state government). The rest preferred the 'respectability' of being Râjpûts.

Duggal: The annual congregation of this birâdarî is held at the temple of its presiding deity, Râjâ Mañdlîk, at Jhîrî.

The **Dûm** community is found throughout Jammû province, though concentrated in Jammû district. The clan is also known as Mahâshâ. The Sañskrit honorific *mahâshay* means 'the great (or exalted) being.' J. Przyluski[xix] believes that the word Dûm derives from Odumbara, an ancient non-Aryan, possibly Austro-Asiatic tribe that had a republican system of governance a few centuries before the Christ. This clan might have been part of the bigger and better-known Saka community. It is believed that the community is aboriginal to the area and once enjoyed some power and importance.[xx] Later, the Dûms were given a very subaltern position in Hiñdu society, despite which they did not convert to Islâm or Sikhism.

The Dûms' own view is that Lord Shiv created them because he needed people to play the ritual drum whenever he danced. They also believe that they are the same as the Jogî community. (See 'Jogî' below.)

The Dûms have traditionally not been landowning farmers, though they mostly live in villages. Instead, they work for their fellow villagers—as farm-hands, drummers and in other capacities. Dûms have traditionally created things out of grass and bamboo. These include sieves, winnowing pans, fans, mats, ropes, baskets, screens and furniture. Almost every fifth member of the Scheduled Castes in Jammû is a Dûm. Their sub-castes include Balgotré, Kalotré, Sivotré and Vilâ-loch (Bilâ-loch). (0.9 per cent of the population of the undivided state, as it stood in 1931, belonged to this community.)

The **Gaddîs** are Hiñdu shepherds. (A few Jammû Gaddîs—there were 76 of them in 1931—converted to Islâm.[4]) General Cunningham argued that the Gaddîs have descended from a clan that the ancients called Gandaridæ or Gangaridae. On the other hand, Dr Jerath believes that in ancient times the Gaddîs were gypsies.

I wonder about the latter. That's because the Gaddîs' lifestyle is not half as nomadic as that of the Gujjars or Bakerwâls. The change of seasons in the mountains mandates some kind of seasonal migration not only for those whose livelihood depends on grass (which gets covered by snow in winter) but also for others (including kings, nobles, civil servants, traders and craftsmen) who seek to avoid extreme temperatures.

So, if the Gaddîs go uphill in summer and come down in winter it does not make them the Hiñdu cousins of the Gujjars and Bakerwâls. For one, their culture is totally different. For another, the Gaddîs do not migrate bag and baggage or spend exactly half the year in the mountains and the other half in the plains. Nor does the entire family migrate. (The nomadic Gujjars and Bakerwâls do all three: they shift the entire family to the other residence for six months at a time.) Typically, a Gaddî family will send one or two young male members to a nearby mountain pasture for a few months in the summer.

The (Muslim) Chopân community of Kashmîr has a similar pattern of migration. However, the Gaddîs normally own their own sheep, while the Chopâns tend sheep on behalf of the rest of the village.

One theory about the origin of the Gaddîs is that they belonged to the Punjãb and Sindh, from where they fled to Jammû and Himâchal Pradésh during the reign of the 17th century Mughal Emperor Aurañgzéb, in order to escape 'persecution'[xxi] and worse. This theory is similar to the one according to which the Gujjars formed their present identity after they were defeated by the 16th

4. Significantly, the area around Delhi, Karnâl and Ambâlâ had Muslim Gaddîs till 1947.

century Mughal Emperor Akbar. Both theories have to be wrong because the Gaddîs' presence in the Dogrâ hills seems to be older than the 17th century. (And the Gujjars were a community a thousand years before Akbar.)

The word *gaddî* means 'the cushion' or 'the seat.' If we accept this theory, then idiomatically *gaddî* means 'the throne' or 'the seat of power.' The Gaddîs believe that Lord Shiv gave the hills of Jammû and Himâchal Pradésh to their community to rule over.

The Gaddîs mostly live in the villages of Bannî, Basohli, Batote, Bhaderwâh, Billâwar, Râmban and Udhampur. Their sub-castes include Aralu, Balouria, Chârak, Chuhân, Harokar, Jarwâ, Katoch, Lalhâl, Parihâr, Shundal and Vîrpurî.[xxii]

Gaddî is not a caste but a community with its own dialect, dress and set of castes. There are Brâhmins and Khatris in this community, with some Râjpûts and Râthîs, too. There is a view that the majority of Gaddîs are Khatris and that their sub-castes are exactly like those of the Punjãbî Khatris. Some inter-marriage has traditionally taken place between the Khatri Gaddîs and the other Gaddî sub-castes. (0.3 per cent of the population of the undivided state, as it stood in 1931, belonged to the Gaddî community.)

In 1931 there were only 177 people in the **Gar-di** (or **Gar-rî**) community of Jammû district. The figure got reversed by 1961, when there were all of 771 Gar-dîs. Just twenty years later their number jumped to 2,181. There used to be some Gar-dîs in Siâlkot (now in Pâkistân). Could they have all migrated to Jammû after 1947, thus swelling the numbers in Jammû, which is their original home?

This is an underprivileged clan of wandering musicians, actors and quack 'doctors.' They sing and play devotional Hiñdu songs and recite folk tales, especially when a child is born or after someone dies, as part of the ritual. (See also 'Jogî' on page 69.)

The **Gujrâti Brâhmin** or **Vedvyâs** or **Biâs** or **Nagar** community is said to have migrated to Jammû from Gujarât. But which Gujarât? The district of that name, which is now in Pâkistânî Punjãb or the state of the same name in Western India? The community normally claims the latter. However, at the same time it believes that its ancestors came from Southern Europe or Central Asia, through the Hiñdukush mountain range. In that case wouldn't the district of West Punjãb be a more likely candidate? However, several members of the community speak the language of Gujarât state. This reinforces the other theory.

They also believe that they are the 'purest' of Aryans. Risley[xxiii] thought that they were Greco-Scythian or Dravido-Scythian. In that case, could they have migrated from Georgia with the Gujjars? I believe that this is the most likely explanation.

The other migrants from Georgia, too, first settled in India in the present-day states of Râjasthân and Gujarât. There they created a distinct culture and language, and then migrated to other parts of west and north India.

Before the communications revolution of the 20th century, there was no contact between the nomadic Gujjars of the Himâlayas and the Hiñdu Gujjars of Gujarât. And yet they speak a similar language though they have been living thousands of miles away from each other for many centuries now.

The Gujrâti Brâhmins are an urban people. Traditionally they have been astrologers. Some of them rose to high military rank under the Sikhs. Pañdit Shyâm jî was the Sikhs' army commander in Jammû.

They are part of the Pañj Gaor group of Brâhmins and have three sub-castes, viz., Nagar, Audhich and Barad. Their internal pecking order of clans is: Vadnagara, Visnagara, Sathodra, Chitroda, Krishnora and Prashnora. Their surnames include Davé, Jani, Joshî, Mehtâ, Pâñdyâ and Râwal.

Within the Brâhmin caste, the Gujrâtis have a unique—and high—position, because of which they are the first to be given food after a death. They are fed on the 12th day after the death. The Gaors are ranked below them. Offerings made to Râhu, the deity, especially if made during an eclipse, are given to this Brâhmin clan.

Lady Ambikâ is the presiding deity of the community. Srî Hatkéshwar is their favourite male deity. They worship him on the Chait (*chaitr*) Pûrnimâ in particular.

Gumâr, Gumiâr, Kumhâr or Prajâpati: This is a community of potters that is found in all six districts of Jammû. Gumâr, the professional name of the clan, is derived from Kumhâr, the Hiñdî-Urdû word for potter. Prajâpati is the ritual name. Sub-castes include Badyâl, Dab, Dafarâ and Manawâ.

Potters are needed in every village, especially for the earthen water pitchers that they make. However, some Gumârs have always lived in the cities because demand for their earthen pots is even greater there. The clan makes earthenware, baked bricks and pottery. Kumhârs also make idols and clay toys. (Sun-dried bricks are generally made by Chamârs.)

Traditionally, this was one of the few communities —in many areas, the only one—that kept donkeys. This made them important because the grain of the village was transported on these donkeys. Around a third of the Kumhârs of undivided Punjāb were Muslims. Like the Hiñdu Kumhârs, they trace their ancestry to Lord Brahmâ himself. For that reason they are sometimes respectfully called the Prajâpatî ('creator') clan. (0.4 per cent of the population of the undivided state, as it stood in 1931, belonged to this community.)

Gurkhâ: A small number of Gurkhâs migrated from Nepal (and the adjacent Indian districts) to Jammû and Kashmîr to join the state Army.

Jain: In Jammû and the Punjãb the community is known by the name Bhâbrhâ. Some feel that the latter word has pejorative implications and should not be used. However, Anita K Billawaria believes that it has been derived from *bhâo-bhalâ* (good intentions). The Jains of Jâlandhar have another explanation for this name. They had a spiritual leader, Bîr Swâmi, who asked them to stop wearing the sacred thread and also informed them that their faith (*bhû* or *bhâ*) was great (*barhâ*).

Jammû's Jain Bâzâr is still referred to by its old name, Bhâbrhâ Bâzâr. Traditionally it was Jammû's most prosperous—if crowded and congested—market. In the 1990s it reinvented itself with glittering shops—made of marble and polished granite—that sell Jammû's famous gold jewellery.

This is an affluent urban trading community. Extremes of non-violence are an article of faith for the Jains. Traditionally the community has been clubbed with the Hiñdus, with whom it intermarries and has much in common. However, several Jains want to be counted as a separate religious community. (Ibbetson,[xxiv] writing in 1916, noted that eleven per cent of the 'Bhábras have returned themselves as Hiñdus.' The 2001 census revealed the same ambivalence, with some Jains asserting a separate identity and others happy to be Hiñdus.)

In Jammû province, as in the neighbouring states, the Oswâl group dominates the community. It belongs to the Shwétâmbar ('white robed') school. Ibbetson describes them as the 'more lax sect of the Jains (who) consider themselves Hiñdus first and Jains afterwards.'

The Jains are often called Baniyâs. Therefore, most Hiñdus place them in the 'third' caste of Hiñduism—Vysyâ. However, some Jains claim to be Kshatriya on the ground that the 'founder' of the faith ('consolidator,' actually), Lord Mahâvîr, was one.

Within the state the community consists of three distinct groups: Sithânîk-bâsi, Mûrtî-pûjî and Térâ-pañthî.

The headquarters of this tiny but enormously powerful—and well-respected—community have traditionally been in Hoshiârpur (Indian East Punjãb) and Siâlkot (Pâkistân's West Punjãb), both being very close to Jammû. Some 40km from Hoshiârpur, in the hills, is a place called Fatahpur. In ancient times there was an elaborate town here, the ruins of which can be seen. Many Jains from Jammû and the Punjãb visit an ancient temple in Fatahpur once every year.

Jañgam: The Jañgams are a colourfully dressed clan of vegetarian religious mendicants and bards. Chirani (Udhampur) is their ancestral home. They worship Lord Shiv and specialise in singing about his legendary wedding with Pârvati Dévî jî. Their language is similar to Haryânvî. Therefore, their ancestors might have come from that state. Jañgam surnames include Daru, Gupt, Lañgoch, Mûl, Shil, Shiv-lîg and Shiv-mûl.

The Jañgams often wear saffron clothes, as well as a 'crown' and symbols of the nâg snake loved by Lord Shiv. Indu Bala Dhar notes that 'each part of [their] robe is symbolic of' some aspect of the presiding deities of their clan—Lord Shiv and Pârvati Dévî jî.

The **Jhîvar** or **Jhîñvar** (the name is shortened to Jhîr in Dogrî) community traditionally fetched water from rivers in inflatable leather bags in summer. They were also palanquin-bearers (Kahâr), fishermen and boatmen. In the era of *The Mahâbhârat* they were fishermen. By the end of the first millennium after Christ they were mostly a community of hunters and were seen as the descendants of mixed unions between Kshatriya men and Râjpût women.

The Jhîvars also call themselves Mehrâ or Mahrâ ('the chief'). They often use the surname Dogrâ. In the early 20th century they petitioned that they should be called Kashyap Râjpûts. However, the Mahârâjâ rejected the claim because, as the Census of 1931 put it, 'it was likely to cause confusion.'

Kashyap is the Sañskrit word for tortoise. It is said that when Sîtâ jî, the Hiñdu deity, got married, people were needed to carry her palanquin. Some tortoises were magically turned into muscular men for this purpose. Their descendants, the Jhîvars, are known as Kashyap Râjpûts for that reason.

Water-bearers of the community say that the great saint Kashyap had once served water to thirty-three deities. They claim to be descendants of the saint, after whom Kashmîr is possibly named. Veena Gupta points out that the community has *gotrs* other than Kashyap—for instance, Atrî, Bhârdwâj and Kaushal. Therefore, they can't be descendants of Saint Kashyap.[xxv] She feels that they are a mixed caste. This seems likely because Jhîvar/ Jhîr is an umbrella caste for sub-castes such as Kahârs, water-bearers, hunters and fishermen. Some Jhîvars are bakers while many others wash dishes for a living.

Nowadays most villages have piped water, so people don't need to fetch water from the river. Palanquins are on their way out. However, till the 1990s some skilled men from this community would fill the same leather-bags with air and swim atop them from the Basohli (J&K) bank of the fast-flowing and vast River Râvî to the other bank, which is in Himâchal Pradésh.

Despite its relative poverty, the community's 'social standing is in one respect high; for all will drink at [the] hands' of its members.[xxvi]

Hiñdu Jhîvars live mainly in Jammû district and the Muslim Mashkî (water-bearer) clan in Mîrpur. (The leather bag is called *mashk*,) Some of the community live in Udhampur. (0.3 per cent of the population of the undivided state, as it stood in 1931, belonged to this community.)

The **Jogî** (yogî, lit.: practitioner of yog[a]) community of mendicants and beggars consists of both Muslims and Hiñdus. In the state this community lives mainly in the Jammû, Mîrpur and Kathuâ districts. There is enormous variety within the community. One sect consists of priests. (See 'Brâhmin' in this chapter.)

Broadly, there are two kinds of Jogîs: i) Devotees of Lord Shiv, who are priests and follow the teachings of Gorakh Nâth. These are the Augar and Kanphattâ Jogîs. ii) Wandering *faquirs* and astrologers, the majority of whom converted to Islâm.

Category 1: Like, say, the Gar-dîs, the Jogîs are professional musicians. However, Hiñdu Jogîs mainly sing at temples and other prayer houses, which gives them an exalted status.

Category 2: Such Jogîs are not everyday beggars. They mainly live on the alms that are given during religious ceremonies—which are held to mark the birth of a child or a marriage, and similar moments of joy.

In turn, on such occasions the Jogîs sing religious songs, to the accompaniment of the one-string *kañk* instrument (called the *ik-târâ* in Hiñdî-Urdû). They belong to the same overall caste as the Dholwâlâ clan, except that the latter people play drums and not stringed instruments. Besides, in the caste hierarchy the Jogîs rank higher than Dholwâlâs but are at roughly the same level as the Dûms.

Animal sacrifice among the Hiñdus of the plains is on its way out. When Muslims—and, till the late 20th century, the Hiñdus—sacrifice an animal they give the head and legs to the Jogîs. Hiñdu Jogîs of the second category eat pork.

Some Jogîs claim to be exorcists and say that they know the secrets of the occult. They also double as medicine-men (called witch-doctors in pulp literature). In the villages some of them till land and also look after cattle—their own as well as that of others.

There is a third category, too: fake Jogîs. Ibbetson notes, '[E]very rascally beggar who pretends to be able to tell fortunes, or to practise astrological and necromantic arts in however small a degree, buys himself a drum and calls himself and is called by others a Jogî.'[xxvii] Jogîs of this kind are the most visible and, unfairly, bring a bad name to genuine Jogîs.

General: Nâth is the generic surname used by the community. However, some use the caste-names Chib and Minhâs. The Râwal (Arabic for 'he who can divine things') clan, after whom Râwalpiñdî has been named, is a Muslim kin of the Jogî sub-caste.

The coming of mill-made cloth has marginalised the talented Julâhâ (weaver) community. There is hardly any **Julâhâ** left in Jammû's once-elite Julâhoñ kâ Mohallâ neighbourhood. Some members of the community go by the name Kolî (that's right, without an 'h').

In the rest of India (Muslim) Julâhâs changed the name of their clan to Sheikh Momin, because they felt that 'Julâhâ' had pejorative connotations. However, there was no such problem in Jammû province where they have traditionally also been called the Bafinda community.

There were all of forty Hiñdu Julâhâs in 1931, and they dwelt entirely in the old Réâsî district.

The **Kâñgar** community (also known as Kañgiyârâ) has traditionally consisted of hawkers who sell low-end consumer goods.

Kapâhî: The annual congregation of this birâdarî is held at the temple of its presiding deity, at Bâbâ Tâlâb on the Akhnoor Road.

Katoch probably means 'the defender of the fort' (*kot*). Or, perhaps, it means 'the upper (*uchh*) rungs of the army.' The Jâmwâl and Katoch clans rank the highest among the Râjpûts of Jammû province. This is a Sûrya-vañshi Râjpût clan that once lived in the Kâñgrâ valley of Himâchal Pradésh. Apparently they had to flee their ancestral homeland when the 17th century Mughal emperor Aurañgzéb's army attacked Kâñgrâ.

Ashok Aima records[xxviii] that when they left Kâñgrâ they took the main idol of their deity, Durgâ Mâtâ, with them, in a palanquin. When they reached Hambal village (in Dodâ tehsil) the idol suddenly grew too heavy to carry. The Katochs took that as a sign that the deity wanted them to settle in Hambal.

However, Hambal was only to be a temporary home. The king of Bhaderwâh drove them out of there. Ever since they have been scattered all over Dodâ-Râmban (Pogal Paristân in particular), Jammû, Kathuâ and Udhampur. All the same, the temple at Hambal remains their spiritual capital. Many of the clan have converted to Islâm.

The Mahâbhârat mentions Susaram Chand, a Katoch king of Multân (now in Pâkistân).

Even though the *mohallâ* called Talâb Khatîkâñ has traditionally been a mostly Muslim neighbourhood, the **Khatîk** (or Khatik) clan of leather-tanners and dyers is essentially Hiñdu.

Labânâ is basically a Sikh community of farmers, truck owners and other transporters. Traditionally this has been a clan of landholders and cultivators.

The **Mâlî** community of Hiñdus is associated with gardening. Mâlîs also serve in temples as attendants. Dr Jerath points out that they got their name from the garlands (*mâlâ*) that they make. (He adds that Muslim gardeners belong to the Kuñjar caste.) The Mâlîs are said to have descended from Lord Brahmâ himself, through his grandson Vishv-karmâ's son Mâlâkâr. The sub-castes of this community include Phûl, Goh and Sainî.

The **Mégh** clan believes that it is a breakaway section of the Brâhmins. Its members weave baskets as well as cloth. Numerically this is one of the most important sub-castes of the state and is found in the Jammû and Udhampur districts. It is said, with good reason, that the Meghs were among the earliest inhabitants of Jammû—till the Jamwâls displaced them. In the past, till perhaps the late nineteenth century, the Méghs would eat carrion. This was held against them. However, by the dawn of the twentieth century they had given up this practice.

Pañdâ Brâhmins called Gorais have traditionally performed death and memorial services for the Méghs. Since at least the twentieth century some Méghs have started doing priestly work for their clan. 1.9 per cent of the population of the undivided state, as it stood in 1931, belonged to this community. (See also 'Bhagat [Kabîr-pañthî'] above.)

Mirâsî: This is a substantial community of jesters and singers—and beggars. Most of them live in or hail from Pooñch. (0.2 per cent of the population of the undivided state, as it stood in 1931, belonged to this community.)

Mochî: This is a community of shoemakers. The Mochîs specialise in making and mending shoes. The Hiñdu Mochîs believe that their illustrious ancestors included the saints Râvî Dâs and Gurû Râmânañd. For that reason they prefer the names Ravidâsi, Râmdâsî and Râidâsî for their community.

The Mochîs have special skills. Therefore, some of them have even in the past been very well to do. The saints whom they revere include Buâ Bâbâ, Bâbâ Mânsar and Bâbâ Surgal, as well as the deities Kali Bir and Nâg Dévatâ. The Mochîs of West Punjãb have been Muslim for several centuries now. 0.3 per cent of the population of the undivided state, as it stood in 1931, belonged to this community. (See also 'Chamâr' above.)

Mohtrâ: The annual congregation of this birâdarî is held at the temple of its presiding deity at Madkolî Phuknâh (Sâmbâ).

Mohyâl Brâhmin: A martial, ruling clan of Sarâswat Brâhmins, which is not supposed to do any priestly work, is called Mohyâl. Dr Sharmâ (see 'Brâhmin' below) has been very generous in her assessment of them. Denzil Ibbetson had a far more cynical—and, hence, more accurate—view. He wrote in 1916, 'They [the Mohyâls] object to be called Brâhmins, as the enlistment of Brâhmins is said to be forbidden in our [British] army. This is their own account. But in Hazârâ proper [now under Pâkistân] the Muhiáls perform priestly functions and receive alms just like other Brâhmins.'

The Mohyâls are divided into seven clans, the names of which are: Datt/ Dutt (whose *gotr* is Bhârdwâj), Bâli, Chhibber, Lao, Bhimwâl, Vaid and Mohan (whose *gotr* is Kashyap).

Many Mohyâls are also called Hussaini Brâhmins. Their 7th century A.D. ancestor Sultân Râhib Dutt, a Hiñdu Brâhmin, lived in the Middle East, perhaps in Iraq. He sacrificed all seven of his sons in the battle of Karbalâ (around A.D. 680) in the cause of Imâm Hassan and Imâm Hussain, the grandsons of Prophet Muhammad (peace be upon him). Dr. Sharma writes, 'Consequently it was decided by the loyalist [sic] of Hassan and Hussain to confer on them the title of Syeed [Syed?].'[xxix] While this community of well to do landlords and soldiers never converted to Islâm, many a Mohyâl was the *pîr* (mystic guide) of Muslim followers.

It is said that the Majâltâ area of Udhampur is named after the Mohyâl community. There is an entire Mohyâl (Chhibber) village in Akhnoor.

Rachhwâ in Rajourî still boasts of the ruins of a splendid seventeenth-century rock-castle of the Bakhshi (Dutt) chiefs of the area. They fled Rachhwâ following the massacres of 1947. There is a Mohyâl population in Sâmbâ as well.

The **Nâî** community of hairdressers has traditionally functioned not only as barbers but also as musicians, messengers and marriage-brokers. In a predominantly illiterate society, they would carry verbal (as well as written) messages—especially invitations—from place to place. To this day some of them act as roadside surgeons. Dr. Jerath believes that the word Nâî is short for the Sañskrit 'Ṇâpikâ' ('he who cleans or trims [other people's] nails').

Muslim barbers were traditionally called Khalîfâ ('the caliph'). In the late 20th century they adopted the surname Salmânî.

A section of the community claims to be Brâhmin by caste and Kulîn by sub-caste. It believes that before the coming of Islâm to India, the word Nâî meant Brâhmin. This section wants to retain its unique identity and wants to be confused neither with the Brâhmin community nor with other Nâîs.

Pañgaliâ: The annual congregation of the birâdarî is held at the temple of its presiding deity at Chiglî Chorî in Râmnagar.

Perné/ Gad Jhîr: Even though this community is also called Bangâlî, its ancestors were among the earliest inhabitants of Jammû. They live near forests and have traditionally buried their dead. Baqar Rizvi writes that many members of the community are 'engaged in...stealing, burglary, highway robbery,...liquor brewing and begging.'[xxx] They perform elaborate pilgrimages to the holy shrine of Srî Mâtâ Vaishno Dévî jî with a specified number of red flags in their hands. The community has four sub-castes: Bambi, Gandhila, Khaché and Ben. The number of flags that a sub-caste can carry has been laid down by tradition. The greater the number, the higher its rank within the Perne community.

Rattal: This is a very tiny community of leather-workers scattered all over the province. They take dead animals away from villages and later work on their hides. They have the surnames Kath, Kulsotrâ, Lakhotra, Mootan, Sargotra and Sundeh.

The **Salehr(h)â** clan has traditionally worked with slate and sandstone, sculpting things, including idols, out of them. They inter-marry with the Batehrâ clan.

Sâñsî: This tiny and backward community is scattered throughout the three Hiñdu-majority districts of Jammû. In the past they were 'engaged in petty thefts, highway robberies and illicit brewing of liquor,' writes Indu Aima.[xxxi] In recent times they have taken to farming. Their sub-castes are Châchû, Gholiyâ, Hañdariyâ, Khanwâl, Lodiyâ, Nañdwâl, Nathuwâl, Maswâl, Sañdyâl, Tagiyâl and Toliyâl. The clan asserts a Râjpût ancestry.

The few remaining traditional sculptors of Basohli-Bilâwar are mostly from the **Saryârâ** (or Sarérâ) community. They also spin cotton into yarn.

Apart from Jammû province, the community is found in Chambâ and Kâñgrâ (both in Himâchal Pradésh). Their sub-castes are Basotrâ, Chalotrâ, Chhagotrâ, Dalotrâ, Dhahotrâ, Gotdo, Khokhar, Kragotrâ, Nagotrâ, Pagatiâ, Padgotrâ, Sagotrâ and Sawâliâ.[xxxii] Their *gotrs* are Bhârdwâj, Kashyap and Vashisth. The community's biggest concentration is around Jammû's Bâhu Fort. Elite Saryaras from the Bâhu area can be very fair skinned and brown haired and can be mistaken for East Europeans. In the chapter on the history of Jammû we have alluded to the original settlers of the Jammû area. It is believed that the Saryaras have descended from those settlers.

The annual congregation of the Dalotrâ birâdarî is held at the temple of its presiding deity at Gore, a village on the banks of the Chenâb.

Sén: In the history of Kishtwâr (Dodâ) this author had pointed out that "it is assumed that the Kishtwâr state was founded in the tenth century AD, possibly by a line descended from the Rajas of Beñgâl, and related to the kings of Suket, Keonthal and Mandi (all three in HP)." The Séns of Kishtwâr and Bhaderwâh believe that they are the descendants of those kings of Gaur-Beñgâl. The tiny Sén community of the province has maintained a distinct identity, though it does intermarry with other Râjpût clans. The presiding deity of their clan is Kâlikâ Dévî.

The **Sikhs of Pooñch** or Pooñchhi Sikhs have descended from Brâhmins, who converted in the early 18th century. They have Brâhmin surnames like Isher and Khajuriâ. Their surnames include Rainâ, Reen, Sassen and Sûdan.

The **Sikligar** community of blacksmiths is spread over much of north India and has its own dialect. In Jammû province this tiny clan is found entirely in Sikligar Dikuliyâñ in the plains just west of Jammû town. The Sikligars are clean shaven Hiñdus but, like many Punjãbî Hiñdus, follow the Sikh scripture, the Guru Grañth Sâhib. It must be pointed out that Bhor Camp, a major Sikh settlement established in 1947, is close to Dikuliyâñ. The Sikligars' inclination towards Sikhism is much older that that. They claim to be Râjpûts from Râjasthân but others see them as an underprivileged group. For that reason they have been classified as a scheduled caste in some neighbouring states, but not in Jammû and Kashmîr.

Sochî: The prefix 'so' is pronounced exactly like the English 'sew' and means the same, too. This is essentially a community of tailors that lives in the Dhansâl-Jhajjar Kotlî-Katrâ area. The Sochîs also work as agricultural labourers. They claim to be Râjpûts and the regional Râjpût Sabhâ (congregation) has accepted them as such.

The **Sonâr** (Swarn-kâr) community of goldsmiths makes jewellery. Muslim goldsmiths are called Zargar. Both clans make ornaments of silver and other metals as well, even though their names only suggest an association with gold. (Zar is Persian for gold and swarn the Sañskrit word for the same metal.) This is an affluent community. In Jammû town their shops dominate the Lakhdâtâ and Jain (Bhâbh-rhâ) Bazârs. Hiñdu goldsmiths have adopted the surname Sarâf.

Tarkhân carpenters sometimes double as painters. They, too, claim descent from Lord Vishv-karmâ. A section of this community in Jammû and the Punjãb converted to Christianity, mainly in the 20th century. Another segment has been Muslim for several centuries now. There are Sikh Tarkhâns, too.

Of those who have remained Hiñdu, the ones living outside the state belong to the Râmgarhiyâ sect. Some Tarkhâns claim Brâhmin or Râjpût descent. This is, respectively, the case with their Bhârdwâj and Malhotrâ clans. Accordingly their sub-castes have 'upper' caste names like Chârak, Darmotrâ, Datt (Dutt), Debgotrâ, Gâñdhî, Rakhwâl, Sabharwâl and Vangotrâ.

Every village needs carpenters and all the better-off villages of Jammû province have at least one Tarkhân family each. (0.6 per cent of the population of the undivided state, as it stood in 1931, belonged to this community.)

Thakkar Nâg/ Nâg-vañshi: All over India some Brâhmins and some Râjpûts claim to be Nâg-vañshis ('the descendants of cobra snakes'). The Nâg-vañshis of Réâsî say that they are Râjpûts of the Sandilya *gotr.* Others accept them as Thakkars, a community that was not admitted into the Râjpût fold till the end of the nineteenth century.

Zarrad: The annual congregation of the birâdarî is held at the temple of its presiding deity in Karyâl Brâhminâ (Bishnâh).

Jammû castes found in other parts of India as well

Brâhmin

Almost all the Brâhmins of Jammû are Dogrâs. A few Punjãbî Brâhmins have also been living in the province for some time now and have mostly intermarried and merged with their Dogrâ brethren. The Brâhmins of Jammû province have mainly been farmers—with the exception of the Mohyâls, who were concentrated in Mîrpur and were in government service (mainly the army).

Jammû district has generally been the Dogrâ Brâhmins' stronghold. Around five per cent of the Brâhmins of the state are Sikhs. Most of these Sikhs had been Mohyâls of the Bâlî community (in Bârâmullâ) or Kashmîrî Pañdits.

Dogrâ Brâhmins have traditionally also been teachers, astrologers, music experts and doctors (of the Indian system of medicine). Some were scholars and writers, too. A few were experts of the scriptures (the Véds). Many of them were soldiers and warriors and a few went on to become great generals.

'The Brâhmin community is highly stratified in hierarchical order, at the top of which stands that clan of the Brâhmins who claim to be the descendants of King Porus. Dattâ, Bâlî, Vaid *gots* are considered the superior Brâhmins,' writes Champâ Sharmâ.[xxxiii] 'They mostly join either military and police service or prefer to run business. They do not enter into marriage with the Brâhmins of other groups.'

In Jammû, the Mohyâls are numerically insignificant, though, this clan had ruled Jammû in the centuries immediately before Christ.

The Brâhmins who count in Jammû are the non-martial ones.

Non-martial clans (*gotr* and *al*) that are at the top of the hierarchy are (in the alphabetical order) Badiyâl, Bhanotrâ, Dharmatt and Khajûria. The prominent *als* are Amlî-âlé, Galbaden-âlé, Karlûpié, Kalhé-âlé, Kalîthié, Khanûrié, Kohdié, Nalé-âlé and Udhampurié. 'Al' is an Arabic word that means 'of' (like 'von' and 'de') and indicates the ancestral region of the clan.

Bhojkî priests offer food to the deities. This clan maintains extreme ritual purity.

Other clans in the top rung are Barû, Balkarhiyâ (Balkadiyâ), Davé and Dûbé (both now of the Chenainî hills; their ancestors probably came from Mahârâshtrâ), Garoch, Goswâmî, Jamwâl (or Jamwâl Pañdit—perhaps originally from Uttar Pradésh), Késar, Lalotrâ (of Basohli), Mañgotrâ, Pâdhâ (Upâdhyâya of Basohli), Pâdhâ (Spolié), Pañt, Paroch, Rainâ,[5] Saddotrâ, Sadotrâ, Samnotrâ, Samotrâ, Tagotrâ, Upâdhyâya, Vaid[6] and Vansotrâ.

Other Brâhmin clans of Jammû include Badgotrâ, Badkuliâ, Bakhshî (a title, misspelt and mispronounced Bakshî), Bâlî, Ballî, Balotrâ, Bamhâl, Banâthiâ, Bannotrâ, Barkuliâ, Basmotrâ (of the Chenainî hills), Basotrâ, Bhâkhrî, Bharéyâl, Bhûriyâ, Bhûyâl (of the Chenainî hills), Bilâñloch, Dobliyâ, Dutt(â), Gabgotrâ, Gañdalgal, Gaor/ Gaur (perhaps of Beñgâli origin), Gautam, Gharâl, Gharhîyâl, Hadotrâ, Kâk, Kalsotrâ, Karnâthiyâ, Kérnî, Magotrâ, Mamolié, Misrâ, Modi, Nâd, Palâsar, Pañdotrâ, *Pañj Traparhiyâ*, *Pañkhail*, *Pañkiyâl*, Parâshar, Patéhâ, *Pavniyâ*, *Phañgailiyâ*, Plâshar, Rasgotrâ, *Sardâriyâ* (the six in italics are from of the Chenainî hills), Sâthé (perhaps of a Mahârâshtrian origin), Sûdan (mainly of Pooñch), Suthrhâ and Takâîyâ.

One does not come across many of these surnames any more. People from the smaller and lesser known clans have opted for the generic Brâhmin surname 'Sharmâ.'

The Jogî (yogi) and Bâwâ clans 'also claim to be Brâhmins,' Champâ Sharmâ writes. She says that the Jogîs are priests at temples of Srî Râm while the Bâwâs do the same work at temples of Lord Shiv. However, the Kanphattâ ('pierced ear') Jogîs are 'priests of Siva and are generally to be found in Sivalâs [temples of Lord Shiv].'[xxxiv] The Jogîs bury their dead. Jogî Gate is a very prominent landmark that almost all visitors to Jammû city have to pass on their way to Raghunâth Bâzâr. The area is dotted with memorials (*samâdhî*) built atop the graves of Jogîs.

5. Rainâ is also a Kashmîrî Pañdit surname and is used by the Dogrâ carpenters of Jammû and neighbouring Himâchal Pradésh.

6. Vaids can be doctor-Brâhmins, Mohyâl (martial) Brâhmins or traders of the Vysya caste.

The Bâwâs accept donations made during or after the death rites of children. For the same reason the Chârjî (Âchârya) and Gujrâti clans do not rank high within the Brâhmin community. There are separate entries in this chapter about these two clans.

The Brâhmins are divided into two broad classes: *purohits* and *pañdits*, the latter ranking below the former. There is also a sub-group called *halbâhâ* ('halwâhâ' or 'those who use ploughs') Brâhmins.

Champâ Sharmâ has an interesting take on the *purohits* (priests). She believes that this is a community descended from Brâhmin men who had married Râjpût women. For that reason they 'enjoyed all the favours' of the ruling Râjpût clan. There are certain ceremonies which only this group can conduct.

The Khajûrias rose to prominence because they were the priests of the Jâmwâl royal family of Jammû. The Bhanotrâs, in turn, were priests to the Khajûrias.

The Pâdhâs (Upâdhyâyas) were court physicians, astrologers and priests to the kings of Basohli.

The *pañdits* perform all kinds of religious functions.

When a 'lower ranking' Brâhmin greets an elder or superior he says *pœrî-péy* ('I fall at your feet'). The 'superior' replies with a 'Râm! Râm!' or a blessing.

Interestingly, the Brâhmins of the hills (but not those from the plains) 'universally eat meat.'[xxxv] In the plains only the Mohyâls have traditionally done so. A Brâhmin colleague from Bhaderwâh assumed that this was a post-1947 trend. However, we now have records which state that several Brahmin clans used to eat meat in the nineteenth century, if not before as well.

Exogamy/ chhinnâ: A Karlûpié, Takâîyâ or Hadotrâ is not supposed to marry a Jalotré. It is considered wrong for a Dûbé to marry a Badiyâl. A Késar can't marry a Badgotrâ or a Mamolié. Similarly, there are rules against marriages between the Pâdhâs and Rakwâl Râjpûts.

The *annual congregation* of the Khajûriâ birâdarî is held at the temple of its presiding deity at Sañgwâlî near the Jatwâl police barricade in Hîrânagar. That of the Barkula birâdarî is held at the temple of its presiding deity, Dâtî Shîlâ Wañtî at Bîrpur (Jammû). The Ganotrâ and Dégyâl Brâhmin birâdarîs hold their bi-annual congregations at the Dévsthân Kharhâ Madânâ (Purmañdal, Jammû). The Balotrâ clan congregates at the *darbâr* (court, temple) of Buâ Paiñthî jî in Sâmbâ every year. The Sapoliâ-Pâdhâ clan does the same at the temple of Buâ Bâbâ jî in Palourâ. The Dûbéy clan meets on Baisâkhî day (13 April) at the Râm Krishn Agatsya Muni temple in Muthî.

History: The great King Rañjît Dév was as good to the Brâhmins (and Râjpûts and, I suspect, everyone else) as he had been to the Muslims. Ganéshdâs Badéhrâ wrote in 1847 that during Rañjît's reign the Brâhmins were greatly revered. They enjoyed what Yale historian Dr Mridu Rai calls 'impressive degrees of autonomy.' Individual Brâhmins as well as Brâhmin villages, each called a *patholî,* had the power to grant sanctuary to rebels as well as those fleeing from the government because they owed money to the state.[xxxvi]

On the other hand, if someone showed disrespect to a Brâhmin, the latter would park himself in front of the offender's house and go on a fast. If that did not work (though it normally was sufficient) the Brâhmin would commit gory suicide at the offender's door. The offender was bound to give in. This set of customs was called *parâh.*

Mridu writes that *patholî* and *parâh* continued into Mahârâjâ Gulâb Siñgh's era. However, Mahârâjâ Ranbîr Siñgh whittled both customs down. *Parâh* was banned altogether, and so was the harbouring of offenders in temples. Besides, Mridu adds, the Brâhmins 'were rendered subservient by being put on the payroll of the [newly created] Dharmarth Trust.'[xxxvii]

Temples and their patrons: Mridu offers another interesting insight. She points out that Dogrâ temples were not territorial. (They still are not—in most parts of India.) This means that the patron of a temple need not belong to that area. Thus, the Umâ-Mahâpati temple at Purmañdal was built during the Mughal era by Râjâ Mân Siñgh of distant Ambar (Râjasthân).

Similarly, Mahârâjâ Rañjît Siñgh, the early 19th century emperor, got the Ékliñgaoñkar temple built at Purmañdal. He also donated 1300 ghumaoñ (a unit similar to an acre) of land for its maintenance.

A temple could have a number of patrons. As a result, the keeper of that temple was neither in the power of the king of the land in which the temple was located, nor dependednt on any one patron. He could, as Mridu says, play one patron off against the other. So great was the number of patrons vying to endow temples and sponsor prayers that the Brâhmins associated with the more important temples 'suffered only from an embarrassment of choice,' she adds.

(5.5 per cent of the population of the undivided state, as it stood in 1931, belonged to this community. This figure does not include the Kashmîrî Pañdits, who were another 1.7 per cent)

Râjpût

The twenty-two clans: King Râm Dév Râthor of Kannauj conquered the Dogrâ hills of Jammû-Kâñgrâ (Himâchal Pradésh) in the first century of the Christian era. Râthor had to vanquish as many as five hundred 'kingdoms'—or so the mediæval Arab historian Ferishtâ tells us. Most of these principalities would have consisted of less than half a dozen villages each. Some, like Jammû and Kâñgrâ (Nagar Kot), were substantial kingdoms even at the time. What we learn from this account is how many tiny ruling clans—all of them presumably Râjpût—there were as far back as the 1st century AD.

A millennium and a half later considerable consolidation—and social stratification[7] —had taken place.

We know this because in the 17th century some hill chiefs from Jammû-Himâchal Pradésh had each to leave a son behind at the Mughal court, as a virtual hostage. Jehâñgîr, the Mughal emperor, gave twenty-one such princes the title 'Miyâñ.' This title was passed down to their descendants.

This group, which represented as many (or, perhaps, twenty-two) ruling clans, ranked at the very top of the Râjpût pecking order. It is not that they became important because Jehâñgîr had given them this title. On the contrary, Jehâñgîr had chosen these twenty-one (or twenty-two) clans because they were the most powerful of the lot.

Balladeers, too, speak of twenty-two Dogrâ kingdoms. These ballads date perhaps to the reign of King Dhruv Dév (AD 1703 to roughly 1733). So we can assume that by the eighteenth century the villages of Jammû had been grouped into twenty-two kingdoms. Occasionally many (or all) of them came under the Jâmwâl (or Jambâl) rulers of Jammû proper.

The rulers (as well as other ranking warriors) of these twenty-two kingdoms belonged to as many Râjpût clans. The Jâmwâls (or Jambâls) of Jammû were clearly at the very top. The other twenty-one clans, along with their ancestral kingdoms, in the alphabetical order, are Balorîâ of Basohli-Billâwar, Bañdrâl of Bañdrâltâ, Bhaderwâhiyâ of Bhaderwâh, Bhadwâl of Bhaddu, Bhatiyâl of Bhotî, Chib of Bhimber (or Bhîmbar), Chib of Kharhî-Kharhyâlî, Chinâsiyâ of Chinâs, Dalpatiyâ of Dalpatpur, Hañtal of Chenainî, Jâmwâl (or Jambâl) of Akhnoor, Jarâl of Râjouri, Jasrotîâ of Jasrotâ, Kañgrâl of Kotlî, Kishtwâriyâ of Kishtwâr, Lakhanpuriâ of Lakhanpur, Mankotiâ of Mankot, Mañgrâl of Pooñch, Réâsîyâl of Réâsî, Sambiyâl or Samyâl of Sâmbâ and Trikotiyâ of Trikot.

Incidentally, some of these Râjpût clans (e.g. the Jarâls of Râjouri) are entirely or mostly Muslim.

Sub-castes: Scholars like SDS Charak[xxxviii] classify the Dogrâ (or Râjpût) community quite differently. They list fifteen groups within the community. These are (i) Jamwâl, (ii) Balorîâ, (iii) Ambarâîyâñ (of Akhnoor) and Shoñklâ; (iv) Chib; (v) Bhalwâl, Rajiâl and Rasiâl (who migrated from Udaipur and Méwâr in Râjasthân to Jammû in the 6th or 7th century A.D.); (vi) Lañgéh; (vii) Rakwâl; (viii) Añdotrâ and Bohdalâ; (ix) Jamal and Salehriâ; (x) Bañdrâhl; (xi) Kishtwâriâ; (xii) Galian; (xiii) Hiuntal; (xiv) Thakkar and (xv) Gaddi.

7. In plain English this means that by the 17th century some kingdoms had become bigger, more powerful and more important than the others. Twenty-two kingdoms had emerged at the top. The other 'kingdoms' were either controlled by these twenty-two or at least ranked lower in the Râjpûts' social hierarchy.

The Jâmwâls believe that they migrated to Jammû thousands of years ago. The 5th century AD is a more realistic date. The branches of the Jamwâl sub-caste include Manhâs, Chârak, Shau, Bhatiâl, Jasrotîâ, Sambyâl, Mankotiâ and Salâthiâ (of Gurhâ Salâthiâ, Jammû). The Balorîâ sub-caste is further divided into Bhadwâl, Bhaderwâhiyâ and Sumbriâ.

The roots of the clans: The Manhâs (or Minhâs) clan probably came from Siâlkot (West Punjãb, Pâkistân), which it had ruled in the 4th century AD and later. This is a community of Sûrya-vañshi Râjpûts who lived on both sides of the fertile and prosperous Jammû-Punjãb border. They are perhaps the descendants of King Akâl Dhar (or Ukâl Dhar or even Ukal Ghar) and are part of the extended Jâmwâl clan.

The Manhâs' most famous ancestor, King Jambu Lochan, son of Ukal Ghar is the founder of Jammû (and also of the Jâmwâl clan). (See 'A history of Jammû state.') Their fifth century AD forebear was called Malhan Hans (aka Man Haras). He was the king of Madr Desh, a Sialkot-based kingdom that included Jammû. The clan takes its name from this ruler. Their traditional ancestral villages included Chaprar, Ghorsuha, Pargwâl and Thub and, later, Barâ Mañgâ and Daryâ Piñd. Unlike the main Jamwâl clan of soldiers, they took to farming as well, which made them fall somewhat in the hierarchy.

King Bhog Pâl migrated from Kulu (Himâchal Pradésh) in the eighth century AD and founded the Balorîâ clan. The Ambarâîyâñs are a Panwar or Parmâr clan that came from Ujjain (central India) four hundred years later.

The Rakwâl group traces its ancestry to Srî Râm, through his son, Kush. They thus are Sûrya-vañshi ('solar dynasty') Râjpûts. This means that their ultimate ancestor is the Sun itself. They were (and still are) concentrated in two villages in the Siâlkot area—Rakwâl and Sujwâl (both in India). This clan originally belonged to the Punjãb. The oldest mention of them in the records of Jammû dates to AD 1450.

There are two main dynasties of Râjpûts in South Asia. The other group is called Chañdr-vañshî ('lunar dynasty') and believes that it was founded by the Moon. The Salâriâ clan (which mostly converted to Islâm) is Chañdr-vañshî. Someone called King Shâl founded the clan. If he is the same as King Shâl Vâhan then he probably lived at the same time as Lord Jesus.

The Jâmwâl, Jarâl, Bhâû and Manhâs clans are said to have migrated from Ayodhyâ (Central India). The ancestral temple of these three clans is in Kalîth (Jammû). They have matrimonial ties with the Ambriyâl and Chib clans. The Chibs are perhaps a branch of the Katoch clan.

The Kâtil clan is better known as Khokhar and is Sûrya-vañshi. Its founder, King Karét, migrated to Jammû around the tenth century AD and settled in Kharîpur village.

Some believe that the Lañgéh clan has descended from Dharmu, a brave warrior who fell out with the establishment in mediæval times. He was something of a Robin Hood and was good to the common man. However, what seems more likely is that Lañg Pâl was their founder. It is claimed that he was a descendant of Karn, the great warrior mentioned in *The Mahâbhârat*. In any case, this is a Kashmîrî clan that migrated to Jammû, around AD 1350.[xxxix]

Also found in Jammû province are Râjpût families whose ancestors migrated from neighbouring Himâchal Pradésh and the Punjāb. The Katoch clan of Kâñgrâ and the Jaswâls of Jaswâñ are perhaps the best known.

Jammû has some families from the Pathâniâ clan of Nûrpur, too. The Pathâniâs are the descendants of Rânâ Bhet, who established the Pathânkot state (in the Punjāb) in the eleventh century AD His elder brother, Gahl, founded the Añdotrâ and Bohdalâ clans, which shifted to neighbouring Kathuâ two hundred years later.

Social stratification: The miyâñs have traditionally refused to plough their own lands—though they might own considerable tracts. Besides, they would never give their daughters in marriage to anyone 'lower' down the pecking order. Non-Miyâñ Râjpûts are called *halbâhâ* ('halwâhâ' or 'those who use ploughs').

During community feasts, non-Miyâñ Râjpûts are seated lower than the Miyâñs. When 'lower ranking' people—Râjpûts, as well as others—greet a Miyâñ, they say 'Jai diyâ.' For that reason, the Miyâñ clan is also called Jaikartâ.

Whenever a Râjpût married a woman from a so-called 'lower' caste, their children were called Râthee and expelled from the clan. In time the Râthees came to form a clan of their own.

The annual congregation of the Jamwâl birâdarî is held at the temple of its presiding deity, Datti Sajawati at Domânâ (Akhnoor Road).

The Thakkars used to be a separate community altogether. They did not use the middle name 'Siñgh,' employing instead middle names like 'Dâs' and 'Chañd.' Agriculture was their main occupation. The Râjpûts, on the other hand, felt that 'service' (employment under the king) was their—the Râjpûts'—domain. The Census of 1931 noted, 'The Râjpûts treated agriculture contemptuously and refused to inter-dine [with] or give their daughters in marriage to Thakkars.' The Mahârâjâ, however, united the two communities and clubbed them together for the census. The Mehrâ community had no such luck—though it had tried hard in the early twentieth century.

(9.7 per cent of the population of the undivided state, as it stood in 1931, belonged to this community. Muslim Râjpûts, with a population of 1,95,449, greatly outnumbered their Hiñdu brothers, of whom there were 1,58,457. Muslim Râjpûts were thus 54.9 per cent of the 3,55,662-strong Râjpût community of the undivided state. The remaining roughly 1,600 Râjpûts must have been Sikh.)

The Vysya caste: The Mahâjan business community

In theory—at least in some 2nd century AD books—the business caste of the Hiñdus is called 'Vysya' or 'Vaish.' In actual practice no one calls them by that name in most parts of India.

Guptâ-Mahâjan—origin and allied castes: The Guptâ-Mahâjan clan is, on average, the wealthiest in Jammû province—with the possible exception of the Jain community with whom, at least at the national level, it shares extensive ties of kinship. The Mahâjans of Jammû have a very long history of living in the Dogrâ hills and, therefore, are closer to their cousins in Himâchal Pradésh than to the Jains of Jammû.

Prof. SDS Charak feels that the Mahâjans are the descendants of mixed marriages between the Baniyâ and Kâyasth clans on the one hand and of the children of Baniyâ-Kâyasth unions with 'girls of the lower Râjpût grades, such as Rathis and Rawats.'[xl]

The Mahâjans and Kâyasths are considered two distinct castes in Western Uttar Pradésh, Delhi and states further north. The Kâyasths are seen as a caste of salaried employees (i.e. bureaucrats and teachers) and the Mahâjans as businessmen. And yet, some kind of a link between the two has continued into modern times even in these areas. (In Eastern UP, Bihar and Beñgâl these two castes have always been one.)

Ibbetson wrote about the Mahâjans of greater Punjãb, '[T]he Mahâjan is a Mahâjan in the hills so long as he is a merchant, but a Kâya[s]th as soon as he becomes a clerk.'[xli]

In some parts of West Punjãb (especially Hazârâ) and Péshâwar in the North West Frontier Province (both now in Pâkistân) there used to be Mahâjans who claimed a Brâhmin origin. They have since migrated to other parts of India. In any case, many Brâhmins keep shops in the hills.

One Mahâjan family migrated, along with the great Gen. Zorâwar Siñgh, from Himâchal Pradésh to Vijaypur (Sâmbâ tehsil, Jammû district) where it built a substantial house.

Today the Mahâjans of Jammû province are found mainly in Jammû district, Udhampur, Kathuâ and Bhaderwâh-Kishtwâr—in that order. Till 1947, when they had to flee, they had a fair presence in Mîrpur as well. Apparently the Mahâjans of Mîrpur 'mostly' had more than one wife.[xlii]

Sub-castes: The Vysya community of Jammû-Himâchal Pradésh consists of the Mahâjan, Sûd and Gosâîñ clans.

In Jammû, the community is further divided into two groups, based on where their ancestral home had been. The post-1947 migrants from Mîrpur are called Mîrpurîs, and the rest—the older Mahâjan families of Jammû—are known as Dogrâ Mahâjans.

Each of the sub-castes of this clan normally has a guardian deity and a fraternity-temple, usually in the ancestral village. Once every year they organise a prayer ceremony and fair at this temple. The better-known fairs are held at Jhîrhî and the shrines of Bâbâ Pohto and Bâbâ Sehej Nâth. These fairs are essentially a device to get the scattered community together once a year.

Sub-castes of the Guptâ-Mahâjan caste of the Dogrâs include Jañdiyâl, Kîlâ, Kalsotrâ, Tiyâlâ, Lammâ, Phavâ, Pargâl, Goyal, Jédéyâl, Béyotrâ, Kañgâl, Bolâ, Buchchâ, Piddû, Pâvâ, Manâth, Kansotrâ, Pachél, Vaid, Lañgar, Phagétrâ/ Phagotrâ, Chunnâ, Bubâthî, Savâr (Savârâ?), Mohotrâ, Lambotrâ and Rohmétrâ.

Mîrpurî sub-castes include: Bagotrâ, Bhagiyâl, Gadyâ, Granâl, Kabotrâ, Kalshotrâ, Khañgal, Khannâ(!), Khariyâl, Pakshotrâ, Paharu, Pandi, Phaniyâl, Ragarly, Rasotrâ, Rotrâ, Sadavartiyâ and Thatthar.

Over the centuries the community as a whole was known by different names, some of them pejorative. The village shopkeeper was—and is—addressed as Shâh jî ('Mr King'), only partly in jest. Lâlâ was a nice title for businessmen which, somewhere down the line, got associated with a generous avoirdupois. Kirâr and Karâr met an even worse fate. Therefore, the titles currently preferred by the community are the Sañskrit–Hiñdi Mahâjan ('the great or exalted people') and the Persian Chaudhary ('the headman'). Some Mahâjan families, especially those from Himâchal Pradésh, had the title Râjâ ('king') as well.

The *annual congregation* of the Lammé Mahâjan birâdarî is held at the temple of its presiding deity, Buâ Dâti Satwati Darvar at Sanyal. That of the Swar Mahâjan birâdarî is held at the temple of its presiding deity at the Brahm Dév Sthân at Râjpurâ (Hîrânagar). The Phawa Mahâjan clan meets every year at the Sujâwatî Mañdir Sthân in the Mill Area of RS Purâ and encourages visitors from out of town to spend the night there. Reghrâ Mahâjans assemble at the Bâbâ Brahm Dév jî Sthân at Cholé dâ Chak near Sâmbâ.

(0.5 per cent of the population of the undivided state, as it stood in 1931, belonged to this community.)

Khatrî

This is a handsome, light-skinned, urban, business community of Hiñdus and Sikhs. While Khatrîs have for centuries been living in places as far apart as Uttar Pradésh (Central India) and Afghânistân, they are mainly a Punjãbi community. They are found in small numbers in the urban parts of Jammû province and Srînagar city.

Ibbetson writes, 'The Khatri occupies a very different position among the people of the Punjãb... [He is] superior to [the other mercantile and shop-keeping castes] in physique, in manliness, and in energy; he is not, like them, a mere shop-keeper.'[xliii]

Having said that, Ibbetson, like several other British scholars (not to mention such Hiñdus as have traditionally claimed expertise in such matters) felt that the Khatrîs' claim to being direct descendants of the Kshatriya caste was of doubtful validity. Captain Burton wrote of 'a race of pretended Kshatriyas who are really Banias of the Nanak-Shahi (Sikh) faith and who trade, and have a large share of public offices. These are evidently Khatris.'[xliv]

True, the word Khatrî sounds tantalisingly like the much-admired Kshatriya. But, as some scholars suggest, it is even closer to *chhatrî* (umbrella). Apparently some Sarâswat Brâhmins had taken the mothers of the present Khatrî clan under their protective umbrella. This was when the violent mythological priest-warrior Parshûrâm had gone on a murderous genocidal spree.

The Khatrîs' own accounts suggest a mixed origin. Khatrîs of the Agniras *gotr* claim descent from fire (which they call Havishmat and Havirbhuja). To me this suggests kinship with the equally fair and good-looking Zoroastrians, who come from roughly the same parts of the Indo-Iranian region. (I know one Nârañg family that claims Iranian Hiñdu ancestry. Many Khatrîs came from the NWFP region of what is now Pâkistân and is close to Iran.)

The Kaushik *gotr* claims to have descended from the moon. Those of the Kaushalya *gotr* believe that the sun is their original ancestor. So, the Khatrîs are without doubt a coalition of three separate clans.

Being an urban people, the Khatrîs of the Punjãb took to English-language education before many other communities did. Therefore, in the 19th century some of them were employed by the government, in the Punjãb as well as in the other areas where they lived. Some of them rose to the highest levels. The Dogrâ Mahârâjâs of Jammû and Kashmîr encouraged some talented Khatrîs to migrate to their state capitals. This process started with the visionary Mahârâjâ Rañjît Dév (1733-82) and accelerated in the early years of the twentieth century. An important example is the migration to the state of the clan of the Diwâns of Eminâbâd.

Because of their education, the Khatrîs rose to high offices in the civil administration, and some in the army.

The main Khatrî population was traditionally in Jammû and Mîrpur. There was always a small indigenous Khatrî presence in Muzaffarâbâd and the parts of the state that bordered the Punjãb.

Even though this is essentially an urban caste, all historical records suggest that every village needed at least one Khatri. And if a village did not have a Khatrî, the thing to do was to steal one from the next village. That's because Khatrîs were needed to keep the accounts, to do all work related to banking and to buy and sell grain.

And in these capacities, Sir George Campbell noted, the Pathâns of Afghânistân "seem[ed] to look at them as a kind of valuable animal; and a Pathân would steal another man's Khatrî, not only for the sake of ransom…but also as he might steal a milch cow, or as Jews might be carried off in the middle ages with a view to render them profitable."[xlv]

Sikh Khatrîs have traditionally been teachers and men of religion. There are some Jain Khatrîs, too. And then there are Gaddî Khatrîs in the upper hills.

The Khatrîs are divided into three main classes. These, in the descending order of their rank, are Bârî, Buñjahi and Sarîn.[xlvi]

The Bârî class has twelve (*bârâh*) sub-castes, grouped into four *barhâ* (high) sub-castes and eight *chhotâ* (of 'smaller' rank) sub-castes. These are: *Barhâ:* Kapûr, Khannâ, Malhotrâ and Kakkar(h)/ Séth. *Chhotâ:* Choprâ, Talwâr, Sehgal, Dhavan, Tañdon/ Tannan, Vohrâ/ Bohrâ, Wadhâwan (Wadhâon) and Mahéñdrû.

The twelve Bârî clans are also grouped into Dhâi-ghar (2½ families), Châr-ghar (four families), Chhé-ghar (six families) and Bârâ-jâto (twelve sub-castes), in that order. These are four concentric circles, with the most exclusive one (2½) at the centre. The least exclusive group lies in the outermost circle and accepts all twelve sub-castes.

Let me explain. The 'number' of 'families' that a sub-caste accepts as equal or superior increases the lower it ranks on the traditional ladder. Thus the number of sub-castes which that sub-caste can give its daughters to in marriage increases.

The Dhâi-ghar clans can marry their daughters only to boys from the top two and a half clans. At the other end are the Bârâ-jâto whose daughters can marry into any of the twelve sub-castes of the Bârî category. (The general principle within the Khatrî hierarchy—and the Hiñdu pecking order as a whole—is that a girl can marry only an 'equal' or a 'superior.' Miscegenation was traditionally forbidden. So the number of families that a girl can marry into gets smaller the higher up her clan is on the ladder.)

The Buñjahi class is divided into four sub-classes and fifty-two (*bâwan-wajâ*) sub-castes. The important ones are the eight sub-castes of the Khukhrain fraternity (birâdari), viz., Ânañd, Bhasîn, Chaddhâ, Sâhnî, Sûrî, Séthî, Kohlî and Sab(h)erwâl.

Next in rank within the Buñjahi group is the Buñjahi Khâs (main)/ Kalâñ (senior) sub-caste. It is further divided into Asli (the real or true), Puccâ (pure)/ Barhâ (big) and Chhotâ (small) Buñjahi.

The Sarîns, too, are divided into Barhâ and Chhotâ groups.

Other Khatrî sub-castes include Ghaî, Chañdok, Mehrâ, Behl, Puri, Vâhî (Wâhî), Vij, Bhallâ, Bédî, Sodhî and Sâhî. Khatrî sub-castes particular to Jammû province include Maiñgî (Méñgî), Gañdotrâ, Nargotrâ, Badérâ (Vadérâ), Kanotrâ, Salhotrâ, Kalsotrâ and Nâgpâl.

The Khatrîs of Jammû province have their own divisions. Those in the plains are called Jhiklî and hill-dwellers are called Dugrî.

The annual congregation of the Méñgî birâdarî is held at the temple of its presiding deity, Mahâdév, at Réâsî.

(0.6 per cent of the population of the undivided state, as it stood in 1931, belonged to this community.)

Arorâ: This is a community of Hiñdu-Sikh Punjãbî traders. Within the state their numbers were not great. There were all of 3,548 Aroras in the state in 1931. They were mainly found in Jammû and Mîrpur. A little less than half the Arorâs of the state—around 49 per cent—were Sikhs. One Arorâ family had converted to Islâm.

References

i Sources for this chapter include

Census of India, the, 1921

Census of India, the, 1931

Census of India, the, 2001

Hutchison and Vogel, *History of the Punjâb Hill States*, (first published in 1933), Vol. I (reprinted in 2000), Department of Languages and Culture, Himâchal Pradésh, Ibbetson, Denzil, *Punjãb Castes* (1916; reprinted in 1993 by Low Price Publications, Delhi.)

Jerath, Dr. Ashok, *Duggar kâ Sâñskritik Itihâs* (1997), Mânvî Prakâshan, Pañjtîrathî, Jammû. (All translations are by this author.)

Siñgh, K.S. (editor) *People of India, Volume XXV. Jammû and Kashmîr* (2004), The Anthropological Survey of India, Manohar, New Delhi. The author's own fieldwork.

ii *People of India, Volume XXV*, page 290.

iii 'Congregations of various Biradris at respective Dév Sthans on Nov 26,' *Daily Excelsior*, 23 Nov. 2004.

iv Ibbetson, op. cit., p. 301.

v Ibbetson, op. cit., p. 333.

vi Ibbetson, op. cit., p. 332.

vii Ibid, page 333.

viii Ibid, page 221,

ix *People of India, Volume XXV*, page 190.

x See the 1921 and 1931 censuses.

xi Ibbetson, op. cit., p. 301.

xii Anita S Billawaria, *People of India, Volume XXV*, page 207.

xiii Ibbetson, op. cit., p. 154.

xiv *People of India, Volume XXV*, page 208.

xv Ibbetson, op. cit., p. 321.

xvi *People of India, Volume XXV*, page 221.

xvii Pp. 336-337.

xviii *People of India, Volume XXV*, page 318.

xix Quoted by Billawaria in *People of India, Volume XXV*, page 325.

xx Ibbetson, op. cit., p. 334.

xxi Ibbetson, op. cit., p. 205 and *People of India, Volume XXV*, page 333.

xxii *People of India, Volume XXV*, pages 333-4.

xxiii *People of India, Volume XXV*, page 380. See also Ibbetson, op. cit., p. 220.

xxiv Ibbetson, op. cit., p.244.

xxv *People of India, Volume XXV*, page 293.

xxvi Ibbetson, op. cit., p. 307.

xxvii Ibbetson, op. cit., p. 235.

xxviii *People of India, Volume XXV*, page 436.

xxix *People of India, Volume XXV*, page 511.

xxx *People of India, Volume XXV*, page 565.

xxxi *People of India, Volume XXV*, page 607.

xxxii B Siñgh, *People of India, Volume XXV*, page 621.

xxxiii *People of India, Volume XXV*, page 284.

xxxiv Ibbetson, op. cit., p. 228.

xxxv Ibbetson, op. cit., p. 218.

xxxvi Rai, Mridu, *Hiñdu Rulers, Muslim Subjects: Islâm, rights and the history of Kashmîr* (2004), Permanent Black, New Delhi. Pages 104-105.

xxxvii Ibid, page 119.

xxxviii *People of India, Volume XXV*, page 268.

xxxix *People of India, Volume XXV*, page 269.

xl *People of India, Volume XXV*, page 474.

xli Ibbetson, op. cit., p. 7.

xlii *People of India, Volume XXV*, page 475.

xliii Ibbetson, op. cit., p. 247.

xliv Ibbetson, op. cit., p. 248.

xlv *Ethnology of India*, quoted by Ibbetson, op. cit., p. 247.

xlvi The next few paragraphs are on the authority of Dr Ashok Jerath, *Duggar kâ Sâñskritik Itihâs* (1997), Mânvî Prakâshan, Pañjtîrathî, Jammû, SDS Charak, *People of India, Volume XXV*, page 447 and Ibbetson, op. cit., pp. 248-250.

5

Muslim Castes

Except for the Mughals, Pathâns and Syeds, *all* Muslims of Jammû are converts from Hiñduism and other native communities. The Census of India (1931) estimated that only 3.2 per cent of the Muslims of the *state* belonged to these three 'alien castes.' It added, 'The remaining 96.8 per cent of the [Muslim] population is due to conversion to Islâm.' Most of them are Sunni.

Almost all clans that converted to Islâm en masse retained the Hiñdu name of their clan. I suspect that it was only when conversion was the decision of an individual or that of one or two families of a clan that they had to take on the honorific Sheikh.

The Muslims of Jammû, Kathuâ and most of Udhampur are Dogrâs because they speak Dogrî (or Punjãbî) at home. I know Muslims in Banni and Reasi who have distinctly Kashmîrî names and features—and who inter-marry mostly with Kashmîrîs to this day—but think of themselves as Dogrâs because their families have been in Jammû for a few hundred years. I also know Muslims from Kargil-Baltistân who have been in Jammû for just three generations but speak Dogrî-Punjãbî at home and think of themselves as Dogrâs.

The reference to Punjãbî is not a slip. Many well to do Dogrâ Muslims speak Punjãbî with each other and equally fluent Dogrî with their Hiñdu friends.

The Muslims of Rajourî and Pooñch are often Chibâlis and those of Dodâ district are often Kashmîrîs. These are non-Dogrâ communities.

The main Muslim clans and sub-castes of Jammû are:

Arâîñ: This Punjãbî community has dominated public life in Pâkistân after 1947. Its members have traditionally grown and sold vegetables. In the state they were found almost exclusively in Jammû province—mainly in Jammû district, followed by Mîrpur. Kathuâ was a distant third. Traditionally this has been a community of landholders and cultivators. (0.6 per cent of the population of the undivided state, as it stood in 1931, belonged to this community.)

Awan: This community of farmers lives mostly in Muzaffarâbâd, Pooñch and Mîrpur.

Bafindâ: This community of weavers lives mainly in Jammû province (Kathuâ, Réâsî, Mîrpur and Pooñch *jagîr*). In Kashmîr there was a small Bafinda population in Muzaffarâbâd. (See also Julâhâ in the chapter 'The Hiñdu-Sikh clans and sub-castes of Jammû.') *Baftan* means 'cotton' in the Persian language. (0.9 per cent of the population of the undivided state, as it stood in 1931, belonged to this community.)

Note: The Kashmîrî Dhoon community, too, is called Bafinda.

Bakerwâl: Even though the name of the community means 'the people with the goats' they actually rear only sheep. They claim that their original home was Swât (which is on the borders of Pâkistân Occupied Kashmîr), from where they migrated to Jammû around the second century BC (and later to Kashmîr). They mainly live in Rajourî, Pooñch, Udhampur, Kathuâ, Jammû and Dodâ.

Like the Gujjars they migrate to the mountain pastures of Dodâ and Kashmîr in summer, so that their flock has good grass to eat. Some Bakerwâls also go to Kargil in Ladâkh—as deep into the Surû Valley as Rañgdum.

Anand Saran notes, 'Though they speak the Kashmîrî language and use [the] Arabic [Persian?] script yet their dialect is identified as Gojri which is the main dialect of the Gujjars.'[i] The Gujjars claim the Bakerwâls as a sub-sect of the Gujjar community.

In terms of clothes (especially the turban of the men and the cap of the women) they are somewhat different from the nomadic section of Gujjars. A very substantial portion of the Gujjar community has for centuries now consisted of landowners, even affluent landlords, which is to say that many Gujjars are not nomads. For that reason, some Muslim Gujjars have always been part of the elite of Jammû, Kashmîr and the Punjãb. They were part of the Mahârâjâ's aristocracy.

On the other hand almost all Bakerwâls are nomads. The Bakerwâl elite is much smaller and of relatively recent vintage. Illiteracy among the Bakerwâls is also much higher.

For several kinds of religious ceremonies the Bakerwâls depend on Gujjar men of religion. That is because the much bigger Gujjar community can afford the luxury of following professions other than their ancestral cattle-rearing. Bakerwâls, on the other hand, still mostly stick to sheep-rearing—and related activities. Like the Gujjars, their holy shrine is at Wâñgat (Kañgan, Srînagar), where they have a religious function every year in July.

Ferocious dogs of a particular breed are trained to guard the Bakerwâls' sheep. The Bakerwâls have always had ponies, too. Tourists (and pilgrims to the Hiñdu holy shrines of Srî Mâtâ Vaishno Dévî jî and Srî Amarnâth jî) pay reasonably well to hire these ponies, adding somewhat to the Bakerwâls' avenues of income.

The **Chañg-garh** clan might possibly be the oldest natives—the aboriginal inhabitants—of Jammû province. Till 1947 they mostly lived in the districts of Punjãb closest to Jammû. After 1947 the Muslim Chañg-garhs migrated to Pâkistân. This is a clan of warrior-farmers and its sub-castes are Bhattî, Bhullar, Chauhân, Khokhar, Manhâs and Tûr. The community converted to Islâm under the influence of Shams Tabréz, the renowned saint of Multân. The men are agriculturists while the women clean and sift grain for merchants. They speak a distinct dialect and prefer to be called Chûbnâ.

The **Chibali** people are those who live in the Chib(h)al region, which is on the left bank of the Jehlum, along the border with Hazârâ. At one stage this region included Akhnoor, Havélî, Méndhar, Nausherâ and Rajourî. They also live in Pooñch. The region got its name from the Chib clan. However, even by the 19th century there were few Chibs left in this, their ancestral, region. (See also 'Chib' under 'Hiñdu-Sikh clans.')

The Râjpûts (as well as other Hiñdus) of the area started becoming Muslims after AD 1465, which was the year of King Dharam Chañd's conversion. The Hiñdu castes and sub-castes of the Chibhal area were Bhawpâl, Jarâl, Jât, Jeehur, Jhakîr, Mañgdâl, Manhâs, Nankâ and Sâhu. Some members of these clans became Muslims.

As we have seen in the chapter about the history of Rajourî, the Hiñdus and Muslims of the area used to inter-marry as a matter of routine. This was especially true of the Râjpûts of both religions. Emperor Jehâñgîr put an end to this in the 17th century.

What he could not eliminate were the Hiñdu customs that the Muslim Chibalis continued to practice. However, once intermarriage stopped, these customs lost some of their vigour. British Raj scholars, writing in 1890, noted that the Muslim Chibalis had retained several Hiñdu customs. To this day they continue to be proud of their Râjpût origin.

Most Chibalis are farmers. Those in the towns have taken to trade.

The clans of Muslim Chibs are Mandiâl, Srâhiâl and Dhériâl. The Ghaniâl people, too, are Chibs.

Domal: Though the Domal Râjpûts mainly live in Rajourî-Pooñch today and speak Dogri, they have some Ladâkh-Gilgit blood in their veins. Apparently, a Hiñdu Mala Râjpût once married a Buddhist Dûm woman in Kargil. They later converted to Islâm and took on the surname Khân. Their descendants ruled Gilgit and Chilâs for a while.

Parmanand Lal writes, 'The community perceive themselves as Muslim Râjpûts. Others consider them of middle rank in the social hierarchy and equal in status with Jaral, Basîth and Gujjar.'[ii]

Most members of this Sunni community are hired farmhands.

Gujjar: As we have seen, this is one of the most important communities of the state, and the only one spread throughout the state, except Leh district.

Traditionally Pooñch has been their citadel, followed by Réâsî and Jammû. Some Gujjars are nomads. All Gujjars have bred cattle and most of them have sold milk and milk-products. Traditionally this has been accepted as a community of landholders and cultivators. (The community has been covered in greater detail in Chapters 3 and 14.) The Gujjars account for 11 per cent of the population of the undivided state.

Hajjâm: This community of barbers mainly lives in Jammû province. In 1931 almost thirty percent of all Hajjâms were Hiñdu. The Sikhs consider it sinful to shave or cut the hair of the head. Therefore, it is a revelation that there were as many as nine Sikh Hajjâms in 1931. (0.5 per cent of the population of the undivided state, as it stood in 1931, belonged to this community.)

Jarâl: This Rajourî-based community was Râjpût Hiñdu before its conversion. Historically they have tended cattle—mainly buffaloes—and sheep. Several Jarâls have been kings and headmen. They claim to have descended from Arjun of the *Mahâbhârat*, through his grandson King Parîkshit, whose descendant in the eighth generation was King Jaisar Rao. Jaisar is said to have founded the Jarâl clan, the name of which possibly derives from Jaisar.

We have considered three theories about how and when they converted to Islâm in the volumes 'Jammû' and 'A History of Jammû.' Parmanand Lal[iii] gives us a fourth—and the least plausible—one: Apparently the 16th century Emperor Akbar once chanced upon a settlement of Jâl (net) weavers. He married one of their women. According to this tale, Akbar's descendants from that Jâl woman are called Jarâl. The problem with this theory is that the Jarâls have a recorded history that dates to at least three centuries before Akbar. Above all, Akbar's son Jehâñgîr, in his memoirs, gives a totally different account.

The Jarâls' villages are mostly in the hills and are perched above certain tributaries of River Chenâb, mainly the Râmgarh, Kalali Jamol and Barot streams.

Significantly, traditionally the Jarâls have had a taboo against eating beef. They use the titles Mirzâ and Yûsuf as surnames of sorts. The Jarâl *nikâhnâmâ* (wedding contract) is normally oral and not written.

Despite having given the area its greatest ruling dynasty, the Jarâls are not at all well off. They often work on the fields of their better-off Hiñdu neighbours. They also make and sell ropes and baskets.

Jât: A little more than eighty percent of the Jâts of the undivided state were Muslim and concentrated in Mîrpur. The rest were mainly Hiñdu. In 1931 there were 5,619 Sikh Jâts, too. After the partition of India, the areas where the Muslim Jâts lived mostly came under Pâkistâni occupation.

B Joardar, writing in 2004, states, 'Majority of Jâts [in the portion under the Indian tricolour] are Sikhs and a few of them are Hiñdus.'[iv] If this is correct then the explanation for this change in the Hiñdu: Sikh ratio can only be explained by the migration of Jât Sikhs from West Punjãb (the area now in Pâkistân) to Jammû. Sikh fertility rates are normally not higher than among the Hiñdus, so that can't be the explanation.

Sikh and Hiñdu Jâts normally marry each other with social approval. Like several other Hiñdu communities, Jammû's Hiñdu Jâts pray at gurudwârâs (as well as at Hiñdu temples), follow many aspects of Sikhism and venerate the Sikh Gurûs.

The Jâts mostly live in the border areas of Jammû province. This is a community of middling to rich farmers. Traditionally it has been a clan of landholders and cultivators. Very few of them are landless. (4 per cent of the population of the undivided state as it stood in 1931, belonged to this community.)

Kashmîrî Muslims live in Kishtwâr, Dodâ, Banihâl, Réâsî, a few villages of Bannî and Lohâî Malhâr (both in Kathuâ), Basohli town, Rajourî, Pooñch and parts of Udhampur. Traditionally this has been a community of landholders, cultivators, government servants and traders.

There are more Muslims than Hiñdus in the **Lohâr** community of ironsmiths, which is mainly found in Jammû province. They are present in all self-respecting villages because every village needs ironsmiths and their twentieth century avatars, the mechanics. (0.7 per cent of the population of the undivided state, as it stood in 1931, belonged to this community.)

Manhâs: This community was Râjpût Hiñdu before its conversion.

Miyâñ: This community was Râjpût Hiñdu before its conversion.

Mughal: This is one of the very few non-indigenous Muslim clans of the state. Though found all over the state, they have traditionally lived mainly in Jammû province—in Jammû city, Nausherâ, Pooñch and Rajourî, with a few clans in Dodâ district. (There are few Mughals left in Jammû city, because of the 1947 exodus of many Jammû Muslims to Pâkistân.) Traditionally this has been a community of landholders, cultivators, government servants and traders.

When did the Mughals first settle in Jammû province? Certainly not with the Mughal conquest of the state around 1586. My guess is that they came in the 18th century, at the invitation of the great Raja Ranjit Dév. Indu Bala Dhar, however, feels that they migrated to Jammû as recently as around 1857. She also has doubts about the true Mughalness of the Jammû Mughals on the ground that *none* of them belongs to the Chughatta or Bartas [perhaps she means Barlâs] clans, which alone she accepts as 'true Mughals.' (Ibbetson had reservations only about a small minority of those who claimed to be Mughals. He did notice a tendency among the 'low' castes to pretend to be Mughals.) 0.8 per cent of the population of the undivided state, as it stood in 1931, belonged to this community.

Pathân: Not everyone called Khân is either a Pathân or even a Muslim. Old Ghenghis was neither. (0.5 per cent of the population of the undivided state, as it stood in 1931, belonged to this community.)

Muslim **Râjpûts** have always outnumbered their Hiñdu cousins 54.9:44.5. Both have traditionally been employed in the army and the civil service. They have also been farmers. (9.7 per cent of the population of the undivided state, as it stood in 1931, belonged to this community. See also the chapter 'The Hiñdu-Sikh clans...')

Râthor(e): The 'e' is silent. This community was Râjpût Hiñdu before its conversion.

Salâriâ: It is said that the Râjpût Salâriâ clan dominated two hundred villages till the seventeenth century when, during the Mughal Emperor Aurañgzéb's reign, exactly half these villages converted to Islâm. These villages were to the west of what is now the Indo-Pâkistân border, in the Siâlkot area. After the partition of India in 1947, many of the Hiñdu Salâriâs chose to live in Indian Punjãb (mostly Pathânkot-Gurdâspur), while many Muslim Salâriâs opted for Pâkistân or 'Âzâd' Jammû and Kashmîr. The Hiñdu Salâriâs who preferred Jammû migrated to the areas immediately east of the border: Hîrânagar, Kathuâ and Sâmbâ. The original *gotr* of the Salâriâs is Bhârdwâj, which makes them akin to the Atsi and Pathâniâ clans of Hiñdu Râjpûts. The Salâriâs rank high in the pecking orders of both the Muslims and the Hiñdus.

In Jammû and the Punjãb a **Sheikh** is someone whose family is a relatively recent convert to Islâm. Not so in India as a whole, where some Sheikh families are the descendants of Arab clans that rank next only to the Syeds in the international Islâmic hierarchy. In the state the Sheikhs live mostly in Pooñch and Muzaffarâbâd. (0.8 per cent of the population of the undivided state, as it stood in 1931, belonged to this community.)

The **Sûdan** or **Sûdhan** community lives mostly in Mîrpur and Pooñch. Traditionally this has been a clan of landholders, cultivators and government servants. (1.8 per cent of the population of the undivided state, as it stood in 1931, belonged to this community.)

Despite the celebrated migration of Central Asian Syeds to the Valley of Kashmîr, the exalted **Syed** community was mostly based in Jammû province, and within that in Pooñch district. In Kashmîr province they were more numerous in Muzaffarâbâd than in the Valley itself. (1.1 per cent of the population of the undivided state, as it stood in 1931, belonged to this community.)

Télî (oilmen) live mainly in Jammû province. Except for one—maybe two—Hiñdu families all Télîs are Muslims. They have traditionally extracted oil from seeds and every large village needed at least one Télî family. In the 20th century they started becoming transporters as well. (0.4 per cent of the population of the undivided state, as it stood in 1931, belonged to this community.)

Thakkar: This community was Thakkar Hiñdu before its conversion.

Pâl: This is a community of Hiñdu converts.

(In the present volume see 'The People of 'Âzâd' Jammû and Kashmîr.')

References

i Siñgh, KS (editor) *People of India, Volume XXV. Jammû and Kashmîr* (2004), The Anthropological Survey of India, Manohar, New Delhi. Page 80.

ii *People of India, Volume XXV. Jammû and Kashmîr* (2004), page 313.

iii *People of India, Volume XXV. Jammû and Kashmir,* page 411.

iv *People of India, Volume XXV. Jammû and Kashmir,* page 419.

6

The Muslims of Jammû Province[1]

'What was it about that city that still draws us back?...Maybe it was that great fellow-feeling. It did not matter what caste, family, tribe or clan one belonged to: we treated one another as if we were members of the same family. We were together when it was time to mourn or celebrate. The people of Jammû were genuinely nice and did not say what they did not mean.'

Rehmat Ullâh Râd, *Memory Lane to Jammû*[2]

King Rañjît Dév (1723-83) set into motion an admirable trend of inviting Muslims to come and settle in Jammû. This continued till almost 1947, when the demand of some central Indian Muslims for an all-Muslim country called Pâkistân gravely affected the living conditions of Muslims elsewhere in India.

Ajmal's is a case in point. He writes,[i] 'My great-grandfather, after getting fed up with [the] high handedness of the British rulers of India, took refuge in the state of Jammû and Kashmîr [and migrated to that state] from Qila Sobha Siñgh, District Sialkot [which is in the Puñjâb and very close to Jammû]. His father and grand father were Zamindars (land owner/cultivators). The Mahârâjâ, based on [the] background of the family, granted him provisional citizenship of the state. He purchased a house in Jammû Tawi (the winter capital of the state) and settled there.'

---

1. The districts later known as Jammû, Kathuâ and Udhampur (plus Leh, in Ladâkh) were the only districts in the state where the Muslims were—and still are—in a minority.
2. Rad, Rehmatullah and Khalid Hasan (eds), *Memory Lane to Jammu,* (Lahore: Song-e-Meel Publications, 2004)

This happened around the 1870s. Jammû was still a haven to which Muslims from all neighbouring states could shift if things got bad for them in their own state. And Ajmal's forefather hardly moved to an underclass existence in Jammû. That he could buy a house shows that he was welcomed into the middle-class of Jammû.

And that was how things remained. The Muslims and Hiñdus of Jammû lived together, thought the same thoughts ('ours is a very clean city'), had exactly the same love for the ice-cold waters of the Canal and the Chenâb, visited the same shrines every Thursday, celebrated each other's festivals, ate almost identical food and had identical reactions to all situations.

Whether it was big-hearted liberals like Malkâ Pukhrâj, Rehmatullâh Râd, Sorayyâ Khurshîd, Muharram Hâshmî and Khâlid Hasan, or right-wing Muslims like 'Ajmal,' they all loved Jammû as much as their Hiñdu-Sikh brethren did, and for the same reasons. Râd, Khurshîd, Hâshmî and Hasan are generous, singularly unbiased scholars, who had to migrate to Pâkistân in 1947. Despite what they went through in November 1947, they have only the nicest of things to say about Jammû, Jammûites and even Hiñdu ceremonies.

'Our clean Jammû'—a shared regional identity: Pukhrâj and Ajmal have separately recorded, "Jammû Tawi was a beautiful and clean town.[ii] It was built on the slopes of a mountain. Rains were common and after every rainfall the roads and streets used to glitter, because the rains had washed them clean. The town of Jammû had a specialty. It had flowing waters on its three and a half sides. On two and a half sides was River Tawi and on one side was a Canal fed by River Chenab. The waters of the Canal were ice cold, because they consisted of freshly melted snow. The Canal passed under River Tawi—the Tawi went over the canal through a man-made aqueduct.

"The inhabitants of Jammû were fond of picnics on the waterside or in the hills. They were also good swimmers. We used to have picnics on the banks of the Canal in summer. We did not go to the Canal on holidays because a large number of people used to come from Punjâb on holidays. During picnics at the Canal, we used to place baskets filled with mangoes, melons, watermelons or milk bottles in the canal and tether the basket to a tree with a rope. This used to 'refrigerate' the mangoes and other fruits and when we pulled the basket out, its contents would be as cold as ice." (And that was how Jammû remained till the 1970s, when 'modernisation' began to sweep away old traditions.)

All lanes in the Mahârâjâs' Jammû were paved with cobbled stones, as in old Europe. This made them easy to clean with a single rainfall. 'You could not find, even if you looked, any mud in Jammû,' Hâshmî recalls. 'This city of clean, stone-paved streets surrounded by hills had a story-like quality as if it were a tale out of Arabian Nights…I found many Italian cities similarly laid out,' Sorayyâ Khurshîd adds. Râd says, 'I do not recall ever seeing garbage piled on the street in Jammû…or puddles of standing water...Municipal water wagons kept [the roads] showered both morning and evening...Those who never knew Jammû would find it hard to imagine what a clean and beautiful city it was.'

Indeed they would, because around 1991 a few greedy engineers made crores of rupees by removing all those hand-chiselled stones and replacing them with ugly cement tiles, which will wear out in no time.

All well-to-do Jammû Muslims, like their Hiñdu brethren, recall that "we used to spend our summer vacations in Srînagar, the summer capital of the state. There we used to live in a house-boat which had two bedrooms with attached bathrooms and a large drawing-cum-dining room. A cook-boat was attached to it which housed the kitchen and residence of servants."[iii]

And yet Hasan says what Pukhrâj echoes, "Somehow Srînagar, where I was born and where I lived more than I lived in Jammû, has never had the same fascination for me that I felt for Jammû. Even today [in 2004], I would gladly return to Jammû.'

The Muslim population increases: During the Dogrâ era (roughly 1820-1947), as now, there were very few Shiâs (Shiites) in the province—or in the state as a whole. However, 'because of the efforts of [Ustâd Ghulâm Hussain] the number of Shiâs grew.' This says something about the freedom of religion in the state—that a Muslim sect could increase its numbers in a kingdom ruled by a Hiñdu.

And it wasn't just the Shiâs. Every census revealed that the Muslims formed a greater percentage of the population than a decade before—in every district, including the Hiñdu-majority districts of Jammû, Udhampur and Kathuâ. In Udhampur, for instance, the Muslim proportion increased from 28.66 per cent in 1911 to 33.37 per cent in 1931. In Dodâ, the Muslim share rose from 53.33 per cent in 1911 to 57.35 per cent in 1941. In Pooñch, the Muslims' ratio went up from 80.27 per cent in 1911 to 85.59 per cent in 1941.

Part of this increase was the result of migration from Muslim-majority areas like Gujrât (West Puñjâb).[iv]

That was how secure the Muslims felt in Jammû.

Shared festivals and customs: Malkâ Pukhrâj was secular because almost all Jammû Muslims of that era, like the Hiñdu-Sikhs, were secular. The only identity that the people accepted was regional, not religious. The Muslims and Hiñdus of Jammû thought of themselves as Jammûites, and not as Muslims or Hiñdus.

For instance, during the spring festival called Basañt the people of both communities put on identical clothes. The men wore yellow turbans while the women wore clothes that were entirely yellow.[v] The Hiñdu festival of Holî became a sore point between the Hiñdus and Muslims in some parts of India in the 1930s. But in Jammû, till 1946 or so the Muslims would not only celebrate it, they would also throw colours on their Hiñdu friends and get smeared in turn.[vi]

Dussehrâ was another festival that the Muslims—who thoroughly enjoyed the nine days of Râm Leelâ before it—celebrated with the Hiñdus. Malkâ Pukhrâj, who says that the Râm Leelâ was enacted for a month, goes into raptures about the beauty of the *bhajans* sung at those performances. Master *ustâds* had composed them, she writes.[vii] (*Ustâds* are normally Muslims.[3] In turn, Hiñdu theatre directors like Master Labhu Râm would stage plays on 'Muslim' themes such as Shîrîñ-Farhâd.)

Master Ghulâm Haider was the other leading theatre director of the era. He would, in turn, stage Punjâbî classics like Sassi Punnu.

Most Hiñdu youths of today might not know that Dussehrâ is celebrated in the month of Bhâdoñ but Râd, writing 57 years after he had to leave Jammû, has not forgotten this fact. Like most Muslims of his generation he knew the story of *The Râmâyan*, which he has summarised with obvious affection in his Urdû book published in Pâkistân, for Pâkistânîs, in 2004. He adds, 'After Dussehrâ, pilgrims would begin their annual march to pay homage to Vaishno Dévî.'

Râd also describes in detail the two Baisâkhi fairs of Jammû. His heart, and those of his family and friends in Pâkistân, still 'begin to dance with joy when we think of the Thâkur's pâlki [palanquin] being taken out on Janam Ashtami, Krishna's birthday, the festival of Holi with the colour-drenched clothes of the celebrants...We recall the festival at Pîr Khoh [a Hiñdu shrine] during Baisâkhi and Jharri.'

Jammû city's annual Muharram tableau was known for its beauty. Hiñdus as well as Muslims would stand on either side of the road when the procession went through the town. People of both communities would set up little stalls (booths) at which *sherbet* and drinking water would be served—free—to the Shiites. 'Indeed,' Pukhrâj writes, 'the Hiñdus put up more booths for they were given to praying for miracles.'[viii]

Hâshmî adds, '[Before the 1940s] Hiñdu-Muslim unity was exemplary. Hiñdus and Sikhs would join the *ta'azia* procession... [and] would set up water points (sabeels) for the marchers.'

Syed Gulzâr Hasan Shâh, a shopkeeper and the patron saint of the idle chess players of Jammû, would lead the procession.

One of the grandest festivals of the year was the Eid é Mîlâd un Nabi. All Muslims and Hiñdus who remember that era still talk of its magnificence.

3. Not that it made a difference. Malkâ Pukhrâj's first teacher was a Muslim but his guru had been a Hiñdu. Whenever the diva heard a particularly good thumri being sung by a pañdit, she would hire him for a month or two—'at a generous salary'—and get him to teach her the thumri as well as the body movements associated with it.

A major procession would be taken out through the streets of Jammû, which would begin and end at the Muslim Hall on Residency Road. The Hall was one of Jammû's major landmarks.

On average, the royal court celebrated one festival a month—and Hiñdus and Muslims took part in them all in equal measure. (See the chapter 'Jammû: 1885-1947' for more about the Dogrâ Mahârâjâs' patronage of Eid and Baisâkhî.)

The people also shared a common vocabulary. Hiñdus would spontaneously use Islâmic expressions like 'that child of Muharram' (which has pejorative implications). Leave alone Punjãbî Muslims, even Baltîs settled in Jammû tell their grandchildren exactly the same folk-tales as do their Hiñdu compatriots.

Among the Hiñdus there is a rule that when a wife's relatives look her up at her husband's home they don't eat or drink a thing there. The idea is not to be a financial burden on the husband, because traditionally the wife did not have an independent income of her own. To this day, the Muslims of Jammû treat Hiñdu women born in their neighbourhood like their own daughters and sisters. If a Muslim woman calls on her Hiñdu girlfriend at the latter's in-laws' home, the Muslim will refuse to eat or drink anything, saying, 'She is our girl. How can we accept food from her husband's family?'

Shared political views: Their political reactions, too, were identical. Balrâj Purî reminds us that 'when Kashmîrî Muslims led by Sheikh Abdullâh and supported by national leaders like Gandhi and Nehru were fighting against the rule of the Dogrâ mahârâjâ, they did not get much support from Muslims—as also Hindus—of Jammû; which [then] was [the] most populated region of the state.

'And when Sheikh Abdullâh and his National Conference had indicated their tilt towards accession to the Indian Union, the Jammû-based Muslim Conference and the Hindu Sabha supported the Mahârâjâ's desire to remain independent. One of the reasons for this decision, cited by the then president of the Muslim Conference, Chaudhary Hameed Ullah, was that "the Muslims of Jammû have never been lacking in showing loyalty and respect for the Mahârâjâ and it is because of this attachment that we did not support the Quit Kashmîr movement (launched by the National Conference for an end to Dogrâ rule)."'[ix]

Significantly, as Balraj Puri and Ershad Mahmud have separately pointed out,[x] 'militancy which started in the Kashmîr region in 1989, did not extend to Jammû.'

The Muslims' impact: Even though the Muslims were in a minority in Jammû town—as well as in what are now the Jammû, Kathuâ and Udhampur districts, they had a very significant impact of the social life of the area.

Within Jammû town the Muslims were concentrated in the Khalkâ ('lower') Mohallâh, Ustâd Mohallâh (named after the Mahârâjâ's Muslim teacher) and Pathânâñ dâ Mohallâh. The Urdû Bâzâr (now called Rajinder Bâzâr), Talâb Khatîkâñ and Dalpatiâñ remain predominantly Muslim to this day. The quiet Vazârat Road was where the very substantial Muslim elite lived—right next to the palatial house of the British Resident. And it was hardly as if the people of Jammû were ghettoised into Hiñdu and Muslim areas. The toniest house in Julâha kâ Mohallâh belonged to a Puñjâbi Muslim. Several rich Hiñdus lived in Talâb Khatîkâñ and the Ustâd Mohallâh. The elite family of Air Marshal Asghar Khan [Chief of the Pâkistân Air Force and a politician in later years] lived in the Pathânâñ dâ Mohallâh.[xi]

The Muslims of Dârûgeerâñ Mohallâ, near Residency Road, had been invited by a seventeenth or eighteenth century king of Jammû to settle in his kingdom and make gunpowder (dârû) for the Jammû army.

The other neighbourhoods with a substantial Muslim population were Jatkatiâñ, Afghânâñ and what is now called Mastgarh.

Jogi Darwâzâ (now Jogi Gate) was one of the last Muslim-majority neighbourhoods to come up before 1947.

Mughalâni Begum, the widow of Mîr Moin-ul-Mulk, who was the Mughals' Governor, was among those who fled to Jammû during King Rañjît Dév's era. She built 'a grand residence in Gañdum [now Kanak] Mañdi. [Till the 1940s] this neighbourhood [was] known as Mohallâ Bégum ki Havéli.' (Râd)

Sardâr Muhammad Akram Khân's havéli in Talâb Khatîkâñ was the other major mansion. Green Gates on Vazârat Road, which this author was allotted as his official residence, was another.

The Muslims, in particular, were very cosmopolitan. Part of the reason was that many of their teachers were (Muslims) from the Punjâb. This had a profound impact on the language that they spoke (Punjâbî at home and Dogri with their Hiñdu friends), their dress and, later, the politics of some young, educated and middle-class urban people. Muslims from places as far apart as Bannu in the NWFP continued to migrate to Jammû as late as in the 1930s. (Non-Muslim teachers, Hiñdus as well as Christians, too, came from distant lands like Shikârpur in Sind.)

Pooñch had a huge martial tradition. Employment in the army would help many Pooñch Muslims serve in foreign lands, rise in status and then settle in the winter capital of the state.

The bow-makers of Mastgarh had migrated from Batâlâ (Punjâb). After guns made bows and arrows redundant as weapons, the only patrons left were children, who would play with scaled down versions. Jammû's (Muslim) bow-makers would also make kites, especially for the (Hiñdu) festival of Janamashtami. This tradition came to an end in 1947.

I revived the kite festival in 1993, with the help of India's foremost experts (who, too, happened to be Muslim) from the walled cities of Delhi and Gujarât. However, under pressure from an influential local newspaper, my department abandoned the festival after my transfer.

The traditional vegetarian Hiñdu way of life does not enable the same kind of familiarity with animals (other than cows and buffaloes) to develop as the Muslim lifestyle does. Small wonder then that Gâmi (Ghulâm Muhammad) Qalander, the barber, owned the city's main pet shop. The majority of tongâs (horse driven carriages) in the province were owned and driven by Muslims.

Jeerâ, another barber, operated a hammâm, a tradition that is more or less lost to India.

The Muslims also had a monopoly on the very difficult art of making sword sheaths that were neither a millimetre too loose nor too tight. (Ceremonial swords were used by the Mahârâjâ's army and police till 1947, and by the upper rungs of the Indian police and army even in the 21st century.)

Shams Dîn was one of the most successful tailors of his time: the others in his bracket also being Muslim.

The Muslims took to newfangled machines with greater ease than the rest. Mistri Abdul Hamid operated a saw machine. Mistri Nazar Muhammad of Ustâd Mohallâ was a sought after motor mechanic.

Chhinj (wrestling contests) are held all over Jammû province after the monsoons. As would happen before 1947, even in the early 21st century wrestlers who happen to be Muslim win at least half of all championships.

Illiteracy and unemployment: Literacy in Jammû and Kashmîr was, and remains, the second worst in India. From all accounts, the Muslims were even more illiterate than the Hiñdus. According to Pukhrâj only half a dozen or so Muslim families were well educated and in senior jobs in the government. All of them were Pathâns. One of them had been the governor of Gilgit—which was one of the highest positions in the state. His sons were colonels and generals in the Mahârâjâ's army.

One reason why Muslim literacy was lower than that of the Hiñdus was that most Muslim women were illiterate. Even in the year 2001, female literacy in Kashmîr and Pâkistân was just a little more than half of that of the men.

Hâshmî notes, 'In those days no Muslim girl was sent to college.' He adds, 'Initially, the Muslims had declared any Western education [even for men] as apostasy. It was this attitude that gave non-Muslims the opportunity to get into higher civil service posts. It was difficult for a Muslim in those days to even get hired as a peon.'

Only a few Muslims managed to receive some education, and the best that the majority of them could hope to do was to join the government as clerks or become ill-paid assistants to some unsuccessful (and normally

Muslim) lawyer. Many young Muslims joined the lower ranks of the police and army.

The rural Muslims of the Dogrâ belt of Jammû-Kathuâ-Udhampur were mostly barbers, carpenters, ironsmiths and weavers. In the cities Muslims were not able to get salaried jobs. So, the youths would either become carpenters, masons and ironsmiths or set up tea stalls. Pukhrâj estimates that only half a dozen or so large shops were owned by Muslims. The Gujjars, of course, sold milk.

Unemployment among educated Muslim youths was rife during Mahârâjâ Pratâp's time. Pukhrâj writes that these educated young men were now too posh to become masons. So, they would idle away their days playing cards or chess, gossiping and ogling pretty flower sellers. At an age when they should have been supporting their parents, they would instead depend on their working-class parents for every rupee that they spent.

When other Muslims saw that even Muslim youths with Masters' degrees were unemployed, they concluded that there was no point in getting an education. They stopped sending their children to school. These children would, instead, spend their time swimming in what used to be the Khatîkâñ pond (it has been built over since) or play other street games. The few Muslim children whose parents forced them to go to school often played truant, perhaps because they found that the majority of their friends did not go to school at all. In any case, Muslim children would begin their schooling a few years later than their Hiñdu peers.[xii]

Mahârâjâ Hari Siñgh tried to give government jobs to educated Muslims. However, by then one generation of educated Muslims had been lost.

Efforts towards literacy

Till the 1910s or so, Muslims and Hiñdus attended mixed schools and colleges of the Western kind. Nusrat was the Second Master of the Sâmba High School. The primary school at Mastgarh had two teachers—Master Dâûd and a 'Pandit jî.' Obviously they had no Urdû equivalent of Vere Foster, for the Pandit jî would painstakingly write all the numbers from one to a hundred on the wooden 'slate' of each student—Hiñdu as well as Muslim. The students would then run their reeds over these numerals in order to learn how to write them correctly.

Mahârâjâ Partâp Singh ensured that no citizen had to pay a fee for primary education. Then, in the 1920s, his successor Mahârâjâ Hari Singh made primary education compulsory for all children in all the important towns. Textbooks and stationery were given to all children free of charge. Because several new schools were opened, the walk to school was greatly reduced. This gave a great boost to Muslim education—and employment, for many of the teachers were Muslim. Hakîm Farîd Âlam, for instance, was the headmaster of the Pîr Mitthâ School.

Somewhere along the way—and most unfortunately—community-oriented schools began to spring up all over India. In Jammû, the Râjpût School was the best known of these. Naturally, the Muslims, too, wanted a school of their own. Nawâb Mehboob Ali Khân Khusrau Jung persuaded the Mahârâjâ to allot the old Gundoo army barracks and the surrounding land to the Anjuman e Islâmiâ. That was how the Akbar Islâmiâ High School was founded.

To begin with the school was a disaster. Hardly any student from the school was able to matriculate successfully. The visionary Sheikh Abdul Azîz changed all that in 1933 when he took over as the headmaster. Within a year he ensured that hardly anyone failed.

All students who passed the school's internal pre-matriculation test were required to spend the night in the school hostel. They could go home for breakfast and, if it was close enough, lunch. After dinner they had to return to the school where teachers would coach them for the matriculation examination till midnight.

Sheikh Abdul Azîz must have done something even more wonderful at home—or maybe it was in his genes. His son, the legendary UNDP economist Mahbûb ul Haq, not only made Pakistan a success in the international financial market in the 1980s, he gave the world the Human Development Index. (Haq studied for a while at Jammû's non-denominational Ranbîr High School.)

All over the world schools compete with each other—especially for sporting glory. Sports teams during the British Râj were normally organised along religious lines. So, when they met on the sports field it inevitably became a clash between the concerned communities.

That is what began to happen every time Akbar Islâmiâ High School played the Râjpût School in the late 1930s and early 1940s. The boys would start fighting each other during the game. Things got so bad that teachers, too, began to take sides. Chaudhari Rehmat Khân, a teacher who had come over from the Punjâb, had to discipline two partisan teachers from the other side with his cane. After that the two teams needed police supervision each time they met on the playground.

The elite Prince of Wales College had students from all communities. As a result everyone was proud of it. Hâshmî points out that it had India's first geology department after Calcutta. He goes to the extent of claiming that it had the biggest campus for any college in India. (Guwahati's university-sized Cotton College, surely, holds that record?) POW College produced the only ICS (Indian Civil Service) officer from the province—and one of only two from the entire state—Qudrat Ullâh Shahâb.

Around the 1930s, young Jammû Muslims began to go to the Aligarh Muslim University for higher studies. 1943 was the year when the biggest batch of Jammûites went to the AMU. At Aligarh, Jammû was seen as the town where all the beauties came from. That reputation vanished after

1947.

Poor support for separatism: Chaudhary Ghulâm Abbâs was one of the few Jammû Muslims to support the theory that the Hiñdus and Muslims were two different 'nations.' He did so despite the fact that a (presumably Hiñdu) chief judge had given the Chaudhary's father employment as a peon in the court 'so that he would get a government salary. The judge was very generous toward Ghulâm Abbâs' father,' Pukhrâj writes. 'He [helped Ghulâm Abbâs' father get] an education for his three sons. Ghulâm Abbâs got a law degree. The second son was appointed as the SDO (Sub-Divisional Officer) in the irrigation department where he earned a great deal of money and lived in style and comfort.'[xiii]

Allâh Rakhâ 'Sâgar' and Abdul Majîd 'Karshî,' who had both received some schooling, were Ghulâm Abbâs' associates. Allâh Rakhâ's father was a wealthy property dealer. The three decided to project themselves as the leaders of Jammû's Muslims. They started asking fellow Muslims for small donations for the organisation of the community's festivals. They would plant stools in the middle of the street, climb on them and lecture passers by on political issues.

Muslims who had thitherto been perfectly at peace with the Hiñdus were, 'because of these men's leadership,' made to realise that some Hiñdus were contemptuous of them. On the positive side, the trio made the Muslims more 'conscious of their dignity and self-esteem.' They also demanded that a certain percentage of government jobs should be reserved for them. The very fact that the three leaders were organising the community along religious lines—something that had never happened before in Jammû and was part of a new phenomenon throughout urban South Asia—meant that some Muslims of Jammû city had now begun to think of themselves as a separate community. Earlier, Pukhrâj writes, 'no one had felt this way.'[xiv]

Pukhrâj was Allâh Rakhâ's neighbour and knew all three men because they would frequent her ustâd's shop. The details that she provides about their lives add up to an unflattering picture of the trio. (It is an honest picture. However, had she written about the average Hiñdu leader of Jammû of that era, the pattern would have been identical—a few years of schooling plus a habit of preying on others.)

Abdul Majîd seems to have been a man who thrived on the miseries of impoverished Muslim litigants. He would 'impose his help' on those simple people when they needed legal advice and force them to pay him for his presumed services. (Touts of that kind flourish to this day, except that they no longer presume to be the leaders of their community.)

In 1930, this group formed the Young Men's Muslim Association in Jammû. It led to the formation, in 1931, of the Muslim Conference for the entire state. (The MC, and its majority faction, the secular, pro-India, National Conference, would dominate the politics of 'AJK' and Jammû and Kashmîr respectively for the next more than seven decades.) Chaudhary

Ghulâm Abbâs BA, LLB, was the founding secretary of the MC.

A chasm appears: Kashmîr has always been a shining example of Muslim-Hiñdu unity. The tiny Hiñdu minority formed a little less than five per cent of the population. But it never felt insecure because the Muslims never gave the Hiñdus any reason to.

The efforts of leaders like Chaudhary Ghulâm Abbâs changed some of that. A day before the Mahârâjâ was to meet the Chaudhary and his associates, Pukhrâj happened to be walking on the bund (embankment) that leads to Srînagar's Amîrâñ Kadal. She 'saw a Kashmîrî pundit, bleeding from his head, running for his life, followed by a Kashmîrî Muslim [who had] a stick in his hands...A Hiñdu-Muslim riot had begun.' (Pukhrâj's book mentions no dates. However, this must have been in 1931.[xv])

Pukhrâj's grandfather caught hold of the pursuer and gave the Pañdit a chance to escape. (I have a theory that liberalism—like prejudice—runs in families.) The attacker told her grandfather, 'I wanted to kill [the Pañdit] because he was a Hiñdu, a pig and a bloodsucker. We have to get rid of these Hiñdus, these *kâfirs* [infidels].'[xvi]

Pukhrâj says that Chaudhary Ghulâm Abbâs had engineered that riot. The Chaudhary had to resort to cheap tricks like those to rally the people, because he knew that the Kashmîrîs loved Sheikh Muhammad Abdullâh and not him. He incensed the people further by alleging that the Mahârâjâ was not prepared to concede the demands of the Muslims whereas, according to Pukhrâj, this was not true.

She adds that the Mahârâjâ's Muslim aides, such as Khusrau Jung, 'lowered their eyes' when the matter was discussed in the court. They knew how the Mahârâjâ had alienated many Hiñdus—especially some 'generals and colonels of his own caste'—by his decision to concede the Muslims' demands.[xvii] The actions of Chaudhary Ghulâm Abbâs and his group seemed to vindicate the advice that these generals had given the Mahârâjâ: 'Do not trust the Muslims.' The Mahârâjâ's Muslim staff, Pukhrâj writes, 'behaved as if they were guilty even though they were in no way responsible for what had happened.'[xviii]

In the mid-1940s a chasm had begun to appear between the Hiñdus and Muslims of the British-ruled parts of India. Thanks to the movement started by men like Chaudhary Ghulâm Abbâs, it cast a shadow, albeit feeble, on the Mahârâjâ's court as well. It took the form of silence, which descended on the thitherto cheerful court. For the first time the staff got unofficially divided along religious lines. Neither group would say very much to the other. Perhaps they did not want to unwittingly say something that might cause offence. Or worse, perhaps they, too, had started believing the nasty things that the right wing of their community was saying about the other.

Festivals were the first casualty. The court still celebrated them, but now

neither community seemed much inclined to take part in the festivals of the other. In the 1940s, both Hindus and Muslims started obstructing religious processions of 'the other community': the Eid Milad-ul-Nabi procession of the Muslims, and the Râm Lila procession of the Hindus.[xix]

Indeed, since 1945 or 1946 every religious festival has been a tense day for district administrations in India and Pâkistân, because in some corner or the other of these two unfortunate countries someone from the other community (in the case of Pâkistân, the other sect) might try to disrupt the festivity of the other.

A province, the citizens of which used to have heroes in common (KL Saigal, 'angel-face' Naseem Bano, the earlier Allâma Iqbâl, Malkâ Pukhrâj, Master Madan, Rattan Nâth Sarshar, Khurshîd, KC Dey and Râm Dulâri) now started drifting apart. When a group of Muslim schoolboys decided to set up a library in 1946 or early 1947, they decided to call it the Jinnâh Library. Hiñdu boys began to give their patriotic symbols a religious touch.

Such was the mistrust that the 'Pâkistân Movement' created that some Muslims employed by the Mahârâjâ's government were suspected of sedition and working for the future Pâkistân dispensation. They were dismissed from government service.[xx]

After the hijrat

More than 1.8 lakh Jammû Muslims found themselves in Siâlkot (Pâkistân) and 'AJK' in November 1947, after their tragic exodus. But only their bodies had migrated. Their hearts were still in Jammû. 'They remained strangers [in Pâkistân] and are so to this day [2004],' Hasan recorded.

Sorayyâ Khurshîd could not get herself to like the guavas, jâmuns or berries of Siâlkot because 'they do not have the taste and aroma' of their Jammû counterparts. Râd would miss the 'cool breeze [that] would rise from the east [on summer nights] at around 10p.m. which we called *dhidoo*.'

Alyâ Kebâbi used to make the best kebâbs in Jammû. It was more than mere nostalgia that made him wind up his kebab stall in Siâlkot after attempting to make Jammû-style kebabs for a year. His problem was that the sheep of the hot plains of Siâlkot did not yield the same delicious mutton, as did sheep fed on the mountain pastures of Jammû.

The *panâh-gazeen* (lit. protection or refuge-seekers) from Jammû, who had been 'happy and well-to-do people in my city of Jammû [were now reduced to] selling odds and ends in the dark and winding streets' of Siâlkot. (Râd)

Gâmi Qalander, who once owned Jammû's main pet shop, would wonder if the monkeys of Pakki Dhakki missed their erstwhile bete noire—the only person in Jammû who could tame the most ferocious of monkeys.

The monkeys must have missed him very sorely because they no longer

are as overwhelming a presence in the town as they used to be till 1947. They migrated to the Bâhu Fort area.

Siâlkot, as Râd points out, is only 22 miles from Jammû. Nostalgic Jammûites now in Siâlkot often go to the ancient Siâlkot fort from which, 'on any clear evening, the Jammû city lights can be seen glimmering in the distance like fireflies.'

The feeling is mutual. Not only the people of present Jammû but also visitors from places as far away as Bengal often go to Jammû's Bâhu Fort and the Bypass to see the lights of Siâlkot, which, through emotion-choked eyes, look like the glistening waves of an ocean and which hold a similar fascination for those who identify with all that unpartitioned Jammû stood for.

References

i From 'My Life In Kashmîr,' a series of articles posted on the Internet by a right-wing Jammû Muslim who later migrated to Pâkistân.

ii This passage is a composite of the identical memories of Malkâ Pukhrâj and 'Ajmal,'

iii Again, both Malkâ Pukhrâj and 'Ajmal' have recorded this.

iv Ibid, page 31, first paragraph.

v Pukhrâj, Malka, *Song Sung True*, trans. and ed. by Saleem Kidwai (2002), Zubaan, Kali for Women, Hauz Khas Enclave, New Delhi 110016, p. 116.

vi Ibid, page 136.

vii Ibid, page 153.

viii Ibid, page 29. The point about the increase in the Shia population is also made on page 30.

ix Puri, Balraj, *Indian Express*, Wednesday 25, February 2004.

x Ibid and *The News*, July 25, 2001.

xi This passage is based on the memories of Malkâ Pukhrâj and 'Ajmal,'

xii Pukhrâj, op. cit., pp. 98-99.

xiii Pukhrâj, op. cit., p. 100.

xiv Pukhrâj, op. cit., p. 103.

xv *Kashmîr in the Crossfire* (London: IB Tauris, 1996) p102-3

xvi Ibid, page 200.

xvii Ibid, page 201.

xviii Ibid, page 203.

xix Alexander Evans, quoting Muharram Hashmi, in Rehmatullah Rad and Khalid Hasan (eds), *Memory Lane to Jammû* (Lahore: Sang-e-Meel Publications 2004) p. 87.

xx See Pukhrâj, op. cit., p. 213.

7

Sikhs in Jammû and Kashmîr[1]

Sukh Jîwan was the Afghâns' Governor of Kashmîr from 1751 to 1762. (For a brief while he ruled Kashmîr independently.) He gave jobs in the Kashmîr army to a number of Brâhmins from the Pathohâr and Kohistân Malth areas of the Punjãb. These Brâhmins included Sikhs as well as non-Sikhs. When they retired they stayed on in Kashmîr.[i]

Sukh Jîwan had provided refuge in Kashmîr to a fugitive prince from Balkh (Afghânistân), as well as his followers. However, the prince was not altogether satisfied with his host. So, one day, he went up to Sukh Jîwan, pulled out a dagger and stabbed him. Contemporary histories tell us that some of Sukh Jîwan's Sikh soldiers rushed in, saw what had happened and killed the prince and his followers on the spot. Fauq writes, "They then went on a rampage in that stretch of Srînagar which lies between Zâldaggar (Nawâb Bâzâr) and Pândân."

During the Afghân period, the Sikhs, like the Kashmîrî Pañdits, rose to high positions in the army as well the civil administration. For example, in 1766 when Nûr ud Dîn Bamzaî was the governor of Kashmîr, the (Afghân) Emperor summoned him to Kâbul for a while. Bamzaî constituted a two-man council to look after the government while he was away. It consisted of Bamzaî's nephew, Jân Muhammad Khân, and Sardâr Gurmukh Siñgh. It is said that Bamzaî had faith in the Sardâr's administrative abilities.

The next that we learn about Sikhs in Kashmîr dates to 1781. Hâjî Karîmdâd Khân was the Governor of Kashmîr at the time. He sent Sardâr Dîwân Siñgh as the head of an army contingent against Bahâwar Khân Khakhâ. The Sardâr was killed in that battle.

In 1819 Mahârâjâ Rañjît Siñgh's army defeated the Afghâns. The brief Sikh era of Kashmîr's history (1819-46) began. Punjãbî Brâhmins—again, Sikh as well as non-Sikh—were employed in the army as well as civil

1. This chapter augments that which is contained in the volume about 'Kashmîr.'

service. However, instead of getting a salary, they were paid in kind (*jins*). These Brâhmins, writes Fauq, were Mohyâls of the Dutt and Bâlî clans. They belonged to the Râwalpiñdî and Jehlum districts of the Punjãb. Those of them who made the transition to Sikhism came to be known as Jinsî Sikhs. In Kashmîr they settled in the Trâl, Karohan, Hamal, Mattan and Budgâm *pargânâs* (mediæval-era districts).

The Sikhs of Kashmîr—*jinsî* as well as others—are landowners and farmers. The Kashmîrî that they speak is not quite the same as that of, say, the Kashmîrî Pañdits or the Muslims.

As mentioned, some Sikhs held high offices during the Afghân and Sikh periods. Then, due to a low level of literacy, came an era of decline. Fauq, who published his book in 1934, when the Dogrâs ruled the state, noted that by his time the Sikhs had once again begun to be employed in the upper rungs of the government, 'thanks to education.' He added, 'In Bârâmullâ and Srînagar they have large *dîwâns* [assembly halls] and Siñgh Sabhâs [fraternities]...There are Sikh *zaildârs* [chiefs of a group of villages] and *numberdârs* [village headmen]. The Kashmîrî Sikhs might not be as sturdy as Punjãbî Sikhs but they are not weak either. Their complexion and the quality of their skin is much like that of the Kashmîrîs...*Zamîndâr* [landlord] Sikhs came to Kashmîr during the Sikh era and have settled in Mattan (South Kashmîr) and Chogal (North Kashmîr).'

The customs of Zamîndâr Sikhs are quite different from those of Jinsî Sikhs. Normally, the two do not inter-marry. The Zamîndârs prefer to marry their children to their counterparts in the Punjãb. They speak Punjãbî at home and dress like the Punjãbîs.

Jinsî women, on the other hand, had, by the late 1800s, given up Punjãbî clothes and taken to Kashmîrî *pheran* cloaks.

The Sikh population in 1891, 1911 and 1931

Recent population figures have been given elsewhere in this trilogy of books. However, historical population figures reveal sub-castes that the more recent censuses have stopped recording.

In 1891 there were 11,399 Sikhs in the state. Of them 5,956 were in Jammû province and 5,273 in Kashmîr. This included 31 Chamâr Sikhs and 12 Dûm Sikhs.

In 1911 the break up of the Sikh sub-castes was: 14 Arorâ, 2,019 Dutt and Bâlî Brâhmins, 369 other Mohyâl Brâhmins, 99 Khatrî, 88 Mazhabî, 44 Râjpût, 38 Sâñsî, 2 Tarkhân, 6 Zargar and 12,067 other castes. Total: 14,894.

The 1931 break up was as follows: 635 Râjpût, 2,069 Kâyasth, 5,232 Labânâ, 42 Kumhâr, 1 Mazhabî, 142 Mégh, 221 Lohâr, 104 Mahâjan, 11,723 Brâhmin, 321 Basîth and 3 Batwâl. Total: 21,453.

Interestingly, the sub-castes of 1931 are quite different from the ones enumerated in 1911. Of the ones that have the same names in both censuses 'prestigious' castes like Brâhmin and Râjpût grew hugely, severalfold, while less fashionable ones declined equally rapidly. The total number of Sikhs, however, grew at a pace similar to the national average. So, obviously thousands of families claimed to be from a different caste in the latter census.

Reference

i Fauq, Muhammad ud Dîn, *Târîkh Aqwâm é Kashmîr* (Lahore, 1934). Reprinted in 1996 by Chinar Publishing House, Srînagar. Pages 113-17. Translated from the Urdu by the author.

8

The People of 'Âzâd' Jammû and Kashmîr

'Âzâd' Jammû and Kashmîr has the worst of both worlds. Its government has 'always been kept on a very tight leash' by Pâkistân, through its Ministry of KANA (Kashmîr and Northern Areas) Affairs, Roger Ballard writes. On the other hand, because Pâkistân pretends that 'AJK' is an independent state, 'the level of expenditure on rural development has...long been a good deal lower in Âzâd Kashmîr than elsewhere in Pâkistân; international aid agencies have been denied access, on the grounds that Âzâd Kashmîr is a "sensitive area"; most strikingly of all, these same grounds are used to justify the routine exclusion of information on Âzâd Kashmîr from virtually all public statistics. Even census data remains unpublished.'[i]

However, some intrepid scholars[ii] have ferreted out the relevant data for the districts of 'AJK,' which may be summed up as below:

District	1991 census projection
Muzaffarâbâd	609,000
Mîrpur	559,000
Bâgh	412,000
'Pooñch'	530,000
Kotlî	476,000
Total for 'Âzâd' Jammû and Kashmîr	**2,586,000 (1,980,066 in 1981)**

Who are the 'Âzâd' Kashmîris?

There used to be Hindus and Sikhs in the market towns of the region till 1947.

Some thirty thousand Hiñdu-Sikhs were driven out of Mîrpur alone and more than one lakh in all. More than 1.5 lakh Muslims felt compelled to leave Jammû province. Sarâf's extremely dishonest figure of three lakh Muslims migrating from Jammû is the result of simple arithmetic. He has deducted Jammû's Muslim population of 1961 from that of 1941 and come up with this figure. He has conveniently forgotten that the 1961 figure of Muslims in Indian Jammû does not include the Muslim population of areas that have been under Pâkistâni occupation since 1947.

As with the Kashmîrî Pañdit migration of 1990, actual numbers are not important. The principle is. And it is a shame that the majority of Jammû's non-Gujjar Muslims had to flee India. Many of them went to Siâlkot, where they set up three 'Jammû mohallâs' (residential neighbourhoods).

The Muslim Sûd(h)ans are the main community in Bâgh and Râwlâkot, which are the northern parts of 'AJK'.

'AJK' has three rival centres of power:

i) Kotlî, where the elite, martial Sûdhans live. (They also live in Râwlâkot and parts of occupied Pooñch.) Since 1947 'AJK' has mostly been ruled by the Sûdhans—in conjunction with the Râjpûts. All important leaders (except Ch. Ghulâm Abbâs, who was a Jammûite) have been Sûdhans. The Sûdhans probably number around four lakh (0.4 million), or roughly 13 per cent of the population. The Râjpûts live in most parts of 'AJK.'

The Pooñchîs are considered a martial race. There were at least twenty thousand Pooñchîs in the Indian Army in World War I. The number tripled in World War II. The Sûdhan, Jarâl, Dhoñd and Satti clans, in particular, have a long and distinguished history of military service.

ii) Mîrpur: The Jâts dominate the town and the area around it. The Sûdhans have traditionally looked down upon the Jâts as peasants. Therefore, the 'AJK' diaspora is mainly Mîrpuri and Jât. After the 1960s it was they who sent in remittances in hard currency—the pound sterling. This gave them the confidence to thumb their noses at the old elite. By the mid-1990s their economic clout also made them politically important.

iii) Muzaffarâbâd is the administrative capital but politically it counts relatively little. The Neelum valley is a neglected outpost. It has had all of one legislator, who is totally irrelevant in the power structure of 'AJK.' Both Muzaffarâbâd and the Neelum resent this. (In 2005 the area was given a second legislator.)

'The Neelum [valley was] largely left undeveloped given it straddles the Line of Control'.[iii] Because it has been 'spared' the scars of development, the Neelum valley still exists in a fairly pristine state. The roofs of its houses, for instance, continue to have roofs made of timber, unlike the Valley of Kashmîr where, as I have lamented in the volume on 'Kashmîr,' shiny—and unseemly—tin roofs have taken over. Its two side-valleys, Jagran and Sorgum, are equally picturesque.

Till 1975, almost half the population—three lakh people—had to gather fuel-wood for themselves, to cook food and heat rooms with. In the 1990s every sixth family had at least one 'forestry case' pending against it. They had been accused of stealing wood or some other produce from government-owned forests. As in Jammû and Kashmîr, the population has grown far beyond the capacity of natural forests to sustain it. Deforestation is the result.[iv]

River Neelum has, since 1948, been the line of control between India and 'AJK' along much of the formal LoC. The people are 'very poor, mainly farmers or migrant labourers.'[v] The sole government hospital in the valley is military. Islâmic Relief, an NGO, runs Neelum's only other hospital, which is in Kuttan. There is a 30MW hydro-electric power project in Jagran.

Food is expensive, because grains and vegetables are mostly brought in from the outside. Thanks to the November 2003 ceasefire, the cost of transporting food fell and so did the prices of food.

There used to be just one road from Muzaffarâbâd—or Pâkistân—to Neelum. It is close to the LoC, where the Indian Army controls the heights above Tithwâl and can easily fire upon—or shell—the road. (In Kargil [Ladâkh] it is the other way around.)

For that reason, Pâkistân first built three bypasses leading from this road and then, in 1998, a road on an entirely different route (Kâghân-Jalkad-Nûrînâr-Shârdâ) into the Neelum. (Similarly, India is building an alternate road in Kargil. In the 1970s, India built the Dhâr-Udhampur road in Kathuâ-Udhampur as a substitute for the vulnerable Pathânkot-Sâmbâ-Jammû highway.)

There must be around eight lakh Gujjars in 'AJK.' In political matters, the Gujjars and Jâts follow the Râjpûts' lead.

The Jâts of Mîrpur: Mîrpur proper, which is in the south, is the home of the Muslim Jâts who have the same Pothohâri Punjâbi culture as the neighbouring Rawalpindi and Jehlum districts of Pâkistâni Puñjâb.

However, ironically, the Jâts have always favoured an independent Kashmîr, as opposed to integration with Pâkistân. They would rather be with the Kashmîrîs, whose language they do not speak a word of, whose customs they do not share and with whom they did not inter-marry in the past.

The reasons are money (remittances from abroad), marginalisation and the Mañglâ Dam.

More than half the foreign exchange remittances received by Pâkistân come from the 'AJK' diaspora in general and overseas Mîrpurîs in particular. Around two-thirds of all those who entered the UK with Pâkistâni passports and then settled there are from 'AJK.' Within 'AJK' they are mostly from Mîrpur district and nearby Kotlî. (The 'Pâkistâni' population in Britain—including that from occupied Kashmîr—was around 0.4 million in 2005.)

In these two districts there are entire villages, located in remote hills, of which more than half the population lives abroad. Remittances have made these villages rich. Writing in 1991, Dr Ballard reported that in one sample village of three thousand people there were as many as five banks and more than Rs. 5 crore on deposit. (See also the chapters on 'AJK' in the volume about 'Kashmîr.')

Mîrpurîs resent the fact that they are not able to invest this wealth profitably. They are unhappy that their money benefits Pâkistân, and not 'AJK.'

The Mañglâ Dam: The water (from the rivers Jehlum and Pooñch) that the Mañglâ Dam stores and the electricity that it generates are crucial for the economy of Pâkistân—certainly of West Puñjâb. But the same dam is a curse for those who live upstream—the Mîrpurîs. The two main towns of the area—Mîrpur and Chaomukh—as well as countless villages, roads, electricity and telephone lines, historic mosques and much fertile agricultural land are the victims of the reservoir.

A very large number of Mîrpurîs, especially people from Dadiâl tehsil, migrated abroad because of the Mañglâ Dam.[1] However, people from the area have a history, which dates back to at least the late 19th century, of going to distant lands in search of employment.

The origin of the Mîrpurî diaspora: Mîrpur was part of a princely state ('Indian India') and not of British India. So, while their cousins in British-ruled Pathohâr could join the Punjâb regiments of the British Indian Army (and they did so by the tens of thousands), the Mîrpurîs normally could not. (Wartime was a different matter.) So, young peasant boys from Mîrpur started going to Bombay to seek employment as stokers on British merchant ships. The nearest railway station from most parts of Mîrpur District was in Gujjar Khân, which, as Dr Ballard points out 'was [a] little more than a day's walk away.'

'Britain's coal-powered merchant fleet continued to expand rapidly during the early decades of [the 20th] century, so the demand for labour steadily increased, and seamen began to be recruited [in] ever larger numbers from an ever wider swathe of villages,' Dr Ballard adds. In Bombay, the Mîrpurîs became a very major presence in the engine rooms of British ships.

---

1. Dadiâl is close to the railway station. For that reason, its people are the most mobile.

The next step was for them to become seamen on British ships, which they did in equally substantial numbers. And then they started settling in Britain.

Till the mid 1970s, most Mîrpurî expatriates were young men and would send remittances to their families, which had mostly stayed behind in Mîrpur. This money—as in, Kerala, India—was initially used to build grand houses. The economy of 'AJK'—especially of Dadiâl tehsîl (sub-district)—boomed.

Mass migration because of the Mañglâ Dam: When the Mañglâ Dam was built, thousands of Mîrpurîs left for Britain in disgust. The lake did little to help the local people, but increased the distance between one point and another—especially in Dadiâl—enormously. This raised the cost of everything in Dadiâl, including that of building houses. Besides, now one could only travel in boats—which were accident prone.

People uprooted from ancestral homes and farmlands because of the dam—called 'affectees' in 'AJK' (from the expression 'affected by the dam')—felt that they had not been compensated adequately.

All this generated an anti-Pâkistân feeling among the Mîrpurîs. The breaking point was a major boat accident in which fifty people from elite families died. The people went on a rampage and seized control of the police station. They also placed the head of the civil administration under 'arrest.' Ballard adds, 'Indian flags were ironically raised over public buildings.' Pâkistân had to drop armed personnel by parachutes to regain control of Dadiâl. Things had got that bad.

Since then, the anti-Pâkistâni feelings of the Mîrpurîs have been expressed through their adoption of Kashmîrî nationalism. By insisting that they are Kashmîrîs they are really saying that they are not Pâkistânîs. Ballard writes, '"*Kashmîr Zindabad! Pâkistân Murdabad!*" they cry with great enthusiasm.' [Long live Kashmir. May Pakistan die.]

But Pâkistân will always cling on to this area with all its might—because it gets most of its electricity and most of the waters of its elaborate system of canals from 'AJK.'

2005: The Mañglâ Dam 'upraising' project: The issue raised its head once again in 2005 when the Mañglâ Dam 'upraising' project was taken up. To win the support of the 'affectees' the Government of Pâkistân promised them an airport in Mîrpur (vital because of its internationally-oriented population), a dry port (again, important because of Mîrpur's linkages with the global economy), new townships, a couple of bridges and a technical college.

Initially this helped Pâkistân win the support of top-notch leaders like Sardâr Attique Ahmed Khân, who in 2005 was the president of the Muslim Conference. Attique campaigned for the 'upraising' despite being greeted with black flags at Dadiâl. His opponents in the rival People's Party had been consistently hostile to the project.

The breaking point for Attique came when work on the gas pipeline being built from Sui in Balochistân to Mîrpur was abandoned. He alleged that 'the equipment [meant for the project] was shifted from [Mîrpur] to the constituency of [Pâkistânî] Prime Minister Shaukat Aziz.' This led Attique to conclude that 'Mîrpur is being handled like a conquered land.'[vi]

A Kashmîrî identity: Ironically, the Mîrpurîs are not Kashmîrîs in the sense that the word is understood within the Valley of Kashmîr—for their ancestors have never spoken a word of the Kashmîrî language. Nor do they practice any of the several uniquely Kashmîrî customs.

All Britons are often called Englishmen (though they might be Irish, Welsh or Scottish), and people from the entire Soviet Union were often referred to as Russians. Similarly, all of Jammû and Kashmîr is sometimes loosely called 'Kashmîr.' The Mîrpurîs (and the people of the so-called Northern Areas) are Kashmîrîs in that sense.

The Mîrpurîs are also quite alienated from the people of the Muzaffarâbâd part of 'AJK.'

The under-representation of Muzaffarâbâd: Not that Muzaffarâbâd and the neighbouring Neelum Valley have been mollycoddled. 'AJK' had three districts in 1947: Muzaffarâbâd, Mîrpur and Poonch. The two latter districts got converted into six districts. This meant that more government employment was created in old Mîrpur and Poonch. The people of these areas now had to walk shorter distances to reach the district headquarters and their administrators could give them more focussed attention. the Government funds flowed into the creation of the new district headquarters—with more to follow every year for their maintenance.

All this while Muzaffarâbâd continued to be a single district—despite having by far the largest population and area among the seven districts of 'AJK.' The Neelum Valley, with a population of 1,45,000[vii] in 2005 and the unique burden of being on the frontline of the Indo-Pâkistân conflict, with all its attendant destruction and suffering, continued to be clubbed with Muzaffarâbâd till 2005, when the government decided to give Neelum Valley the status of an independent district.

Muzaffarâbâd is greatly underrepresented in the state legislature. It has only six seats there, while Mîrpur (including Bhimber), the population of which is 9 per cent smaller, has seven seats.

The Quréshîs of Kuñdal Shahî (and Chilâs and Kâghân):[viii] The mountainous Kuñdal Shahî area (c.5,000', 74km. from Muzaffarâbâd) is in the 'Neelum' valley—where the Jâgrâñ Nâllâh meets the Neelum River/ Kishen Gañgâ. It is close to the Neelum Valley Highway. British records refer to the area as Darral—that being an Anglicisation of Dular, a village in the area. The LoC is quite close. In the west, separated by mountains, some of them around 15,000' high, is the fascinating Kâghân valley.

Kuñdal Shahî is now the headquarters of the *tehsîl* (sub-district), because Athmuqâm was too close to the LoC for comfort—it was within the range of the Indian artillery.

Almost all the two thousand or so people of Kuñdal Shahî are Quréshîs. They speak a unique dialect, which the few non-Quréshîs of that town used to derisively call *râwrî*. The Kuñdal Shahî language has no other formal name.

Sheikhs, Mughals, and Syeds form less than ten per cent of the population of the town and speak Hiñdko—which is the main language of the rest of the Neelum valley. (The Gujjars, of course, speak Gojri. Shînâ is spoken in Phulawai and Taobat (Tao Butt) and Pashto in Dhakki and Changnar (Chaknot). Kashmîrî is spoken in some villages.)

Like all South Asian languages spoken by a tiny population, the language of Kuñdal Shahî—the one spoken by the Quréshîs—is dying out. Around the 1970s, Quréshî parents stopped speaking to their children in their own language, and opted, instead, for Hiñdko. (The same is true of Puñjâbi, Dogrâ and affluent Kashmîrî parents in India and Pâkistân. They have thrown in their lot with the more populous language of their region—Hiñdi-Urdû.)

The Quréshîs' ancestor, Kamâl Khân, belonged to Tijjar (Sopore, Kashmîr), from which he migrated, around AD 1700, to Muzaffarâbâd, before settling in Kuñdal Shahî.

However, one of his four sons, Hâtim Khân, put down roots in Kiân Sharîf, in the wooded Jâgrâñ valley, where déodâr trees with world-class timber grow. (There is also a famous Islamic shrine in Kiân Sharîf.) Some descendants of another son, Shâh Gul, now live in Gosher (Chilâs) where they are called the Timré clan. Others of Shâh Gul's clan have settled in Andhérâ Bélâ (Kâghân).

The Quréshîs of Kuñdal Shahî are descended from Sikañdar and Haidar, the two sons of Kamâl Khân who stayed on. Haidar's clan marries non-Quréshîs as well. That probably is the reason why this branch normally gives the area its headman—wider acceptability. Sikañdar's descendants have retained the purity of their bloodline.

The Hiñdko-speaking Miyâñ clan of Kuñdal Shahî is descended from an Islâmic scholar and teacher. He came here in the 18th or 19th century at the request of the Quréshîs, who continue to consider the PPP-leaning Miyâñs the political leaders of the area. Interestingly, as Rehman and Baart point out, even though the Miyâñs are Déobañdis (austere, strict Sunnis), most of the people of Kuñdal Shahî belong to the (rival, more liberal, more relaxed) Barélvi Sunni sect. The *pîr* of Choorâ Sharîf (Attock) is their spiritual leader.

Being ethnic Kashmîrîs, the Quréshîs used to look to Srînagar for all their material needs, as well as for education. The forced division of the state in 1947 changed all that.

References

i Ballard, Roger, 'The Kashmîr Crisis: A View From Mirpur,' *Economic and Political Weekly,* 1991 pp. 513–17. Dr Ballard is with the Centre for Applied South Asian Studies, University of Manchester.

ii Kishtwâri, Wali Mohd. Aseer, *Focus on Jammû and Kashmîr* (2003) Crescent House Publications, Jammû. Page339.

iii Evans, Alexander, 'Kashmîr: A tale of two valleys,' the manuscript of an article based on a lecture that Mr. Evans delivered at the Royal Society for Asian Affairs in December, 2004.

iv Evans, op. cit., p. 8.

v Evans, op. cit., p. 6.

vi 'Mîrpuris may withdraw support to Mañglâ Dam: [Attique] Khân,' *Greater Kashmîr,* 30 Jan, 2005.

vii 'Pak to have 8th district soon,' *Greater Kashmîr,* 6 Feb 2005.

viii Rehman, Khawaja A. and Baart, Joan L.G., 'The Language of the Qureshis of Kundal Shahi in Âzâd Kashmîr' a prepublication draft, January 9, 2004.

9

The Handicrafts of Jammû

(There are separate chapters on 'Basohli miniatures' and 'Wellside Sculptures'.)

Note: Some of the handicrafts mentioned here are made mainly for the local, rural market. Others are made for particular markets. Certain types of blankets, for instance, are meant to be sold mainly at the pilgrim centres of Uttarakhand and Uttar Pradesh.

Almost all handicrafts that have found a market among tourists are sold in and around Jammû's Raghunath Bazar.

Bamboo products

Baskets have traditionally been made of bamboo, in Kathua district in particular. Since the 1960s, other items, too, have been made, such as flower vases, fruit bowls, furniture, lampshades, magazine racks, paper trays and table mats.

Blankets

The finest woollen blankets of the province are woven in Kishtwar. The best ones come in red-and-white or grey-and-white. Kishtwar also makes blankets in natural colours but you can get that variety almost anywhere. Vegetable and mineral dyes are used.

There are some villages in Kathua, notably Ghagwal on the highway, which make blankets all the year around and sell them at local fairs.

Other places where blankets are woven are:

i) Kathua district: Banni, Billawar

ii) Udhampur district: Basantgarh, Duddu, Lâti, Ramnagar

iii) Dodâ district: Bhaderwah

iv) Poonch

v) Rajouri

Brass, copper and other metal work

Apart from vessels for domestic (mainly kitchen) use, Jammû's smiths make hookah bowls, idols and items made of hand beaten sheet metal. The Dastkari Hât Samiti points out, 'Large brass vessels called *sangla* made by pouring molten brass into mud-moulds is a dying craft, practised by a handful of artisans. Jammû city, Udhampur, Sâmbâ and [Basohli] practise this traditional craft.'

Calico and chintz

Sâmbâ used to have a flourishing cotton weaving and calico-printing handloom industry. The year 1947 changed all that. The talented craftsmen of Sâmbâ all fled to Pakistan. In the 1970s, the government launched an effort to revive the industry. In calico-printing, blocks of wood, with designs carved on them, are smeared with vegetable dyes and then pressed on cotton cloth.

Masnads and jajams are cotton sheets that have been printed thus. They are often used as floor coverings. More commonly, they are spread atop mattresses and divans (eastern sofas) in eastern-style, floor-based living-and dining-rooms.

Journalist Suraj Saraf, quoting the handicrafts-expert D.N. Saraf, writes, "Maharaja Ranjit Singh of Punjab seeing wide popularity and demand for chintz, offered to settle master chintz printers from Sâmbâ in Lahore. They, however, refused saying that the peculiar and fast tints of chintz could be produced only with the water of a particular tank in Sâmbâ.

The two-nation theory and the partition of India in 1947 ensured that the printers migrated to Lahore anyway, but without their art. India lost the artists, the artists their beloved town and its water and the world this art.

Also made in Sâmbâ and elsewhere in Jammû province are quilt covers, bedspreads, table-linen and running fabric.

Carpets

Carpets made in Jammû are normally meant for budget-customers. They are made at government-run handicrafts centres in Kathua, Poonch and Udhampur.

Chikri wood

On the one hand they tell you that the chikri tree is rare, there's just a few thousand left in the world. On the other they use its wood to make these kitsch toothpicks and matchboxes that aren't even great art. Besides, the matchboxes can't even be struck with a match for a light.

Chikri wood has a fine grain and what an expert describes as 'a light yellow colour.' The wood is hard. Therefore, it is excellent for carving on. If only it were used for higher forms of art.

The one truly smart trick they have is combs with a hollow tube in the middle, and teeth above and below this tube. Two-sided combs, to wit. You can fill oil into the tube and then seal the mouth of the tube with a tiny wooden stopper. There are minute holes all along the shaft of this tube. Oil oozes out through them into the teeth of the comb. So, when people, especially women with their long plaits, comb their hair, the hair get oiled automatically. Apparently Mughal princesses would use these combs. Makes sense, because Thanna Mandi was on the Mughal Road.

One good use this wood is put to is in the architecture of the houses of the hill folk: to make carved pillars, doors and other fixtures.

Other products: Ashtrays, bowls, cups, spoons and table knives. Ordinary combs are also made.

Durries

Durries are thick sheets made of cotton. They are used as inexpensive floor coverings, or placed under mattresses on beds. They are made in several parts of Jammû.

Embroidery

Shawls are embroidered the sozni way in the Kathua, Poonch and Rajouri districts.

Crewel embroidery is done in the Poonch, Rajouri and Udhampur districts.

Staple (ari-work) embroidery is done in the Kathua, Poonch, Rajouri and Udhampur districts.

Chamba roomals are scarves and large handkerchieves that have been embroidered on both sides. Thus there is no 'negative' on the reverse, made up of the ends of threads. In fact, the same image appears on both sides of the cloth. This very clever technique must have originated in Chamba (HP). The artists use a curved needle that travels from the obverse to the reverse and back in a circular movement. This way both sides are embroidered at the same time—and with the same pattern. There still are artists in Jammû who can make such kerchieves. However, hardly anyone purchases their works and I fear that this ingenious art will soon disappear from Jammû the way it has from Basohli.

Footwear—Gujjar and Bakerwal

The Gujjar and Bakerwal nomads wear colourfully embroidered, laceless shoes, somewhat like moccasins. They are almost exactly like the *jootis* the Mughals would wear, curved upwards at the tip. I think similar shoes are still worn by some Rajasthani tribals. The designs have obviously descended from the Persians, through the Mughals. However, the shoes are made of hard leather and thus are very, very heavy duty. So heavy duty that experts I had invited from the Central Cottage Industries Emporium chain felt that only 'lite' versions would be suitable for the delicate feet of city girls. (City men might not be bold enough to wear such colourful shoes outside their homes. Leather soles wear out much faster than, say, rubber soles.)

These shoes are made in various villages on the nomads' migration routes. One such village is near Thein (Basohli), well away from the main road. Machhedi and Banni which, too, are in Kathua district are a little less accessible but the shoes they make are even better.

Modified, upmarket, versions are sold near Jammû's Raghunath Temple.

Footwear—other embroidered

Jammû city has a tradition of moccasin-like shoes embroidered with *zari* (gold or silver thread). The Dhakki Sirâjân is one place where this is still done.

Some of these shoes are sold near Jammû's Raghunath Temple.

Jewellery

Jewellery normally doesn't count as a handicraft because the designs rarely stick to tradition. And yet if there is one craft in which Jammû dominates the northern region, it is jewellery. Jammû has its own distinct urban designs, for which there is considerable demand among wealthy Delhiites in particular. Just as carpets have brought enormous affluence to a certain class of Kashmîri businessmen, jewellery (and dry fruits) have made some Jammûites very rich. The top jewellers are concentrated in the Jain Bazar area of Jammû city. The Julaha ka Mohalla is the other place to look for jewellers.

Traditional rural Dogra designs are still reproduced. Dogra jewellery of the hills tends to be, well, not exactly loud but not understated either. Nose-rings, for instance, are extra-large with a large precious stone embedded. Bangles, the *chhaunk phool* (a metal cap), silver anklets and talismans (*tâveez*) are among the favourites of the hill-folk. They prefer jewellery made of pure or alloyed silver.

Jewellery—Gujjar and Bakerwal

Women of the nomadic Gujjar and Bakerwal tribes wear truly exotic, chunky jewellery. It is mostly made of silver or white metal. Some of it is even made of brass. These Muslim tribals migrate ('oscillate' is the word academics use) between Kashmîr and Jammû. However, they get their jewellery made almost entirely in Jammû, and by Hindu jewellers at that. It could be so because these jewellers have, over the centuries, got to understand their nomadic clients' needs and tastes. The Basohli sub-division has half a dozen jewellers who make jewellery for the Gujjars, in addition to standard Jammû-style ornaments. These jewellers are to be found in some large, semi-urban villages.

As the Sub-Divisional Magistrate of Basohli this is one of the crafts I tried to popularise in the rest of the country. It has, what handicrafts-expert

Kalpana Manglik calls, a 'dramatic quality'. And it is relatively expensive. Experts from the Central Cottage Industries Emporium (CCIE) chain came over at my invitation and agreed with me about the price and exoticness. However, they also pointed out that this heavy jewellery, designed for very tough women, might rupture the delicate ears and noses of city girls. So, we tried out 'lite' versions. That consignment met with some success in Delhi. I got posted to distant, landlocked Zanskar (Ladâkh) and could not pursue this little mission.

Gujjar-Bakerwal jewellery is also made and sold at Bhaderwah, Dodâ, Kathua, Kishtwar, Reasi and Sâmbâ (which is on the Jammû-Pathankot-Delhi highway).

Lacquer woodwork

Also known as lathe-cum-lacquer work, this craft is practised in many parts of India, including Jammû city. The finished products are painted a deep brown and then coated with a transparent film of lacquer. Most goods made through this process are low end and kitsch: toys, rolling pins, table lamps, candelabras, bowls and vases. In the middle-rung are things like 'bed-legs,' the four posts that cots rest on. My favourites are *peerhas*, which Suraj Saraf describes as 'squat-low chairs.' These are traditional chairs, the seats of which are made of cotton or straw-ropes. Their backs look like those of normal chairs. However, *peerhas* have no legs, only stumps that lift the seat just above the ground.

Woodwork is done at Kahna Chak (a suburb of Jammû city), and Mirth/ Bernali (Kathua). (See also the corresponding section in chapter 17 'Kashmîri Handicrafts').

Leatherwork

Vijaypur and Khour, both in Jammû district, are where Jammû's best leatherwork is done.

Mats

The Dastkari Hât Samiti reports that 'Sungwali, Nagari Parole, Airwan, Good and Kore-Punee villages in Jammû region [produce] mats, baskets, hand fans and other household articles from [the] dried leaves of palm trees.' These villages are mostly in Kathua district. Palm trees grow in very few parts of the state. However, feudal elites, as well as the not so well to do, have for centuries used these products.

Painting, miniature

I was able to revive this art at Basohli in the 1980s. Since then alumni of the school that I founded have fanned out to Udhampur town, Jammû city and Kathua town, where they now practise the art. (See also chapter 10, 'Basohli paintings'.)

At various times during the 17th, 18th and 19th centuries, miniature painting also flourished at Jammû proper, Poonch, Mankot (Ramkot), Jasrota and in various other small princely states in Jammû province. In neighbouring Himachal Pradesh this art received patronage at Chamba, Nurpur, Kulu, Mandi and Guler. Together, the Jammû and HP schools of painting are known as the Paharhi (hill) School. The paintings of Garhwal (Uttarakhand) can be included in this school.

Early Basohli paintings are known for their vibrant primary colours. Human faces and trees are stylised, rather than realistic. Most Paharhi paintings ignore depth and perspective.

(See also the chapters "The Basohli School of Miniature Painting" and "The lesser known miniature painting schools of Jammû province.")

Perfumes

Two kinds of *attar* (Eastern perfumes) are made in Jammû, jasmine and rose. They are sold at one of the corner shops at the City Chowk. Perfumes sold near the Jama Masjid, Talab Khatikân, are mostly made in Kannauj (Central India).

Phulkari/ Bâgh

This is a craft native to Punjab and Haryana. However, it has some exponents in Jammû, too. I suspect that even in this case the craftsmen have mostly migrated to Pakistan. Phulkari is a colourful sheet of cloth, every millimetre of which is covered with embroidery. It has a posh, glossy look, because the thread used for the embroidery is unfinished, home-dyed, silk-floss.

Women often wear shawls made of phulkari. However, some even get *qameezes* (long shirts) made of cloth that has been embroidered thus. Because phulkari is very expensive (and, in Jammû, a dying art) such shawls are heirlooms, passed down from generation to generation. I know at least one family that has framed its heirloom phulkari shawl in glass.

Phulkari is done in the Kathua, Poonch, Rajouri and Udhampur districts.

Pottery

The *math* is a speciality of the Jammû region. This is a big jar in which all kinds of grains are stored, often for a year or even more. Because the clay had been fired at a very high temperature, this kind of a jar can last several generations, unless it drops and breaks.

Sculpture

The art lives on in places like Basohli, where some Saryârâ families carve figures, in relief, on stone quite inexpensively. (See also the chapter on 'Wellside Sculptures'.)

Shawls, pashmina

Basohli pashminas are nowhere near as finely woven as the ones made in Kashmîr. However, nor are they as expensive. In terms of both quality and price they occupy a place between the pashminas of Ladâkh and Kashmîr. The weavers of Basohli are ethnic Kashmîris.

Silk

There is a silk factory in Jammû city, near Resham Ghar. Its products are sold at the factory itself and through emporia of the state government. The Dastkari Hât Samiti observes, 'In Jammû villages women make [tasselled] ornaments to bind their hair while men [weave] fine cords to tie their pyjamas.'

Straw products

Baskets, containers of all kinds, mats and trays are made from a particularly resplendent straw in Kishtwar proper, Sangram Bhata and Sarkoot (all in the Kishtwar sub-division of Dodâ district). Kalpana Manglik notes that these are 'delicately decorated with bright woollen strands of threads.'

Till the 1950s even the feudal elite would sit on straw mats on the kitchen floor when they ate their meals. *Binnas* (coiled mats) were particularly popular, because they had a springy, cushioned feel, and had intricate patterns woven in. They are still used in rural households, as are *nadas* and *parandas.* The 'ethnic' crowd sometimes uses *binnas* as wall decorations.

A *nada* (or *nârhâ*) is a waistband, an inch thick cord used like a belt in pyjamas and gowns. A *parândâ* is a braid tied at the end of women's plaits. The *nârhâs* and *parandas* I know of are made of cotton thread, though. It is on the authority of Suraj Saraf that I say that these are made of straw as well. Scholar and civil servant Anil Goswami tells me that the length of the *nârhâ* and the styling of its tassel used to be a major fashion statement among men till the 1940s. Mr Saraf writes that these "thick tufts had become almost a status symbol." The *paranda* seems to have had a similar hold on fashion-conscious rural women, if Punjabi folk-songs are anything to go by.

Terracotta toys

These are still made in certain rural areas. The ancient terracottas of Ambaran (a village near Akhnoor in Jammû district) show Greek influences and are on display at major museums in India and abroad.

Wickerwork or willow basketry

Various kinds of baskets and trays are made in Bhaderwah and Dodâ city.

Crafts that you can't take home

Wood carving

Unlike in Kashmîr, the finest wood carving in Jammû is meant for architecture, not furniture. Go to Jammû city's City Chowk, or the uphill slope just before the Raghunath Temple, and you will still find elegant windows and doors. (There is a very fine balcony between Gurudwara Sunder Singh and the Raghunath temple.) Elsewhere in town there are temples with stately carved doors. (The Bahu Fort has a thick, tall, heavy door with iron spikes for intruding elephants. However, it has been painted over and robbed of some of its glory.)

Door jambs, carved windows and even carved balconies are found in the rural areas, especially in Basohli and Billawar. In the 1980s, I found a craftsman, a Muslim of Kashmîri origin, who could still make such doors. His family had migrated to Basohli around the 16th century. He made a tall, four-door panel for my court at Basohli. It has fine compound arches and carving. You can look it up at the court of the SDM in Basohli.

10

The Basohli School of Miniature Painting

The first school

The earliest available evidence of painters flourishing at Basohli dates back to the reign of Raja Kirpal Singh (1678-95). His grandfather, Raja Sangram Pal (1635-73), had cultivated a taste for miniature paintings through his friendship with Dara Shikoh. (Dara was the heir apparent to the Mughal throne and one of the greatest ecumenicists ever born in India.) Contact between the Basohli and Mughal courts began at least as far back as in 1590.

The first Basohli school is known as the Basohli Qalam. 'Qalam' literally means 'pen'. Figuratively it means 'school' (in the sense of 'style' or 'genre'). Therefore, a miniature painted anywhere in the world in the Basohli style would belong to the Basohli 'qalam' or 'school'. Contemporary artists living in several Punjab Hill States painted in this style.

The style was in vogue from roughly 1675 to around 1750. Its distinguishing marks were bold lines, dense, hot, emotional colours and—easiest to identify—deep, red borders. Trees were stylised and the eyes of the women portrayed were abnormally big and fishlike. The women's foreheads would be large, almost like receding hairlines. Typically, these miniatures were painted on stiff, cardboard-like paper and often were 9" × 12" in size. Postcard-sized miniatures, too, were fairly common. Their borders would be plain, broad and either red or mustard yellow.

Under Raja Amrit Pal, who married the daughter of Jammû's King Ranjit Dev in 1759, Basohli became a feudatory of Jammû.

The second (Kangra) school

Around 1750, after the death of his patron, Raja Balwant Singh of Jammû, Nainsukh, an artist from Guler (HP), went to Basohli to paint for Amrit Pal.

Thus began the second school of miniature painting in Basohli. Two related styles flourished during the century that followed. They are known as the pre-Kangra and Kangra qalams, even though they were painted in Basohli as well.

Eyes and limbs were now painted with a gentle brush. The idea was to be as close to reality as possible. Therefore, stylisation was given up. The foliage shown was lavish. The line became delicate and clear. Colours mellowed down to soft, pale pastels. Shades supplemented primary colours. An overall sophistication was achieved. Borders were pink.

Of Nainsukh's sons, the lines of Kama and Gaudhu terminated early. Nikka, the second son, returned to Guler and proved the fecund one. Ranjha, the third son, stayed on in Basohli, on land gifted by Amrit Pal to his father Nainsukh. Raja Bhupendra Pal got Ranjha to paint for him.

Of Ranjha's sons, Sukhdayal died young, while Gursahai went on to become a painter of repute. Little is known about Gursahai's son Dhananjay. However, about Deviditta, the other son, we have evidence that he migrated from Basohli around 1856. By that year the Pal dynasty of Basohli was no longer in power. Jammû had taken over the kingdom.

Deviditta first went to the Lahore court. When Lahore was annexed by the British, he went to the Patiala court. He died in 1876, leaving behind an unmemorable son, Shiv Saran, upon whose death this line of Basohli painters came to an end.

Themes depicted by artists of the two schools mentioned above were varied. They ranged from the religious (the *Ramayan* and the *Gita Govinda*) to the secular (nayikas, i.e. pretty 'heroines'); from the historical (Nal-Damyanti) to the contemporary (portraits of local Rajas); and from the literary (Ragmala) to the mundane (self-portraits and illustrations for manuscripts).

Among the earliest paintings of the First School were pictures of Lord Shiv and the Devi, as well as scenes from the *Bhâgwat Purân* and the *Rasmanjari* of Bhânu Datt. Refinements in the style took place during the reigns of Dhiraj Pâl (1693-1722) and Medini Pâl (1722-36). There is reason to believe that Devi Dass painted Basohli's celebrated *Rasmanjari* in 1694-95. Manaku's version of Jaya Dev's *Gîta Govinda* is dated to 1730.

The third school

I stepped into the picture 123 years after the last miniature had been painted in Basohli. In 1979 I was freshly out of college and into the Indian Administrative Service. A senior asked me if there was any particular Sub-

Division that I wanted to be posted as the Magistrate (SDM) of. I volunteered for Basohli, with the explicit intention of reviving the art.

Several people told me that it couldn't be done. No one knew how to make those colours any more. Nor those brushes. No one in Basohli knew where Nainsukh's descendants lived. However, some helpful local people told me of an ageing grocer (*pansâri*) in Jammû who still sold the minerals from which the colours were made. The pansâri very kindly taught me exactly how each colour was made.

Sharma, a young teacher from Basohli, was one of the persons who were convinced that the art could not be revived. He told me, "There's an old artist in Kangra [HP] who considers himself lucky if he is paid Rs. 5 for a [postcard-sized] miniature painting."

Rs. 5 were then worth around 40 US cents. The sum was an insult to a painting that took almost two days to create. If that was going to be the fate of the school I had in mind, there was no point in going ahead. I gave up.

Then one day it occurred to me that this Kangra-based artist was a lead worth following up for its own sake. By now young Sharma had disappeared and it took me several months to trace him out. All that he knew was that the artist lived in a village called Rait.

As crows fly, Rait must be less than fifty kilometres from Basohli. But a mighty river and a state boundary separate Basohli (Jammû and Kashmîr) from Rait (Himachal Pradesh). I had to obtain special permission to take my official jeep into another state.

However, once we reached Rait we got more than we could have dreamt of. The artist, Chandu Lal Raina, then 68, showed us copies of the art journals *Marg* and *Roop Lekha* dating to the late 1950s and the early 1960s. In these journals the eminent art historian Dr BN Goswamy had conclusively established that Chandu Lal was a descendant of the prolific Nikka (whose son Gokal begot Ram Dayal, whose son Lachhman in turn begot Chandu Lal).

Dr Goswamy had, in his articles, lamented that the only connection that Nainsukh's descendants now had with art was that one of them painted signboards and advertising hoardings while another made engineering drawings as a draughtsman in Chandigarh.

I requested Chandu Lal to return to the land of his ancestors. I even offered to pay him a salary equal to what I was being paid in the country's highest-ranking civil service. Chandu Lal was tempted but said that he was too old to migrate. So, could I employ his son Sat Prakash, then in his early twenties, instead? I did.

On Dussehra day, 1980, Sat Prakash Raina launched the third school of miniature painting at Basohli. Since then, every year the government has been paying eight local students a small scholarship to study the art. (Others are welcome, minus the stipend.) It's a two-year course. Therefore, at any given time there are sixteen students in the school. Lalit Kumar, one of the brightest alumni of my school, joined the staff as a teacher a few years later.

Other alumni have since gone on to set up privately-run branches of the school at Udhampur, Jammû and Basohli itself. For a while, in the 1980s, there was a branch at Kathua as well. This proliferation of branches makes me hopeful that the third school won't die out in a hurry again. That's because it is dependent more on the market than on feudal patronage.

Not that the market is less capricious. Basohli was only one of the many schools of Indian miniature painting that became extinct after 1850. Two things had happened together. The British took over Indian kingdoms, the rulers of which used to patronise these paintings as well as their painters. (In the case of Basohli, the kingdom was taken over by a more powerful neighbour.) Around the same time, European presses started printing pictures of Indian deities at a fraction of the cost of a hand-made miniature. (In the late 19th and early twentieth centuries the average Basohli miniature sold for Rs. 3.)

Colours, paper, brushes

The third school uses the same colours as had its precursors. These colours are mostly made of minerals dissolved in water. Sometimes, vegetables, leaves, oils and oil-soot are used. One particular shade of yellow is obtained by feeding a cow with the leaves of a mango tree, collecting its urine the next day, drying the urine and dissolving the powder thus produced in water. Real gold and silver foil are used in some of the more expensive paintings.

We also use the same brushes as before. The shaft of the brush is normally made of the central reed of the feathers of certain birds. Sometimes bamboo reeds are used for this purpose. Hairs for the tips of these brushes are taken from the tails of squirrels. Brushes with which borders are painted have as many as 72 hairs, because no precision is required. Those with which eyelashes are drawn might have just one or two hairs. Other brushes come in between.

Before placing them in a brush, each hair is tugged at both ends. If the hair snaps in the middle, it is rejected. The tips of these hairs are also examined. If a hair with a split end manages to get into a brush, it will divide the other hairs of the brush into two groups. A line drawn with such a brush will, therefore, be blurred. So, hairs with split ends, too, are thrown away.

All Basohli miniatures are painted on stiff paper. The paper is made by fusing together waste-paper obtained from the used *bahis* (account-registers) of Sialkot. Sialkot is now in Pakistan and officially there's no trade in wastepaper between India and Pakistan. However, there's enough wastepaper from pre-partition Sialkot still going around (or being brought over clandestinely) to keep the present generation of Basohli artists in business. In any case, only a few hundred miniatures get painted in a year at all the branches of the third Basohli school put together. You just need three or four used account-registers a year for those many.

A thin coat of gum is smeared over each painting after it has been completed. This invisible film protects the colours from moisture, though not always from light. These paintings fade gradually if exposed to sunlight in particular. In any case, paintings were kept in albums in Indo-Islamic Asia, and not hung from walls. (Some Hindu religious pictures are displayed on the mantelpiece, though, and are replaced after soot from oil lamps dirties them.)

These paintings are supposed to be waterproof, at least in theory. You dip them in a jug of water and the colours are not supposed to run. In practice, while the colours don't flow from the paper into the water, they do tend to spread slightly into the neighbouring colours, to produce a blur where sharp lines used to be.

After they have been smeared with gum, the paintings are placed, face down, on a smooth, flat stone slab. The slab is the size of A 4 paper and about an inch and a half thick. The stone is as smooth as marble. It contains the fossils of ancient leaves and is found only in mountains that are covered with snow throughout the year. (That perhaps is why it is known as *barfâni patthar* or 'snow stone'.)

Then a cylindrical 'pestle,' the size of a microphone and made of a different but equally smooth stone, is rolled firmly over the reverse of the painting. This smoothens out any kinks and air bubbles that might have crept in when the sheets of Sialkotiya paper were stuck together. After the obverse has been painted on, these paintings tend to curve inwards. Therefore, more importantly, the rolling of the 'pestle' straightens the painting out.

In the year 2005, a good price for a miniature the size of a newsmagazine, with just one human figure painted on it, would be Rs. 800. Add Rs.150 to Rs. 200 for every additional human figure.

11

The Lesser Known Miniature Painting Schools of Jammû Province

At various times during the 17th, 18th and 19th centuries, miniature painting also flourished at Jammû proper, Pooñch, Mankot (Râmkot), Jasrotâ and many of the smaller princely states of Jammû province.

In neighbouring Himâchal Pradésh this art was patronised at Chambâ, Nurpur, Kulu, Mañdî and Gulér.

Together, the Jammû and HP schools of painting are known as the Paharhi (hill) School. The paintings of Garhwâl (Uttarakhand) can also be included in this school.

History: According to one theory, the Paharhi School originated in Mankot, a princely state in Jammû province, around AD 1650. Raja Mahipat Dév (1660-70) is the first known patron of a Paharhi School.

Charak and Billawaria believe that the style travelled from Mankot to Basohli during the reign of Raja Kirpal Siñgh Balauria (1678-93). It is a plausible theory, because the Mankot school is, arguably, a decade or two older than Basohli's better-known (and much longer lasting) school. Against that background it is difficult to agree with Dr D.C. Sharma[i] that 'the home of the Pahari Miniature is stated to be originated in the State of Basohli.' Besides, it is a fact that artistic activity in Basohli picked up only during Kirpal's reign and no Basohli miniatures on paper are available from before his time.

However, the kings of Basohli had been going to the Mughal court since at least 1590. Kirpal's grandfather, Raja Sangram Pal, was a friend of the Mughal prince Dara Shikoh.

It is even possible that Bhupat Pâl of Basohli was once of the crown princes whom Emperor Jehângîr had kept hostage in Agra from 1613 to 1627, Dr Sharma suggests that he might have picked up a taste for miniature paintings at the Mughal court.

Therefore, it is as likely that the inspiration for the Pahârhî Schools came from Agra-Delhi as from Mankot. My personal vote, as I will argue below, is for an indigenous origin.

At the time Jammû proper was ruled by Hari Dév (c.1656-92). Miniature paintings on paper flourished in what is now Jammû city towards the end of his reign, and probably started then.

There is a theory that the style then travelled to Kâñgrâ (Himâchal Pradésh), with the kings of which the rulers of Jammû and Basohli had matrimonial relations.

The style: Some scholars theorise that 'the style owed much to the Mughal art of Shâh Jehan's period.' I find it difficult to agree, because Mughal art was far more refined. It is true that the Paharhi Schools sprang up around the time that the puritanical Mughal emperor, Aurañgzéb, was in power in Delhi. Therefore, many scholars believe that these hill schools were set up by painters from the Mughal court, who had to leave Delhi because the austere Aurañgzéb would not patronise them.

Well, firstly, these hill schools had started coming up just before Aurañgzéb assumed power. Secondly, stylistically they are nothing like Mughal paintings. (Of all Paharhi Schools, indeed of all Râjpût schools, the Jammû School comes closest to Mughal miniatures.)

Most importantly, thanks to Dr BN Goswamy's efforts we now have the family tree of the Basohli painters. It indicates that Nainsukh was from Gulér and had served as an artist at the Jammû court before migrating to Basohli. Therefore, the Second Basohli School (the Kâñgrâ Qalam) had no Mughal connection.

India has had a very old tradition of wall paintings. Wall paintings from the ninth and tenth centuries AD are still extant. Kashmîr has a history of illustrated manuscripts as well as stand-alone paintings that date to ancient times, There are references in Kashmîr's *Nilamat Puran* to a tradition of painting, perhaps on parchment, that is older still.

Paintings on paper are a tradition brought to most parts of India by the Mughals and other rulers of Central Asian origin. (Orissa had paper paintings around the 10th/ 11th century AD, though.) By at least the 14th century the Kashmîrîs were painting on paper.

I suspect that the Paharhi painters took the idea of using paper, as well as the dimensions of individual mainiatures, from the Kashmîrîs or, maybe, the Mughals but retained the colours and style of their own wall paintings.

Could Nainsukh's family have migrated from Kashmîr to Gulér? His 21st century descendants will be very happy if this can be proved. They use the surname Raina, which everyone associates with the Kashmîrî Pañdits. However, Nainsukh's descendants do not have a trace of the ethnic Kashmîrî Pañdit in them—neither the language, nor the customs and certainly not the matrimonial links that the Kashmîrî Pañdits of, say, Pooñch or even HP retained with their cousins in Kashmîr. Nainsukh's descendants are accepted as local Dogrâ Rainâs of the *tarkhân* (carpenter) caste in Jammû and Himâchal Pradésh.

Dr Sharma believes that stylistically at least one painting done by Mohad (sic) Joo of Kashmîr has much in common with Paharhi miniatures. Now this is eerie: my research reveals a Kashmîrî surname (Raina), and Dr Sharma finds an artistic similarity with Kashmîr.

So, the theory about artists having fled Delhi because of Aurañgzéb is silly because they had started painting in the hills several years before Aurañgzéb took over in Delhi. They could not have fled in anticipation because Aurañgzéb was not the crown prince. On the other hand, there does seem to be reason to believe that the artists might have come from Kashmîr, which had a fabulous tradition of miniature paintings—in the Indian as well as Central Asian styles.

Early Basohli paintings are known for their vibrant primary colours. Human faces and trees are stylised, rather than realistic. Most Paharhi paintings lack depth and perspective.

What were these paintings used for? The biggest single use was as icons in the prayer room. Today the Hiñdus light lamps before prints of paintings. Before colour printing was introduced, hand-painted miniatures were the only option. This is why many antique paintings have been darkened by the soot of oil lamps.

To this day, when a well-off girl gets married in the Dogra hills, her parents gift a few paintings (or prints) of Hiñdu deities to her husband's family.

Customs like these ensured that there was always a demand for miniature paintings in the hills.

Reference

i Sharma, Dr D.C., 'Origin of Jammû School of Pahari Paintings,' *Daily Excelsior*, 30 September, 2001.

12

Wellside Sculpture

Bathing-wells and sculpture: 'Bathing well' is a rather poor translation of what in Urdu would be called a *baoli* (bâ-ow-lee), and in Dogri a bâñ. These are wells in the sense that fresh water keeps coming from under the ground. They are not ponds with accumulated rain-water. But they are not deep at all. Often these bâns in the hills of Kathua and Udhampur districts are at the ground level; at the most you'll have to climb down two or three steps.

Elegant, low stone walls surround these baolis because traditionally everyone, including pretty young women, would bathe without a stitch on at these wells. This custom is fast disappearing. But while it was there, on several occasions it landed the undersigned in embarrassing situations (that is, if 'embarrassment' is the word I am looking for). Since most Indians sit on the ground while bathing, the older walls were rarely more then three or four feet high. While the walls themselves, made of large stone bricks, might or might not be carved, often you will find nice sculptures placed against them: on the inner side. Normally these are grey stone tablets, the size of a coffee table book, only slightly thicker. The image on them is carved, on one side only, in relief, rarely more than an inch and a half (3.5 cm.) deep. Some of these sculptures are *a roundel* (i.e. 3D), e.g. Shivlings.

These baolis do not have roofs. As a result the sculptures tend to get eroded by the rain and the winds and lose their sharpness over the decades. So, in 1981, as the Sub-Divisional Magistrate of Basohli, I took to trying to salvage some of the better pieces. (Being an amateur weightlifter, I'd carry them on my shoulders to my jeep, and thus managed to collect some 30 pieces for a little gallery that I started in my office in Basohli town.) Because this is an art-form that I still haven't seen any articles or books about, I asked my village based staff to make a thorough inventory of the sculptures lying around the wells of the almost 150 villages under my jurisdiction. The typical well has six or seven such pieces, of which perhaps two would not have been eroded beyond recognition.

These sculptures serve (or should that be 'served'?) various purposes. The most obvious, of course, is religious. Hindus like to bathe before offering prayers. So, it is nice to have an idol of your favourite deity at the place where you bathe. As mentioned above, apart from idols in relief, there are bullet-shaped Shivlings as well.

Coiled snakes: The snakes of the *kandi* (semi-arid) areas of Jammû are poisonous. They kill several people every year. Therefore, they need to be propitiated. As a result, reliefs of coiled snakes are a recurring theme in these sculptures.

The clan deity: Most clans have special reverence for one particular deity. Some wellside sculptures are images of this 'clan deity.'

Other stone tablets, especially those created after the 17th century, depict famous Dogra warriors such as Baba Jitto and Data Ranpat.

Warriors on horses: There is a place called Ghorha Galli ('the mountain pass of the horses') in the forests of Gool-Gulabgarh, a mountainous region in Udhampur district. The horses that give the pass its name are not real horses at all. Instead, they are huge stone reliefs, typically as big as a portable blackboard and maybe six inches thick, showing men (kings?) atop horses. Mr Mehmood-ur-Rehman, an idealistic and creative civil servant, got some of these sculptures shifted from Ghorha Galli to what now is the Dogra Art Museum of Jammû.

The finest, and biggest, of the genre come from Ghorha Galli. However, every tenth baoli in the Basohli-Billawar hills has a smaller relief (as I said, the size of a coffee table book) of a warrior sitting on a horse.

Warriors: Sometimes the warrior portrayed is a foot-soldier, an infantryman. He normally has a sword and shield in his hands.

Satis: Most intriguing, and disturbing, are the countless reliefs of ordinary women. This is the *sati* (ritual suicide) genre. (These genres have been named thus by me; sati is an expression only educated people would use in the hills.) These are sculptures of women who had unhappy marriages, which drove them to suicide. (Typically they would jump off a cliff.) It is believed that the spirits of such women continue to hover around unless provided, through prayer and by carving sculptures like these, the peace that they seek. These reliefs are too small for the faces to have any details. In any case the guys who sculpt these stones are no Michelangelos. The sculptors just carve broad lines, and one sati looks much like another.

And yet there are variations. Sometimes there are two women in the relief. This indicates that the sculpture is for the peace of the souls of two women who had killed themselves together. In one instance, the woman featured on the stone tablet was shown holding a child. I was told that this particular woman had jumped off a cliff along with her child.

According to art historian Lalit Gupta the sati could be shown 'riding a palanquin that is carried by bearers.' Somehow I have never come across such a sculpture in Basohli or Billawar, the two tehsils where I did my fieldwork. Gupta adds, "When she stands alone, [the sati] is usually shown holding a 'Kalasa' [vessel] or fan in one of the hands. There are also memorial stones where hero on horseback and Sati riding a palanquin are shown together."

Memorial stones: Gupta says that some of these stone tablets are "memorial stones that are locally called 'Mohrâs'... [These] represent a dead ancestor or one who has died an unnatural death, died for a cause or all those dead relatives and others whose spirits demand [the] setting up of a 'Mohrâ.'" Apparently the more restless of these spirits appear in the dreams of their relatives. They then demand that a mohrâ should be sculpted in their memory, or else they will not be able to rest in peace. If a mohrâ is not created as demanded by the spirit, it possesses the offending relative and makes his life miserable. A mohrâ, thus, is a mystic device meant to give peace to restless spirits.

'Saheeds': Gupta adds that some of these memorial stones are dedicated to *'saheeds'* (presumably, martyrs). He writes that 'sati' stones are also known as *shîlabantis* and *syabaties*. Gupta says that "memorial stones suddenly seem to proliferate after [the] 15th-16th centuries and their presence is felt all over the countryside." Could it not be possible that memorial stones made in the 14th century or before have been worn flat by the rain and the winds?

Other sculptures: In the hilly parts of Kathua and Udhampur the best place to find these sculptures would be a *baoli*. However, in the plains of the Jammû and Kathua districts they are mostly found under sacred trees and in the compounds of rural temples.

The saryârâ sculptors of Basohli: This art was about to die when I chanced upon it around 1980. The reason was that no one was ordering such reliefs, or indeed stone sculptures of any kind, any more. (Temples now use kitschy, factory-made plaster or ceramic idols.) There was just one family of *saryârâs* (a scheduled caste) left, and even they earned their bread and butter as *raj mistrys* (skilled masons). Sculpture was something that they did on Sundays, and then mainly to please me. I pumped in some government money to get Bansi Lal's family to train others in this art, so that it did not die out with this family. A rival Saryara sculptor emerged after I left and is doing marginally better business. Government funds can keep the Dogra Hill School of Wellside Sculpture (the name that I have given this art-form) alive only for one generation, at best two. Only public demand for sculptures can sustain sculptors in the long run. If people stop bathing at wells, because they now have bathrooms at home or because they are too coy (because of Sanskritisation) to bathe in the open, then naturally demand will remain at near zero.

Equestrian warriors have become a thing of the past. With urbanisation so have snakes in the inhabited areas. 'Mohrâs' dedicated to ancestors, however, are one genre still in demand. Let's hope suicides and *satîs* also decrease or, better still, disappear. So will, in a generation, this art.

13

The Performing Arts

Song, Dance and Theatre

The three sub-cultures of the Dogrâs: The Dogrâs live in much of Jammû province and the adjoining parts of Himâchal Pradésh. The land that they inhabit is divided into three regions: (i) the mountains where Jammû and Himâchal Pradésh meet, (ii) the semi-arid (*kañdî*) foothills, and (iii) the plains close to the Punjãb.[i]

The mountain belt stretches from Bhaderwâh (Dodâ) to Pânchairi, upper Chenainî, Mântalâi, Lâtî and Kud (all Udhampur) and the adjacent mountains of Bannî, Basohli and upper Bilâwar (Kathuâ).

The *kañdî* belt straddles Jammû-Kathuâ. It is sandwiched between the hills (north and east) and the plains/ national highway (south and west).

The plains, in turn, lie between the national highway (north and east) and the border with Pâkistân (south and west). It includes Hîrânagar, R.S. (Ranbîr Siñgh) Purâ and Kathuâ. The region borders the two Punjãbs: Indian and Pâkistânî. At Chhamb, it is on the LoC.

The plains should, logically, be influenced by the culture of the far more populous Punjãb. However, the adjoining parts of Indian as well as Pâkistânî Punjãb can, instead, be said to be part of the Dogrâ continuum. The people of Gurdâspur and Hoshiârpur (India) and Siâlkot (Pâkistân) have traditionally ruled over or been ruled by Jammû. The same sub-castes live on both sides of the Jammû-Punjãb border. They prefer to arrange marriages with each other rather than with the other people of their respective states. (In the case of Siâlkot this practice came to an end in 1947.)

Most of the plains of Jammû district are located in an area known as Bhajowath. Mohan Siñgh writes, '[This] is the area between [the rivers] Râvî and Chenâb, especially the area of Manaver and Chhamb—Pâkistân had captured this area during Indo-Pak wars in 1965 and 1971—Pallâñwâlâ, Nâgbani, Karloop and Batehrâ-Manihal.'[ii]

Each of the three regions has its own culture.

Folk Dances

The dances most popular in Jammû include the kud, phummani, chowki, kikkali, dhamma-chada, dandras, chhajjâ, sohadi, ghuraié, bhâñgrâ, giddâ and the dholak dance. The dances of the hills are normally part of the shared Dogrâ heritage of Jammû and Himâchal Pradésh. Punjâbi dances like the bhâñgrâ and the giddâ are popular in the plains of Jammû—in R.S. Purâ, for instance.

These dances are performed at fairs, religious and harvest festivals and weddings.

Bhagat or **Bhagataiñ:** This is an ancient form of folk theatre found all over north India. It is a branch of the more famous *nautañki*[1], with the difference that bhagat (lit. 'devoted' or 'devotee') theatre has its roots in religion. In Jammû (and some neighbouring parts of Himâchal Pradésh) the themes have, since at least the nineteenth century, been totally secular and related to the everyday problems of the audience.

The actors follow a plot and a rehearsed script. However, they also ad lib, according to the mood of the mostly rural audience. By and large the theme is sombre, and the story, normally, has a suitable moral. But the telling, almost invariably, is funny—in fact, sarcastic. Rapacious moneylenders, hidebound priests and confidence tricksters are among the favoured targets.

The Bhagatain of the Dogrâ hills is enacted on a flat ground in the open, normally the village square. This is unlike its Central Indian namesake, which is performed on a temporary stage constructed on any suitable street. Because these performances are held well after sunset, in the past the 'arena' would be lit by torches (*maséré*).

I suspect that the bhagat theatre of the Dogrâ hills owes some of its origin to wrestling, because the ground on which it is performed is called an *akhârâ* (wrestling ground). Its cousin, jagrâtâ (see below) has performances called *chhiñjan*. Chhiñj is the Dogrî word for 'wrestling match.' Besides, the repertory groups that perform bhagat or jagrâtâ have organisational structures much like that of an Indian wrestlers' *akhârâ*: with a stern, veteran guru at the helm.

These actors are not itinerant. Each *akhârâ* has resident actors. (*Akhârâ*, in this sense, also means 'repertory company.' It originally meant 'a brotherhood of wrestlers who have their own wrestling ground.' Certain religious fraternities, too, have their own *akhârâs*.)

Among the most famous bhagat groups of the 20th century was the one based in the Mohallâ Bhagatiyâñ of Arniâ (Bishnâh, Jammû). The art is passed on from guru to disciple, down the generations. However, as often happens in India (and Pâkistân), not only in folk theatre but also in classical

1. Some scholars feel that *nautañki* and *bhagat* are exactly the same.

music, gourmet cooking and miniature painting, the skill normally stays within the extended family or clan, with gurus mainly teaching their own children and nephews. The reason is—especially in the high arts—nepotism, a desire to keep the skill within the family. But equally often no one wants to learn certain arts and crafts because of the low social status attached to practising them as a career.

In the case of bhagat theatre there is some debate about whether it is necessarily a subaltern caste art. Most scholars feel that bhagat theatre started out as an act of religion. In those days people of all castes would take part. However, when it degenerated into ribaldry, it got relegated to ill-paid hereditary professionals. Vishwa Nath Khajuria writes, 'Obscenity and vulgarity became a part and parcel of [bhagat performances]. The performers of Bhagat theatre are called Bhagatvae and are from the low [sic] castes.'[iii]

Till the middle of the 20th century such performances were an essential part of wedding and *muñdan*[2] ceremonies. These two rites—which are performed on most Hiñdus only once in a lifetime each—are held on dates decreed auspicious by astrologers. To this day Kashmîrî Muslims want the best chef that they can afford to cook their daughter's wedding feast. If he has already committed himself, they postpone the wedding to suit the celebrity chef's convenience. Similarly, in Jammû, people wanted the best *bhagat* troupe that they could afford: and if it had been booked by someone else for that date, they would wait for the first auspicious date when that troupe was available.

However, all that is over now. People want glittering, modern, urban pop at their weddings—and not a group of poverty-stricken rural actors. Mohan Siñgh observes that the lack of state patronage in the democratic era after 1947, too, has led to a decline of this form.

The folk theatre of Kashmîr (*bhâñd pather*) is almost identical in many ways. It, too, delivers important political and social messages in a humorous—and, sometimes, bawdy—manner. Its practitioners, too, use the surname Bhagat. It is reasonable to infer that both belong to the same clan, except that the branch in Kashmîr has converted to Islâm.

Bhâñgrâ:[iv] The *bhâñgrâ* of the Dogrâs is quite different from its infinitely better known Punjãbî namesake. The steps, the beat (*tâl*), the music and the clothes worn are totally different. Dogrâ bhâñgrâ dancers normally carry a long bamboo stick, around seven or eight feet long, with a brightly coloured ribbon tied at the top. Some Kathuâ troupes carry bows and clubs. Punjãbî bhâñgrâ dancers never encumber their hands with anything heavier than a handkerchief. Besides, the Jammû bhâñgrâ 'is full of theatrical elements.'[v]

The clothes worn, too, are totally dissimilar. In the Punjãb the male dancers wear a long shirt and a *tehmat* (ankle-lenth, wrap-around skirt). In Jammû, writes Mohan Siñgh, 'Till 1980 the [male dancers] wore red and

---

2. Ritual shaving (tonsuring) of the head of 3-year-old male children.

yellow undershirts' and 'jâñghiâs (handmade underwear).' The Jammû dancers obviously found it embarrassing to wear jâñghiâs in co-ed company. So, since the 1980s, they, too, have been wearing tehmats. When dancing to *lohâniâñ* or *sadâñ* (see below) they wear clothes typical to the Dogrâ region—the turban, long shirt (kurtâ) and ghuttanâ.

Indeed, the two bhâñgrâs are quite unrelated to each other, except for the similarity of names and the fact that both are associated with Baisâkhî (April 13 or 14). Both use the same double-sided drum (*dhol*), but so does much of North India.

Baisâkhî is the enormously popular harvest festival of the Punjãb. Till the second half of the 20th century, it used to be huge in the plains of Jammû as well. Baisâkhî is when the new year of many Hiñdu communities begins. The rabî (winter) crop would be in the process of being harvested and the farmers would have received some of their bi-annual paycheck. (The next instalment arrives around Diwâlî, in October-November.)

Dancers (and spectators) would come from all over the Bhajowath plains of Jammû-Siâlkot to perform at (or simply watch) Baisâkhî festivity. The biggest bhâñgrâ competition was held at Airvan (Kathuâ). Winning at Airvan on Baisâkhî day was so important that rival groups sometimes came to blows with each other.

With the partition of India in 1947, the festival shed some of its sheen, because Siâlkot went over to Pâkistân, even though Airvan remained in India. Then, in 1965, Pâkistân captured Chhamb—which is another major Baisâkhî-bhâñgrâ area. The festival—and the dance identified with it—lost even more lustre. Bhâñgrâ was now confined to some tehsils such as Kathuâ, Hîrânagar and R.S. Purâ. The dance vanished from Jammû City, and got diminished in the villages.

Till, writes Mohan Siñgh, in the year 2001 'the State Government [meaning me, my second in command, M. Ashraf and the Deputy Commissioner of Jammû, Raj Goyal, helped by the hotel owners and travel trade of Jammû] organised an annual festival [the Jammû Festival, which] has become a regular feature [ever since].'

Siñgh adds, 'This festival encouraged the folk artists of Dogrâ Bhâñgrâ [to regroup themselves] and a powerful folk form came into existence once again.'

As the author of that festival, Mr Mohan Siñgh's words are extremely gratifying for me, though the motives that he has imputed (that 'insurgency' in Kashmîr 'compelled' us to create the said festival) are incorrect. Our aim (I was the Tourism Commissioner and Secretary of the state at the time and Mr Ashraf the Director-General) was altogether altruistic. We wanted to showcase Jammû's culture in order to encourage tourists visiting the shrine of Srî Mâtâ Vaishno Dévî jî to linger on in Jammû for a few extra days. The Festival has gone on to become an institution.

The Punjãbî bhâñgrâ is energetic. Its Jammû counterpart is often funny because the dancers 'mak[e] hilarious gestures with ejaculation of sudden rhythmical notes, popularly known as *boliâñ* [in Jammû as well as the Punjãb],' Dr Jerath adds.

Soft and slow songs are sung during the Jammû bhâñgrâ—normally between two fast dances. These could be pithy ballads called *lohâniâñ* or one-verse songs called *sadâñ*. Both deal with tales of love, heroism, disaster and, above all, local scandals and other interesting happenings (including tragic ones) that have taken place in that group of villages. Only a few songs prove good enough to be handed down the generations. That is why most of the songs sung during a bhâñgrâ are of recent vintage. When these songs are sung, the dancers, who had embedded themselves in the audience, come out in ones and twos and dance their way to form a circle. Spectators are encouraged to join the dancers.

The *swâñg* is a dance performed by a male cross-dresser. Typically, he puts on a red feminine *chunni* (large head-and-body scarf) and amuses the audience through facial expressions and movements of the body rather than words.

A **chhajjâ** is a float (as in a pageant). The most popular chhajjâ of Jammû looks like a peacock and is made of cardboard and coloured paper. This float would be taken through the town, especially on the afternoon of Lohri (around the 13th January). Some men would beat drums. One young man would dance with the float, while others would dance at a slight distance. Somehow this tradition, once popular in all three Dogrâ regions, started petering out in the 1980s. (I have tried to revive this tradition through the annual Jammû Festival, which is held in mid-April but without great success.)

Choukî: This is not a dance that everyone can perform. When a *chélâ* (lit.: disciple) of the Mother Goddess gets into a trance it is said that the deity has entered him. A drummer taps a beat on the *dholki* (drum). A small ensemble of musicians play their instruments and, if it is a public occasion (Dussehrâ, for example), a huge crowd gathers to watch. The *chélâ* starts swaying his body in a rhythmic manner. This is known as 'giving a *chouki*' (*chouki dénâ*) or 'filling a *chouki*' (*chouki bharnâ*).

Giddâ: This is an all-female dance of the plains. It is somewhat different from its Punjãbî namesake. Men are not prevented from watching the giddâ, but it is not a dance performed in public. Instead, it is danced at home, in the courtyard or in a hall, if the family has one. While no one needs an excuse or season to dance the giddâ, women tend to perform it at weddings on when a child is born.

The women move in a circle to the beat of the *dholki* drum, as they sing *boliâñ* (verses that rhyme). After the circle has performed one full rotation, two of the women, one from each end of an invisible axis, break away from the circle and start dancing by themselves—normally at the centre of the circle. The beat picks up, gets faster and then returns to the original pace. That is when the song being sung also returns to its refrain. The circle might then do another rotation. Even if it does not, two more dancers break away and start dancing in the centre, but differently from how the pair before them had. Once again the singing picks up—so do the steps of this duo—and then returns to the original beat and refrain. This process continues till all the women have danced in pairs.

Gitlu is the dance of the Râmnagar area. It is performed to the accompaniment of love songs.

Hirnâ: This is the dance of Lohrî (normally, 13 January), which is the peak of winter and after which date the winter starts abating. It is also the dance of Makar Sañkrâñti, which comes a day later. If there's been good news in the family in the preceding year—the birth of a boy or a wedding—that household feels obliged to host a hirnâ performance. It is danced mainly in the mountain belt. In many ways it is similar to kud, the generic dance of the said region. However, it is secular and faster paced. Besides, performers wear deer masks on their heads. Drums and cymbals provide the music.[vi]

Jagrâtâ: A jagrâtâ is an all-night wake—one spent singing mostly cheerful songs about the Mother Goddess. This tradition is called jâgran in the Hiñdî-speaking parts of India and jaggâ in some Dogrâ areas. Interestingly, in Delhi, Haryânâ and the Punjãb the Mother Goddess in question is, almost invariably, Srî Mâtâ Vaishno Dévî jî. But in the Dogrâ hills it could well be the deity's local manifestation.

Rich people organise jagrâtâs at home, if it is spacious enough—and invite friends and relatives over to participate—without looking for a reason. Others do so in the village square to celebrate a wedding, the birth of a child or a muñdan. A *sukhan* is a ritual—such as a jagrâtâ—undertaken as a thanksgiving to a deity for granting a specific prayer.

The songs are sung by a troupe of professional singers and musicians called *bhagats* (devotees). Their leader is known as the *védak.* The ensemble includes drums (the *tablâ* and/ or a *dholki* or two), a brass pitcher (used for percussion) and, normally, a harmonium.

There is no stage. The players perform on the same flat ground that the audience sits on. A large picture of the Mother Goddess is normally placed on a specially constructed platform overlooking the ground. The platform is often decorated a garish red.

The wake begins with Ganésh Bañdanâ (i.e. vañdanâ or worship of Lord Ganésh), in which the audience stands up and participates. Some of them—normally one person from each family—go up to the image of the deity and place some money or an offering in kind at its feet.

The nightlong performance consists of two halves. The first act, called *chhinjan* or *akhârâ*, starts after dinner and lasts till the stroke of midnight. This is the secular part of the ceremony. It consists of staging the legend of any one of almost two dozen local heroes. Mohan Siñgh points out that some of these heroes and heroines are Rânî Keran Mehi, Râjâ Rasâlû, Rûp Basañt, Jaimal Fattâ and Amar Siñgh Râthaur. The védak either asks the audience which story they would like to see performed, or he tells them what he plans to stage, and asks them if they have any objection. After a consensus has been built, the show begins.

Someone from the troupe then gets up and gives the audience a gist of the story in a 'dramatic manner.' He does this through energetic gestures and melodramatic speech. Thus does he try to whet their appetite for the performance. The other members join in and the story is then told in verse. While they follow a script, there is much ad libbing, depending on the mood of the audience. As is the Indian (and Pâkistânî) tradition, if the audience likes the performance people keep getting up during the show to give money to the players, who notice the money but keep performing without pausing. The money boosts their morale, for it means that they have been appreciated. This encourages them to innovate and take risks by adding new elements to the story on the spot.

The second half, the *jagrâtâ* proper, is religious. It begins with the spectacular lighting of the sacred flame at exactly twelve in the night. The show continues till sunrise. The story of the great mythical King Harîsh Chañdr, his Queen (Rânî) Târâ Mati and Rukmani is now recited with devotion, according to a set script, with no room for improvisation—or even abridgement. The worship of Mâtâ Rânî (the Mother Goddess) is woven into the story of this generous and truthful king. The audience gets charged with religious fervour and periodically interrupts the recitation with slogans in praise of the Mother Goddess.

This is the tradition in the Dogrâ hills, though jagrâtâs elsewhere in India are different.[vii]

Kud (pron. exactly like 'could') is the quintessential dance of the Dogrâ mountain belt. However, there is no standard kud. It varies from region to region. The dance is sometimes called *dhékû*. However, Dr Jerath points out that dhékû is the name of the ceremony of which the kud is but one part.

I did my fieldwork in the 1980s in Bannî valley, where the kud can be as energetic as what was then—and still is—being danced in urban discotheques. The music was as fast paced as the then popular 'new wave.' I would watch in amazement as my grossly obese Muslim *patwârî* (village revenue official) danced vigorously and remarkably deftly—alone and in groups of three or four—to totally secular songs, some of them composed by him. (He later helped me translate local folksongs.)

However, neighbouring Bhaderwâh is considered the real capital of kud. And the kud of Bhaderwâh is totally different—and is much slower and always done in groups. It is performed in honour of the snake deity (Nâg Dévatâ) or the clan deity in the campus of a temple or in an open space near the village.

The date is chosen not at random but after scanning the local Hiñdu calendar for an auspicious date. Each important temple has a fixed date on the Hiñdu calendar on which its annual kud is held. Such temples include Mântalâi, the shrine of Puddhar Dévatâ and Sañkhrî Dévatâ (Pânchairi).

After group prayers are offered to the deity—normally in the forenoon—a ram is slaughtered in a ritual sacrifice. The assembled devotees then sit down for dinner (or, sometimes, lunch), after which the designated dancers form a circle and the dancing begins. These dances are normally held at night after the monsoons are over. By then it would be autumn and quite cold in the mountains. So the dance is often performed around a biggish fire.

Even in parts of Dodâ district the songs sung during the dance are normally secular, often being love songs. Sometimes it is not a full song but just one line that is repeated again and again. At Mântalâi this refrain is *Sabâh mérî tit tariyé*, Dr Jerath writes. He adds, "The performers move two and a half steps forward and a step backward and the perimeter of the circle so formed goes on increasing with more and more dancers coming into the fold....[The music is provided by the] flute, [various types of] drums, Ransiñghâ, a sort of bugle, Manjirâ, a type of cymbal, and bells."

The dancers, all of them being men, wear the Sunday-best of the Dogrâ hills—a turban, tight pyjamas and a long (ideally, calf-length) shirt[3] that is tight till the waist and loose below it, with a cummerbund at the waist.[viii]

Phummani is a folk dance of the young men of the semi-arid *kañdî* belt. It is performed around August-September on the occasion of Guggâ Naumî, which is a religious festival celebrated the day after Janamashtamî. Dr. Jerath writes,[ix] "Phum[m]ani is related to a musical term [which, in the local language,] means rhythmical movement of the body with gestures, popularly known as mudrâs."

An arena is consecrated for Guggâ, a deity. Dancers from the neighbouring villages travel to this arena. Some of them carry the idol in a procession, normally in a palanquin. The people dance *dandaras* as they move with the palanquin. Dancers sway this way and that, like Nâg Dévatâ, the snake-deity would. An ensemble of drums, trumpets and cymbals provides the music.

The procession is taken out on the eighth day (ashtmî) of the month according to the Hiñdu calendar. Formal worship is conducted in a yagya (ancient Védic ritual around a sacred fire) on the ninth day (naumî). A *chhinj* (wrestling match) is held on the tenth day (dashmî). People from the Jogî community sing *karak* songs dedicated to the deity.[x]

After 1947 the Guggâ Naumî festival started losing its popularity. In many villages people stopped celebrating it. In 2004 the headman of Burn, a village on the road to Amb-Gharotâ, some thirteen kilometres from Jammû

---

3. The shirt often ends above the knee, because calf-length shirts are expensive and difficult to maintain.

city, persuaded the people of his village to resume Guggâ Naumî celebrations. The festivity (called *gagail*) lasts three days, during which devotees worship Râjâ Mañdlîk or Guggâ Chauhân, a folk deity who is said to have travelled through Jammû province. According to the legend he spent some time in the Kot-Bhalwâl area, which includes Burn.

Tamachrâ or **tamhacharhâ** or **jagarna:** Mohan Siñgh, who is an authority on Dogrî theatre, calls tamachra 'the operatic folk theatre of Duggar.'[xi] In fact, this all-female theatre is closer to the neighbourhood—or family—pantomime of Britain.

In most parts of India, a few days before a couple is to be married, all the close male relatives and friends of the groom form a wedding procession, normally headed by the groom. They travel to the bride's home where the couple gets married. This all-male procession then escorts the bride to her husband's home.

In traditional India—and, outside the biggest cities, all over India to this day—marriages are arranged between families that live in villages and towns quite far apart from each other. So, the men of the groom's family had to walk for several days to the bride's village and back. Even today, when railway trains and chartered buses have reduced the time, they still have to travel at least half a day each way: and are away from home for around three days. Unless, of course, it is a same-city marriage.

So, what do the womenfolk of the groom's family do while the men are away? In the Dogrâ hills the groom's mother is required to stay awake till the *lâmâ-phéré* (Hiñdu ritual vows) are over in the bride's village. The precise time of this ceremony is known weeks in advance, so even without telephones she knows when she (and the other women) can go to sleep. The other women have no ritual compulsion to be awake. However, they are concerned about the safety of their men, who run the risk of being attacked during the longish journey. (Indeed, since ancient times thieves and highwaymen are known to have descended on wedding processions on their return journey. They try to molest the bride and, more importantly, attempt to steal the jewellery and other dowry that she would be bringing with her.)

Not only women whose husbands, brothers and fathers are away, other female friends and neighbours also join in as a kind of a support group and meet at the groom's house. These women range from little girls to grandmothers. To cheer each other up—and to keep the groom's mother company during her wake—they stage a joyful 'opera.' It is an opera only to the extent that it is a play in which people sing, and not recite, their dialogues. Jag(a)rna literally means 'wake' in the British—but not Irish—sense.

The women often stay awake till the *pajéki* (a ceremony held to welcome the newlywed couple, when they return with the wedding procession). The atmosphere is jovial also because with the men away the girls all get to spend a relaxed evening together.

The women sing for the happy married life of the young couple. This aspect of the rite is called Dalassi Pair Pana and is conducted by the wife of the local barber. The elder women of the groom's family sing under the direction of the barber's wife.

One of the larger rooms of the groom's house—or the veranda—is cleared of all furniture and becomes an 'auditorium.' The women close all doors so that none of the neighbourhood boys can see what's going on inside. But it is also part of the tradition that the boys always make an attempt. They perch themselves as noiselessly as they can on the shaky branches of trees or on precarious rooftops—because all the pretty girls of the neighbourhood would be singing and dancing inside.

The performance begins after dinner and continues till sunrise.

There is no script or plot. The women make up the story as the play progress. It is all very impromptu. One or two women who can play the *dholkî*—the standard Indian two-sided drum—provide the music. The other women clap together to provide rhythm. While there might be solo passages in the songs, most of the songs are sung in unison.

These irreverent 'operas' poke fun at everyone: especially the menfolk of the groom's extended family—i.e. the men of the host's family who had left home a few hours before. The male parts are, naturally, played by women. They do not use elaborate make up to play men. Instead, Mohan Siñgh writes, some women make an instant turban out of their *chunni* (long scarf) or place the end of their plait between their nose and upper lip to signify a moustache. Or they coil their plait into a bun—a top knot—above their head to suggest a male saint. Or they put on male clothes or hats for the same effect.

In the last few decades of the twentieth century people in the bigger cities started abandoning the tradition of arranging marriages between families that live very far apart from each other. In same-city marriages the wedding procession travels in a cavalcade of cars and returns home with the bride within a few hours. Therefore, the women of the groom's family don't have to stay awake for even a single night. For that reason the Tamachra/ Jagrna tradition has almost disappeared in the cities. However, in the hills—as well as in the *kañdi* belt—it is still very popular among the Hiñdus.

Folk ballads: Art historian Lalit Gupta writes, 'Many ballads and songs which are sung by folk singers known as 'Gar-di' or 'Yogi' and 'Dares' are typical features of Jammû region.

'Dogrâ folk ballads are of two types [namely, Barâ*n* and Karkâ*n*]. 'Bar' is a corruption of [the] Hindi term 'Bir' which means brave or chivalrous. Since these ballads treat the theme of prowess and adventure, they are called 'barân' or the ballads of heroism. 'Karkân' on the other hand have a religious and spiritual character. 'Barân' are usually [more] stirring than 'Karkân' because the [former] appeals to the feeling of mystery and romance. These weave a halo of undaunted valour around the characters which grip the heart and arouse the feeling of hero worship.'

References

i Dr Ashok Jerath and Mohan Siñgh have made this point separately in their various articles cited here.

ii Siñgh, Mohan, 'Dogrâ Bhâñgrâ,' *Daily Excelsior*, 3 June, 2003.

iii Siñgh, Mohan, 'Bhagatain: The Popular folk theatre of Duggar,' *Daily Excelsior*, 17 August, 2003.

iv Siñgh, Mohan, 'Dogrâ Bhâñgrâ,' *Daily Excelsior*, 3 June, 2003, and Jerath, Dr. Ashok, 'Famous folk dances of Jammû,' *Daily Excelsior*, 20 June, 2004.

v Siñgh, Mohan, 'Dogrâ Bhâñgrâ,' *Daily Excelsior*, 3 June, 2003.

vi Jerath, Dr. Ashok, 'Famous folk dances of Jammû,' *Daily Excelsior*, 20 June, 2004.

vii Siñgh, Mohan, 'Jagrata: the epic theatre of Duggar,' *Daily Excelsior*, 29 June, 2003.

viii Jerath, Dr. Ashok, 'Famous folk dances of Jammû,' *Daily Excelsior*, 20 June, 2004, and Khajuria, Nishikant, 'Râmnagar's Gitlu, Dodâ's Kud aware people of their alive culture,' *Daily Excelsior,* 28 November, 2003.

ix Jerath, Dr. Ashok, 'Famous folk dances of Jammû,' *Daily Excelsior*, 20 June, 2004.

x '*Gagails* mark Râjâ Mañdlîk's Guggâ Naumî celebrations,' *Daily Excelsior,* 9 September, 2004.

xi Siñgh, Mohan, Tamachra: the operatic folk theatre of Duggar,' *Daily Excelsior,* 20 July, 2003. See also Jerath, Dr Ashok, 'Famous folk dances of Jammû,' *Daily Excelsior*, 20 June, 2004.

KASHMÎR

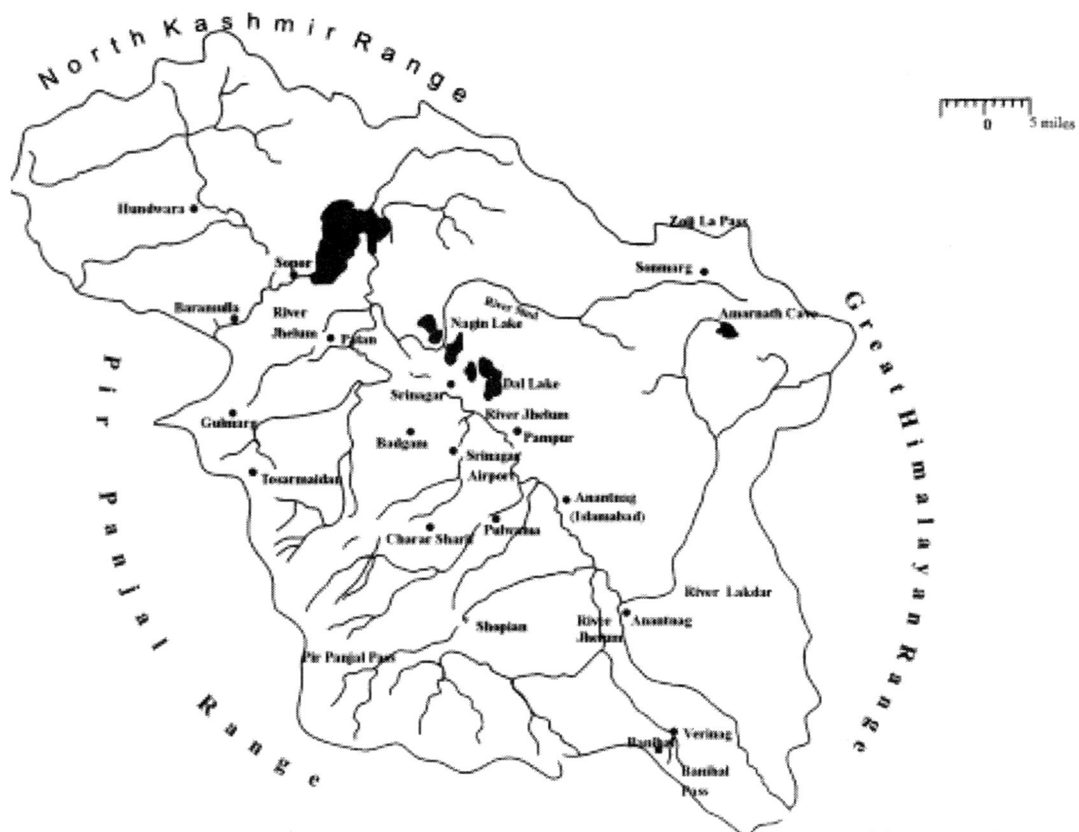

Map not to Scale

The Valley of Kashmir

14

The People of Kashmîr

Hari Singh's Jammû and Kashmîr: Population and area

Mahârâjâ Hari Singh's Jammû & Kashmîr was the largest princely State in India, ahead even of the Nizam's Hyderabad. It was two-thirds the size of the massive Bombay Presidency of British India. It was divided into the Kashmîr and Jammû provinces each headed by a Governor (now known as Divisional Commissioner). Ladâkh district was under a Wazir-e-Wazarat (now Deputy Commissioner, Collector and District Magistrate).

In 1941, the population of the State was 40,21,616 (i.e 4.02 million). 77.11% of the people were Muslim, 20.12% were Hindu, 1.64% Sikh and 1.01% Buddhist.[i]

Kashmîr was divided into four districts and Jammû into five, each under a Wazir-e-Wazarat. The districts, along with their tehsils (in brackets) and, in the case of Bârâmullâ and Reasi, niabats, were:

Kashmîr province: *Ânañtnâg* (Ânañtnâg, Kulgam, Awantiporâ and Srînagar); *Bârâmullâ* (Bârâmullâ, Srî Pratap Singh Pura and Uttar Machhi Pura. Niabats: Gurêz and Sopore); *Muzaffarâbâd* (Muzaffarâbâd, Urî and Karnah) and *Astore* (Bunji was under a revenue assistant, not a tehsildar).

Not including Ladâkh, Kashmîr had an area of 8,539 square miles (approx. 22,200 square kilometres). In 1941, its population was 17,28,686 (i.e. 1.7 million).

Jammû province: *Jammû* (Jammû, Samba and Akhnoor); *Mirpur* (Mirpur, Naushera, Bhimbar and Kotli); *Udhampur* (Udhampur, Ramban, Ramnagar, Bhaderwâh and Kishtwâr); *Reasi* (Reasi and Râjourî. Niabat: Gulabgarh) and *Kathuâ* (Kathuâ, Jasmergarh and Basohli).

Jammû had an area of 12,401 sq. miles (approx. 32,200 sq.km.). In 1941, according to Daya Sagar, its population was 20,01,557 (i.e. 2 million). Journalist-historian B.P. Sharma has a slightly different figure for the population of Jammû province. He puts it at 19,81,433. Either way, the

Muslims, with a population of 12,15,676 in 1941, were in an overwhelming, 66%, majority in Jammû province as well.

Ladâkh district: (Tehsils: Ladâkh, Kargil and Skardu.)

The area of Ladâkh, including Kargil, Skardu and the Gilgit division was 63,554 sq. miles (approx. 1,65,000 sq.km.). Its population in 1941 was 3,11,915 (or 0.3 million).

Bunji tehsil was in the Gilgit division till 1935-36. That year the lease of the trans-Indus 'ilaqa' (region or tract) was transferred to the (British) Government of India. In turn, the cis-Indus area was added to Ladâkh district. Bunji was later detached from Ladâkh district and put directly under Kashmîr province.

Jammû and Kashmîr after 1947: Population and area

Population and territory: Jammû and Kashmîr: Total Area: 2,22,236.0 sq.km (including Pâkistân Occupied Kashmîr/ POK and China Occupied Kashmîr/ COK). Of this 45.62% is actually with India. 78,114 sq. km. (35.15%) are under POK; Pak gifted 5,180 sq. km. (2.33%) to China. COK is 37,555 sq. km. (16.9%).

Population of the state, as in 2001, not including the occupied areas: 98,86,585. Decadal growth of population in the State: 1980s: 32.56%; 1990s: 24.56%. Population density: 98 per sq. km. Literacy: 53.57% (males: 64.60; females: 41.61).

Census: The last two censuses in the State were conducted in 1981 and 2001. The census scheduled for 1991 could not be held. So, the State government made some projections about what the population of the fourteen districts of the State must have been in 1991. These projections have been mentioned in the chapters about districts.

In 1981, the population of the Valley of Kashmîr was 31,34,804 (3.1 million), or 52.35% of the population of the State. Jammû province had a population of 27,18,213 (2.7 million) or 45.39% of the total. Ladâkh, which is part of Kashmîr province but not of Kashmîr Valley, accounted for the remaining 2.2%. The population of the entire state was 59,87,389 (5.9 million).

In 2001, the population of the State was 98,86,585 (9.8 million). That of Kashmîr Valley was 53,15,096 (5.3 million) and of Jammû province was 42,90,871 (4.2 million). There were 2,22,598 (0.2 million) people in Ladâkh (Leh and Kargil).

Districts as in 2004: In 1947, the State lost the following districts to Pâkistân: *Kashmîr*: Muzaffarâbâd (partly), and Astore. It also lost the Bunji tehsil. The Urî and Karnah tehsils remained with India. *Jammû:* Mirpur (partly). The erstwhile *Ladâkh district*: The Skardu tehsil and the Gilgit division.

Since July 1979, there have been the following fourteen districts in the State: Kashmîr province (which includes the Ladâkh region): Ânañtnâg, Bârâmullâ, Budgâm, Kupwârâ, Pulwâmâ and Srînagar. Kargil and Leh make up Ladâkh. Jammû province: Dodâ, Jammû, Kathuâ, Poonch, Râjourî and Udhampur.

Kashmîr Valley: The Major Linguistic Groups as in 1981

Language	Number of persons who speak it
Kashmîri	28,06,441
Dogri	2,943
Gojari	2,55,310
Ladâkhi	471
Punjâbi/Pahârhî	41,181
Lahanda (Pothwari)	21
Urdu	3,830
Balti	811
Shina (Dardi)	12,159 (Mainly in Guréz)
Tibetan	796 (A small refugee population in Srînagar)

Population and Literacy: It might seem from the following table that between 1981 and 2001, despite more than twelve years of militancy, Kashmîr did very well on the literacy front. But is this true? The answer is both 'yes' and 'no.' In absolute terms the spread of literacy was, indeed, very good. In all districts, except Srînagar, the proportion of literate people more than doubled. However, when compared with Jammû province, Ladâkh (Leh and, notably, Kargil) or the rest of India, the relative performance was not at all satisfactory.

	Popn 2001	Lit % 2001	Male %	Fem %	Lit % 1981	Growth %	Gender
Jammû & Kashmîr	**98,86,585**	**53.57**	**64.6**	**41.61**	**32.68**	**3.41**	**900**
Kupwara	6,35,354	40.27	52.76	26.83	18.82		
Baramulla	11,54,591	43.9	55.4	31.39	20.62		
Srinagar	12,11,379	58.38	67.72	48.05	33.31		
Budgam	5,24,633	38.47	49.63	26.53	17.86		
Pulwama	6,27,284	46.87	58.14	34.93	22		
Anantnag	11,61,855	43.65	54.86	31.51	23.1		
Kashmîr Valley	**53,15,096**	**47.88**	**59.29**	**35.15**		**3.68**	**907**

(Popn.= Population. Lit '01= The percentage of the total population that was literate in the year 2001. Male= the percentage of men who were literate in 2001. Fem.= the percentage of women who were literate in 2001. Lit '81= The percentage of the total population that was literate in the year 1981. Growth= the average annual per cent rate of growth of the population between 1981 and 2001. Gender= the number of women for every 1,000 men.)

Religion: The majority of the people of the State are Muslim (64.19%), followed by the Hindus (32.24%) and the Sikhs (3.47%). The 69,706 Buddhists of the State made up just over one percent of the population in 1981. The Buddhists are concentrated mainly in Leh and Kargil districts, and in a few villages (1981 population: 1,113) in the areas of Dodâ district (of the Kishtwâr sub-division, to be precise) that border Ladâkh.

Within the Valley, the 1981 census recorded that 94.96% of the people were Muslims and 3.95% were Hindus. The Sikhs, who live in certain parts of Bârâmullâ, Pulwâmâ and Srînagar districts, constituted just over one percent of the Valley. There were around 500 Christians.

In Jammû province, the Hindus were in the majority (66.32%), followed by the Muslims (29.6%) and the Sikhs (3.3%). There were around eight thousand Christians in 1981.

A similar religion-wise analysis based on the 2001 census had not been done till mid-2003. However, based on an analysis of the 1981 census and the totals of the 2001 census, some mathematical projections have been made about what the religion-wise break-up would have been in Kashmîr province (including Ladâkh) in 2001 (had the mass-migration of the Hiñdûs not taken place):

District	**Buddhists**	**Christian**	**Hiñdûs**	**Jains**	**Muslims**	**Sikhs**
Kupwârâ		32	11,300		5,45,069	2,462
Bârâmullâ	3	180	22,972	14	10,99,40	16,670
Srînagar	299	356	1,01,063	92	10,91,58	10,768
Budgâm	19	163	16,391		599,004	8,769
Pulwâmâ			17,163		658,604	11,166
Ânañtnâg		61	32,043		10,67,12	6,567
Leh	94,374	265	3,478		17,708	313
Kargil	21,865	138	2,536		87,392	255
55,46,609	**1,16,239**	**464**	**2,06,946**	**106**	**51,65,88**	**56,970**

The Muslims

Not all Kashmîri Muslims are descendants of local Hindus who had converted to Islâm, though most of them certainly are. The Syeds, for example, trace their lineage to Prophet Muhammad, peace be upon him, through his daughter Hazrat Fatima and his son-in-law Hazrat Ali. They are thus of Arab origin. The Syeds migrated to Kashmîr in substantial numbers. In 1372 and 1393 respectively, seven hundred and three hundred Syeds fled from Iran to Kashmîr. This was in addition to Syeds who migrated as individuals before and after. The migration of Turks (not just from Turkey but from other parts of Central Asia, as well) was much bigger in terms of numbers: their descendants are spread all over Kashmîr and Poonch. There are entire villages of Turks in Bârâmullâ. They speak Pahârhî, a variant of Punjâbi, at home.

Those whose ancestors had migrated from Baltistan or other Dard areas (mostly in POK) are another major presence. Several Shias have an Iranian connection: either their ancestors had migrated from Iran to Kashmîr or some of their relatives went over from Kashmîr to Iran (sometimes via central India). In Iran, the religious leader Ayatollah Khomeini was known as Khomeini Hindi (Khomeini of India) because of his ancestral links with Kashmîr and central India.

In Gutlî Bâgh near Ganderbal (Srînagar district) there is a tiny tribe of Pushtûns who still speak their ancestral language, retain several Pushtûn customs and have a leadership structure of their own. Their eyes are often green, their features distinctive.

The Muslim diaspora

Ethnic Kashmîrîs have for centuries lived in Râjourî, Poonch, Kishtwâr, parts of Udhampur (notably Reasi), several parts of Dodâ district (especially Banihâl) and even Kathuâ (in Basohli, Banni and Lohâî Malhâr). Zâñskâr has several hundred ethnic Kashmîrî Muslims who came over from Kishtwâr, rather than directly from Kashmîr. Many of the Muslims of Chambâ (HP) are ethnic Kashmîrîs. Some of the Argons of Leh had a Kashmîrî ancestor.

I have always wondered if the Kashmîrî Muslims of many of these regions went over as Muslims: or went there as Hiñdûs and later converted to Islâm. In the case of Kishtwâr, Râjourî and Poonch one can say with certainty that a Kashmîrî diaspora existed in these regions well before the advent of Islâm.

The manufacture of shâwls (and famines) took Kashmîrî Muslims to several parts of Jammû and the Punjâb, notably Amritsar (from which they have since migrated, perhaps to Pâkistân) and Lahore (where they still live in big numbers). By 'ethnic Kashmîrî' I mean someone whose ancestors spoke the Kashmîrî language at home. Thus the people of Mîrpur (POK) don't count: even though internationally they are the most vocal 'Kashmîrîs.' Nor do the people of the 'Northern Areas' of POK. Mîrpurîs and the people of NA are from J&K, but are not ethnic Kashmîrîs.

Trade in shâwls made the Kashmîrîs go as far as Lucknow and Calcutta (Kolkata). However, I believe that the tiny Kashmîrî community of Bihar has to do with the Kashmîrî King Yusuf Shah Chak's 16th century exile there, and not shâwls. And the elite Kashmîrî Shia diaspora that stretches from Lucknow to parts of present-day Pâkistân to Qom in Iran, I suspect, has to do with the mobility (and matrimonial links) that any educated elite has across regions and nation-states.

Bombay, too, has always had a small Kashmîrî Muslim community. Nawab Ahsanullah Khân of Dhaka (formerly Dacca) was an eighteenth century noble of Kashmîri origin. Since the early nineteenth century there has been a Kashmîrî (Hiñdû as well as Muslim) population in Kâbul.

After 1947 (especially after 1990), a substantial Kashmîrî Muslim community has come up in Delhi. More than half of them either trade in apples and mutton, or manufacture carpets. However, almost as many of them are professionals.

Before 1947, the Muslims of Lahore would derisively call the Kashmîrîs 'hatows.' During the preceding century or two, well-to-do Muslims from the Punjâb, Jammû, Uttar Pradesh and some other parts of South Asia had started treating the Kashmîrîs as social inferiors and would avoid matrimonial alliances with them.[1] This humiliation is one of the main reasons why the Kashmîrîs, led by Sheikh Muhammad Abdullah, preferred India over Pâkistân in 1947.

When Pâkistân-inspired militancy started in 1989, as if on cue the Urdu newspapers of Kashmîr started receiving letters from Pâkistân, asking to be forgiven for having used the pejorative expression 'hatow.'

How things have changed since 1947. Today if a person has even a drop of Kashmîrî blood in his veins he proclaims it proudly. From novelist Salman Rushdie to writer M.J. Akbar and actress-fashion model Katrina Kaif, people everywhere are celebrating their Kashmîrî roots.

---

1. It wasn't always so. In the 15th and 16th centuries Kashmîrî royalty routinely intermarried with other South Asian royal families of that era: especially those of Delhi and Kabul. King Shahâbuddîn of Kashmîr and Sultân Ahmed Khân of Kabul married each other's sisters. Ahmed's daughter married Shahâbuddîn's brother, Qutbuddîn. Shahâbuddîn's daughter married the son of Feroz Shâh, king of Delhi (and much of India). Feroz Shâh, in turn, gave three of his daughters in marriage to Shahâbuddîn's family. (-From *Târîkh-e-Kashmîr* by Syed Ali, sixteenth century A.D.)

   I suspect that the snobbishness of the Muslim elites of North India towards Kashmîrî Muslims was limited to the period during which the Valley had lost its political independence.

   Part of the reason must have also been that the North Indian Muslim elite was mainly of ethnic Sheikh (Arab), Mughal and Pushtûn stock. They saw locally converted Muslims as an underclass (*the ajlâf*). They would mostly marry people of their own ethnic groups. On the other hand the population of these three elite groups in Kashmîr is extremely minuscule. The Kashmîrî Muslim elite consisted mainly of local converts.

And in the matrimonial market, middle-class as well as elite Muslims from all over India are quite happy if their daughters get married to Kashmîrî Muslim men from similar backgrounds. (Working class Kashmîrî men married similarly placed Bangladeshi women in large numbers in the last few decades of the 20th century.) Kashmîr's enormous economic prosperity since 1947 is an important reason. Another factor is that other Indian Muslims feel that because the Muslims are in a majority in Kashmîr, they do not have to live in fear of riots and discriminatory treatment by organised groups.

The Hâñjîs

The Hâñjîs are a very poor, mostly illiterate, people who live in boats on the lakes and, sometimes, rivers of Kashmîr. Tourism has brought some prosperity to some Hâñjîs living in Srînagar, though.

Origin: Theory i): The Hâñjîs claim to be the descendants of Noah, who is one of the prophets of Islâm. (His Hiñdû incarnation, Manû, has an even higher, if controversial, status among the Hiñdûs. He is the one who codified the Hiñdû law.)

Theory ii): Raja Parbat (or Pratap) Sen brought boatmen over from Sangaldip (perhaps Srî Lanka). This theory is the one most widely accepted.

Theory iii): The Hâñjîs believe that they are of Kshatriya (warrior/ ruler) stock. Lawrence said that they were of the Vaisya (business) caste. However, traditionally they have been at the very bottom of the hierarchy. In anger they often call their fellow Hâñjîs by the Kashmîrî word for the so-called 'untouchable' people.

Theory iv): Some Hâñjîs claim to be of gypsy stock.

Sub-divisions: Based on their profession and lifestyle, Hanjis can be classified into nine sub-groups. These, in the descending order of their internal hierarchy, are (i) Demb-Hanz (those who grow vegetables on the Dal Lake), (ii) Gəri-Hanz (those who gather siñghârâs/ water-nuts on the Wular Lake), (iii) Bahatchi-Hanz (those who live in bahatch and war boats), (iv) Dûñgâ-Hanz (those who own dûñgâ passenger boats); this group has its own hierarchy, depending on the location of the Dûñgâ, (v) Gad-Hanz (fishermen) and (vi) Haka-Hanz (those who collect wood from water bodies).

The other three sub-castes, but not in any particular order, are the Shikârâ-Hanz (those who ply shikârâ boats), Mata-Hanz (those who deal in wood) and Houseboat Hanz (a very well-to-do lot).

In which parts of the state do they live? On the Dal Lake (the elite), the Wular (the next in rank), the Ânchâr, the Tsont-i-Kol (between Dal Gate and the old golf course of Srînagar) and on the banks of the Jehlum. Before the Nallah Mâr canal of Srînagar was disastrously turned into a road, choking up a historical outlet for the excess water of Srînagar City, the 'lowest' sub-caste of the Dûñgâ-Hanz used to live there.

Majid Hussain, who estimates that around 12% of the Hâñjîs are literate, points out that they also live on the Jehlum: between Khanâbal (near Ânañtnâg town) and Chattâbal (Srînagar city).

Gujjars and Bakerwâls

The Gujjars and Bakerwâls (pron. 'bucker-wâl') make up around 18% of the population of the State. Almost all Bakerwâls and many Gujjars are nomads. The Gujjars (go= cow) tend cattle (mainly buffaloes) and the Bakerwâls (bakrî= goat) herd sheep. A very large section of Gujjars have permanent homes and are not nomads. They are part of an all-India community that is mostly Hiñdû. However, in Jammû and Kashmîr and the neighbouring areas of Pâkistân and occupied Kashmîr (and, to an extent, in Himachal Pradesh, Uttarakhand and north Punjâb) all Gujjars and Bakerwâls are Muslims.

Origin: Theory i): Some Gujjars believe that their ancestors came from Georgia (which, they believe, was once called Gurjia or Gurjaristân), a Central Asian republic formerly in the Soviet Union. These cowherds are supposed to have migrated from Georgia to India through Iraq, Iran, Afghânistân and Baluchistan, before settling in Gujrât (a district in Pâkistân's Punjâb province).

Theory ii): Cunningham, a British Raj scholar, wrote that the Gujjars' ancestors were the Kushan and Yachi tribes of the Eastern Tartar community (also of the erstwhile Soviet Union). The Tartars are a Turkic people.

Theory iii): The Muslim Gujjars' Hiñdû cousins still live in Râjasthân and Gujarât, especially in Kâthiâwâd. They speak the same Râjasthâni language and look similar. Therefore, the Himâlayan Gujjars could well have migrated from these parts of western India to the Himâlayas, perhaps in the 6th and 7th centuries AD.

In which parts of the state do the Gujjars live? In all districts of the State, except Leh. The nomads among them spend almost exactly six months each in the plains and on mountain pastures. The winter home in the plains is in Jammû or Kathuâ (or Pathânkot/ Gurdâspur in neighbouring Punjâb). The summer home in the mountains could be in Jammû province (Dodâ or Udhampur) or Kashmîr (Urî, Ganderbal, Ânañtnâg, Daksum, Wâñgat/ Kangan, above Dâchîgâm or in one of several pastures in the other districts) or even Kargil/ Zâñskâr. Gujjars also live in big numbers in Râjourî and Poonch.

Physical appearance: The nomadic Dodhi ('milk') Gujjars and Bakerwâls are normally tall and well-built. They live long, walk tall and erect and suffer from few ailments. The men are around six feet tall, extremely muscular and have long beards (dyed red with henna when they start greying). They all wear turbans and the shalwâr-qameez. The women wear colourful clothes and jewellery that are not very different from those worn by tribals in Râjasthân and Gujarât.

However, Gujjars who have given up their nomadic life and have settled down are neither tall nor muscular nor even disease-free. They walk with the same slouch as the rest of us and have a similar life-expectancy.

Annual migration: Every mid-April the nomadic Gujjars and Bakerwâls migrate from the plains of Jammû to the mountains. They return in October. Each journey takes around two weeks, because it is done on foot, and they take their flock (and horses) along. Increasingly the Gujjar elite has taken to doing the journey by jeep or truck, leaving it to their servants to trek up (or down) with the flock.

The summerhouses of the nomads are very simple mud and dried-grass structures called '*kothâs*' and '*bandîs*'.

Politics: The Muslim Gujjars of the State are quite close to their Hiñdû brethren in central and western India. The better-off ones meet each other frequently. In every war with Pâkistân they have helped the Indian Army enormously. In 1965, it was a Muslim Gujjar, Lâl Dîn, who alerted the Indian Army to the fact that Pâkistânî infiltrators had entered India. He was awarded a *Padma Shri*, a high national award, for this. In 1999, some Bakerwâls in Kargil told the Indian Army that Pâkistânî forces had captured the unguarded mountain peaks of that district.

The Gujjars and Bakerwâls, like most other rural Muslims of the state (and parts of Pâkistân), follow their own customary law, and not the Muslim Personal Law (shariat). They keep their disputes out of the courts. A committee of their elders settles all their disputes. The Gujjars have a high sense of ethics and propriety. Therefore, they have relatively few disputes in any case.

The Dard-Shîn People of Guréz

The Dard-Shîn community of Jammû and Kashmîr[ii] lives in Kargil (Ladâkh) and Guréz. It is an ancient community that once had a major presence in the areas between (and including) north-eastern Afghânistân and central Tibet. The theory is that the Dardic Aryans came to (undivided) India, established settlements in the Pâmîr region and then branched out to Chitral and Gilgit. The ancient Greeks and Romans knew about, and were in touch with, this handsome Indo-Aryan community.

Early references: Herodotus mentioned this community. Pliny and Ptolemy wrote that the Dards lived in the mountains on the eastern border of River Indus. This is the region corresponding to present (undivided) Ladâkh and Kashmîr. Sir Aurel Stein, the 19th century British scholar, wrote, "The Daradas [mentioned in *The Râjâtarañginî*] are the modern Dards... Their seats, which do not seem to have changed since the time of Herodotus, extend from Chitrâl and Yâsîn [both in POK], across the Indus regions of Gilgit, Chilas, and Bunji [also in POK] to the Kishengangâ Valley in the immediate north of Kashmîr. The tribes inhabiting the latter valley [Kishengangâ] are meant in most of the passages in which the chronicle [*The Râjâtarañginî*] mentions the Daradas or Darads."

The Dardistân region is mostly in the Northern Areas of POK and partly in India (Guréz, Tilail and Drass). The Dâ-Hânu region of Ladâkh has a sizeable Dard population but is not a part of this 'belt.'

The people: There is near-unanimity among anthropologists that the Dards are Aryans. Indeed, some Aryan 'nationalists' from Germany have been celebrating the unadulterated Aryanness of the Dards of Dâ-Hânu in Ladâkh. This fascination among some Germans for the Dards probably has its origin in Leitner's writings, in which he had certified the Dards' Aryanness.

They have a caste-system very similar to that of the Hiñdûs. The castes, in the traditional order of hierarchy, are: (i) Ronu or Renue (ruling class), (ii) Shins (religious sect), (iii) Yashkun (cultivators), and (iv) Dum (menial class). Incidentally, the caste name Dum is also found among the Muslims of the plains of Kashmîr and among Hiñdûs of, Jammû, again at the same place in the hierarchy.

The Dards of Guréz are entirely Muslim. In Kargil many Dards retain their old faith, some have been influenced by Buddhism and many have converted to Islâm.

Language: The Dard-Shîn people speak Shînâ, a language that is rapidly heading towards extinction. The Dards have taken to Urdû both in the Indian State of Jammû and Kashmîr and in POK. People in Chilas and Gilgit have switched to Urdu in a bigger way because their area is not as inaccessible from the plains of Pâkistân as the Guréz Valley (see 'Bârâmullâ') is from the rest of India. This language and the related culture are somewhat better maintained in Guréz, and flourish best in Kargil (Ladâkh).

Shîna is much like Hindi-Urdu and, sometimes, English. ('Two' is 'du' and 'three' is 'tera/ tre.') Their language is very Indo-Aryan. Actually, it is eerily close to Sañskrit. For instance, they call the sun 'suri' (from the Sañskrit 'surya'). Their word for 'hand' is 'hath.' The 'tongue' is called 'jeeb'.

Politics: The people of Guréz have consistently been nationalists. They have excellent relations with the Indian Army and have stayed away from the militancy of the 1990s. In all elections to the national Parliament and the State legislative assembly, especially those held after 1989, the people of Guréz-Tilel have turned up to vote in huge numbers. (As have the people of Tangdâr, Urî, Budgâm's Tsrâr-i-Sharief and Srînagar's Kangan.)

During the 2002 elections I discovered why. Around 11 in the morning I was accosted by an angry youth near Dâwar (the ancient capital of the Dards). He complained that the officers at the polling booth were clearing the long queue of voters at a very slow pace. At that rate all the adults of the village would not be able to vote by 4pm, when voting would come to an end.

Mathematically speaking he was absolutely right. But where in the world did one hundred per cent of the adults turn up to vote, I argued. In any case, I explained that all voters who entered the compound outside the booth before 4pm were entitled to vote, even if it meant keeping the booth open till seven in the evening.

In the event, voting continued in most parts of Gurêz till slightly after eight that night. Every single adult who was present in that village (and many other parts of Gurêz) and was not seriously ill came to vote.

Apparently, the community elders had ordered all Gurêzîs working, studying or otherwise living in Srînagar, Jammû, Bârâmullâ town or even Delhi to return to Gurêz to cast their vote. Surely this makes the populace of remote and, often inaccessible, Gurêz one of the most democracy-conscious people in the world.

Ethnic groups: The Dard-Shîns are the oldest inhabitants of Gurêz. The Chak royal family, which ruled Kashmîr in the 16th century and had influenced Kashmîr's politics in the two preceding centuries, was of Dard stock. A hillock in Gurêz is named after this clan and a spring after Habbâ Khâtoon, a poet who married a Chak king.

There is also a small community of Kashmîrîs in Dâwar and Bagtor. And then there is a clan that was, till the 1950s, called Thag (the same as the Hiñdî-Urdû 'thug'). They are somewhat darker skinned than the Dards and Kashmîrîs and are believed to have come from the plains of central India. They settled in Gurêz and Kishtwâr (Dodâ, Jammû), perhaps to escape the anti-thuggee campaign of Lord William Bentinck (1738-1809). They converted to Islâm and borrowed the surname Lone from their Kashmîrî neighbours. (See also the chapter on 'Bârâmullâ.')

The Kashmîrî Pandits

In 1981, there were 1,24,078 Hindus in the Valley, or just under four percent of the population. Of these, around five to ten thousand Hiñdûs would have been the Punjâbis and Bhaderwâhîs living in Srînagar City and Baramulla and the handful of Dogrâ Rajpûts settled in the rural areas. The rest were all Kashmîrî Pandits, a tiny, talented community of Brâhmins.

By way of comparison, writing in the 1890s, Lawrence recorded that there were 52,576 Hiñdûs in Kashmîr. Of them, 28,695 lived in Srînagar and the small towns. Another 23,881 Hiñdûs lived in the rural areas.

By 1931, their population had grown to 64, 809 in all of Kashmîr (in a population of 13.31 lakh/ 1.33 million, or 4.86% of the total).

However, those are not all the Kashmîrî Pandits that there are. Over the centuries an equally substantial Kashmîri Pandit community has grown outside the State in Delhi, Allahabad, Lucknow, the Punjâb, Himachal Pradesh and even Madhya Pradesh. They do not speak Kashmîri any more but retain their customs and till the 1950s would almost invariably marry within the community. (Most still do.) The Pandits who continue to live in Kashmîr call their cousins (who migrated to the rest of India before the twentieth century) 'Butt Punjayb.' ('Butt' and 'pun' pronounced as in English).

Within the State, there have for centuries been a few thousand Kashmîrî Pandits in Kishtwâr, plus a few families in Poonch-Râjourî. Since 1947, another few thousand have settled elsewhere in Jammû province, mainly in Jammû City.

Migration has been a recurrent theme in the history of this mostly light skinned community. Quite a few people from Mangalore (Karnataka), most of them equally fair skinned and with surnames like Rai and Rao, say that their ancestors were Kashmîrî Pandits who had migrated from Kashmîr around the 9th century AD. So do several Saraswat Brâhmins of Mahârâshtra and Goa.

Today the Kashmîrî Pandits of the State celebrate their main festival, *Shivarâtrî*, on two different days, according to whether or not their ancestors had migrated from Kashmîr during the reign of Sultan Sikander, the so-called idol breaker (1389-1413). The Pandits believe that all but eleven families of Kashmîri Pandits fled the Valley to the plains during this period. The descendants of these eleven families form a tiny minority called Malamâs. They celebrate *Shivarâtrî* according to Kashmîr's own, lunar calendar.

(The route that the fleeing Kashmîrî Pandits, locally known as the Butts, took while leaving the Valley corresponds to what is now known as the National Highway between Srînagar and Jammû. There is a place on the highway called Batote, or butt-vat: 'the path that the Butts took.')

Shortly after Sikander came the great Emperor Zain-ul-Abedin. He persuaded the Kashmîrî Pandits who had fled to return to Kashmîr. The descendants of this group, which constitutes the majority, are called Bânamâs. Having lived in mainland India, they had taken to celebrating *Shivarâtrî* along with other Hindus, and do so to this day. (The words Malamâs and Bânamâs mean 'lunar calendar' and 'solar calendar' respectively.)

All Kashmîrî Pandits are Shaivites, worshippers of Lord Shiva. However, their main temple is the Râm Hanumân inspired Khîr Bhawânî at Tulınulâ near Srînagar. The Shankarâchârya, the Shiva temple that towers over all of Srînagar, is frequented more by Dogrâ Hindus and tourists.

The Afghân rulers of Kashmîr (1752-1819) patronised this highly educated community, appointing them to high office not only in Kashmîr but taking them along to Kabul and giving them even higher positions (including Prime Minister) there. (To get an idea of the depth of Afghân-KP amity, see also 'Surnames and nicknames' in this chapter.) This was the first major State patronage that they received after Sultan Zain-ul-Abedin (1420-70).

The Sikhs and the Dogrâs succeeded the Afghâns. Because of their high literacy the Kashmîrî Pandits continued to man the middle and lower bureaucracy, a few families rising to the top. In the twentieth century many of them became lawyers, doctors, journalists, scientists, playwrights, artists and teachers. Their skills were in demand in the Mughal bureaucracy, too. The Nehrus, who were the '*kotwals*' (police chief) of Delhi under the later Mughals (nineteenth century), are the best known example. After the accession of the State to India in October 1947, some Pandits also took to commerce: an upmarket grocer's here, a pharmacy there and the occasional luxury hotel. At the time of their migration in 1990, just under 19,000 Kashmîrî Pandits (or almost every sixth Pandit) were government servants.

Because of the unfortunate events of 1990, more than ninety percent of the community left Kashmîr between January and April, hoping to return as soon as things settled down. Militancy, however, continued in a big way for more than a decade. During this period the Kashmîrî Pandits set up house mostly in Jammû City but also in Udhampur, Delhi, Mumbai and the USA, doing very well in the professions, even commerce.

The name that the community goes by is somewhat misleading. Very few Kashmîrî Pandits are priests. Mrs. Jaijaiwanti Parimu, a writer and educationist whom I consulted for several details used in this section, estimates that only around a seventh of the members of her community actually performed religious duties at any stage of history. This sub-group is called Bâchh Bhatt and has surnames like Zadoo, Ganzoo (not Ganju), Kharoo, Sharma and Dutt.

The majority of Kashmîri Pandits are Kârkuns: professionals and civil servants. In the second half of the twentieth century, even among those whose ancestors were priests very few had any connection with their ancestral function any more. (This is true of the Brâhmins of many other parts of India as well. It is impossible to find Jammû Brâhmins who are willing to act as full-time priests at any of the hundreds of temples lying unmanned in Jammû.)

The Kârkuns consider themselves socially superior to the priestly clan. Traditionally the two did not inter-marry. The division between the Kârkuns (government servants) and the Bâchh Bhatts (priestly class) took place during the reign of Sultan Zain-ul-Abedin aka Budshah (1420-1470). The Sultan had employed several Kashmîrî Pandits in his government. It is believed that it was this State patronage that led to the formation of two clans within the community. Budshah's time must have been one of enormous ferment and reorganisation in this community: it was also then that the Malamâs-Bânamâs division took place.

(Historian GMD. Sufi adds, 'A third section is the Jotish or astrologer class which intermarry (sic) with the Kârkun.')

However, none of these sub-groups deigns to marry members of the Bohri sub-group. 'They eat and live differently,' I was told. This group is supposed to have converted briefly ('for one night') to Islâm before coming back to the Hindu fold. Now, mere conversion does not change food habits and other customs, and certainly not immediately. I once came upon a reference to a clan of Vohras (Punjâbi Khatris: who belong to the business caste) who had migrated to Kashmîr in late mediæval times and got absorbed in the Kashmîri Pandit community. My theory is that the Bohris are descendants of those Vohras.

So, can non-Brâhmins become Brâhmins? Studies conducted by the Anthropological Survey of India, under the scholar-civil servant Singh, indicate that caste was not as rigid as the British Raj would have us believe. While studying mediæval Kashmîr, I noticed that (Muslim) Rainâs had descended from the Rajpût warrior caste. Some (Hindu) Kashmîrî Pandits have the same surname. Clearly, a handful of Rainâs remained Hindu even after the majority of their clan had converted to Islâm. These Rainâs, who probably numbered one or two hundred, were too few to maintain an independent identity. For one, Hindus can't marry within their own clan, so you need other clans to marry into. So, these Rainâs probably merged with the Pandits, who weren't too numerous either.

Kashmîri Pandit elders don't reject my theory outright. I am told that there are Kârkun Rainâs, priestly Rainâs as well Rainâs whose ancestors were Rajpûts. (Some Rainas of Jammû-Himachal are carpenters.) The Vohrâs (or Bohrâs or Bohrîs) might likewise have latched on, without having been accepted fully.

At the bottom of the Kashmîri Pandit ladder have traditionally been the cooks and chefs: the '*wâzâs*' and '*kânders*', mostly from the Deosar area. Today, even this group is too literate to cook for others, and has entered the professions. So, now the Kashmîrî Pandits get their '*wazas*' and '*kanders*' from Kishtwâr.

The mass-migration of the Kashmîrî Pandits in 1990 has blurred a lot of intra-caste distinctions, though. This includes distinctions between the Bohrîs and the Pañdâs, the kânders and the wâzas.)

(The kânders are mostly nânwâîs [rural bakers]. The Hiñdû wâzâ or wâz came from Luk Bhawânî and Ânañtnâg. The Pañdâs are almost entirely from Mattan.)

Surnames and nicknames

So deep-rooted was the Kashmîrî Pandits' friendship with the Afghâns and their identification with Afghân culture that they adopted Persian/ Afghân surnames such as Adeeb (literateur), Râzdân and Bakâyâ and Safâyâ (both connected with the treasury). They also adopted Central Asian, and thitherto Muslim, titles such as Bakhshi and Chaudhari. (The last two titles were bestowed on Hindus, Muslims, Sikhs and even Christians throughout the sub-continent.) Durranis are Afghâns and Mirzas are Turks: but the Kashmîrî Pandits were given these two surnames, too. More interestingly, they took on names apparently connected with the Islâmic religion: Qazi (Islâmic judge) and even Mulla (Muslim priest). Above all, you will find Agas among

Kashmîrî Pandits. (An Aga is a Muslim spiritual-cum-temporal leader, headman, and aristocrat, normally a Shia from Iran.)

Sometimes you can tell about a Muslim's ancestry by his surname. All genuine Syeds, of course, are descendants of the Holy Prophet Muhammad, peace be upon him, and thus of Arab origin. Meers, Mirzas and Bandeys are supposed to be Turks but, as we have seen, this isn't always the case. In most of South Asia a Khân is supposed to be a Pathan (Pushtûn), but in Kashmîr and Kargil it's a title given to countless others. Some of the rural Turks that I have lived with go by the name Khân.

Muslims with surnames like Pandit, Bhat/ Butt, Wânchoo, Wâni, Khândey and Ganâi are descendants of local converts.

There is a huge tradition of nicknames in Kashmîr: among both the Muslims and the Pandits. I have a colleague called Abdul Ahad who at one stage was obsessed with the teaching of history. So, he was nicknamed Ahad 'History'. Another colleague's father owns Victory Carpets. So, the common man knows her as Tanveer 'Victory'. Those who lived by the canal (neher) were reportedly given the name Nehru and those by a bridge (kadal) Kadlabju. Parimu means 'the foreigner,' perhaps referring to some ancestor who had come from or gone abroad. (It is this name that suggests that some foreigners, possibly Jews, were absorbed into the Kashmîri fold well before the advent of Islâm. There is a neighbourhood called Pârimpurâ, 'the township of the foreigners'.)

Normally, however, there's a tinge of sarcasm, even malice, in these names. A professor who went on to earn a name as a principled politician was nicknamed 'Siyasi' (the political one) during his years as a teacher, because even then he dabbled a lot in politics.

Over the centuries these nicknames (called rehtchh or simply rets) have hardened into surnames. Mushran means 'ugly like a fierce demon'. Mothers warn their children that if they don't behave a 'mushran' will gobble them up. Briefly, around 1990, Bombay had a film actor whose ancestors had been saddled with this surname. The literateur Chakbast had ancestors who ate sour rice (tsok= sour). Khar (including Kher, as in the film actor) means donkey. Hâk(t)sar is a worm that feeds on the hâk variety of spinach. Thâl(t)soor is a person who steals utensils (thâli), and this is the name of a ranking family.

Char people and sweepers, unfortunately, had been assigned an extremely low position in Hindu society in particular, and in South Asia in general. In Kashmîr they are known as wattals. An eminent Kashmîri Pandit family once gave refuge to some wattals. As a result the host family and its descendants have the surname Wattal.

Most illustrative of this phenomenon is the family now called Taing. A mulberry tree (tul) grew in their backyard. Out of fear that they would be, teasingly, nicknamed Tul, they got the tree uprooted. This resulted in a pit (khoda) where the tree used to be. So, they were promptly nicknamed Khodâ. This bothered them and they brought some earth to fill up the pit with. However, they got more earth than was required and a small mound (taing) of earth was created where the pit was. Not to be outdone, their detractors decided to call them Taing.

References

i. Most of the figures in these paragraphs are from Geo-administrative order of Mahârâjâ's J&K by Daya Sagar, *The Daily Excelsior*, Jammû, February 11, 2001. Administrative units and figures regarding area have been shown as they stood on the 14th August, 1947.

ii. Sources include Majid Hussain's website and the photocopy of an anonymous case study 'Gathering history from the ground: a case study of Guréz and Tilail.' The language used in the two is sometimes identical.

15

Were the Kashmîrîs Jews?

There is a whole body of scholarship that seeks to prove that the Kashmîris (including the Pandits) are one of the lost tribes of Israel. Some of the arguments in favour are fairly convincing and are based on similarities of language, customs and facial features.

While touring a Kashmîri village with Mridu Rai, then a University of Columbia-based scholar and now with Yale, we came upon a circular Kashmîri bread (the tsacheroo) which looks and tastes exactly like the Jewish bagel. Thus, clearly there was considerable cultural exchange between Kashmîr and ancient Israel and possibly the migration of a few Hebrews to Kashmîr.

However, there is no historical evidence of a major migration from Israel. Besides, some of the 'evidence' given in support of the theory is childish.

For example, when the Kashmîris address a person with respect they call him 'joo.' This, we are told, is the same word as 'Jew.' Therefore, the Kashmîris are Jews! Firstly, ancient Jews would hardly call each other 'Jew'. Yahood, and its derivatives, would be more common. Secondly, in Ladâkhi 'joo' means the same as in Kashmîri. So, does that mean that the mostly Caucasoid Kashmîris are descended from the Mongoloid Ladâkhis? Or that the Mongoloid Ladâkhis too were Jews? Preposterous. The fact is that 'joo' is a cousin of the Central Indian 'ji' and is used in exactly the same way, in both Kashmîr and Ladâkh.

Besides, there is absolutely no trace of the Jewish religion anywhere in Kashmîr.

Not homogeneous

In any case, the people of the valley of Kashmîr do not belong to one, homogeneous ethnic group.

Only a small minority of Kashmîrîs has those 'Jewish' facial features, especially noses. Only around one half of all Kashmîris are even light skinned.

The other half, especially the poor and those in the villages, are born with the same complexion as that of most central and South Indians/ Pâkistânis and with similar features, too.

A very large section of the population of the State, in Kashmîr, Jammû and Kargil, consists of the nomadic (and 'settled' or zameendar) Gujjars (cowherds) and Bakerwâls (shepherds). Some Gujjars trace their ancestry to Indian states like Gujarât and Râjasthân. Others claim that their ancestors came from the former Soviet republic of Georgia (which, they say, is an abbreviation of 'Gurjaristan').

An equally big community is that of the Pahârhîs. They, too, are Muslims, but they speak a language similar to Punjâbi. Then there are Kashmîris of Dard origin.

The Syeds of Kashmîr are all of central Asian (Irani) or Arab (mainly Iraqi) origin. Then there is a substantial Turkish population. Not all Kashmîris with the surname 'Khân' are of Pathan (Pushtoon) stock. 'Khân' has been a local, Kashmîri title since mediæval times. All the same, there is in Kashmîr a small community of Pushtoon origin.

Some Kashmîris use the surname 'Mughal'. It stands to reason that almost two hundred years of Mughal rule would have left at least a small Mughal clan behind. Surely, Mirza Haidar Dughlat, the first 'Mughal' to rule Kashmîr, would have started a small Kazakh line, too. After all, he came to Kashmîr with an army.

There is also a small clan of Tibetan Muslims in Kashmîr.

Historians from neighbouring Kargil claim that people from their district first populated the Valley. And, as everyone knows, the first king of Kashmîr to convert to Islâm was Rinchen Shah, a Ladâkhi prince of Tibetan origin.

Many of the Shias of Kashmîr produce family trees going back to Iran and Iraq.

Origins of the belief

There is no reference to the Kashmîris, or even some of them, having migrated from Israel (or anywhere other than the Indian plains) in any of Kashmîr's several splendid histories. The *Râjâtarañginî* and its sequels don't mention it. The anonymous *Baharistan-e-Shahi* (16th and 17th centuries) doesn't either. Nor do the mediæval historians Syed Ali or Bîrbal Kâchrû.

So, this belief essentially originated in the late 19th century. British Râj scholars, some of who were past-masters at spreading divisive tendencies, noted that several Kashmîris had Jewish faces and hooked noses of the Hebraic type.

The theory is that when King Nebuchadnezzar started murdering Jews in Palestine, most of them fled to safer lands. Kashmîr was one of them.

The belief started taking root in the 20th century. That was when some Kashmîri scholars, Pandit and Muslim alike, were trying to assert an identity that had nothing to do with the rest of India (or Pâkistân). Muslim scholars from places as far apart as Lahore (Pâkistân) and Bijnore (UP) fuelled the belief. The majority of Kashmîris have obviously descended from Hindus who had converted to Islâm. Therefore, it became necessary to prove that Kashmîr's original Hindu population was itself of Jewish origin.

Pandit Hargopal Kaul was one of the first Kashmîris to do so. His *Târîkh-e-Guldastâ-e-Kashmîr* refers to the oldest mention of migration to Kashmîr. This is contained in the memoirs of a man who had never visited Kashmîr: the Mughal Emperor Bâbur. All Babur did was to speculate that the word 'Kashmîr' might have derived from '*Kash*', a tribe from the hills, which had migrated through the Sind pass. Even he did not talk of Jewish origins or lost tribes of Israel.

The only other mediæval reference to this belief is by Dr. Francois Bernier (1620-1688) who noted that 'the inhabitants in the frontier villages struck me as resembling Jews'. So, till the 19th century all we have are stray mentions in the accounts of foreigners that some Kashmîris resembled the Jews. Nothing in Kashmîr's own formidable historiography. Certainly nothing about migration from Israel.

The arguments for and against

Historical references

For: Al Beruni, the noted historian (A.D. 973-1048), travelled to places close to Kashmîr, perhaps up to Râjourî. Aziz Kashmîri, the author of some excellent books on the subject, quotes him as saying of the Kashmîris, 'They are particularly anxious about the natural strength of their country and, therefore, take always much care to keep a strong hold upon the entrances and roads leading into it… In former times, they used to allow one or two foreigners to enter their country, particularly the Jews. But at present do not allow any Hindu whom they do not know personally to enter much less other people.'

This explains the numerous imprints of Jewish culture on Kashmîr: on the Kashmîri language and on the beliefs of the Kashmîri people. It also indicates how the bagel might have come to Kashmîr.

Mathew feels that 'the white Huns (Naphtalites, [were] one of the lost tribes of Israel).' This dynasty ruled Kashmîr from c.A.D. 528 to around A.D. 600. Its members were custodians of the sun temple at Mârtañd.[1] They had certainly come from a country in the west, possibly Afghânistân. Thus, the white Huns could well have been Jewish. From the histories it would seem that just a handful of them — not more than a few dozen — had sought refuge in Kashmîr. So, even if they were Jewish they would account for an infinitesimal proportion of the population.

1 And from Mârtañd they migrated to Keralâ where they came to be known as Nambûdirî Brâhmins, Mathew adds.

For: The hill known currently as the Shankarâchârya hill was called the Gopâdri hill/ Jyesth Lidder/ Jyestheshvar in older times: Most Kashmîri Muslims believe that this is the Throne of Solomon (Takht-e-Suleiman). This is adduced as proof of the Kashmîris' Jewish origin.

Against: Not just the Jews but Muslims and Christians, too, hold Solomon in high regard.

More important, it is on record that it was the great 14th century Persian saint, the Shâh-é-Hamadân, who named Kashmîr the Bâgh-e-Suleiman, the Garden of Solomon. All references to the Garden or Throne of Solomon date to after the 15th century.

In any case, there is a theory that Christ lived in Kashmîr. According to it, the Garden and Throne of Solomon have been named after a Persian noble called Suleiman, and not the Biblical Solomon.

For: The boatmen (hânjis) of Kashmîr claim to be descendants of Noah.

Against: The story of Hazrat-e-Noo (Noah) is identical to that of the Hindu saint Manu (Ma-noo). So this argument gets us nowhere.

For: Some of the arguments in favour of the 'Kashmîris-are-Jews' theory border on the ridiculous. Votaries of the theory approvingly quote Pt. Hargopal Kaul's strange, self-contradictory statement, 'Muslims are tall, strong and vulgar like Jews, with the exception of the gentle ones.'

Against: Neither community is (or was in Pt. Kaul's time) vulgar. The Jews have dominated Europe's (and now New York's) world of science, commerce, classical music, psychology and the social sciences for more than three centuries now. The handicrafts, cuisine and historiography of Kashmîr have no equal in South Asia. The Kashmîris are certainly taller than Jammûites. But by absolute standards (and by those of the neighbouring Gujjars, Bakerwâls and Punjâbis) most Kashmîri men are of medium height.

For: Moses (Musa) is a very common name in Kashmîr.

Against: Is it? I find it more common among the very Indo-Aryan Gujjars of the Himâlayas. I know Tamil and other Muslims called Musa. (The Tamilians are supposed to be of Mediterranean Caucasoid descent.) Does this prove that the Jews and Tamilians, too, are of Jewish origin?

Similarities between the Kashmîri language and Hebrew

Against: It is argued that there are many words in the Kashmîri language that correspond to Hebrew words. Thus Kashmîri must be an offshoot of Hebrew. Indeed, there are many such words. However, Urdu-speaking Muslims of Central India and Pâkistân also use most of these words. Let us look at some of the words offered as proof:[i]

Hebrew	Kashmîri	The meaning	But...
ab	bab	father	'Bab' is further from 'ab' than the 'abba' and 'abu' used for 'father' by Urdu-speaking Muslims. 'Ab' is an Arabic word.
Aoh	auh	'Oh!'	Hindi-(and English-) speakers, too, use this exclamation.
Akh	akh	one	Hindi, Urdu and Punjâbi have similar words for 'one': eik, ik.
Arah	arah	saw	Hindi-Urdu speakers use the word 'ârâ'.
Ahad	ahad	one	Urdu speakers use 'vâhid', a derivation of 'ahad', to describe the singular. The name Ahâd is from the Holy Qur'ân.
Adar	chadar	blanket	If words like this are 'proof,' then the whole argument collapses. All North Indians use the word 'chadar,' which is from the Persian language.
Aaz	âz	today	Hindi-Urdu speakers use 'âj'. Most traditional Kashmîrîs say 'z' when they mean 'j'. Clearly âz is âj pronounced in the local fashion.
aosh	aosh	tears	Corresponds to the Sañskrit 'ashroo'.
Abital	abtal	under water	Derived from 'ab', which in Urdu-Persian, too, means 'water'. 'Tal' has a meaning similar to 'under' in Hiñdi-Urdu as well.
and	gand	knot	The Kashmîri 'gand' is identical to the Punjâbi 'gand' (also meaning 'knot') and the Hindi-Urdu 'gânth'. Resemblance with the Hebrew 'and' is far-fetched.
Bâl	bâl	spring	Corresponds to the Urdu 'bâoli'.
Beneh	beneh	sister	Corresponds to the Hindi 'behen' (sister) and the Urdu-Arabic 'binnat'.
Dafah	dafah	to turn out	It's the same in Urdu.
gair	gair	not related	It means the same in Urdu.
ghabar	gubar	young son	Corresponds to the Urdu-Punjâbi 'ghabroo' (youth), as well.
jâl	jâl	to deceive	Means the same in Urdu, too.
jabur	jabur	to force	'Jabar' and 'zabar' have the same meaning in Urdu.

Contd,

mazah	mazah	to taste	'Mazah' means '[to] taste' in Urdu, whereas in Hebrew it means 'to suck'. Which is closer to the Kashmîrî word?
Mehar	mahar	dowry	Now this is too much. 'Meher' is an Arabic word, an Islâmic concept, which has travelled to all Muslim lands, not just Kashmîr.
noor	noor	light	Again hardly unique to Kashmîr. 'Noor' means the same in Arabic and Urdu and is from the Holy Qur'ân.
qadam	qadam	step	Means the same in Urdu.
qabar	qabar	grave	Means the same in Arabic and Urdu.
qatal	qatal	murder	Means the same in Urdu.
rasah	razah	confirmation	The Kashmîri word is, in fact, closer to the Persian-Urdu 'razah'.
Sahar	sahar	dawn	Means the same in Urdu.
sidiq	sidiq	truthful	Means the same in Arabic-Urdu and is from the Holy Qur'ân.
shas	shas	breathing	'Breathing' is 'shwas' in Sañskrit and 'sâns' in Hindi.
Tuok	thook	spit	Means the same in Hindi-Urdu.
tumum	tamam	all	The Kashmîri word is, in fact, closer to the Urdu 'tamam'.
Zabeh	zabeh	to slaughter	Means the same in Urdu.
zinah	zinah	adultery	'Zinah' is an Arabic word, an Islâmic concept, which has travelled to all Muslim lands, not just Kashmîr.
ziker	ziker	to remember	Means the same in Arabic-Urdu. and is an Islâmic concept.

The conclusion is obvious. The Kashmîrî language got these words not from Hebrew, but from Arabic (through Islâmic texts) and Persian. The Quran Sharief, the Hadith and many Islâmic texts are in Arabic. Almost all Islâmic concepts are in either Arabic or Persian. Almost 95% of the population of Kashmîr has been Muslim for several centuries now. There were contacts with Arab soldiers (and one prominent Arab refugee, Hameem) even before Muslim missionaries from Irâq and Irân came to Kashmîr. As for Persian, it was the court and literary language of Kashmîr between the 15th and early 20th centuries.

Now, Hebrew is very similar to its sibling, Arabic. It has much in common with neighbouring Persian, too. Is it, then, very difficult to see why there are so many Hebrew (or Arabic-Persian) words in the Kashmîri language? As we have seen, they are there in Urdu, too. If the presence of Hebrew words in a people's language proves that they are Jews, then all Indian, Pâkistânî, Afghân and Persian Muslims, too, must be Jews.

For: The above, however, are only words of caution. The fact is that there are an equal number of Hebrew words in the Kashmîri language that are not found in Urdu. The word for 'cruel', Aziz Kashmîri points out, is 'Nebuchadnezzar' in Hebrew and 'Buchnasar' in Kashmîri. Srînagar has a suburb called Harwan. In Urdu, '*Harwan*' is spelt the same as '*Hâroon*', the Muslim name for '*Aaron*'. All this clearly shows an exchange of ideas between the two languages, even if it doesn't prove that both peoples are of the same race.

Similarities in architecture

For: Apparently the tiles found at the Harwan ruins have motifs identical to those found in Babylon: cocks, deer, men with beards, Roman numerals (which Aziz Kashmîri calls 'Hebrew figures'), women with water pots, and so on. Kashmîri says that the walls at Harwan are made of pebbles, which is also true of the architecture of Syria and Palestine. (And, may I add, of Dogrâ Hiñdû architecture.)

Regarding the Mârtañd temple, Kashmîri quotes Dr. James Ferguson as saying, 'The temple is a very small building, being only 60 feet in length and 38 feet in width; the width of [the] façade, however, is eked out by two wings as adjuncts which make it of 60 feet; also it realizes [sic] the problem the Jews had so earnestly set themselves to solve—how to build a temple with three dimensions equal but yet not cubic.'

Against: It is argued in support of the arguments 'for' that 'The ancient monuments and ruins near Awantiporâ, Mârtañd Temple at Kreveh Matton and at the Sulaiman [Shankarâchârya] hill, Srînagar, are that of Israelis in structures, stone eves, and constructions and in no way represent the Buddhist or Hindu Art. [sic]'

Such arguments are so easy to shoot down that they provide cheap cannon fodder to opponents of the 'Kashmîris are Jews' theory. The three monuments listed are identical in style to their Hiñdû contemporaries in Jammû province. They are also very similar to the 10th-13th century Hindu-Buddhist Angkor Wat temples of Cambodia.

Aziz Kashmîri is on much firmer ground when he cites authority to show that there are Greek influences in the architecture of the temples of Mârtañd and Harwan. Of course, there are. And in the temples at Nârâ Nâg and Awantiporâ as well. The pillars/ columns, the triangular cornices and the pediments are all Hellenic. But the Greeks and the Jews are two very different peoples.

Names of places, castes and tribes

For and against:

An attempt has been made to show that the names of Kashmîri villages, castes and 'tribes' have been mentioned in the Bible. Now, the Bible, especially the Chronicles, lists a few thousand names—of people and places. If you are prepared to stretch sounds a bit, you can find names from any given part of the world in the Bible. (Abba, the name of a 1970s Swedish pop group, is an acronym. It derives from the first letters of the names of the four members of the group. Yet, as they told the world, their name is there in the Bible: 'Abba, the father.')

I have cross-checked with the Bible each Kashmîri name offered as 'proof.' The results are as follows:

Names of places

It is argued that 'it is obvious that when Banni Israel settled in Kashmîr, they kept the very names of the places, which they had in their own motherland.' (Emphasis mine.)

Place in Kashmir (or nearby)	Name mentioned in the Bible	Reference	On cross-checking with the Bible I found that it was...
Achâbal	Ash'bel	Gen. 46:21	the name of a person.
Amairah	Am-a-ri'ah	I Chron. 23:19	the name of a person.
Araham	Ara	I Chron. 7:38	the name of a person.
Arahbal	Arah	I Chron. 7:39	the name of a person.
Asham	Ash'i-ma	II Kings,17:30	a place, but it is closer to the Sañskrit 'Ashimâ.'
Astor	Ash'toreth	I Kings, 11:5	the name of a goddess.
Barzilla	Bar-zil-la'i	I Kings, 2:7	the name of a person.
Beithpoer	Beith-pe'or	Deut., 34:6	a place. A good argument. (But see 'Christ in Kashmîr.')
Doru	Dor	I Kings, 4:11	a region. Good argument.
Gadha	Gad	I Chron. 2:2	the name of a person.
Gilgath	Gol'go-tha	Matt. 27:33	a place. But the similarity is extremely weak.
Harwan	Ha'ran	II Kings, 19:12	the name of a person.
Hasbal	Hesh'bon	Deut., 4:46	a place, but the similarity is extremely weak.
Himas	Ha'math	Numbers 13:21	a place.
Keran	Che'ran	I Chron. 1:41	the name of a person.

Contd.

Kishtwâr	Cush	Gen. 10:6	the name of a person. He is the son of Ham and father of Ra'a-mah. You decide if Cush is closer to 'Kishtwâr' or to Lav.
Ladâkh	La'a-dah	I Chron. 4:21	a person. Is even predominantly Mongoloid Ladâkh supposed to be Jewish?
Leh	Le'hi	Judges 15:9	a place. Ditto: the Mongoloid Ladâkhîs are the least likely people in the world to be Jewish.
Ludu	Lud	I Chron. 1:17	the name of a person.
Moab	Moab	Deut., 34:6	a place.
Poonch	Phe-ni'ce	Acts, 11:19	'a distant place.'
Shopian	Sho'phan	Numbers 32:35	a place. Convincing.
Tibet	Tib'hath	I Chron. 18:8	'a city near Chun.' Convincing.
Urî	Urî	Exodus, 31:2	the name of a person.

Conclusion: Some of the arguments are convincing and some rather far-fetched. Most of the arguments 'for' are based on very weak phonetic similarities.

Names of communities

For and against: When I read that quintessentially Kashmîri names like Kaul, Dar, Dhar, Rainâ, Razdan, Magre, Moza, Katru and Wani were mentioned in the Bible, I was convinced that no further proof was needed. The Kashmîris were Jews: all native Kashmîris were. However, on cross-checking these nine names with the Bible I only found Moza there in its pristine form. For the rest one has to stretch things a bit. And as for the clan name 'Kaul', it resembles not a Biblical name but the English word 'caul.' This word does not occur in the translations of the Bible into most other languages.

Here is the factual position. You decide how close the resemblance is.

Name of Kashmîri clan	**Name as mentioned in the Bible**	**Reference**
Amal	A'mal	I Chron 7:35
Atal	At'tai	I Chron. 12:11
Bakru	Be'cher, Boch'eru	I Chron. 7:6, 8:38
Bal, Bala	Ba'al	I Chron. 5:5
Dar, Dhar	Dor (a region, not tribe)	I Kings, 4:11
Dum	Du'mah	I Chron. 1:30

Contd.

Gaddar	Ge'dor	I Chron. 4:4
Gadha	Gad	I Chron. 2:2
Guni	Gu'ni	I Chron. 7:13
Haroon	Hezron	I Chron. 2:5
Hukak	Hu'kok	I Chron. 6:75
Ishui	Ish'u-i (good point)	I Sam. 14:49
Kanah	Ka'nah (place)	Jos. 19:28
Kar	Ca-re'ah	II Kings 25:23
Katru	Ke-tu'rah	Gen. 25:4
Kaul	Caul (see note)	Isa. 3:18
Lavi	Levi	I Chron. 2:1
Mâleh	Ma-al'eh (a place)	Jos. 15:3
Magrey	Ma'gor	Jer. 20:3
Mallek	Mal'luch	I Chron. 6:44
Mearah	Me-ar'ah	Jos. 13:4
Minto	Min'nith	Judges 11:33
Moza	Mo'za	I Chron. 8:36
Mushi	Mu'shi	I Chron. 6:19
Naiku	Nechoh	II Kings 23:29
Nehru	Nahor	I Chron. 1:26
Pau	Puah	I Chron. 7:1
Rainâ	Rinnah	I Chron. 4:20
Razdan	Rezon	I Kings 11:23
Réshî	Rhe'sa	Luke 3:27
Shamir	Sha'mir	I Chron. 24:24
Shora	She'rah	I Chron. 7:24
Thapal	To'phel	Deut. 1:1
Tiku	Te-ko'a	I Chron. 2:24
Wani	Va-ni'ah	Ezra 19;36

(Notes: Mallik is a title found among Central Asians, Indonesians, Indian Hindus and Muslims everywhére, 'Caul' is an English word for either a membrane or the smooth part at the back of a woman's hat. From the context 'caul' appears to be a part of the human body. As used in the Bible, 'caul' probably means 'A portion of the amnion, especially when it covers the head of a fetus at birth.[ii] '*Nehru*', as a surname, probably did not exist till the 17th or 18th century AD. On the other hand, the Biblical name 'Nahor' is closer to the Central Indian/ Bengali 'Nahar'. Kar is a Bengali name, too.

Therefore, the Bengalis must all be Jews. Besides, both communities like the cinema. '*She'rah*' is a feminine first name. '*Haroon*' is the Arabic name for '*Aaron*'. It is popular in several parts of South Asia and the Muslim world, especially Pâkistân's Sind. It is hardly a name unique to Kashmîr. '*Wani*' is pronounced 'woin' as well. '*Vaniah*' is closer to the north Indian 'Baniya' and the Tamil 'Vanniyar'. You decide whether the Kashmîri 'Réshî,' meaning saint, is closer to the Sañskrit 'rishî,' also meaning saint, or the Jewish Rhe'sa, which is a name with no assigned meaning. Atal is a Sañskrit name from the Hiñdû texts. And it does not resemble At'tai at all.)

Customs

For: The Jews say nasty things about you behind your back. So do the Kashmîris. Therefore, the Kashmîris have descended from the Jews.

Against: In that case the entire population of the world is Jewish.

That ('For' above) is the kind of logic used by votaries of the theory. Both peoples sleep naked at night. Therefore, they are of the same stock. (People in most cold lands sleep naked at night. The British have traditionally done so. The people of Kargil [Ladâkh], Banni [Jammû], Sweden and many parts of Northern Europe still do. Does that make them all Jews?)

Jewish priests sound trumpets; Kashmîri Pandit priests blow into conch shells, 'thereby confirming the fact of being the descendants of Israelis or Jews'. (Hindu priests blow into conch shells in most parts of India. Thus, all Hindus must be descendants of the Jews.)

Kashmîri bridegrooms sometimes live permanently with their in-laws, rather than with their own parents. So do some Jews. (The Buddhists of Ladâkh have an elaborate institution, the *makpa*, to sanctify such an arrangement. Hindus and Muslims of the rest of South Asia sometimes do the same. Therefore, the Mongoloid Buddhists must all be Jews, too.)

One of the most ridiculous arguments in favour of this belief is this: 'The Kashmîrîs circumcise their male children and so do the Jews. Therefore, they belong to the same race.' Now, as we all know, Muslims everywhere have adopted male circumcision. Obviously this 'sunnat' (tradition) came to Kashmîr with Islâm — as did so many Jewish customs and words that Islâm has absorbed worldwide. Had the Jews—and not Muslim missionaries—brought this custom to Kashmîr, then even Kashmîrî Pandits would have adopted it. After all, Jews are supposed to have come to Kashmîr several centuries before Islâm did, and even Kashmîrî Hiñdûs are supposed to be the descendants of Jews.

The very fact that not a single Kashmîrî Pandit clan practises circumcision proves that neither they nor the majority of Kashmîrî Muslims have descended from the Jews. (The ancestors of most Kashmîrî Muslims were Hiñdûs before their conversion to Islâm.)

For: Boats: The end of oars that dips into the water is shaped like a heart in both lands. Both have flat-bottomed boats and gable-roofs. (The ends of most Kashmîrî oars are circular: though it is possible to glimpse the shape of a heart in them.)

Childbirth: Women in both lands bathe forty days after a child is born to them.

Clothes: The traditional costumes of women in the two lands are supposed to be similar.

Dance: Apparently Jewish women, too, dance to songs as in the case of the Kashmîri 'roph'/ 'roef'. The movements of the two dance forms seem to be similar.

Graveyards and tombs: Both plant brimage trees in their graveyards. Both have a tradition of east-west tombs. The Kashmîris later accepted the Muslim norm of north-south tombs. Aziz Kashmîri gives us a list of some east-west tombs: Hâroon (i.e. Hârvan), Râjpurâ, Syed Bladur Sâheb, Koker Nag and Awantiporâ. More significantly, he points out that there is an ancient tomb in the graveyard at Bijbehera that has a Hebrew inscription. This conclusively proves that Kashmîr had a Jewish connection at some stage. (At least one grave in the Malkhah cemetery of Srînagar has a Sañskrit inscription. It is the grave of a Lodi prince, not of a local convert. All that this grave proves is that Sañskrit was still respected then.) In any case, there are only a few east-west tombs in all of Kashmîr. They were, thus, not a widespread practice.

Worship: There is a stone called '*Kâh Kâh Pal*' at Bijbehera (Anant Nag). It is said to be the stone of Moses. It is believed that eleven (kâh) people can together lift the stone with their fingers. (The figure eleven represents the tribes of Israel.) Bârâmullâ has a similar stone.

Muslims are not supposed to worship anyone but God. Yet many Kashmîri Muslims go to the shrine of Harut and Marut, close to the Mârtañd Temple (Anant Nag). They ask the angels that are supposed to live there to get their prayers answered. This practise is certainly unIslâmic. Some say that these angels were worshipped in pre-Islâmic Babylon. Aziz Kashmîri writes that the name of the village where this shrine has been built is Chahi Babel. That only deepens the mystery.[2]

Conclusion

The Kashmîris do not all belong to the same ethnic group. Some of them certainly have facial features resembling those of the Jews. Indeed, there are some Hebrew words in the Kashmîri language. Most of these words are also Arabic words and are found in every Muslim land. Some Jewish customs

---

2 Or does it? My investigations reveal that the name of the place is "Chhattâbal." One has to be slightly imaginative to read 'Chahi Babel' into this very Kashmîrî name. There is a Chhattabal in Srînagar, too.

and beliefs, too, are found in Kashmîr. There can be no doubt that Jews used to visit ancient, pre-Islâmic Kashmîr at the rate of one or two visitors a year. They were particularly honoured guests. This explains their stamp on some aspects of Kashmîri life. Some of them must have settled in Kashmîr and accepted Hinduism (and later Islâm). That explains why some Kashmîris, Hindus and Muslims alike, have the 'prominent noses' that have intrigued European travellers so much. The descendants of these 'foreigners' (parimûs) would account for less than one per cent of the population. However, the vast majority of Kashmîris have not descended from Jews.

References

i. The first three columns above, as well as all arguments in this section 'For' the belief, are based on Aziz Kashmîri's *Christ in Kashmîr.*

ii. The American Heritage® Dictionary of the English Language, Third Edition © 1996 by Houghton Mifflin Company.

16

The Clans and Sub-castes of Kashmîr

Two of my teenaged Kashmîrî friends complained that they knew nothing about the clans and sub-castes of Kashmîr, I believe that most Kashmîrî students share this quest. They are curious to know about their own origins and, more important, that of their friends. However, they don't know where to ask. The best place to do so is the two-volume, 1,200-page *Târîkh Aqwâm-é-Kashmîr* by Muhammad-ud-Deen 'Fauq' (Lahore, 1934).

The next best is the summary of family names and clans drawn up below[1]. Adfer and Mehreen wanted to be able to tell a person's origins by his surname. When I was talking to them, a Palestinian married to a Kashmîrî lady got interested in our conversation. He wanted to know about his wife's community. This chapter might serve at least the limited purpose that Adfer, Mehreen and the Palestinian had in mind.

Many Kashmîrî names are so evocative that they contain their own history. Nicknames (many of them offensive) and professional names that have become surnames fall into this category. Other names (like Dâr with a soft d) are so obscure that one can only guess about their origins.

Rich Mosaic

What we need to remember is that though the population of the Valley is very small (around 55 lakh/ 5.5 million in 2004), Kashmîrî Muslim society is a very rich mosaic of ethnic groups. I once met a young Ghilzaî (who is from an Afghân clan) in Srînagar. There is a single Vadéhrâ (Siñdhî) family, which has been in the Valley since the 19th century. There are around a thousand Tibetan Muslims, too.

---

1. This is a summary of the work done by Fauq, Lawrence and Kashmîr's old historians, together with my own field and academic work.

The blue-eyed Pushtûns of Gutlî Bâgh are, of course, in a class of their own. Because of militancy there was resistance to organising tourism festivals in Kashmîr[2]. So, members of this brave, straightforward community went all the way to Jammû, with their rare pedigreed horses, and stunned everyone there with the wealth of their culture.

In Kashmîr there is a substantial Dard community, some Ladâkhi Muslims in the Sonamarg area and Srînagar, around a thousand Baltîs, a small clan of Effendîs, a very big Turkish community and all of thirty people of the Lahanda (Pothwari) group.

Kashmîrî society is incomplete without Hazratbal, and that venerable shrine without the much-respected Bâñdés. This handsome, pink-skinned clan from Central Asia is, today, as much a part of Kashmîrî society as the Syeds, who are of Arab origin.

But then who is an indigenous Kashmîrî? Or for that matter an aboriginal Indian? We say that foreigners started ruling Kashmîr in 1586. But what about the two dynasties before the Mughals, namely the Shâhmîrîs and the Chaks? At least the Chaks had been in the Valley for two or three centuries before they ascended the throne. In the case of the Shâhmîrîs they weren't even native born. They became kings in less than three decades of migrating to the Valley. Similarly, the White Huns were probably from a foreign land, too.

The tiny Kashmîrî Pandit community has so many sub-groups that I suspect that some clans consist of just two or three households each. And they are not the only Hiñdûs, or even Brâhmins, that there are in the Valley. There is a small Dogrâ Râjpût community in the villages, and a major clan of Bhaderwâhî Râjpûts in Srînagar city. There are Punjâbî Hiñdûs not just in Srînagar, but also in the villages of Urî. They did not flee the Valley in the 1990s because their area remained uniquely peaceful.

A smart teenager in a designer skirt and black stockings came to my office in Jammû in 1990 and asked me where Christians from the Valley should register as migrants. She mentioned that she was related to one of India's best known fashion designers, who is a Punjâbi Hiñdû. I cross-checked her information. I learnt that the couturier's uncle had, indeed, converted to Christianity. As had several Kashmîrî Pandits who were employed by one of Srînagar's elite Anglican schools.

Kashmîr used to have a small Jewish community. They ran the town's most respected nursing home. I am permanently linked to it because I was born there, and was delivered by Dr Gabbé. (At the time my father was posted in Srînagar.) The Jewish community of Kashmîr came to an end with her.

---

2. Till, in 2002, I decided to hold a festival anyway, without spending a single rupee of state government funds. I did it with the help of hotel, houseboat and shikârâ owners. They chipped in, despite the fierce opposition of a few newspapers, and despite a small section of the tourism industry boycotting the festival. The spring festival has, since, become an institution.

In this chapter I have mostly used phonetic spellings, rather than the way that the names are actually spelt. I have cited from old censuses because after a while the Census of India stopped listing people by their caste.

Kashmîr has so many clans and sub-castes that I have been able to list only a few, the more populous ones.

Many surnames are common to the Muslims and the Hiñdûs. Many Muslims have retained their pre-Islâmic surnames, while some Hiñdûs have taken on Afghân, Persian and even Arabic surnames.

The Muslims

Caste and social stratification

Caste exists with religious sanction only among the Hiñdûs and Sikhs, Buddhists (from Ladâkh to Japan and Korea) and Zoroastrians[3]. Islâm (like pristine Sikhism and Buddhism) is egalitarian. And yet, as Imtiaz Ahmed and his team demonstrated, some social stratification and caste-like features exist even in Muslim societies, not just in the Indian sub-continent but also outside it.

Ahmed and his colleagues, most of them being eminent Muslim sociologists, had published their findings in a groundbreaking classic of the late 1960s called *Caste and Social Stratification among Muslims in India*, a book whose broad conclusions (and title) I am quoting from memory.

The first thing that they noticed about Indian Muslim society was that it was divided into two broad categories: the Ashrâf (Muslims who had come from West and Central Asia) and the Ajlâf (local converts). The former ranked much higher than the latter. Converts from the Râjpût caste of Hiñdûs were somehow sought to be accommodated in the first category, but weren't always accepted as Ashrâfs.

The Ahmed-led study was really meant for the plains of India, Bâñglâ Désh and Pâkistân. Of relevance to my Kashmîrî friends seeking their roots is the hierarchy within the Ashrâf category. All the researchers observed that the Syeds sat at the very top, followed by the Sheikhs, Mughals and Pathâns (the correct word is 'Pushtûns'), in that order. As I said, in some parts of India, Muslim Râjpûts managed to migrate from the top of the Ajlâf category to the bottom of the Ashrâf group. (In Urdû the word *shurfâ* is used for Ashrâfs.)

Syeds, Mughals and Pathâns have been explained below. What really needs explaining is the second 'caste,' namely Sheikh. If the Syeds are exalted because they are the descendants of Prophet Muhammad (pbuh), the Sheikhs rank second because they are mostly the descendants of the Four Righteous Caliphs and are also of Arab origin.

---

3. And, yes, there used to be a very elite Pestonjee family and a Parsi Bagh in Srînagar.

The Sheikhs are Siddîquîs (descended from Hazrat Abû Bâkr Siddîq), Farûquîs (descended from Hazrat Omar Farûq), (the descendants of Hazrat Usmân Ghanî) Usmânîs, some Ghanîs and Umavîs and Alvîs (the non-Syed descendants of Hazrat Alî Murtazâ). And then there are the two great Arab clans closest to Prophet Muhammad (pbuh): the Ansârîs and the Qurêshîs.

Now the bulk of Muslims everywhere consist of converts from the original people of that land. The new converts normally take on the title 'Sheikh.' What's more, they often adopt the name of an Arab tribe, normally the one of their spiritual master.

The best examples of this are some thitherto-underprivileged Hiñdû castes that took on Arab clan-names upon their conversion to Islâm. The weavers of much of the Indian sub-continent all became Ansârîs, the butchers all became Qurêshîs and the barbers all became Salmânîs.

Traditionally, a north Indian or Pâkistânî Qurêshî of Arab origin would not marry into a family of butcher Qurêshîs, or even treat them as social equals. The same is true of the other Arab Sheikhs in relation to their local namesakes.

In the context of Kashmîr, Imtiaz Ahmed's main thesis doesn't quite apply because Islâm came here almost entirely through preaching-led conversion, very little through inward migration and not at all through conquest. In the rest of the sub-continent there was a substantial inward migration of the Syeds and Sheikhs from West Asia, of Mughals from Central Asia, of Arab traders to Kerala, Bombay and Lakshadweep and of Pathâns from Afghânistân and the frontier. Therefore, the (Arab) Sheikhs are the Muslim elite of North India, Hyderabad, Bombay and Pâkistân.

In Kashmîr the number of (Arab) Sheikhs, Mughals and Pathâns is insignificant. The Syeds are as respected in Kashmîr as they are throughout the world of Islâm. After them I have listed the Afghâns, the Mughals, the Râjpûts and the (locally converted) Sheikhs. Fauq used this order. It corresponds roughly to the order accepted all over the Indian sub-continent, as observed by Imtiaz Ahmed and his team, writing three decades after Fauq. (Within each category I have used the alphabetical order.)

In Kashmîr one does not hear the words Ashrâf and Ajlâf, except among some academics. And yet there is a tacit division. On the one hand are the Syeds, the Afghâns, the Mughals and converts from the Hiñdû upper-castes (the Muslim Râjpûts and the Sheikhs).

On the other hand are converts from the former Hiñdû underclass. Fauq called them the 'adnâ aqwâm' (lower castes). Perhaps we can call them the 'underprivileged sections of society.' I have used the more cumbersome but also more PC (politically correct) expression 'Castes associated with culture and specialised professions.'

Ashrafisation

One of the sidelights of Ahmed's thesis is the expression 'Ashrafisation.' It is obviously the Muslim equivalent of legendary sociologist M.N. Srinivas' 'Sañskritisation.' Both are phenomena in which the subaltern castes take on the ways of the so-called upper castes.

Writing more than half a century before even Srinivas, Lawrence noted, 'Of late years the Dûms[4] of Kashmîr have steadily assumed the [clan-name] of Ganai, much to the annoyance of the original Ganais. To make matters worse, the gardeners and butchers have also taken a fancy to the [clan-name] Ganai. The boatmen of Kashmîr have settled on the name Dâr as a patent of respectability, and Musalmâns of the other [clans] are now annoying the Ganais and Dârs by asserting that they were originally Dûms and boatmen. Some [clan-names] are, however, restricted to men of lowly pursuits, and the [clan-name] Sufi, which is said by some to be of Brâhman origin is chiefly found among market-gardeners, bakers, and servants. Pâl is another such [clan-name]. The barbers of the valley do not aim so high as the butchers and boatmen, and have contented themselves with appropriating the [clan-name] of Thakur; but there is nothing to prevent Abdulla, the Dûm, from calling himself Abdulla Pañdit.'

Similarly, a clan of fake Syeds is the so-called Syed Makar tribe.

The most important things to note in the context of Kashmîr are: (a) The Mughals of Kashmîr came here as migrants and men of religion, for which they are greatly respected. They did not come as rulers. Therefore, they do not have the same privileged status here as in North India and Pâkistân. (b) The Afghâns ruled over Kashmîr too briefly, and far too much by remote control, to have left behind a Pushtûn ruling elite of the kind that existed in the rest of the sub-continent. (c) Muslim society in Kashmîr is more homogenous, more egalitarian and less stratified than in the rest of the sub-continent. No one bothers much about how fancy your pedigree-table (family-tree) is. Only your present status matters. d) Above all, the Sheikhs of Kashmîr are mostly converts from the local castes. Very few of them are the direct descendants of the Four Righteous Caliphs.

The Syeds

Prophet Muhammad (pbuh) had only one surviving child, Hazrat Fâtimâ. She married Hazrat Alî, who was the fourth Righteous Caliph of Islâm. All Syeds are the descendants of Prophet Muhammad (pbuh), through his daughter Hazrat Fâtimâ and Hazrat Alî.

Bulbul Shâh is the first known Syed to have come to Kashmîr. This was a few years before A.D. 1320. Given below is a partial list of some Syed surnames, with a few words about the founders of these clans.

---

4. Lawrence said that the Dûms were of *shûdr* origin.

Sometimes non-Syeds adopt Syed names. Some Syed names are also the names of sûfî orders founded by a Syed of that name. Members of such orders adopt the name of their order as their own surname. So there is no guarantee that the Hamadânî, Naqshbañdî or Qâdirî next door is a Syed. I know at least one Kashmîrî Pandit called Jalâlî.

Andrâbî Imâm Hussain was the beloved grandson of Prophet Muhammad (pbuh). Syed Muslim was his descendant in the fourteenth generation. The Syed migrated from Hejâz to Andrâb (in Afghânistân). His clan lived in Andrâb for nine generations. In the tenth generation came Syed Ahmed Andrâbî, who migrated to Kashmîr with Syed Alî Hamadânî.

Mantaqî-Baihaqî Syed Hussain Mantaqî founded this clan. Hemigrated from a town called Baihaq (Khurâsân) to Kashmîr during the reign of Emperor Budshâh @ Zain-ul-Abedin (the 15th century). The clan is known as Mantaqî because they were experts in the science of *mantaq* (logic).

Bukhârî Syed Jalâl-ud-Dîn Bukhârî was a renowned saint. His fame spread from Bukhârâ (Uzbékistân) to all parts of India. His descendants are called the Bukhârîs. The first of his clan to come to Kashmîr was Syed Alâuddîn Bukhârî. This was during the reign of Sulân Sikander (1389-1413). The 1911 census revealed that there were 9,237 Bukhârî Syeds in the state.

Dâhbîdî This clan is descended from Makhdûm Âzam Syed Ahmed 'of Kâshân' (actually he was from Khurâsân). Even among the Syeds of Kashmîr, few are aware that a branch of this tiny clan exists in Kashmîr. It once occupied a very high status. However, by the end of the 19th century they were confined to performing religious rituals. They were relegated to the darning and bookbinding professions. Some of them have traditionally lived in the Lâl Bâzâr and Naushehrâ neighbourhoods of Srînagar.

Davârkî This line comes from an Irâqî town called Davârak, which is near Baghdâd. Allâmâ Mîr Syed travelled from there to Hérât. After a brief stay in Hérât he migrated to Kashmîr during the reign of Emperor Budshâh @ Zain-ul-Abedin (the 15th century).

Gîlânî See 'Qâdirî' below.

Hamadânî Hazrat Amîr Kabîr Syed Alî Hamadânî came to Kashmîr in AH 781 (late 14th century AD). The Hamadânî Syeds are from his line.

Jalâlî Syed Hussain Sabzwârî, son of Syed Alî, founded this clan. Their order can be traced back to Imâm (not king) Zain-ul-Abedin. The tomb of Syed Hussain Sabzwârî is in

Gupkâr village, by the banks of what used to be the Gagrîbal lake (Srînagar).

Naqshbañdî There are two Naqshbañdî clans in Kashmîr. Their founders were: i) Hazrat Khwâjâ Khâvind Mehmûd Naqshbañdî Attârî, who came to Kashmîr in the early 17th century AD and ii) Hazrat Khwâjâ Syed Abdur Rahîm Naqshbañdî, whose ancestral kingdom was Tashkent (Uzbékistân) and who migrated to Kashmîr in the early 18th century. Both were descended from a line of Bukhârî Syeds.

Qâdirî Shâh Abul Hassan and Shâh Muhammad Fâzil Qâdirî were brothers. They were related to one of the greatest saints of Islâm, Hazrat Ghaus Âzam Sheikh Abdul Qâdir Jîlânî. They came to Kashmîr, through Péshâwar, in A.H. 1090 (17th century AD) with a large group of followers. They founded one of three Qâdirî lines in Kashmîr. The three lines are based in Khânyâr, Rétaing and Nowgâm Shâhâbâd respectively. All Qâdirîs are not Syeds. However, all Qâdirî-Gîlânîs are. (G and j are interchangeable when we switch between Arabic and Persian-Urdû. Thus, Gîlânî and Jîlânî are the same.)

Rufâî Syed Muhammad of Isfahân was an eminent saint. He was popularly known as 'Rufâî.' He migrated to Kashmîr during the reign of Emperor Budshâh @ Zain-ul-Abedin (the 15th century). He first lived in Srînagar. However, he soon found that the city was not quiet enough for his meditations. So he migrated to Bârâmullâ.

Rizvî Syed Hussain Rizvî, a saint, migrated from Qom (Irân) to Kashmîr in the 15th century AD Budshâh @ Zain-ul-Abedin was the emperor of Kashmîr at the time. He had got a splendid garden created for himself at Zainagîr (Sopore). He gifted it to the saint. The word Rizvî is derived from the name of Hazrat Imâm Alî-ar-Razâ, the founder of the clan.

Yasvî Alvî All Alvîs are the descendants of Hazrat Alî, from wives other than Hazrat Fâtimâ. Therefore, they are not Syeds as such. However, the Yasvî Alvîs are Syeds. They come from the line of Hazrat Sultân Khwâjâ Ahmed Yasvî through Imâm Muhammad bin Al Hanafî. Ultimately, like all Syeds, their family tree goes back to Hazrat Alî. The name 'Yasvî' is derived from Yas or Yasû, which is a town in Turkestân. Khwâjâ Ahmed Yasvî Naqshbañdî belonged to this town. He migrated to Kashmîr in the 18th century.

The Quréshîs

The Quréshîs are descendants of the exalted Quré sh tribe of Arabia, which was founded by Nazar-bin Kanânâ. Some of the greatest names in Islâm, including Prophet Muhammad (pbuh) himself, are from this tribe. The Syeds and the Quréshîs are thus of the same stock and a similar ancestry. Like the Syeds, the Quréshîs came to Kashmîr from west and central Asia.

The first of this clan to come to Kashmîr was Syed Muhammad Quréshî. He was thus both a Syed and a Quréshî. He migrated to Kashmîr in the 14th century AD as a member of the entourage of Hazrat Amîr Kabîr Syed Alî Hamadânî.

The Afghâns

During the Afghân period not only Kashmîrî Muslims but also Kashmîrî Pañdits were appointed to senior government positions in Kâbul. Many of the Muslims stayed on, never to return to Kashmîr. During the same period a substantial Kashmîrî Muslim diaspora formed in what was later called the North West Frontier Province of Pâkistân (now Khyber-Pakhtunkhwa). Fauq writes that in the early part of the twentieth century almost a half of the Muslims of Péshâwar proper were of Kashmîrî origin. However, he added that the ethnic Kashmîrîs had given up their customs and blended so well with the 'Pathâns' (Pushtûns) that they have begun to look like good 'Pathâns'.

Similarly, those who migrated *to* Kashmîr from Afghânistân or the NWFP have given up their language and customs to blend with the Kashmîrîs. One of the few exceptions is the Pushtûn tribe of Gutlî Bâgh (Gâñderbal). They still speak Pushto at home.

Lawrence adds, 'The most interesting colony is that of Kuki Khayl Afridis of Dranghaihâma, who retain all the old Pathân customs, and still for the most part speak Pashtu... Another colony of Pathâns is that of the Machipurias but by intermarriage with Kashmîrî women the Machipurias have lost most of the characteristics of the Pathân... The Machipuria Pathâns belong to the Yusufzaî section...

'Pathâns came to Kashmîr in the Durrani time [generally called the Afghân era], but many were introduced by the Mahârâjâ Gulâb Singh, who granted them jâgîrs [estates] for service on the frontier. In Bhiru [Beeru, Beerwâ?] many villages are held by Swâtis and Bonairwâls.'

The surname Khân indicates nothing. In Kashmîr many Khâns are of purely local origin. It was a military title. The Khâns of Kargil are mostly indigenous Kargilis, who had this title even before they converted to Islâm. Genghis is the world's best known Khân. And yet he was neither a Pushtûn/ Pathân, nor even a Muslim. (He was an animist.) All the Turks of the hills of Bârâmullâ call themselves Khân.

In 1911, there were 52,263 Pushtoons in the state. Of these, 30,338 claimed to be Khâns. Several Muslim Râjpûts of Mîrpur told the census authorities that they were Pushtûns. The proportion of Pushtûns in post-1947 Jammû and Kashmîr might not be the same. Almost the entire Pushtûn elite of Srînagar migrated to Pâkistân after the partition of India.

The Afghân clans of Kashmîr are:

Kukî Khél

Kant

Khatkî

Khyberî

Niâzî

Sado-zaî

Yûsufzaî

Dispute: Fauq classifies the Khâñd or Khâñdé clan among the Afghâns. Lawrence puts them among 'Brâhmin farmers.' The balance of evidence indicates conversion from a native clan,

Mughals

Sir Walter Lawrence mentions only five Mughal clans: the Mîrs, the Bég-Mîrzâs, the Bâñdés, the Bachhs and the Ashâîs. Urdu-Persian histories mention others as well.

Ashâî This clan migrated to Kashmîr from a village called Aishâwar (Khurâsâñ). Their actual title was Aishâwarî. However, over the years it seems to have got shortened to Ashâî. An old history of Kashmîr, the *Rozatul Abrâr*, calls them 'an eminent bloodline.' The first of the clan to come to Kashmîr was Khwâjâ Sangîn Shâh of Hamadân. He accompanied Hazrat Amîr Kabîr Syed Alî Hamadânî to Kashmîr in the 14th century A.D. The Khwâjâ and his sons were shopkeepers and manufacturers.

They would divide their various duties in a very disciplined manner. From *ishrâq* (the voluntary namâz offered well after sunrise) to *peshin* (or *zuhr*, the obligatory prayer offered after it is noon) they would be available in their shop to attend to customers. Then they would leave for the workshop where their goods were made. They would stay in the workshop till *asr* (the obligatory *namâz* offered between *zuhr* and sunset/ *maghrib*). They would offer their *asr* prayers at a mosque and would stay in the mosque till it was time for *ishâ* (the obligatory *namâz* offered after it is night).

There is a theory that the clan got the name Ashâî because its members would emerge from the mosque only after the *ishâ* prayers.

The elder who brought the *moo é muqaddas* to Kashmîr was an Aishâwarî. If we accept the first theory about the

Ashâîs, then Khwâjâ Nûr-ud-Dîn would have been from this clan.

Bachh/ Bachh A very elite Mughal bloodline is that of Genghiz Khân. This clan is called Chañgézî in much of Asia. Mîr Muhammad Alî @ Mîr Alî Bukhârî, an eminent religious scholar who belonged to this clan, came to Kashmîr during the regime of Emperor Budshâh. His descendants included the illustrious Mîr Nâzuk Niâzî Qâdirî and the martyr Qâzî Mîr Mûsâ. The emperor granted him an estate. The maulânâ served the people of Kashmîr sincerely and well. His descendant Qâzî Mîr Ibrâhim, son of Qâzî Sikañder, was the first of the clan to use the name Buchh. Bachh and Buchh are said to be Kashmîrî words that correspond to the Sañskrit 'vats' (father).

The Buchhs are a branch of the Mîr clan.

Bâñdé The 1911 census document mentions that this clan had been put in jail for being headstrong and outspoken. What? The entire community? And by whom? When? Was this in Kashmîr? The census doesn't say. And no other history even hints at this.

Another history tells us that during the era of the Shâhs (presumably, Kashmîr's own sultâns), some 'Chughts' [i.e. Mughals of the great Chughtaî clan] came over from Turkestân to Kashmîr. They were given an estate in what is now called Bâñdîpur.

This is a very tiny clan. And yet they have produced a number of eminent men who find mention in almost all Urdû-Persian histories.

We all know that when Budshâh was still a prince, he 'accompanied' Amîr Tîmûr (Taimûr) to Samarqand (Uzbékistân). 'Forced to accompany' would be more accurate. 'Taken hostage' comes closest. In any case, Tîmur placed the young prince in the care of one Khwâjâ Badiullâh (or Badiuddîn). The Khwâjâ was a native of Turkestân, but had become a part of the Lahore aristocracy. Young Budshâh stayed with the Khwâjâ for a very long time. Most historians say that he was allowed to return to Srînagar only when Tîmûr died. Others record that when Tîmûr left India, the prince went back to Srînagar.

Either way, the Khwâjâ escorted the prince back to Srînagar. Sikander But Shikan was the King of Kashmîr at the time. He organised celebrations on his son's return. He also gave the Khwâjâ an estate in Kashmîr. Fauq says that the Kashmîrîs are 'experts are distorting words, giving them weird shapes and rendering them meaningless.' (True, but don't all Indians do this? Don't the people of Lucknow change the name of their city to 'Nakhlau,' don't Jammûites interchange syllable, don't the Punjâbîs of Pâkistân change my name to 'Péjî'?) Well, the people of Kashmîr did distort the name of this particular elder to 'Bâñdî bâbâ' and 'Bâñdé bâbâ.' The name stuck to his descendants.

There is a magnificent Bâñdé lane in Bâñdîmar. The ruins of its mansions speak of the splendour that once was.

Bég(h), It is a Turkestânî tradition that army officers who display exemplary bravery on the battlefield are given the title 'Bég.' The word means 'leader' or 'chief.' Variants of the title include Bak (pron. buck), Bag (pron. bug) and Bey (or Bay). In Turkey, too, the titles Bay and Bak were given to senior army officers. Some Bays and Bégs went on to acquire the highest title of the land, Pâshâ. The best known example is that of Gâzî Anwar Pâshâ.

In 1911, there were 280 Bégs and Mîrzâs in Jammû, 6,595 in Kashmîr and 30 in the frontier areas. The two main Bég clans of the state are based in Srînagar and Ânañtnâg.

Gânî The first Mughal to come to Kashmîr as a conqueror was Mîrzâ Haidar Dughlat Gurgân(î). There can be no doubt about the Mughalness of the Gurgânîs. (I say this because Lawrence left them out.) There is a note in a Persian history that reads, 'The Gurgânîs are famous [i.e. better known] as the Gânîs.' Historian Hassan, too, feels that these are two names of the same clan. The Gânîs live in Kashmîr and the Punjâb. Some came to Kashmîr as men of learning. Mîrzâ Haidar Dughlat also left behind a few soldiers and administrators.

Jân (See 'Mîr' below for events leading to the migration of some of that family to Khoihâmâ.) The martyrdom of Qâzî Mîr Mûsâ generated enormous sympathy for the family, which began to flee Srînagar for the villages. Some even fled to the Punjâb. 'Jân' is a Kashmîrî word that means 'the nice' or even 'the beloved.' The branch that fled to Khoihâmâ was affectionately called Jân because everyone liked them for their own good nature and out of sympathy for Mûsâ.

Mîr If the name Mîr is used at the beginning of a person's name (e.g. Mîr Jâvéd Shâh), it is a title, especially of people of the Syed and Shâh clans. To find out what that person's caste is, look at his last name. On the other hand, if Mîr is used as a last name (e.g. Jamshed Mîr), it indicates that the person is a Mîrzâ. This is true of Kashmîr and the Punjâb. In other parts of India different conventions apply. For instance, in

Hyderabad (South India), even genuine Tâtârîs use Mîr as a title, before their given name.

Mîr is a Turkish word. It means 'officer' or 'chief.' There are schools of thought which say that Mîr is short for Amîr or Mîrzâ. It is the people of Mughalistân (Maghûlistân) who made the use of this title widespread.

Mîr Alî Bukhârî migrated from Turkestân-Mughalistân to Kashmîr during the reign of Emperor Budshâh (15th century). He had received this title well before his migration. *Rozatul Abrâr*, a mediæval history, notes that 'God had given the Mîr a very ample number of children. God also gave him a lot of wealth,' As a result, the clan founded by Mîr Alî Bukhârî is quite numerous in Kashmîr and the Punjâb. The Kashmîrî Mîrs of the Punjâb are of this clan. In Kashmîr they live in Srînagar city as well as in the villages.

The Mîr family used to intermarry frequently with the Syeds. For instance, Qâzî Muhammad Sâleh, son of the martyr Qâzî Mîr Mûsâ, was married to a Syed.

Another reason why this clan is so widespread is that it prospered during the Mughal era in Kashmîr. Qâzî Mîr Mûsâ was a disciple of Sheikh Hamzâ Makhdûm. The spiritual heirs of Makhdûm Sâheb had invited the Mughals to take over the administration of Kashmîr (in the 1570s and '80s).

One reason why some of them fled Srînagar (not only to the Punjâb, but also to rural areas within Kashmîr, notably Khoihâmâ) was because the then king of Kashmîr, the hot-headed Yâqoub Shâh, went after them hammer and tongs. Because they were not ethnic Kashmîrîs, many of the clan could consider fleeing all the way to the Punjâb and then settling there.

The fact that Sâleh was an ethnic Mughal must have helped him advance in the new power structure after 1589.

Till the 19th century the order in which this title was placed in a name helped tell a Syed from a Mughal, at least in Kashmîr and the Punjâb. Syeds used Mîr as a title. However, by the end of the 19th century such distinctions began to get blurred. Even Mughals started using Mîr as a title, i.e. at the beginning of the name.

However, even to this day, in rural Kashmîr and the Punjâb genuine Mughals still use the word as a surname, at the end of the name.

Many Mîrs enjoyed temporal power and wealth till the end of the Dogrâ era. The palatial house of Khwâjâ Azîz Mîr in

Râjpur, Pulwâmâ, for instance, is testimony to this. In Chhatergul, Budgâm, the Dogrâs' *zaildâr* (chief of a group of villages), too, was a Mîr.

In 1911, there were 1,210 Mîrs in Jammû, 16,008 in Kashmîr and 28 in the 'frontier' areas.

Rafîquî This is a very well known clan. Their family-tree goes all the way back to Khwâjâ Sangîn Shâh (see 'Ashâî' above). Thus, the Rafîquîs are an offshoot of the Ashâî clan. This particular branch was founded by Khwâjâ Tâhir Rafîq Ashâî Suharwardî, who was a great-grandson of Khwâjâ Sangîn Shâh.

I have written about the Bambâs in a separate chapter. Some of them claim to be from Turkey. In that case they ought to be classified with the Mughals. However, the ancestry that I have mentioned in that chapter is based on very sound authority, including Fauq's. Lawrence adds, '(They) take wives from the Hatmâl and [Khakhâ] families of the country below [Bârâmullâ]. They give daughters in marriage to [Syeds]. Batkot is the old home of the [Bambâs] in Kashmîr, and when they die they are brought back to the beautiful burying-ground, still kept up in Batkot. The heads of [Bambâ] families are addressed as Râjâ, and the tract in which they live is known as Rajwara.'

Râjpût Muslims

All historians, from Kalhan of *The Râjâtarañginî* to Sir Walter Lawrence agree that in ancient times Kashmîr was ruled by kings who were Râjpûts. However, Fauq laments that the original *got(r)* of none of the present-day (Muslim) Râjpût clans is known. He singles out the Bhatti clan of Kashmîr and the Punjâb as being the exception. (*Got(r)s* are bloodlines; somewhat like sub-castes.)

While I respect Mr. Fauq's research enormously, the fact is that most Muslim Râjpûts have retained their old surnames, if not *got(r)s*. Thus, the Mâgré clan was called Mâgrésh before its conversion. In olden days, according to some historians, the Dârs were called Dâmars.[5] Till a few centuries ago they were called Dâñgars. The Nâiks have retained their Hiñdû name, as have the Pâls, Gakkhars and Râthors.

There's an interesting twist to this. It might solve the problem of the lost-to-memory *got(r)s* of the Râjpûts of Kashmîr. Fauq quotes a book called *Râjpût Goteiñ* ('The bloodlines of Râjpût clans') which makes a sweeping statement. It says, 'Evidence of Râjpût governments has been traced right up to Kashmîr. Because Râjpûts ruled over Kashmîr for a very long time therefore we believe that most of these Râjpût clans were Bhattîs.' Great logic. Makes life so simple for us self-styled anthropologists.

5. Lawrence writes, 'The Dâmars are said to be descendants of Sudras, the lowest of the four Hiñdû castes.'

The first modern census of the (united) state of Jammû and Kashmîr took place in 1851. It listed the following as being the best-known farming communities (read: rural chiefs and landlords) of Kashmîr: Pañdit, Sofi, Butt, Ittoo, Tâñtré, Khâñdé, Ganâî, Rainâ, Dâr (hard d), Râther and Rishî.

Now all eleven clans were classified in the said census as [Muslim] 'Brâhmin farmers'. This could be due to ignorance about caste on the part of the (mainly British) compilers of the census. Or, perhaps, several centuries after they had converted to Islâm it was difficult to say who was what before conversion. At least in theory the caste system has allotted the work of farming to the Kshatriya (Râjpût) caste. However, over the centuries some major 'martial' clans of soldier-farmers emerged among the Brâhmins as well.

By 1891, the census authorities seemed to realise that they might have erred about many of the aforementioned communities. That the Pañdits and Butts were 'Brâhmin farmers' is beyond doubt. The structure of the name Ittoo (or Yittoo), too, might suggest a Brâhmin origin. The Rishiîs might also have been Brâhmins before they accepted Islâm.

Incidentally, as my senior Mr. Mehmood ur Rehman pointed out, in Kashmîr if a person is called 'Pañdit' he will invariably, without exception, be a Muslim (ditto if he is called Butt; Hiñdûs use the spelling and pronunciation Bhat).

Lawrence classified the following (Muslim communities) as being of Kshatriya stock: Mâgré, Tâñtré, Dâr (hard d), Dâñgar, Rainâ, Râther, Thâkur, Nâik. Surprisingly he left out the Ganâîs.

Bhattî These are Chanderbansî Râjpûts. In the ninth generation after Lord Krishn there was a king called Râjâ Gaj. Fauq quotes a belief to the effect that this king founded the city of Ghaznî which, the story goes, was originally called Gajnî (get it? gaj-nî). He also cites a history that says that Râwalpiñdî was originally called Ganjîpurâ and was Gaj's capital. The Bhattis are Gaj's descendats.

Cunningham, the 19th century British army general cum historian, was of the opinion that the Bhattîs ruled over Kohistân Namak and Kashmîr from their capital at Ganjîpurâ, Râwalpiñdî. They ruled over Kashmîr till AD 1239, he adds. (This mystifies me. I am not aware of any Râwalpiñdî-based ruler controlling Kashmîr during that era. It is possible, though, that the Râwalpiñdî-based ruler was a general overlord to whom Kashmîr owed allegiance. Kashmîr's own histories make no mention of this.)

Dâr (with a hard d) There is unanimity among all scholars that the Dârs are of Kshatriya stock. They were great warriors in ancient times, and were the overlords of a major portion of the Valley. They are mentioned in *The Râjâtarañginî,* which refers to Koshthak, a famous Dâr of the Lehar (Lâr) area. He died on the battlefield. His wife was so distressed that she sat on his funeral pyre and committed sati. She did this, as Fauq points out, to keep her Râjpût-glory intact. Sati, as we know, was never widespread. It was always an upper-caste, and within those castes an elite, phenomenon.

Dâr (with a soft d)

Little is known about the origins of this community. Dâr (with a soft d) is certainly not a variant of the better known Dâr (with a hard d). According to one theory, Dâr (with a soft d) is actually a suffix, *-dâr* (the keeper, lord or owner of), as in Tehsîldâr (the chief of a sub-district) and Thânédâr (the head of the police station). Since this is a Persian suffix, it would seem that this community had held important positions in the power structure during mediæval times.

Kakr(h)û

The Gakhrû, Gakkhar(h), Khokhar and Âwân clans are inter-related. Some believe that these are all of Arab or Persian origin. Others classify them as Râjpûts. Old records show that at least the Gakkhar(h)s were Hiñdûs, and Râjpûts at that, when Mehmûd of Ghaznî came a-calling. This was in the tenth century AD Ferishtâ specifies that they were 'infidels' at the time.

The Gakkhar(h)s joined the Râjpût alliance against Mehmûd. At Péshâwar the Gakkhar(h)s and some other Râjpûts martyred between three and four thousand Muslims.

Throughout the history of the Valley, the Gakkhar(h)s crop up from time to time as a clan of fierce warriors.

Khatân

Mahârâjâ Gulâb Singh always depended very heavily on this brave clan of warriors, of whom he was extremely fond. In turn, the Khatâns always stood by their king during every crisis and whenever sensitive operations had to be carried out. The Chib Râjpûts of Mîrpur (Jammû) were the clan best represented in the forces that had the Mahârâjâ's confidence. The Khatâns are a branch of this clan.

When Zorâwar Singh led the Punjâb-Dogrâ army into Ladâkh to annex it in the 19th century, this clan was in the forefront. While the Punjâb-Dogrâ army won the war, the Khatâns lost a lot of their men, especially when they entered western Tibet. The Khatân clan was almost wiped out in that war. All male adults of this clan, except a youth who had not yet joined the army, were martyred. The Mahârâjâ summoned this young man, Shér Alî, and appointed him the head of the department that looked after the army's horses.

The Mahârâjâ took Shér Alî under his wings. When the Mahârâjâ went to Kashmîr he took Shér Alî along. Shér Alî fell in love with Kashmîr. He told the Mahârâjâ that he wanted to settle in the Valley. So the Mahârâjâ granted him an estate of 400 acres in Nâgâm (Budgâm).

Lone Lawrence classified the Lones (the e is silent) in the Vysya (business) caste. The clan believes that it migrated from Chillâs to Kashmîr. Neither claim is backed by evidence.

The clan, as Stein pointed out, has always been involved in the political power structure of its area, and sometimes of all of Kashmîr. It is first mentioned in *The Râjâtarañginî* as the Loniâ clan, during the reign of King Harsh (AD 1101). Stein wrote that the Lones seemed to be a very important part of the rural population of Kashmîr. All evidence indicates that they were a land-owning and farming community. The Vysyas, on the other hand, used to stick to shopkeeping and trade.

Mâgré The Mâgrés are a very old, pre-Islâmic ruling clan. There are countless references to them in the chapter 'A History of Kashmîr.' The name derives from Mâgrésh. In 1931, there were 7,668 Mâgrés in the state. They are also found in Jammû province and in the Punjâb.

Nâik The name of this clan derives from the Sañskrit word for 'leader' or 'chief.' (Fauq says that it means 'the wise one' or 'thinker' in Sañskrit. It is, therefore, the Kashmîrî equivalent of mantaqî.) Some scholars have classified the Nâiks as Brâhmins. However, as Fauq argues, not everyone in the learned professions was a Brâhmin.

What is certain is that this is a community of rural chieftains. They pop up in the history of Kashmîr at regular intervals. And they have always been a force to reckon with.

During the short lived reign of Queen Sugañdh Rânî (AD 921-923), the Nâiks teamed up with the Tântrés to kick up such a violent storm that the queen had to abdicate.

Then in Budshâh's time they entered into a matrimonial alliance with the family of Pâñdû Chak of Trehgâm.

When the Mughal Emperor Akbar attacked Kashmîr the clan's response varied. The Nâiks first resisted the invaders. Then Ibrâhim Nâik and Shañgî Nâik sensed that the war was going in favour of the Mughals. Some time between 1586 and 1589 they switched over to the would-be victors. However, Qâsim Nâik stuck it out and valiantly resisted his eponymous enemy, Mirzâ Qâsim Mîr Behrî.

Parré Like the Lon(e)s and Shâlîs, the Parrés are a clan of soldiers and farmers. Along with the Lones, they were always considered good fighters. There were 15,497 Parrés in Kashmîr in 1931.

Rainâ[6] This is an illustrious clan of rulers. Their history has been given in some detail in the chapter 'A History of Kashmîr.' In 1931, there were 3,873 Muslim Raina Râjpûts in the state.

Râther or **Râthor** In the various histories of Kashmîr they are referred as Râther, Râthor and Râo-thor, etc. They are of the same stock as the Janjûâ clan. They are Yaduvanshî Râjpûts, of the dynasty of Lord Krishn. In 1931, there were 39,725 of this clan in the state.

Shahmîrî This clan ruled over all of Kashmîr, as sultâns, longer than any other 'indigenous' Muslim dynasty. However, it depends on what one means by indigenous. Even the Shahmîrîs had migrated to the Valley from the frontier region of Svâd Kanîr (Swât) in AD 1315, during the reign of King Singh Dev or Sambha Dev. The political history of Kashmîr from AD 1320, till the beginning of the 16th century is really the history of this much-loved dynasty. (The correct pronunciation is both Shahmîrî and Shâhmîrî. Most authorities prefer the latter. Fauq has used both pronunciations, at different places.)

Tântré Some scholars feel that the word has been derived from 'tâñtric' and that this clan lived off the earnings of magic and mystic talismans. I have my doubts. Warriors don't peddle amulets. But then the Kashmîrî Pañdits accept the Tântrés as Brâhmins. The 1891 census listed them as Brâhmin farmers. They certainly are a soldier-farmer community. But were they Brâhmins? Sir Walter Lawrence listed them among the Râjpûts. In ancient records they are called the Tantrin clan. There were 5,478 members of this clan according to that census. By 1931, the number had increased to 12,253.

Thag The Thags claim to be Chanderbansî Râjpûts. Thag (or Thug) means highwayman (dacoit). However, the Thags have a better explanation. They say that their ancestor was a 15th century Râjpût from Chenaini (Udhampur, Jammû). He decided to go to Kashmîr because he had heard so much about Emperor Budshâh's sense of justice.

On the way he met a Muslim ascetic who converted him to Islâm. Budshâh found him talented and appointed him to a high rank in his army. Presently, the Râjpût Muslim from Jammû married a Kashmîrî woman.

6. This is a name that conveys nothing. A Rainâ can be a Brâhmin, a Râjpût or even a Dogrâ carpenter.

One day the emperor told the officer, 'You can ask me for any favour.' The newly converted officer replied, 'All I want is enough land to spread my prayer mat on.'

Now a prayer mat hardly takes up less space than a bath-towel. The emperor was pleased by his officer's simplicity. But the Râjpût's wife was offended that her husband had let such a good chance slip by. She told the emperor, 'My husband should have asked you to grant him enough to look after the needs of his children, himself and me.'

Budshâh remarked, 'This man has turned out to be quite a *thug*. He created a good impression on me by asking for nothing, but he got his wife to give me a long shopping list.'

In 1931, there were around 4,000 members of this clan. They are found in Bhaderwâh, Kishtwâr, Srînagar, Râjourî, Ânañtnâg and Pâdar. See also the section 'The Dard-Shîn People of Guréz' in the chapter 'The People of Kashmîr.'

Sheikhs

In most Muslim lands, new converts are called by the honorific Sheikh. However, in Kashmîr certain former-Brâhmins still choose to be called 'Pañdit.' This is a group that once specialised in medicine and education. They retain their old caste-name in part because it is the only surname that they have, and in part, as Fauq implies, because of the prestige attached to it. However, as elsewhere, they are called Sheikhs (and Khwâjâs) as well.

In 1911, there were 3,326 Pañdit Muslims in the state. Their number had increased to 3,584 by 1931. The male: female ratio was 100:87. In the middle of the 19th century many Pañdit Muslims migrated to Amritsar, Siâlkot and Lahore.

Âkhûn Historian Hassan wrote that there were four kinds of Mullâs: i) The kind that lives off the earnings of mosques, acts as imâms and educates male children. Such people are called 'Âkhûn,' which is the Persian word for teacher. This category includes clans called Maulvî, Qâzî, Mallâ, Mullâ, Muftî and Âkhûn. ii) Gorkan. iii) Ghusâl: This is the Persian word for those who wash and cleanse corpses before burial. iv) Farmers.

Bâbâ Like 'Shâh' this is not the name of a clan or tribe. Instead Bâbâ and Shâh are honorifics by which the community around them used to address likeable and respectable families. Bâbâ is also a title associated with the Syeds and other saints.

Butt/ Bhat This is a surname shared by Hiñdûs and Muslims alike. The Butts are almost certainly of Brâhmin origin.

Drâbû Drabîyâr is a neighbourhood in Srînagar. According to one theory, people of this area who have migrated to other neighbourhoods or villages are known as Drâbûs. A more likely theory traces their origin to the Drabagâm village of Budgâm. They were called Drâbû when they migrated to Srînagar. The place where they built their houses came to be called Drabîyâr, and not the other way around.

Ganâî Most Ganâîs trace their ancestry to local Râjpûts. This is a very old clan, certainly older than the reign of Emperor Budshâh. They were active members of Budshâh's nobility, and also close associates of Sheikh Nûr-ud-Dîn. In Kashmîrî folklore they have a reputation for wisdom.

Ishberî Ishber (or Îshâ-ber) is a now-affluent neighbourhood near the Nishât Garden and close to the Dal Lake. In the *Râjâtarañginî* it is mentioned as the place where a Jesus-(Îshâ-) like saint was crucified, buried in a vault and resurrected. The village is also a major pilgrimage of the Hiñdûs. The original inhabitants of the village were known as the Ishberîs when they migrated to the city. Many of them were Brâhmins,

Kaul Historian Hassan wrote that the Kauls were the highest ranking Brâhmins. After conversion to Islâm, too, the clan produced several eminent men.

Kut Râj It is said that the ancestors of this clan used to be the rulers of Multân. They migrated to Kashmîr when they were dethroned in Multân and needed employment. They captured the present Budgâm area during one of Kashmîr's numerous civil wars.

Makhdûmî There are three kinds of Makhdûmî clans in Kashmîr. i) The descendants of Bâbâ Alî Rainâ, who was the brother of the enormously respected 16th century saint, Makhdûm Sâheb. ii) Those who have been managing the legacy of Makhdûm Sâheb during the last five centuries. iii) The residents of the Kalâshpurâ neighbourhood.

Malik This is a title of Central Asian origin, conferred by the Sultâns of Kashmîr on their nobility (courtiers, rural chieftains and senior civil and military officers). It is not the name of a caste-group or clan. The rulers of Kashmîr also gave this title to the guardians of the highways to central India and Turkestân. Fauq says that all Maliks were Hiñdûs before their conversion.

Mallâ See 'Âkhûn.'

Mântjû or **Mântjî** This is one of Kashmîr's pre-eminent clans in terms of learning and the 'knowledge of developments in the world of religious and secular scholarship.'

Mattû (with soft t's)	Khwâjâ Dâûd, a Kashmîrî, was an expert in 'the science of all things that are manifest.' However, he did not know how to get into a spiritual trance. He once went to meet the legendary saint, Khwâjâ Habîbullâh Naushehrî. The saint cast a glance at Dâud and rendered him unconscious. On that day he learnt the art of spiritual ecstasy. Mattû is a Kashmîrî word that roughly means 'he who is possessed' or 'the entranced one.' Ever since, the descendants of Khwâjâ Dâud have been known as the Mattûs. (Incidentally, it is because of a Persian verse written by Khwâjâ Habîbullâh Naushehrî, a mediæval saint, that we know that a 'prophet' and a 'king' [the king of kings?] is buried in Rozâbal.)
Mullâ	See 'Âkhûn.'
Pañdit	See the first two paragraphs of this section.
Pîrzâdâ	This is not the name of a clan or sub-caste. Each important disciple of a Syed *pîrs* (hereditary saints) was called a Pîrzâdâ (lit.: 'the son of a pîr') or even simply 'Pîr.' Even *pîrs* who are not Syeds are known as *pîrs* if they have a significant number of disciples, a following.
Putlû	The name is derived from the Kashmîrî-Urdû word 'putlâ,' which means 'idol.' This community retained its pre-Islâmic name even after conversion to a faith that opposes idol worship. When they were Hiñdûs they either made and sold idols, or were keepers of idols at temples.
Qâsmî	In Srînagar, there once was a saint called Hazrat Sheikh Muhammad. Sheikh Qâsim Bahâî was his grandson. Qâsim's descendants are now known as the Qâsmî Pîrzâdâs.
Rishî (or **Réshî)**	The word is supposed to have been derived from the Sañskrit 'rikhî.' In 1891, there were 6,290 members of this community in Kashmîr. In 1911, there were 7,686 Rishis, including 459 in Jammû province and 22 in the 'frontier[7].' By 1931, their numbers had increased to 10,288. The male: female ratio was 100:82. This is significant, because the Rishî saints were entirely men and celibate. Clearly, over the centuries the Rishis became a clan, a community. Even Fauq traces the origin of this community to the Rishî saints.
Sâdhû	The ancestors of this major clan were highly literate and, to quote Fauq, worldly-wise. The clan has several sub-castes, including Mor (pronounced like 'more'), Budchî, Mârû,

7. Essentially the areas now in Ladâkh and what Pâkistân called the Northern Areas.

Sheikh, Mâtak, Qâzî, Mashehdî and Shâh. Much of the clan migrated to Lahore during the Sikh era.

Shâh See 'Bâbâ.'

Shâl Kashmîr has been making pashmînâ (cashmere) shawls since the ancient period. (See the chapter on 'Shawls.') However, the word shawl (or, more correctly, shâl) came to Kashmîr only in AD 1542, with Naghz Beig. Till then this garment was called 'pombar,' which is the Kashmîrî-Sañskrit compound word for 'robe' or 'garment.' By the mediæval age Kashmîr had a flourishing trade in shâwls. Merchants who traded in them and grew quite wealthy in the process, as well as their descendants, are called Shâls.

Sûd The Sûds of Kashmîr were known for their learning, which they would pass down the generations. Fauq feels that this is a pre-Islâmic surname that the Muslims retained after their conversion. Some of them were among the closest companions and disciples of Makhdûm Sâheb.

Tâk This is a trading community. Apparently they are the descendants of the three talented sons of a wealthy Hiñdû of Srînagar. 'Tâk' means 'three.' The other theory is that two Hiñdûs of Srînagar converted to Islâm. One of them went to Bîjbehârâ all alone (*tâk*). So he came to be called Tâk. The other brother went to Kâshghar for several years. On his return he settled in Shopiâñ, where he came to be know as the Kâshghar Tâk.

Top Gurû/ Topé Gurû These days the Top Gurûs are people who make caps. Top Gurû or Tope Gurû is a huge humongous clan, being a coalition of smaller groups. For example, if a Lone or Butt were to start making caps, they, too, would be called 'Top Gurû.'

However, historically some very respectable people have sported this name. Maulânâ Muhammad Âbid was a leading cleric of Srînagar. Once he went to his spiritual master wearing a newfangled cap. The master remarked indulgently, 'Here comes a Top Gurû.'

Trambû Trambû is a fruit that grows in the Gurêz area. People who traded in it are called the Trambûs.

Vândar Vândar and vandar are the Kashmîrî-Hindi word for 'monkey.' For some reason this clan came to be saddled with this, er, moniker. Khwâjâ Ishâq Vandar (18th century AD), a leading saint, is the first of this clan to be mentioned in a historical record.

Woin or **Wânî** or **Wâin** — Before conversion to Islâm the Woins probably belonged to the Vysya (business) caste. Even after conversion to Islâm they continued to be businessmen. The area of their trade has historically included Ladâkh. There were 59,487 Woins/ Wânîs in the state in 1911, and 72,113 in 1931. Some of them migrated to the Punjâb, where they have held high offices.

Martial Brâhmins

Pâl — Lawrence classifies the Pâls among the Brâhmins. He probably based his theory on mediæval historian Ferishtâ's note that '(King) Jai Pâl son of Asan Pâl belonged to the Brâhmin community.'

Fauq disagrees. He argues that Jai Pâl was related to the King of Ajmér and that Ajmér was 'obviously' ruled by a Râjpût king. Therefore Jai Pâl, too, must have been a Râjpût. His point is that no Brâhmin would have married into a Râjpût family.

The caste system was never as rigid as modern scholars assume. There is no reason why a Brâhmin could not be related to a Râjpût king. In any case there is a theory that not all Râjpûts are of Kshatriya origin. Some are of martial-Brâhmin stock as well.

On the authority of Ferishtâ and Lawrence I believe that the Pâls are of Brâhmin origin. Which is not to say that they were Kashmîrî Pandits. They are of martial-Brâhmin stock.

Some other important clans

Âwân or — There were 27,588 Âwâns in the state in 1911, most of them in Poonch (Jammû).

Bachâ — Bachâ is Kashmîrî Hiñdî Urdû for 'lad' or 'young boy.' In Kashmîr the word has a specific meaning as well. A *bachâ* is a pretty young lad who dances for a living. There is a very respectable clan of traders of this name in Sopore.

Chak — This clan and its history have been discussed in considerable detail in the chapter 'A History of Kashmîr.' Lawrence states that they were certainly not converted from the local Hiñdûs, that they came from Chillâs and were Dards.

Dév — This is an eminent clan of ethnic Kashmîrî Muslims who live in Bhaderwâh and Kishtwâr.

Dîwânî — Khwâjâ Ishâq Jîlânî (died AH 826/ 14th century) founded this clan. He was 91 when he was martyred on the orders of Tîmûr's son Shâhrukh Mîrzâ. He was buried in Jîlân. Khwâjâ Sibgatullâh belonged to the third generation after Ishâq. He migrated from Hérât to Kashmîr during the reign of Sultân Sikañder (late 14th century). Sibgatullâh was a senior member of the ruling elite of his native land. So Sultân Sikañder granted him an estate in Kashmîr. He also gave Sibgatullâh a high rank ('Dafâtar Sultân Âlâ' or 'the Offices of the exalted Sultan'). As a result his descendants are known as the Dîwânîs.

Hâpat Hâpat means 'bear.' The founder of this clan killed two bears in a single day in the Ânañtnâg area.

Haqqânî Shâh Qâsim Haqqânî belonged to the fifth generation of the dynasty of Pîr Shams-ud-Dîn Shâmî. The Pîr was an associate of Mîr Syed Alî Hamadânî. (14th century AD) He was a fearless advocate of the truth (*haq*). Therefore, he came to be known as Haqqânî.

Întû (Or **Aintû** or **Entû**.) This clan used to sell the lids of clay vessels. A few families of this clan live in Sopore.

Jahâz This family was dominant in Kashmîr's pashmînâ (cashmere) trade, which in Mughal times (16th century and even before) flourished in the Punjâb and during the Sikh era made enormous profits in Western Europe. (See chapters 17 and 18 'Handicrafts' and 'Shawls.') Jahâz means 'ship.' A pashmînâ trader from Kashmîr once loaded a fortune in shawls onto a ship that was meant to go to France. The ship got caught in a storm and was diverted to some other land. News spread in Kashmîr that the ship had sunk. Later when the ship reached France, safe though much delayed, there was much jubilation in Kashmîr. The trader's friends promptly named him Jahâz (the ship).

Kannû Kannû is a kind of grass. It yields a fibre with which the Kashmîrîs have traditionally woven shoes (*polâ harû*). The Hiñdû women of Srînagar were the biggest patrons of these leatherless shoes. A persian couplet suggests that this family got such shoes made for 'Hiñdû *zanân* (women).'

The Kannû family has produced eminent men of learning and religion, including Muhammad Asraf Yakta, Allâmâ Amânullâh (died AH 1152/ 18th century AD) and the celebrated Khwâjâ Khairuddîn Baldémarî. Trade was the Kannûs' day job.

Kâûsâ (Kawoosa) This clan is not ethnic Kashmîrî. However, no one knows the name of the country from which it migrated to Kashmîr. The Kâûsâs have been in Kashmîr since at least the fifteenth or sixteenth century AD. The first Kâûsâ to find mention in a recorded history was Mullâ Yûsuf. One Nadîm Shâhjehânî introduced him to the court of a Shâhmîrî king. This was to draft a reply to the King of Rûm. The Mullâ did it so well that the king admitted him to the royal court. After that this clan flourished under the Shâhmîrî kings.

Khatîb This is a clan of ethnic Kashmîrî Muslims living in Bhaderwâh and Kishtwâr (both in Jammû province). The founders of the clan used to read the *khutbâ* (sermon).

Mughal Some Kashmîrî and Punjâbî Mughals use the surname 'Mughal.' Before the Mughals annexed Kashmîr (in 1586-89) there had been two major historical figures who used this surname: Hâjî Mughal and Sûfî Mûsâ Mughal. Hâjî Mughal was a pupil and disciple of Sheikh Saifuddîn. He is buried in the courtyard of the seminary of Syed Muhammad Aman (Amîn?) Bakhshî. Sûfî Mûsâ Mughal was a disciple of Makhdûm Sâheb. He had a cheerful and attractive voice, a contemporary record tells us. Clearly, both had migrated to Kashmîr before the Mughals began to rule the Valley. (I wonder: could Sûfî Mûsâ Mughal have persuaded his mentor and fellow disciples to invite the Mughals to rule Kashmîr?)

During the Mughal era in Kashmîr there was a Khwâjâ Hayât Mughal. A village called Hayâtpurâ in the Awantipur area is named after him.

Shâlbâf This is a Persian surname that means 'the maker of [pashmînâ] shawls.' The Kashmîrî name for this clan is 'Khañd-wow.'

Shonthû The founder of this clan was very circumspect (*shontû*) in his speech. He would weigh things over thoroughly before offering his opinion on anything.

Sûfî This community has descended from various Hiñdû clans, most of them Brâhmin. Because of their close association with sûfî saints they were given the general title Sûfî.

The Turks The Turks first came to Kashmîr during the pre-Islâmic era. Three (non-Muslim) princes from Turkestân ruled over Kashmîr for a total of 42 years. The Turks attacked Kashmîr during the reign of King Jai Singh. Then during the era of King Sahadev (1301-1320), Zulchû @ Zulqadar Khân devastated Kashmîr. Was Zulchu a Turk? Many historians say that he was. But them, as Fauq says, in Kashmîr all Muslim invaders are called Turks, even Tîmûr and Mehmûd of Ghaznî.

Today most of the Turks of Kashmîr are farmers. Some migrated from Muzaffarâbâd as recently as in the early 19th century. When their fellow Muslims from newly-created Pâkistân ravaged Kashmîr in 1947, the Turks of villages like Larî Dorâ (Bârâmullâ) personally escorted the microscopic Hiñdû community to the safety of distant Srînagar. Like most

Muslims of Kashmîr, this community has an excellent record of race relations.

Vakîl Mullâ Abdus Salâm was an eminent scholar of the Mughal era. He was the brother-in-law of Murâd-ud-Dîn Khân, through whose good offices he managed to become a lawyer (*vakîl*) in one of the Mughal courts. The name has carried down to his descendants. (Not all Vakîls of Kashmîr, leave alone India as a whole, belong to this clan. However, Abdus Salâm's is the main Vakîl clan of Kashmîr.)

Castes associated with culture and specialised professions

Bâñd These are talented singers, actors and satirists. They have been mentioned at several places in this book, especially in connection with festivals. Also spelt Bhâñd. They have eponymous counterparts in parts of the Punjâb, too.

Chopân Kashmîrî (as opposed to Bakerwâl) shepherds.

Dom According to Lawrence the Doms or Dûms were *shûdr* (underprivileged) Hiñdûs before their conversion. Makes sense, because there are underclass Dûm Hiñdûs in Jammû as well.

Gallâ-bân The Gallâ-bâns (or Galbâns, or Galwâns) rear horses. One such horse-rearer, called Galwân, used to provide horses to British officers of the Râj. He learnt a smattering of English and went on to author an early-20th century pidgin classic called *Servant of the Sâhibs.*

Hâñjî There is a detailed section on the Hânjî boatmen of Kashmîr in the chapter 'The People of Kashmîr.'

Wâtal These are the charpeople of Kashmîr. Their festival at Hazratbal used to be a major annual event. Thanks to prosperity, many of them have given up their ancestral profession but also some of their customs.

The Kashmîrî Pañdits

The number of Kashmîrî Pañdit clans is so large that my list is at best a sample.

The Qistbâshî Pañdits

This is a community that used to collect taxes in ancient and mediæval times. They took on the names of whoever or whatever they collected taxes from. Their names are quite unflattering, because they mean things like 'ass.' The names actually mean '[people who collect taxes from]...'.

Âram This community used to collect taxes from the ârams (vegetable-growers) for the government. There is a major

	neighbourhood in Sopore called Ârampurâ, where vegetable-growers live. The word is derived from the Sañskrit âramak and is mentioned in the *Râjâtarañginî.*
Baqâyâ	Baqâyâ is the Persian word for 'that which remains' or 'arrears.' This community used to collect tax arrears for the government.
Gazarbân	If you read the chapter 'Traditional routes between Srînagar and Muzaffarâbâd' you will come across references to customs houses. The Gazarbâns were people who collected this duty.
Gurû	Surprise. Gurû does not mean what you think it does. In Kashmîr this is a community of cowherds and milkmen. Gurû is the Kashmîrî word for Gujjar. People who taxed the Gujjar cowherds or were patwârîs (juniormost but powerful revenue officials), too, were called Gurûs.
Khar or **Kher**	(Khur, actually.) Khar and khur mean 'donkey' or 'ass.' This clan used to collect taxes from those whom we now call 'pony-owners.'
Krâl	Krâl means potter. Krâlapurâ in Srînagar is where the potters have a major presence. The Krâls used to collect taxes from potters.
Manwatî	Manwatî is a weight equal to a little more than a kilogram. The rice crop would be measured by the *manwatî.* People who collected taxes on the rice crop were called Manwatî.
Nehrû	Neher means canal. Don't ever believe the legend then this community used to live next to a canal. The fact is that the Nehrûs used to collect water-taxes and taxes levied on embankments where boats would land.
Qâzî	Hiñdûs as well as Muslims who collected taxes on gold (and on gold related disputes) were called Qâzî. I always thought that a Qâzî was necessarily a Muslim religious judge. This particular use of the word, instead, derives from *qazâyâ*, which means 'dispute, case, [law] suit, quarrel.'

Important Clans of the Kashmîrî Pandits

Below are likely explanations for the origin of some of the best known Kashmîrî Pañdit surnames. If you read the section 'Surnames and nicknames' in the chapter 'The People of Kashmîr' before you read the table below, you might appreciate that many of these names started off as a joke,

You will notice in this chapter that people come to be known by the name of their ancestral village only after they migrate to some other village of town. I suppose that makes sense. Pam French is certainly British. So, I believe, is Andre Deutsch. No one within France would need to be called 'French' or 'Francais.' It's only when you migrate to another land that your ancestral land becomes a mark of your identity. That's the way you see yourself and that's how the natives of your adopted land see you.

Arz-bégî All over the Indian sub-continent illiterate people go to petition-writers to draft their letters and applications. Such people are known as Arz-bégîs.

Atal See Thalal.

Badhû or **Bajû** In Kashmîr, as in 19th century Punjâb, Hiñdûs, Muslims and Sikhs consider it auspicious to give their children this name. It is said to make the person so named live very long.

Bakhshî Muslims as well as Hiñdûs who were accountants in the army and distributed salaries were known as Bakhshîs.

Bazâz This is a large clan spread over Central India as well. Their ancestors used to sell cloth.

Bhân Bhân(u) means 'the sun.' This is a very ancient clan. Their traditional home is the Bhân Muhallâ, which is between the Habbâ Kadal and the Fateh Kadal.

Chakâ The founder of this clan was the last of twelve children. Apparently his parents were slightly embarrassed at having such a large brood.

Chakbast Chak means 'a plot of land.' Such plots were (and often still are) granted by the government of the day to farmers and others. Officers who oversaw such land grants were called *chakbasts.*

Fota-dâr/ Fotedâr The founders of this clan were senior officers of the Mughal treasury. (The literal meaning of this Persian-Arabic name would be 'a person with, er, testicles.' However, no respectable dictionary supports such an interpretation.)

Gandnû The name refers to 'a bunch (of flowers).' Apparently this family was in the bouquet-making trade.

Gurtû This is an offshoot of the Râzdân clan. They belong to the Kûchâ Râzdânâñ of Gand Al-hamar. One of this clan, Pt. Mukund Râm Gurtû, migrated to Lahore in the middle of the nineteenth century and was the first Kashmîrî to publish a newspaper.

Hakîm This Arabic word means 'the doctor' or 'the healer.' Fauq feels that there must have been doctors in this clan, which gave them their name.

Handû Handû is the Kashmîrî word for 'sheep.' Apparently, the founder of this clan was 'as fat as a sheep.'

Hazârî Sardâr Hazâr Khân was the governor of Kashmîr during the Afghân era. Fauq's theory is that the Hazârîs were his trusted

	lieutenants. I thought that they had something to do with the Hazârâ district.
Ishberî	Same as among Muslims.
Jawân Shér	This is an Afghân name. There was an Afghân governor by this name. His 'reader' (judicial clerk) took on the surname of his boss[8].
Kâchrû	A very old elite family. It has produced eminent historians and writers.
Kakrû	There is a village called Kakrû Guñd near Achhâbal (Ânañtnâg). That's where the Kakrûs came from. Fauq believes that the Koker Nâg spring is named after this clan. (But the standard theory is that the spring is named so because it looks like the claws of a *koker* [chicken].)
Kalposh	Kalposh is a cap worn by Hiñdû as well as Muslim women. A male of this clan once wore a kalposh as a joke. His clan came to be known by the name.
Kannû	The name is derived from the Kashmîrî words for 'tasteless,' 'food without salt' and 'as thin as water.' Once a saint from Rainâwâri, Miâñ (Mânak) Shâh, asked a Kaul, 'What was the food at the feast like?' The Kaul replied, 'Tasteless. Thin as water. There was no salt in the food.' The saint commented, 'In that case you are a Kanîn Kaul.' The word gradually changed to Kannû.
Kanzrû	Kunzer is a major satellite village of Gulmarg and Tañgmarg. That's where the Kanzrûs (or Kunzrûs) come from.
Kâr	This clan comes from a village called Kârhâmâ in tehsil Handwârâ (Kupwârâ) in north Kashmîr. That's where the Kârs come from.
Karvâîyûñ	Karvâîyûñ means 'hot water' as well as 'those who sell peas.' This sub-sect actually belongs to the Dév Shândliya clan and are Malmâs pañdits.
Kât(h)jû	Kâthéshwar was an ancient pilgrimage near Tanki Kadal in Srînagar. In the Dogrâ era a new temple was built on its foundations. The Kât(h)jû clan lived in this neighbourhood.
Katwâ	This is a sub-sect of the Wâzâ clan. Katwâ is the Kashmîrî word for 'small cooking vessel.
Kilam	These are the former residents of Killam, a village in Kulgâm tehsil (Ânañtnâg).

8. Taking the name of the boss' clan was quite widespread. In Lolâb, within forty years of Dogrâ rule a (Muslim) clan began to call itself 'Dogrâ' because its members had served the Dogrâ rulers for two generations.

Killa-wât An Englishman named Col. Watt supervised the construction of the Pahalgâm road. He had a Kashmîrî Pañdit man Friday called Kailash Nâth. In Kashmîr 'Kailash' normally gets shortened to the nickname 'Killa.' Because of his association with Col.Watt, he (and his descendants) came to be called Killa-wât.

Kotrû Kotrû or Kotar is the Kashmîrî equivalent of the Hiñdî-Urdû word *kabûtar* (pigeon). Apparently, the founder of the clan had a large number of pet pigeons.

Kurâz Kurâz is the name of a fierce animal.

Lâbrû Literally, 'the profiteer.' Lâb(h) is Sañskrit for 'profit' and 'benefit.' This is a clan of businessmen.

Lâl These are Kashmîrî Pañdits whose ancestors had served under Punjâbî *lâlâs* (middling businessmen).

Lañgar or **Lañgrû** A lañgar is a community kitchen. The founder of this clan was the chief administartor of some ancient, government-run, community kitchen.

Langû Langû means 'the lame one.' Fauq feels that the founder of the clan was lame. But would people call someone with specially abled limbs 'lame'? I wonder. My guess is that the original Mr. Langû was merely faking it. People saw through his sham and started teasing him.

Mallâ or **Mullâ** No, this name has nothing to do with Muslim priesthood. It's just a coincidence that the two words are identical. There are two theories about their origin: i) They were vegetable-growers (*malyâr*) or, as is more likely, they collected *malyâr* taxes. ii) They are the original residents of Srînagar's Mallâpurî neighbourhood (near Ganpatyâr). This clan has truly distinguished itself in Allahâbâd and other parts of central India, as jurists as well as brave soldeirs.

Mantû This sub-group is related to the Manwatî clan. *Man tî* means one and a half *sér* (almost one kilogram). The legend, almost certainly apocryphal (because it so resembles the etymology of Manwatî), is that the founder of the clan had eaten a *man tî* of rice in a single meal.

March-wâñgan The name literally means 'red chilli.' This moniker was given to a hot-tempered clan.

Misrî Misrî means 'the Egyptian.' I had always thought that names like Misrî and Parimû ('the foreigner') suggested that these clans had come from foreign lands. They could possibly be the Jews who keep popping up in theories about the origin of the Kashmîrî people. Fauq has a different spin. He says that the first Mr. Misrî was the local agent of an Egyptian trader.

Motâ Fauq's theory is that 'motâ' means 'fatso,' the same as in Hiñdî-Urdû. The founder of the clan was horizontally enhanced, according to Fauq.

Mubaî or **Mumbaî** This is the pen-name of a Kashmîrî Pañdit family whose members had gone to Bombay (which, even then, was called Mumbai by the local people). One of this family was a well-known journalist, who wrote for a community magazine.

Munshî This is a sub-caste of the Tikkû clan. Munshîs are (accounts) clerks. There was a very celebrated Munshî during the Sikh or Afghân era. He gave up his ancestral surname and preferred to the called Munshî instead. Apparently it was a big thing to be a Munshî in those days.

Mushrân Mushrân means 'ugly like a fierce demon.' The word is the stuff of popular Kashmîrî curses. This community has been living in central India since at least the 19th century AD. I don't buy the theory that the original Mr. Mushrân was truly challenged in the looks department. That's because a) the present generation is quite nice looking, and b) one doesn't remind homely people that they are that. Obviously, this nickname came off as a joke.

Nâlâ This is the nickname of a clan of Dattâ-tréya Kashmîrî Pañdits. Apparently, they were the superintendents or protectors of a stream (nâllâh).

Ogrâ This is a sub-sect of the Dattâ-tréya clan.

Pâmporî The Kashmîrî Pañdits of Pâmpore (Pulwâmâ) are, regardless of their sub-caste, called Pâmporî by the people of Srînagar.

Pehelwân Pehelwân means i) a champion, ii) a successful wrestler and iii) a member or retainer of the Pehalvi dynasty of Irân. I always assumed that the Pehelwâns of Kashmîr belonged to the third category. Fauq, however, tells us about the legendary Gawâb Pehelwân, who belonged to this tiny clan. His point is that this was a clan of muscular athletes. He adds that among the Kashmîrî Pañdits the other champion athletes were the Shérâs and among the Muslims the star wrestlers were from the Sabahâ clan.

Peshin Peshin means 'evening.' It is also the Persian word for the *zuhr* prayers. Apparently, the ancestors of this clan were government servants whose main duty started after the *peshin* prayers.

Pîr Pîr Pañdit Pâdshâh (16th century AD) was one of the greatest Kashmîrî Pañdit saints ever. His temple is in Bata-yâr, Âlî Kadal. The Muslims, too, respect him enormously. All Kashmîrî

Pañdits who sport the surname Pîr are descendants of the disciples of this saint, who was also called Rishî Pîr.

Pûrbî Literally, 'the easterner.' This is a 19th century moniker given by some officials in Delhi to a Kashmîrî Pañdit who held high office under the Nawâbs (rulers) of Lucknow (a city which is to the east of Kashmîr and Delhi).

Qulî This name came to Kashmîr from Afghânistân. During the Afghân era there were two famous Afghân chieftains—Târ Qulî Khân and Nûr Jañg Qulî Khân Durrânî. Kashmîrî Pañdits who grew close to (and/ or received employment under) these chiefs took on their surnames.

Raghû or **Ragû** No, this clan did not get its name from the Prince of Ayodhyâ. The name, instead, means 'the skinny one.' Apparently the founder of this clan was slightly built.

Sabû This clan would perform priestly (*purohit*) functions in Srînagar town.

Saprû The Saprûs were the first group of Kashmîrî Pañdits to learn the Persian language. (This was in the reign of Budshâh, in the early 15th century AD)

Sas Sas is a mainly vegetarian dish. Apparently the founder of this clan was asked what he had eaten at a feast that he had been to. He replied, 'Sas.'

Shagâlî This clan came over from Kâbul with the Afghâns. Their founder had the title 'Mîrzâ' and the surname Shagâlî. His given name was Mal or Mamal.

Shâlâ The Shâlâs are the residents of Shâlâ Kadal (near Habbâ Kadal).

Shanglû Shanglû literally means 'a person with six (*shay*) fingers (*ungal*).' Apparently, the first Shanglû had six fingers in one of his hands.

Shargâ Shargâ means 'parrot.' People with parrot-like eyes, too, are called Shargâ. This is a sub-caste of the Kauls. The Shargâs migrated to central India and produced eminent littérateurs.

Shâyar Literally: the poet. The founder of this clan was an eminent poet of the 18th century, when the Mughals were fading and the Afghâns were on the ascendant.

Shér A very brave and well-built clan, renowned for its physical prowess. According to a legend, the founder of the clan had grappled with a 'lion' (presumably, a leopard).

Soporî This clan migrated from Sopore to Srînagar in ancient times.

Sukâ The name refers to a sour kind of yeast. It derives from the Sañskrit 'sur-âhâr' ('to drink alcohol').

Sukhiyâ There are some families of Kashmîrî Pañdit *purohits* that are called sakh, sikh or even sukh. In central India they are called Sukhiyâ.

Sultân These were the agents and representatives of the sultâns of Kashmîr. They took on their masters' title.

Thalal Thalal means 'to collide (against someone or something).' It also refers to people whose broad foreheads indicate a high rank. The name Atal is certainly derived from Thalal. (In the chapter 'Were the Kashmîris Jews?' I have argued that Atal might be a Sañskrit word. It is. However, the Kashmîrî names Qâzî, Walî and Gurû only by a coincidence sound like identical Arabic and Sañskrit names. Similarly, it is possible that the two Atals might be totally different words.)

Thussû There's a village called Thus in the Kulgâm tehsîl of south Kashmîr. When the Kashmîrî Pandits of Thus migrated to Srînagar they came to be called Thussû.

Tîmnî The correct pronunciation is Tâî-manî. Fauq's guess is that this clan might have descended from the *munîs* (ascetics).

Tork or **Turk** or **Turkî** Fauq's theory is that such Kashmîrî Pañdits as were the agents of Turkish traders started calling themselves after their employers. Kashmîr's close links with Turkey and Turkmenistân date to well before Islâm came to either land. There were Turks (*turushk*) in the pre-Islâmic armies of Kashmîr. Can't the Kashmîrî Pañdits who bear these names be of Turkish stock? Kashmîr has a very substantial population of (Muslim) Turks in the hills. They are quite poor and speak a form of Punjâbi or Pahârhî at home.

Ukhul or **Vukhul** or **Wukhlû** The Ukhuls live mostly in central India and the Punjâb. Their Kashmîrî ancestors were (and cousins still are) known as Vukhul or Wukhlû. An Ukhul is a stone on which dirty wet clothes are beaten during their cleaning. Because there were no washermen or laundries, such stones were kept in every neighbourhood. Kashmîrî Pañdits in whose houses these stones were placed were called the Ukhuls.

Vichârî In Sañskrit, Vichârî would literally mean 'the thinker.' Fauq supports this theory. However, I suspect that this clan came from the Vichâr Nâg area.

Vishen The clan has been named after its founder. Vishen is the Kashmîrî word for Lord Vishnû.

Walî Surprise. Walî is derived not from the Muslim word for saint but from walû (see below).

Walû A walû is a hole in the wall through which the Kashmîrî chimney lets smoke escape to the outside. Apparently the man who invented this chimney-hole was given the title Walû.

Wânchû Fauq writes that no one is sure about how this name came into being. It is perhaps a variant of Wântû or Wânchî.

Wângnû Wângan is the Kashmîrî word for brinjal (eggplant). This vegetable might be great for health but it is the favourite of very few people. The founder of this clan was either excessively fond of this unpopular food or hated it so much that his friends started calling him by this name in order to tease him.

Wântû A wântû is a walnut without a kernel, or with a very inadequate seed.

Wâtal My friend Rattan Wâtal told me that 'Wâtal' means 'sweeper' or 'charperson.' The wâtals were 'untouchables' under the caste system. Some of Rattan's ancestors gave the wâtals shelter for a few days. This, in the eyes of their hidebound contemporaries, was enough to pollute Rattan's ancestors. So, Rattan's ancestors came to be called the Wâtals.

Wâzâ A clan of chefs and cooks.

Wazîr According to Fauq, Kashmîrî Pañdit employees in the offices of Mughal and Afghân governors and viziers came to be called Wazîrs themselves.

I have no doubt that the ancestors of at least some present-day Kashmîrî Pañdit Wazîrs were full-fledged viziers themselves.

Zâbû This is a sub-sect of the Râzdâns. Apparently one of their ancestors was slightly built, hence the name.

Zâdû This is a clan of *purohits* (priests). Zâdû means 'land,' more accurately 'wetland.' The Zâdûs are a people who live deep inside the inhabited part of a town or village: in the downtown, so to speak.

Zutshî Also called Jotshî. This is a clan of astrologers.

Prominent émigré clans

The prominent émigré Kashmîrî Pañdit clans of the 19th and early 20th centuries were:

Chhachh- Chhatâbal is a suburb of Srînagar. It is also known as Chhachhbal. The Râzdân Pañdits used to live there. Pañdit Kishen Dâs of this family migrated from Kashmîr in 1757. He first went to Lucknow and Benâres. His family came to be called Chhachh-balî because of their ancestral neighbourhood. His grandson, Pañdit Gañgâ Râm held a commission in the army and was posted in Delhi during the Marâthâ era.

Dar During Emperor Aurangzéb's era, one of his army contingents was stationed at a border post near Muzaffarâbâd. The commandant got talking about roots with one of his juniors, Shiv Pañdit. He asked Shiv to tell him about his ancestors. Shiv was too embarrassed to admit that he didn't know. So, he wrote to his elder brother Parshist Pañdit in Srînagar to mail him the details. Parshist, too, expressed his ignorance. However, he penned down what he knew for sure. That was about the two preceding generations. This helped them trace the family's roots up to Mérû Pañdit, who had come to Kashmîr with the army of Empress Nûr Jehân. The two brothers then decided that they would maintain a careful record of the history of their family.

As a result the Dars are the only Kashmîrî Pandits—according to Fauq the only [ethnic] Kashmîrîs—who have a detailed record of the history of their family.

Lawrence notes that the Dar family has 'probably been the most influential' of all Kashmîrî Pandits. But, he adds, 'proverbs suggest that their influence has not been beneficial.' The proverb in question is: 'The Dars like doors should be locked up.' (My interpretation: Losers are jealous of all prominent families. Besides, in Dar there was a pun too delicious to resist. 'Dar' also means 'door.')

Dattâ-tréya Even before the era of *The Mahâbhârat* there lived in a village near Bârâmullâ a Sañskrit scholar and poet called Atrî. His wife Anusûyâ, too, was a great scholar. His work *The Atréya* is an important extant work on religion. Their son, Dattâ-tréya, founded the bloodline named after him.

Ghamkhwâr This is essentially a Delhi and, before 1947, Lahore clan. It consists of a handful of households. Basically they are Kauls. They migrated from Kashmîr to Âgrâ at the invitation of Emperor Akbar's government. His son, Emperor Jehâñgîr, kept them in his inner circle in Lahore and Kashmîr. Emperor Shâh Jehân patronised them in an even bigger way. He gave them their highest rank. He made them *mansabdârs* with a rank of 5,000. He also gave them a large estate and house in Delhi. (The name literally means 'he who eats sorrows,' or 'he who is always in a state of sorrow.')

Haksar In the Uttar Machhipurâ area of Bârâmullâ there is a village called Hâkchharpurâ. The pañdits of this village are variously called Hâkchhar, Hâksar and Haksar.

Kâk 'Kâk' is the Kashmîrî word for 'elder brother' or 'respectable elder.' The founder of the clan was a respected pañdit who became a *sâdhû* (saint). People would call him 'kâk' out of respect. His descendants are known as the Kâks.

Kaul This is one of the oldest bloodlines among the Kashmîrî Pandits. According to Sañskrit histories, a kaul is a person who destroys all worldly desires and rises above them. A very large number of Kashmîrî Pandits who do not use the surname Kaul actually belong to this clan. There are as many as thirty-six branches of this huge lineage. These are Aimâ, Bâbû, Bamchuñt, Bâmzaî, Bajû, Chaudhari, Dâñder, Dâñgar, Drâbî, Dont, Hâk, Jalâlî, Jinsî, Jotâ, Kâk, Kaptî, Kasû, Kothédâr, Ladâkhi, Manjzîn [Magazine?], Mañdal, Mozâ, Makhnas, Nigârî, Ograâ (or Vagrâ), Padar, Pehelwân, Râfiz, Sâheb, Shargâ, Shogâ, Sangârâ, Salmân, Sultân, Totâ, Zamîndâr, Tilwân.

Kichlû, 'Kichlû' means 'long beard.' Apparently, the founder of the clan had a long beard. This family earned a name for itself in Lahore, where they were Déwâns in the court of Mahârâjâ Ranjît Singh. Déwân Rattan Chañd was famous for his long beard. Most of the branch that stayed on in Kashmîr converted to Islâm.

Madan The Madans are a clan of Râzdâns who used to live in the Madan Mohallâ near Habbâ Kadal, Srînagar.

Mattû (with hard t's) The Mattûs, Kâchrûs and Fotédârs are members of the same *gotr* (bloodline): Patswâmin Kaushik. The best theory about the origin of the name is that it is derived from *math* (seminary). The keeper of a Sañskrit-school and or religious seminary would be called a mathû.

Rainâ The Rainâs are the same people as the Râzdâns.

Râzdân 'Râzdân' seems to be a Persian word that might mean 'the confidant.' However, the 1891 census says that it is a corruption of the Sañskrit 'râjâñk.'

Tikkû A Brâhmin of Srînagar had no children of his own. He adopted a Râjpût child. The pañdits put a *tilak* (smear made of sacred herbs) on the child's forehead and said, 'This boy was not born a Brâhmin. But he has become a Brâhmin through adoption.' The descendants of that child are known as the Tikkûs.

Trisal A branch of the Dar family returned to Kashmîr in the mediæval era and produced eminent members. Later the family of Nékû Pañdit adopted a Râzdân Rainâ youth called Mansâ Râm from a village called Trisal in Pulwâmâ. His descendants are called the Trisals.

Miâñ Râjpûts

A few clans of Dogrâ Râjpûts of the ruling family were given estates, mainly in the Deosar tehsil. Many of them chose not to migrate from Kashmîr in the 1990s.

Even in the 19th century they had taken so completely to Kashmîrî ways that there was little resemblance between them and their cousins in Jammû. Some of them started marrying Kashmîrî Pandits. Thus some of them merged with the only other Hiñdûs that there were in their part of the Valley.

17

Kashmîrî Handicrafts: and how to purchase them

Basket-work

(See 'Wicker-work' below.)

Carpets

History: Legends abound about how the world has been in awe of Kashmîrî carpets. Mahârâjâ Ranjit Singh of Punjab so fell in love with one that he is said to have found pleasure in rolling on it. I can vouch for a true, 21st century story: We have in the J&K Government Arts Emporium a brilliant 15' x 18' carpet that has been around the world at least twice, looking for a customer. Of the few who could afford it, most found it too big to fit their houses.

Carpet making was brought to Kashmîr from Samarqand by the much loved 15th century Kashmîrî emperor, Zain-ul-Abedin (aka Budshah). However, after a while, perhaps because there weren't enough rich buyers, the craft died out.

Akhund Rahnuma, a Kashmîrî, was Jehangir's Governor of Kashmîr (1614-18). He went to Andijan in Turkestan (Central Asia), on his way back from the Haj pilgrimage. There he learnt how to make carpets. He also brought tools of the trade back with him. In turn, he taught his fellow Kashmîrîs how to make carpets. That is why all carpet makers greatly respect his tomb in Gojwara (a residential neighbourhood in downtown Srînagar).

Vegetable dyes ceased to be made in the late 19th century, under the influence of European customers. Dyes used ever since have been chemical: aniline and alizarin. Initially these were imported from Europe.

However, British custom cut both ways. In 1902, the Viceroy of India, Lord Curzon, paid £100 for a Kashmîrî copy of what is perhaps the most famous Eastern carpet in the world — the AD 1536 Persian carpet at the Ardabil mosque in Kashan. This led to a burst of creativity within Kashmîr. Besides, it were British businessmen who took Kashmîrî carpets to the USA, exhibiting them at the Chicago World Fair of 1890. A huge market thus opened up. Other Englishmen, like Devergue and, later, Hadow, ensured, through the export of Kashmîrî carpets, that the workers got good money.

Some Kashmîrî carpet-makers migrated to Amritsar in the 19th century. (See also 'Shawls' below and 'The history of Leh'.) They were known as the *qâl-bâfs* (short for *qâleen bâfs*, or carpet makers). Till the 1947 Partition of India, the Kashmîrîs of Amritsar even ran a rival centre of carpet manufacture. After 1947, I suspect, they went over to Pakistan and merged into that country's superb carpet industry.

In the second half of the 20th century, Kashmîr's competition with carpets made in Pakistan and Iran see-sawed. Iran went through a burst of oil-inspired affluence in the 1970s. Iranian labour first turned far more expensive than that in Kashmîr and then became too posh to stay in the trade at all. Kashmîr filled the vacuum, and with style. In the late 1980s, when Iran became poor again, its carpets once again became competitive.

Kashmîr's own troubles of the early 1990s led to its top carpet-makers setting up additional factories in South Delhi, mainly in the Qutab Minar area, without shutting down their Kashmîrî operations.

Kashmîr's carpet-makers have earned millions of dollars since the 1950s. Much of this has been invested in some of India's most expensive real estate: behind the Taj in Bombay, in Bangalore's leafy Cantonment, in Jaipur and, of course, all over Delhi.

Patterns, designs and themes: Carpets made for consumption within Kashmîr would use subdued colours, their tints 'perfectly blended'. However, customers of the British Raj preferred brighter hues.

Because Kashmîr's carpet industry is doing extremely well, it is always looking for new ideas and designs. Therefore, Kashmîr's carpet manufacturers routinely use (authentic) designs from their Persian, Turkish, Turkman, Caucasian, mediæval Kashmîr-Mughal and Jaipur-Mughal heritage.

GMD Sufi says, 'Both shawls and carpets manifest ...the allegorical language of the passions and virtues of the people of Kashmîr. Some of the productions tell the story of the lives of famous personages, others depict historical episodes, poetic fantasies or religious and philosophical themes.'

The Dastkari Hât Samiti lists the better known designs thus:

i) *Mohtashan Kashan:* A central medallion is surrounded by floral motifs. This is a celebrated Persian design.

ii) *Syrk Turkman:* The Syrk tribe evolved this type of rug in ancient times.

iii) *Shikârgâh:* Hunting (shikar) scenes were a staple of Mughal miniatures. Such paintings are blown up and reproduced in 'Shikârgâh' carpets. Personally, I take a very poor view of miniatures that are blown up in size: in Kashmîr or in Madhubani (Bihar, Central India). All the shortcomings of Eastern portraits become evident and get amplified in enlargement.

iv) *Kashmîr Qum:* This kind of carpet has a Persian pedigree. In it the design consists of panels that are repeated.

v) *Turkman Princes Bukhara:* In such carpets the design is based on a candle-stand.

vi) *Kashmîr Mughal:* Here the designs are geometric with a floral effect.

vii) *Kashmîr Kashan:* The Tree of Life is portrayed in this type of carpet. Sometimes flowers, animals and birds, too, are shown.

Purchasing a carpet: These are the things to consider, the questions to ask:

i) Is the carpet made of 'silk on silk' (i.e. a silk '*pile*' or 'upper surface' on a silk *base*)? Or does it have a silk pile on a cotton base? Or a mixture of silk and wool on a base of cotton? Or wool on a cotton base? The price would vary accordingly.

The base of woollen carpets is always made of cotton. This is true of most silk carpets, too. If the base is made of silk, the 'fringe', too, would be of silk. Such a carpet would be very expensive. Sometimes, some of the important motifs in a woollen carpet might be made of silk.

ii) How many *knots* are there per inch when you look at the lower surface of the carpet? The greater the number of knots, the more expensive the carpet will be and the longer it will last. Many carpet shops now keep an eyeglass and a 'footrule' to let you count for yourself. Turn the carpet upside down. Then choose the portions where you will count the knots. Scan at least three different parts of the carpet, randomly selected, on the lower surface (i.e. the 'reverse' or the base). The number of knots per square inch used in Kashmîrî carpets varies between 18x18 and 22×22. (It could also be a number like 18×20.)

iii) Does the pattern lack *symmetry*? Sometimes the design at one end of a carpet is bigger or smaller than its opposite number at the other end.

iv) Have one or more *lines* in the design been *skipped* altogether, making the pattern look odd?

v) The *outlines* of the motifs on a carpet should be firm and 'crisp'. If they are blurred, insist on a huge discount-or avoid.

vi) The *edges/sides* of the carpet should be straight and perfectly parallel to each other. A wavy edge, or the length/ breadth at one end being smaller/ larger than at the opposite end, shows shoddy workmanship.

vii) *'Art' silk* means 'artificial,' not 'artistic,' silk. The Kashmîrîs call it 'staple'. It is also known as 'mercerized cotton'. 'Art silk' carpets cost around a third of their cheapest pure-silk counterpart, but more than wool. Please, please satisfy yourself on this count. A thread randomly selected from such a carpet will burn quickly, because it is synthetic. Real silk burns slower. 'Art silk' shines much like the real thing. One foolproof test for amateurs is the *weight.* 'Art silk' carpets weigh one and a half times as much as the same size in silk. For example, a 3' × 5' silk carpet should weigh less than 4 kg. The same size in staple will be more than 6 kg.

viii) What is a 'seventy-five percent silk carpet'? The upper surface, the pile, of such a carpet might be of pure silk, but the base of some other material. So, as a *percentage* of the total amount of yarn used, the silk content might be 75 or 80%.

ix) What if the number of *knots* you find on counting is less than what the dealer had promised? Count a few more 'square inches' at different places and take the average of the lot. There will be reason to disbelieve the dealer only if the average is less than what he had said.

x) What are single and *double knots*? Stroke the pile (upper surface) of the carpet with your hand. If it consists of double knots, the pile will bend when stroked in one direction but remain straight when stroked in the other direction. Single knots are fluffy. They behave in the same manner in both directions. You can also make out double knots by looking at the 'base'.

xi) Are there carpets *without knots*? Yes, some carpets are tufted instead. These are far less durable. And less stiff and less firm to touch.

xii) Did *you* choose the carpet showroom/ factory, or did a 'middleman' take you there? Remember, the middleman gets a commission (and not just on carpets and not merely in Kashmîr; this happens in most parts of the world).

You can watch a carpet being made. In Srînagar almost all carpet factories encourage you to do this.

Carpets are made in all six districts of the Valley, namely Srînagar, Budgâm, Kupwârâ, Pulwâmâ, Bârâmullâ and Ânañtnâg.

Carpets are sold in Srînagar at showrooms in and around Residency Road, Polo View and the Bund, and also on the Boulevard. They are also sold at carpet factories on the outskirts of Srînagar — on the way to the Shalimar, and on the way to Hazratbal.

Chain-stitching

Such stitching is done not by a needle but by a hook, called an **ari** (pron. â-ree). Hooks are more efficient than needles because they embroider the same surface much faster.

The base used most commonly is pre-shrunk, white, cotton cloth. The thread can be of wool, silk or cotton. In the best (and most expensive) pieces i) only the finest woollen thread is used, and ii) a very large number of tiny stitches are used — the tinier, the neater and the more, even the better. The cloth used as the base is not meant to be seen at all and is covered entirely by the stitches. A special golden coloured thread is used in this craft. Sometimes threads of 'staple' are used instead of woollen threads.

The craft is not very old. It was invented after '*gabbas*' were. Therefore, at most it must have started in the first half of the 19th century.

The design: The background is always in one single colour and consists of a number of concentric circles, each the size of a coin. The motifs and figures of the foreground are more brightly coloured.

Fabrics that chain stitching is done on include cotton, dosooti, hand-woven cloths, silk and wool.

Uses: Chain-stitched fabrics are used for curtains, cushions, floor coverings, garments, soft-leather and upholstery. (See also 'Crewel' and 'Gabbas' below.)

Chain stitching is done in the Ânañtnâg, Bârâmullâ, Kupwârâ, Pulwâmâ and Srînagar districts.

Copperware

Items made of copper are mainly for the local market. They are not very upmarket either, despite their obvious beauty. As a result, of all Kashmîrî handicrafts, they are the best value for money. The price is decided by the weight of the metal used and by the amount of ornamentation (*naq-qâ-shee*).

Types of utensils made: '*Samovars*', ingenious vessels in which a low fire burns in the lower third and tea smoulders in the upper portion, are popular with tourists as well. So are copper bowls and plates. Other utensils made of copper include cooking vessels, cups, ladles, trays and tumblers,

The motifs used are very stylised. They come in both relief and intaglio. (See 'Walnut' below for 'intaglio' and 'relief.') '*Badam*' (almond), the Chinâr leaf, flowers, intertwining vines, leaves and '*the mehrab*' (Islâmic arch) are among the most popular motifs. Abstract designs, too, are used. The designs are then oxidised to make them stand out against the background. Products made of copper are beaten, embossed, engraved or just plain.

The Kashmîrîs have mined copper for more than a thousand years now. Copper mines were a major source of income for the 15th century Emperor Budshah.

The coppersmiths of Kashmîr work with brass as well. Many have descended from families of silversmiths. Increasingly copper trays are being fitted onto wooden bases.

Copper products are made mainly in Srînagar city. Within the city, the following localities are best known for their products: Bohri Kadal, Fateh Kadal, Jâmâ Masjid, Nalamar, Rainawari, SR Ganj and Zaina Kadal.

Copperware is also made and sold in Srînagar at Anchar, Bahloochi Pora, Batak Pora, Bota Kadal, Gojawar, Kalnath Pora, Onta Bawan, Makhdoom Pora, Naoshera, Pazwal Pora, Sikh Bâgh, Syed Sâheb, Terigari Pora and Tuluwari.

Crewel-work

Crewel-work is a form of embroidery. The broad principles are the same as in chain-stitching (see above). However, here the cloth used as the base is seen clearly because its surface is covered with chain-stitched embroidery only where there is a motif, not everywhere. The colours are not as bright either. The base is normally white or off-white cotton. (Dosooti is normally the cloth used. See 'Gabba' below for more about this cotton cloth.) The woollen thread used in the embroidery employs just two or three colours at a time. Only single-ply thread is used.

Chain-stitching is normally used in wall hangings, bedcovers and rugs/ 'carpets'. Which means that these products are sold by the piece and have definite borders. '*Crewel-work*', on the other hand, is normally used in curtains. It is also used in upholstery, tablecloths, cushion covers, bedcovers and a roundish shopping bag unique to Kashmîr. '*Crewel-work*' is rolled into bales and sold by the metre. Therefore, there are no borders at the top or bottom of the cut-pieces, because they are not individual works of art.

This is a European, perhaps British, craft brought into Kashmîr in the late nineteenth or early twentieth century. 'Crewel' is the name of the thin worsted yarn. '*Crewel-work*' is the name of the embroidery.

Crewel-work is done and sold at: In Srînagar city: the Bund, Dal Gate, Karan Nagar, Karfali Mohalla, Nawab Bazar, Nawa Kadal, Nayeed Kadal, Nowhatta, Safa Kadal, Tangporâ Mohalla, Tarabal and the Third Bridge.

'*Crewel embroidery*' is done in all six districts of the Valley, namely Ânañtnâg, Bârâmullâ, Budgâm, Kupwârâ, Pulwâmâ and Srînagar.

Embroidery

A 1st century AD plate found in the ruins at Harwan, near Srînagar, shows a woman wearing an embroidered shawl. At some stage this art, like many others, died out. Mîr Syed Ali, who came to Kashmîr from Hamadân in the 14th century, revived some of the Valley's lost arts. Artisans from Iran accompanied him and settled in Kashmîr. Emperor Zain-ul-Abedin (1420-70), aka Budshah, encouraged more craftsmen to come over from Iran. Some of them were experts in embroidery. As a result there are Iranian features in Kashmîrî embroidery.

Most of the motifs used are floral. However, sometimes the patterns can be geometric. They are drawn on cloth with the help of paper stencils. The craftsman then fleshes out the pencil drawings with coloured thread pulled by a steel needle. Zari embroidery alone is done by women. All other kinds of embroidery are the preserve of men. The Srînagar and Budgâm districts are the main centres of embroidery.

The kinds of stitches used in Kashmîrî embroidery include the buttonhole stitch, the chain stitch, the herringbone stitch, the knot stitch, the satin stitch, the slanted stitch and the stem stitch.

There are two broad categories of embroidery in Kashmîr:

a) *Jâlik-doozi:* This is embroidery on large-sized cloth, to be used as furnishings (curtains, bedspreads, table cloth and the like). It is employed only in four kinds of crafts: i) 'crewel embroidery', ii) '*namdas*', iii) '*gabbas*' and iv) fur-based crafts.

This art is also known as 'wool-work'. The strokes used are broad. The thread used is, invariably, wool. The motifs are inspired by flowers, leaves-especially the distinctive Chinâr leaf, fruits, especially the almond—and birds and wild animals. Of course, these motifs are stylised and rarely realistic.

b) *Sozan-kâri:* This is embroidery done on cloths of a smaller size. It is used in garments: women's shirts, stoles and pashmina and ruffle/raffal shawls. It is also used in furnishings. The motifs are finer, more delicately wrought and far more difficult to create than ordinary embroidery. The thread used, too, is much finer and normally silk. As a result each motif takes that much longer to create. The stitches used are herringbone and darn. The craftsmen are called '*sozan-kârs*'. '*Sozan-kâri*' is of two kinds:

i) *Rafgar ka'am:* This is the embroidery done on shawls and garments made of ruffle/raffal as well as on pashmina. Men wear this kind of embroidery on gowns, coats and mufflers. Women use it on western dresses, Indian saris, pherans, handkerchiefs and coats. It is also used on tea cosies, cushion covers, bags and pillowcases. Of course, it is best known as the embroidery done on shawls. (See also 'Shawls' below.)

ii) *'Zar doozi':* This craft is also called 'tilâ kâri' or 'tilâ' work. 'Zar' and 'tilâ' both mean 'gold'. In this craft, first a pattern is traced out on the cloth base (or 'ground') in pencil, using a paper stencil. The pattern will consist of motifs that can be large or small. The size depends on how much gold is intended to be woven into the garment. The cloth is then embroidered with two kinds of thread. The first kind is made of gold. (Thread made of gold is either white or golden.) The second thread-usually silk or cotton-is used to bind and fasten the golden thread.

'Zar doozi' is normally done on *'pherans'* and women's shawls.

Do-rukha or 'two-sided' embroidery is an art still found in Kashmîr and Chamba (Himachal). It used to flourish in parts of Jammû (notably Basohli). In this the needle so winds its way through the cloth that the same pattern is woven on both sides of the cloth, sometimes using different colours on each side. (See 'Shawls' below.)

Main areas where embroidery is done: i) Srînagar district: Bashpura, Botapura, Ganderbal, Harwan, Naoshera, Soura and Zakura.

ii) Budgâm district: Budgâm proper and Chadoora.

iii) Ânañtnâg district: Craftsmen in certain villages of Ânañtnâg embroider *'dosooti'*, *'gabbas'*, *'namdas'*, *'pherans'* and shawls (pashmina as well as ruffle/ raffal).

Zari embroidery is done in the Ânañtnâg, Pulwâmâ and Srînagar districts.

Fur

Officially, trade in most varieties of fur, animal skin and horns is banned. However, Kashmîr has a hoary tradition of fur for every income-group. Which means that very inexpensive fur caps and leather gloves have traditionally been available in the Kokker Bazar-Lal Chowk area of Srînagar. Leopard–and bear – skin occupy the upper rungs of the fur hierarchy. The skins of various smaller cats, jackals, rabbits and domesticated animals like kids (young goats) and sheep are also used.

The Kashmîrîs have been using fur since the beginning of recorded history. Towards the end of the 19th century a new chemical, rexine, was introduced. It revolutionised the industry, because it gave leather a soft, glossy texture.

Fur and leather items that Kashmîr specialises in include jackets and coats, gloves, bags, caps, carpet slippers, cummerbunds and belts, shoes and boots, and cushion covers. These items are often embroidered in the *'jâlik-doozi'* style. (See 'Embroidery' above.)

Before the bans started coming into place, Kashmîr had a substantial export trade in fur and leather goods.

Gabbas

A *'gabba'* is a rug which is either made of old, recycled woollen blankets or of shreds of *pattu* (local tweed). *'Gabbas'* are generally called 'carpets for the common man'.

There are four kinds, the first three being specialties of Ânañtnâg town. i) *Dal guldâr*: This is an appliqué style. At the centre is a star, called the *chand* (which, incidentally, means 'the moon'); ii) embroidered *'gabbas'*; iii) a combination of appliqué and embroidery; iv) the printed *'gabbas'* of Bârâmullâ. In types ii) and iii), designs are embroidered on the finished product. The motifs are drawn from animal and plant life or nature.

'A kind of a refined patchwork,' is how an officer of the British Raj described the appliqué variety. The shreds are dyed in various colours, mainly in bright primary colours. They are then joined together in a manner in which the seams are concealed, sometimes by embroidery. The patterns are mostly geometric.

In the case of '*gabbas*' made of whole blankets, the blanket is first dyed and then embroidered with coloured woollen threads. These threads are of double-or triple-'ply'. This kind of work is known locally as *feetay ka kâm.* Such '*gabbas*' are mainly meant for local customers and normally are custom made.

Chain stitched rugs, too, are a variety of '*gabba*'. (See 'Chain-stitching' above.) The cloth used in chain stitched '*gabbas*' is totally different from that used in ordinary '*gabbas*'.

The shape is almost always rectangular. The size rarely exceeds 9' × 12'.

Sometimes '*gabbas*' are also used as curtains.

The fanciest '*gabbas*' use broad-cloth and 'barrack blankets,' instead of old blankets as their raw material. At other times the yarn used is staple (see 'Carpets' above), not wool. This makes '*gabbas*' look like carpets: and at a fraction of the cost.

Normally a cotton lining is sewn onto the reverse of '*gabbas*'. Sometimes this lining is filled with wool to give the gabbâ a soft, cushioned feel.

No one knows for certain how *'gabbas'* originated. One theory is that an Afghân refugee called Abdul Rehman brought this craft to Kashmîr when, in a village near Trâl, he made a small, embroidered woollen rug to be placed on the saddle of the horse of his host, Kamal Butt. The type of embroidery that he had used was '*jâlik-doozi*''. (I assume that this happened in the 18th century.)

According to another version, there lived in Islâmabad (Ânañtnâg), also in the 18th century, a poor tailor called Lassa Tota. He could not afford a new bed-sheet. So he stitched together shreds of cloths of different colours to make a sheet. The result was so attractive that other tailors started imitating his work.

In any case, '*gabbas*' started out as rugs for the poor man. As they grew in elegance, even the rich started buying them. Towards the last quarter of the 19th century they started being made in Bârâmullâ and, by the 20th century, in Srînagar.

In my family we purchase sheets of 'dosooti' cloth that are slightly bigger than the '*gabba*'. This is a heavy cotton cloth, of which the yarn is 'double twisted'. The Handloom Development Corporâtion makes it in Kashmîr. However, it is made in many other parts of India as well. It is sold at traditional textile shops everywhere in India. We give the '*gabba*' and the '*dosooti*' to our neighbourhood tailor in Delhi, who sews the '*dosooti*' behind the '*gabba*'. So when we place the '*gabba*' on the floor (or drape it on a wall) it is the '*dosooti*' that touches the floor or wall. This gives the '*gabba*' weight and body and thus prevents the '*gabba*' from crumbling on the floor. It also makes sure that its sides don't curve upward. The '*dosooti*' lining also makes the '*gabba*' last longer.

The art would have died out but for the patronage of Ranbir Singh (1857-85). The Mahârâjâ invited to Srînagar the four best '*gabba makers*' of Ânañtnâg to make tents (*shamianas*) and floor coverings for the government. The Dogrâ rulers were fond of this craft. It is said that once when Ranbir's father, Mahârâjâ Gulab Singh (reign: 1846-57) was travelling through rural Kashmîr he met an elderly man who offered him milk and fruit juice. The Mahârâjâ was given a '*gabba*' to sit on. He was so impressed by the '*gabba*' that he asked for one.

Sold at: i) Ânañtnâg: Various shops in the town.

ii) Srînagar: The so-called Central Market, the Khadi Bhandars and Polo View.

*Made at:*i) Ânañtnâg district: Ânañtnâg proper, Anchidora, Chatter Gul, Mattan, Shangas and Qazigund.

ii) Bârâmullâ district: Uri.

iii) Srînagar district: Makharporâ and Sazgariporâ.

Jewellery

Kashmîrî jewellery has been influenced by a) Central Asia (e.g. the silver charm-cases worn on caps) and b) the Empress Noor Jehân, who brought with her intricate designs thitherto unknown in Kashmîr. The jewellers of Kashmîr have, since, internalised the art and their products are distinct in shape, size and boldness of strokes.

The ornaments are made of gold, silver, brass, copper, tin and even a fine kind of clay. Precious stones used include opals, carnelians, bloodstones, agates and turquoises.

Some of the most popular jewellers in Srînagar are grouped around the Hanuman Mandir of Amira Kadal. There are some in the Lambert Lane, too.

Traditional jewellers are grouped around the Third Bridge. They also make leaves of silver and gold, and fine copperware. Other localities in Srînagar where good jewellery is made and sold are Khanyar, Mira Masjid and Râjourî Kadal.

Retail outlets can also be found in Ashraf Mohalla, Bataporâ, Beeruni Andarwari, Kala Doori, Kangri Mohalla, Lakhriporâ, Shamsawari and Sheeshgari Mohalla. Some of these outlets also sell, by the kilogram, old jewellery that had once been worn by Gujjar and Bakerwâl women.

(See also 'Copperware', 'Silverware' and 'Turquoise work' in this chapter.)

Kângris

Unlike boats and ceilings, you *can* take a '*kangri*' home. However, chances are that you might not want to, except perhaps as an inexpensive curio, because you would have no use for a '*kangri*', even if you live in Siberia. Only a Kashmîrî knows how to handle this body-warmer, which causes stomach cancer, burns all over the body and fires in wooden houses.

A *kâñgrî* is a bowl-shaped clay-pot enclosed in a basket made of willow. It has a wide, open mouth at the top. The pot is the size of a football. The hard willow basket ensures that the user does not come in touch with the red-hot pot. There is a willow handle above to carry the *kangri* with, and a flat bottom for it to rest on. Sometimes there is a little spoon, made of silver or wood, and called the *Kânij*, dangling from the handle.

Kashmîrîs place live coals in the clay pot and take the whole thing inside their loose '*pheran*' gown (which is slightly different from the smart, tight variant popular in Central India these days). It keeps the user warm at the peak of winter, but at the aforementioned cost to health. The *kâñgrî* is the Kashmîrî equivalent of the hot-water bottle and is similarly taken to bed.

History: The word is possibly derived from i) '*kâni*' (the switch) '*gar*' (maker); ii) the Sanskrit '*kut*' (small) '*angâra*' (fire-place), or iii) the Sanskrit '*kâstha-angârika*' (also: 'little fire-place'). A 19th century British historian had the gall to suggest that around the 17th century some Jesuit Father from Italy might have brought this contraption from Florence, Italy, where it is known as the '*scaldino*'. (Kashmîr had no recorded contact with the Jesuits in that age. Leh, which did, never knew the '*kangri*'. But then everything worthwhile in India—including the Taj Mahal – is supposed to have come from Europe, according to such historians. In the case of the *kangri* there are definite references in 12 century AD Kashmîrî literature to such a contraption.)

Ritual significance: The *kangri* is used in Muslim as well Hindu rituals.

Made and sold at: i) In Srînagar: Batmaloo and Habba Kadal; ii) In Bârâmullâ: Sopore; and iii) Kupwârâ: Lolab. The *kangris* of Sopore and Lolab are particularly hardy.

Lacquer woodwork

Also known as lathe-cum-lacquer work, this is not one of Kashmîr's more subtle crafts. Nor is it unique to, or even mainly practised in, Kashmîr. Articles made of wood are covered with a bright, shiny film of lacquer. The colour below this film is a deep, artificial looking brown. Items thus made include abacuses, bedsteads, child-walkers, ladles, rice measures, rolling pins, spinning wheels, stools and toys.

In Kashmîr the craft is centred around Ânañtnâg.

Leather

Partly because of political correctness and partly because of changing tastes this is a dying craft. Till the 1960s and '70s, the Bund would be overpowered by the strong odour of leather jackets, bags, portmanteaux, gloves, caps and upholstery. Prices are low by any standards.

Kashmîrî leather's speciality was that it lasted very long. The 19th century British veterinary surgeon, William Moorcroft, was an expert in horses, and thus saddles. He wrote, 'A fabric of much greater importance to Great Britain than that of damasked sword-blades, is that of Yirak leather, or leather suited for saddlery...The leather was strong, solid, heavy and pliable, without any disposition to crack. Some of the pieces had been in use eighteen or twenty years, and were none the worse for constant wear.'

The British attributed this superiority to the method of tanning. The 1890 *Gazetteer* says, 'The skins, after being cleaned, are placed in a vat of clean water, with a layer of pounded galls between every two skins; a man is employed to tread them down daily, from morning to night, for twentyfive days, fresh galls being added every fifth day. They are then hung to dry...(The skin) is then put into water again and trodden, and rubbed until all greasiness disappears, when it is polished by being well rubbed with a blunt iron instrument.'

Products: Gloves, jackets, shoes (leather as well as suede) and suitcases. All of them are hand-stitched, often to a design specified by the customer.

Sold in Srînagar at: The Bund, Dal Gate, the Fourth Bridge, Polo View, Residency Road and Zaina Kadal.

Made in Srînagar at: Ahsan Sâheb, Ali Kadal, Amda Kadal, Bahlochiporâ, Dabtal, Dalal Mohalla, Fateh Kadal, Hazratbal, Kachgari Masjid, Kalamdan Pora, Kani Mazar, Khajaporâ, Lal Bazar, Nalabal, Nawab Bazar, Patther Masjid, Rehbab Sâheb, Sadarbal, Sehyar, Sikh Bâgh, Thag Bab Sâheb, and Urdu Bazar.

Mats

Those who live in houseboats have traditionally both made and used mats. These are placed under the bedding and carpets, to provide additional warmth. The poor all over Kashmîr use these tough mats, known as *waggu*. They are made from *pits* (reed mace), a plant grown in swamps. Some such mat-making goes on in the Dal Lake itself, in the inner 'lanes' behind the tourist houseboats. Kalpana Manglik, an expert, rates the mats of Lasjan, which is south of Srînagar, as the best in Kashmîr.

Namdas

(Pron. num-dâ, if singular.) These are inexpensive floor coverings or rugs made of pressed felt, and patronised by the middle classes. They are used mostly in the winters because of the warmth they provide. '*Namdas*' are usually made of a mixture of wool and cotton yarn: the greater the proportion of wool, the more expensive the '*namda*'. You can leave the cotton out, but never the wool. Cotton is used mainly to provide bulk. Besides, cotton gives a '*namda*' its strength and durability.

The fibre is pressed into shape manually. '*Namdas*' are then embroidered, with cotton or woollen thread, in the 'chain-stitch' (see above) tradition. They can be round, oval or rectangular. Sizes vary between 2' × 3' and 9' × 12'. The amount of wool used in a namda can be anything between one and eight kilograms.

This craft is believed to have been developed in Central Asia around the first century AD. '*Namdas*' were imported in large numbers from Yarqand till the beginning of the 19th century. Central Asian '*namdas*' were plain and unadorned. They were imported into Kashmîr and embroidered in the '*jâlik-doozi*' style. They were then re-exported to the rest of the world. This trade was at its peak during the First World War. Around 1929, the USA became a major customer.

It is estimated that 2,00,000 plain '*namdas*' were imported into Kashmîr every year till 1940. Because of this enormous demand, around 1929 the craftsmen of Kashmîr started making '*namdas*' locally. In the beginning the number of '*namdas*' made locally was small and their quality inferior. In 1938, a full-fledged '*namda*' industry was set up in Kashmîr. As a result, by 1941 Kashmîr stopped importing '*namdas*' altogether. Which was just as well, because in 1947 the route to Yarqand was closed off because of the changed political situation.

In Srînagar they are sold at the so-called Central Market, the various Khadi Bhandars, Polo View and Rainawari.

They are made at: i) In Srînagar district: Aqalmir, Channa Dora Mohalla, Chhargari Mohalla, Chamadoori, Dekhdarhar, Dhakahbab Sâheb, Doomporâ, Gojwara, Jamalatta, Kani Mazar, Khanwari, Malporâ, Koker Bâgh, Makhdoom Kocha, Mehraj Gunj, Rang Masjid, Sehyar Nawab Bazar, Sukaliporâ, Umar Colony, Wantaporâ and Zahidporâ.

ii) In Kupwârâ district: Kupwârâ town.

Paper

In the chapter on Kashmîrî art, I have mentioned Kashmîr's handmade paper. I have so much historical material (and not very old stuff as well: apparently this legendary paper was being made till the early 20th century) on Kashmîr's fabled paper that I could devote a full chapter to it. But what's the point? You can't go out and purchase it because it's not being made any more. It is almost a mission with me to revive this art. Wish me luck.

Papiér Mâchè

(pron.: pâp-yay mâ-shay) As its French name suggests, this craft uses mashed paper as its raw material. Delicate designs are then painted on this base, which is also lacquered. The craftsmen themselves used to call the art the '*Kâr-e-Qalamdâni*'.

The Process: Paper is soaked in water till it is reduced to a very soft pulp. After that it is pounded. A liquid adhesive is added to the mashed material. The mixture is smeared over a *vasal* (mould). When it sets and dries it is painted upon and then varnished to add gloss. Periodic varnishing over the years adds to the gloss. (The craftsmen's own varnish is perfectly colourless and transparent. It is made by boiling the clearest '*copal*' [sumdras] in pure turpentine.)

There are three or four different grades of papiér mâchè. The grading depends on how fine the pulp to which the paper had been pounded was. This fineness in turn determines how smooth the finished good will be. Prices vary widely according to the smoothness of the finish. They also depend on whether pure gold leaf was used in the designs or bronze dust or mere golden paint was. Real gold lasts much longer and its colour does not fade or tarnish.

The best pieces should be able to hold hot water.

In addition, there is-and has been since at least the 19th century—imitation papiér mâchè. Cardboard, wood or even leather is painted over in the papiér mâchè style for those who can not afford the real stuff. If you press cardboard with the tip of a finger, it will give slightly. Real papiér mâchè won't. (Nor will wood, though.)

Most *designs* are brightly coloured. Intricate branches with ornamental leaves are a favoured theme. Human and animal figures, too, come up now and then.

History: Like many other crafts, this was brought to Kashmîr by the great Sultan Zain-ul-Abedin. Experts were invited from Samarqand (Uzbekistan) and, for some historical reason, this art became the monopoly of the Shias (Shiites) of Kashmîr. Syed Turâb, who lived in the 19th century, was the most celebrated practitioner of this craft in recent centuries. Its local name is *kâr-e-qalamdâni* (the art of the pen-case), perhaps because historically pen-cases were the most popular papiér mâchè product. It is also known as *kâr-e-munaqqash* (painted work).

Lhasa was traditionally a major market for Kashmîrî papiér mâchè. So was Paris.

According to the Dastkari Hât Samiti, 'Mughal kings often commissioned entire communities of craftsmen to make gifts as well as decorative panels and other items for palaces.' The *bârâdarîs* (pavilions) of the Mughal gardens at Nishat and Shalimar have panels made of papiér mâchè. Most of them date to the 17th century and have, therefore, faded considerably.

Uses: Almost anything can be made of mashed paper. Table lamps, tables, picture frames, folding screens (which serve as room-dividers), vases, trays, just anything. In the early twentieth century some imaginative shawl-manufacturers got cartons made of papiér mâchè to send their shawls to Paris in. (There the empty cartons were resold separately.)

Items made of papiér mâchè and sold in shops include bangles, bowls, boxes, cabinets, Christmas-tree ornaments, cups, dressing table sets (to keep toiletries and jewellery in), mirror-holders, panels, photo frames, screens, table and pedestal-lamps, vases, wall-plaques and writing sets (pen-case, paper-knife, writing pad and stationery holder).

Sold in Srînagar at Alam Giri Bazar, Amira Kadal, the Bund, the so-called Central Market, Dal Gate, Hari Parbat, Hassanabad, Hawal, Nagin, Nowpura, Polo View, Rainawari, Residency Road and Zadi Bal.

Made in Srînagar at Adalat Masjid, Akilmir, Alamgiri, Amda Kadal, Aram Mohalla, Aram Pora, Arwat, Bâbâporâ, Bagwan Pora, Baharbar, Bota Kadal, Budoo Bâgh Chinkral Mala, Cyana Mohalla, Doniporâ, Hassanabad, Hasi Bhat, Kachi Mohalla, Kaka Mohalla, Kamgarporâ, Khajan Pora, Khushal Sar, Lal Bazar, Langiporâ, Madeen Sahib, Mandibal, Mughal Mohalla, Pazwal Pora, Pokherbal, Shamsawari, Sheshgari Mohalla, Shri Bhat, Sikh Bâgh, Syed Afzal, Syedporâ, Vichar Nag, Zadibal and Zari Mala.

Made in Bârâmullâ at Delina and Wagoora.

Made in Pulwâmâ at Gangoo and Suttsoo.

Pashmina

(See 'Shawls' below.)

Perfumes

Kashmîrî perfumes have been an obsession of mine since the early 1990s, when I discovered that Srînagar and Jammû had fairly nice traditions of making traditional *attar* perfumes. (Attar is a Greco-Turkish system, blended with India's own.) It's a dying art because modern young ladies in India prefer subtler, factory-made, Western or Western-style perfumes. Jammû has just two varieties of attar, jasmine and rose. Kashmîr has at least a dozen.

It is difficult to obtain traditional Kashmîrî perfumes today. Apparently this was always so. The 1890 *Gazetteer* records, 'The '*atta*' [attar?] of roses made in Kashmîr used to be considered superior to any other; it never appears, however, to have been an article of commerce.' It still isn't.

In Kashmîr, the almost odourless walnut oil (see the chapter on 'Flora') has traditionally been used as the medium for extracting the perfume of jasmine, iris (*zambak*), narcissus (*yimberzal*), daffodil (*nargis*), chamomile (*babeena*) and the yellow rose (*zeba*). One weight of these flowers is put into a bottle containing three weights of the oil. The bottle is placed in sunlight for forty days, by which time the oil acquires the perfume of the flower.

Towards the end of the 20th century this traditional method was gradually phased out in favour of more western-inspired methods. However, Kashmîrî perfumes are strictly herbal in origin.

Since these perfumes are made on a very small scale, you will normally be able to purchase only perfumes-of-the-season. The few shopkeepers who sell Kashmîrî perfumes rarely have out-of-season perfumes, even though these perfumes are very stable and, if stored in sealed bottles, can last for years. If the bottles are left uncorked the perfumes gradually evaporâte. Therefore, they make excellent room-fresheners.

Some of the better known perfumes

Firdaus: This is made of the juices of the yellow Batposh flower, which blossoms in April and May.

Saffron/ Zâfrân: This perfume is extracted from saffron (see 'Flora').

Kot: This perfume, like turpentine, is extracted from a tree: in this case in June, July and August.

Jasmine: This perfume comes in two colours, red and yellow. It is extracted from flowers that are yellow, white or blue.

Bred Mushk: A seed, also called '*Bred Mushk*', yields this perfume. The seed looks like a raw almond. The tree bears a yellow flower and fruit in March-April and, if sufficiently sunny, in February as well.

Rose: This perfume is extracted from the petals of roses. The roses are pink *(Kashmîrî gulab)* or red (*Roosi gulab*). 'Gulab' means 'rose,' and 'Roosi' means 'Russian.'

Amber: A tuber that, naturally, grows underground, yields this perfume which, too, is somewhat like a resin.

Ishq pechân: A light blue flower that blossoms in March and yields the perfume of the same name.

Sandalwood: This perfume is extracted from sandalwood (which is purchased from the South Indian state of Karnataka).

Kashmîrî perfumes are normally sold as concentrates. They are pure extracts. As a result they appear to be more expensive than attars from other parts of India and Pakistan, which have been diluted in white oil. Nor are colours added to Kashmîrî perfumes.

Kashmîrî perfumes have, for that reason, often been used to make bath waters fragrant. One drop of a Kashmîrî perfume is normally sufficient for a tub full of water.

Sold at Lal Chowk and Amira Kadal.

Pherans

Traditionally this has been a loose, rough, plain, tweed cloak for men as well as women. It has been transformed by the Delhi market-place into a pretty, embroidered, long-shirt for women, which fits snugly atop the *qameez* (long-shirt) worn with the *shalwar* (loose trousers) and which is now made of some fine cloth such as 'ruffle/ raffal'. The neckline is now invariably embroidered and at least a foot long. The cuff and hem, too, are embroidered with ari-work. (Ari: see 'chain-stitching' above.) The embroidery can be up to an inch thick. The Khânqâh-e-Mualla area of Srînagar (near the Shah-e-Hamadân shrine) is the best place for such deep embroidery.

It is believed that the word *pheran* is a corruption of the Persian *peh-râ-han* (lit. 'garment'). This would imply that the Mughals brought this dress to Kashmîr. But why would they? They never wore anything like this themselves Answer: The Mughals did this to de-martialise the thitherto brave Kashmîrîs, by making them wear this sloppy dress. So the theory goes.

Increasingly, there's evidence that the '*pheran*' has been in Kashmîr since much before the Mughals. A 15th century miniature painting that I came upon shows people in '*pherans*'. Besides, the Persian language came to Kashmîr more than two hundred years before the Mughals.

Pottery

The glazed 'Dal Gate pottery,' brown, white or green, is made in the neighbouring Rainawari area. Glass powder is used for the glazing. 'Martabâns' are the most popular products made thus. These are large vessels in which pickles are preserved, sometimes for as long as a year or even two. Curds are set in smaller brown pots made of the same material. Dinner sets, tea sets and vases are some the other items made of glazed pottery.

Less fancy, unglazed pottery is used in the rituals of the Kashmîrî Pandits, especially during Shiva Ratri. The Kashmîrî equivalent of the 'hot-water bottle' is the *kangri* (see above). The pot inside the *kangri*, as well as the tobacco-receptacle of the *hookah*, are the other commonly used items of pottery.

Glazed as well as ordinary pottery is sold in Srînagar at Dal Gate, Habba Kadal, Ishber, Kral Khud and Rainawari.

The pottery of Tsrar (Chrar)-e-Sharief is known for its colours, normally blue and red. Sometimes flowers, green or white, are drawn on the pots.

Shahtoosh

(Also known as 'toosh'. See 'Shawls' below.)

Shawls

(See the chapter on 'Kashmîrî Shawls.')

Sherbets

'*Sherbets*' are a by-product of the Unani (*yu-nâ-ni*) method of making medicines. Though Unani literally means 'Greek,' this is the system of medicine found in all Muslim lands, including mainland India. However, as in the rest of South Asia, colas are edging '*sherbets*' out of Kashmîr as well.

Though this art has survived into the 21st century, it might not last into the second half of the century.

Kashmîrî '*sherbets*' are made mainly in the Fateh Kadal area of Srînagar. The houses and shops on the road outside the Khânqâh-e-Mu'alla are the hub of this craft. Mostly people of the Kosgar caste make Kashmîrî '*sherbets*'. The Kosgars have now started joining the professions. Some of them have become medical doctors. There are, thus, very few left behind to make '*sherbets*'.

The method: The ingredients used are chiefly flowers and herbs. These are put into a large cauldron (*deigh*) on a base of water or some other liquid. The cauldron is then heated, preferably on a log-fire. A *sarposh*-like lid is placed atop the cauldron. These are thick and heavy lids made of metal, often with fine patterns etched on them. They are not flat. Instead, they rise towards the centre, and right in the middle there is a small peak. They, thus, look somewhat like the domes of Islâmic mosques.

During the making of '*sherbets*' these lids (*sarposhes*) are placed upside-down atop the cauldron, the peak pointing downwards. After a while, steam begins to rise from below. It collects on the convex surface of the *sarposh* and condenses there as a liquid. [Because the convex lid has been placed upside-down, it is concave now.] This liquid slides down towards the peak, from which it starts dripping down. There's a receptacle below the 'peak' which receives the thick, concentrated *sherbet*.

The '*sherbet*' is then stored in large glass pitchers.

Custom-made: The best '*sherbets*' are made to order, with ingredients used in the precise ratio desired by the customer. For some reason *sherbet* makers do not stock glass-bottles to sell their product in. So, take empty bottles along. Or you will wind up paying a small fortune for the bottle.

Silk

Karnataka and Bengal and Benares have always produced more silk than Kashmîr. Raw silk loses some of its weight during boiling: Kashmîrî silk loses the most in the world (25 to 30%). (In Japan, and in other parts of India, the loss is around 20 to 22%.) A study conducted by the State government around 1983 indicated that this meant that the silk industry of Jammû and Kashmîr was less efficient and more wasteful than elsewhere. However, going through 19th century records I noticed that this has always been so and might even be a characteristic of Kashmîrî silk.

The silkworm of Kashmîr is smaller than elsewhere and feeds only on mulberry leaves (vs. four kinds of leaves elsewhere). Mughal historians noticed that 'the mulberry (was) little eaten. Its leaves (were) reserved for the silkworm'. Later administrations, like the Dogrâs, preserved the mulberry tree by law.

History: While silk might have been made in Kashmîr as early as in 2,000 BC, that's only a guess. The earliest references to trade in Kashmîrî-silk date to around the 14th century AD/ It would be taken to Bukhara in Central Asia and thereafter sold in places as far apart as Damascus and Europe. The Mughal emperor Jehangir as well as his father's historian, Abul Fazl, both mention that silkworms' eggs were imported from Gilgit and Tibet.

A recurrent theme throughout history has been that the quantity of silk produced in Kashmîr was 'insufficient for domestic purposes'. (This reference is from Moorcroft, 1824, during the Sikhs' rule.)

Around 1855, there was an epidemic among the silkworms of Europe. So, Italian experts came over to Kashmîr and took back 25,000 ounces of seed. Mahârâjâ Gulab Singh had by then made his Chief Physician, Hakim Azim, responsible for all silk-related matters. His son, Hakim Abdur Rahim, along with a Punjabi partner, carried the tradition forward, using a few kilograms of seed smuggled into Kashmîr from Kabul, concealed in walnut shells.

During Mahârâjâ Ranbir Singh's reign, silkworm seeds were imported from China and distributed among rural people. To add to the cosmopolitan pedigree of Kashmîrî silk, expertise was brought in from Murshidabad (Bengal), around 1870. Under Bengali supervision one silk factory each was set up in Ânañtnâg town and Srînagar (at Haft Chinâr). Both were called the Murshidabad factories. Later a silk factory was established at Raghunathpor, near Naseem Bâgh (Srînagar), which was called the Berhampore Factory! The Bengali connection was thus augmented.

In 1895, Sir Walter Lawrence wrote that Kashmîrî houses were 'suited to the requirements of silk rearing' because they were 'well ventilated and the Kashmîrî knew how to regulate the temperature.' GMD Sufi adds, 'The mulberry seed (in Kashmîr) is purer and better strained than the foreign seed.'

The Dogrâ Mahârâjâs' contribution to the silk industry of Kashmîr was enormous. However, it is difficult to agree with the Dastkari Hât Samiti that 'Silk-weaving was introduced to Kashmîr by Mahârâjâ Pratap Singh' (reign: 1885-1925). For one, his own ancestors had done a splendid job in this respect.

Kinds of silk products made in Kashmîr: Charmose satin, chiffon, chinon, crepe, habutti silk, satin and tabby. Scarves, saris and silk cloth are among the products made. The saris are mostly printed outside the state.

Purchase: It is always safer to purchase silk from the Government Silk Factories at Raj Bâgh and Ram Bâgh. You know what you are getting. But the private shop at Raj Bâgh, next to the factory, is cheaper, and shops on Residency Road cheaper still. Please go to these private shops only if you are certain that you can tell the difference between real and artificial silk, or if the shop has a good reputation. I can't. So I got conned by a private shop once.

Silverware

'*Sher-e-Kashmîr*' Sheikh Abdullah used to present ornamental Chinâr leaves, made of silver, to special friends. Gen. KV Krishna Rao, Governor of the state in the 1990s, revived this tradition. You get these leaves only on order (takes 10-12 days) and you pay only for the silver. The craftsmanship normally comes free. (The silver cannot, by definition, be pure. It has to be alloyed with a bit of some other metal to make it possible to work on.)

Lotus leaves are the other indigenous product made of silver. However, much of Kashmîr's silver-work follows the traditions of the rest of North India and of the Raj. Other items made of silver include bowls, boxes, cigarette cases, cups, dinner sets, goblets, plates, tea—and coffee—pots, trays, trinket-boxes, tumblers and vases. All these are made by hand.

Silversmiths are to be found in most major towns of Kashmîr. They are concentrated in Srînagar city, though. There are good silversmiths in Lambert Lane (off the Residency Road) and next to the Hanuman Mandir in the Amira Kadal area. Most of them double as jewellers. Silverware is also made and sold in Srînagar at Kalashpor, Râjourî Kadal, Zaina Kadal and Zarab Khânâ.

Turquoise-work

This kind of jewellery is, essentially, 'mosaic in brass'. Tiny pieces of turquoise are dyed and then set in brass. This method is used to make ashtrays, boxes, brooches, ear-studs, jewellery, necklaces and vases. This craft came to Kashmîr around the late 19th century.

Walnut

Walnut is the preferred wood for furniture, cabinets and, indeed, the construction of houseboats, because of the glow that comes from within the wood, because of its grain and because of its colour.

The grain is most pronounced—and the colour the darkest, almost black—in the root of the walnut tree. At the other extreme are the branches-light, almost blonde, in colour and with almost no grain. The trunk comes in between on both counts. Because of this the wood of the root is the highest-priced, that of the branches the cheapest and the trunk in between.

The colour of wood can vary hugely between one part of the same tree and another. So, the lighter part is dyed to look exactly like the darker part. However, many people like the natural variation in shades. Therefore, craftsmen often don't dye smaller handicrafts like trays and bowls made of walnut wood.

Seasoning: Unseasoned walnut wood can warp. Wood that has been left to 'season' for two years after the tree had been cut, is the best. That way all the moisture embedded in the wood evaporâtes and the wood does all its shrinking before it is converted into furniture. The best wood has the best grain: so the densely packed rings of the tree need to be shown off in the final product. Purchasing a felled walnut tree and leaving it to season for two years naturally increases the final price by that much.

Knots are not a defect. However, many customers don't like them. So, the manufacturer tries to hide them artfully during the sawing.

The patterns carved on the wood can be in relief (figures rising above the main surface) or intaglio (carvings below the surface). The deeper the carving, the more expensive will the product be. In 'semi-carving' the grain of the wood is what stands out rather than the carving, which will be just a thin strip along the edges (with, normally, a motif in the centre).

There is also an inferior type of walnut tree called the *zangul*, which does not bear fruit. Its wood isn't as strong, either, and has no grain. Sometimes in a piece of furniture all the visible parts are made of normal walnut wood, but parts which are not seen from the outside are of *zangul*. This lowers the price.

The furniture that you buy should be of wood which is at least one inch thick. Less than that will be cheaper but will also last much less.

Maintenance: Wax polish is the best. Varnish isn't, because it hides the grain and changes the colour.

Other products: Boxes, bedsteads, bowls, cabinets, cupboards, furniture, panels and screens. This author's invention—and a very elegant one, if I may say so myself—is a cabinet that stores 1200 CDs but can be broken down into four modules of 300 CDs each.

Made and/ or sold in Srînagar city at the Bund, Dal Gate, Hari Parbat, Hassanabad, Hawal, Kawdara, Nageen, Nalamar Road, Nowhatta, Polo View, Rainawari and Safa Kadal.

Made at: i) In Srînagar: Akal Mîr, Amda Kadal, Bag-e-Goji Lankar, Bagwan Pora, Bota Kadal, Budshah Mohalla, Channa Mohalla, Daliporâ, Dekhdar Har, Fateh Kadal, Hamâmbal, Hathi Khân, Kachri Mohalla, Kak Sathoo, Kalamdan Pora, Kani Dewar, Kani Mazar, Khajporâ, Khudporâ, Lal Bazar, Madeen Sâheb, Mandibal, Mîr Masjid, Narwara, Patliporâ (Payeen), Shah Mohalla, Shati Bâgh, Shri Bhat, Syed Hamid Pora and Urdu Bazar.

ii) In Budgâm: Shankarporâ.

iii) In Kupwârâ: Tangdar, Trehgam.

Wickerwork or willow basketry

I had been looking at those inexpensive baskets all my life, displayed at shops in the Dal Gate and Hazratbal areas of Srînagar, never giving them much thought, because basket-work has traditionally been considered low-art. In the late 1990s, however, I started getting calls from friends in Chandigarh and Bombay to get them clothes-bins and 'boxes for magazines and books' made of the same willow-rushes. Suddenly, imaginative new uses were being found in the luxury market for Kashmîrî basket-work. If you plan to take them to the hot plains, please purchase them unvarnished and keep sprinkling them with water periodically, to make them last longer.

Going through the taxes levied by Kashmîr's own Sultans (1320-1586), I noticed that basket-work was one of the items to be taxed. That tells us how old the craft is.

In the early 20th century an experiment was conducted to grow British (weeping) willows in Kashmîr. It worked. In fact, because of the fertility of Kashmîr's soil, the twigs produced were longer than in even England itself.

Products: Baskets, clothes-bins, containers for bottles (so they don't break in transit; and to make it easier to hold very hot bottles), lamp shades, picnic hampers, shoe-racks, sofa sets and tables. The medium is so flexible that almost any kind of container can be made of wickerwork.

Made at: i) In Srînagar city: Anchar, Hazratbal and Soura; ii) In Srînagar district: Ganderbal, Haren and Shalabag; iii) In Ânañtnâg: Doru and Qaimoh; iv) In Budgâm: Tsrar-e-Sharief.

Woollen articles

Blankets and other woollen articles are made in Bandipore, Budgâm, Beerwah, Chadoora, Gurêz, Hañdwârâ, Inder Gadodar, the Lolab valley, Magam, Nadihal, Pulwâmâ, Shopian, Sopore, Tarzoo, Tiiail and Trâl.

Crafts that you can't take home

The Khatam-band ceiling

You might find the ceiling of the room in your houseboat or upmarket hotel made of polished wood, with pretty, geometric patterns on it. The 'base' of the ceiling would be flat, like ceilings everywhere. However, regardless of the design, after every two or three inches in every direction there would be raised surfaces, made of thin strips of wood, no longer than two or three inches each. The patterns could be squares, rectangles, octagons, diamonds or any design that could possibly be made with little strips of wood. Each strip is about ¾" wide, about an inch thick and as mentioned, two or three inches long. The flat surface above (yes, above) these strips is not one long, flat board, either. It is made of hundreds of flat little pieces of wood, cut into squares, rectangles of whatever the pattern demands. Typically, these flat pieces are around 3" × 3", and as thick as a scale/ foot-rule.

'*Khatam-band*' ceilings, thus, are made of a very large number of tiny pieces of wood. The flat pieces alternate with the strips. They are fitted together—without a single nail—as in a jigsaw puzzle.. These ceilings cost a fortune, but entirely because of the labour involved in fitting thin, flat pieces into grooves inside the thicker strips. (Each thin-flat piece has to fit into grooves in the four to six thick strips that surround it.) The wood is free, because it consists entirely of the waste wood generated while making windows, doors, wall panels and floors for that house.

Mirza Haidar Dughlat brought this art, called the '*khatam-band*', from Central Asia to Kashmîr in the 16th century. The wood used is a mixture of dark walnut and lighter coloured pine. The better known (Muslim) shrines of Srînagar and all the Dogrâ palaces of Kashmîr have excellent '*khatam-band*' ceilings. The palace at Chenaini (Udhampur, Jammû) has a decaying '*khatam-band*' ceiling.

There are several dozen different '*khatam-band*' patterns. However, many of the classical designs are no longer being executed. The Chhattabal area of Srînagar is a good place to find experts in this craft.

Pinjra-kâri

(Also known as '*zâli-pinjra*' and '*achhi-dâr*'.)

'Pinjra' means 'cage.' 'Kâri' is a suffix that means '-work.' Thus, together the two mean 'cage-work.' 'Zâli' seems to be the Kashmîrî equivalent of the Urdu 'jâli,' which means net, 'wire-net', 'wire-mesh' or 'grate'.

Pinjra-kâri, thus, is a kind of openwork or latticework. It is done on fences, doors, railings, ventilators, room-partitions, screens and windows.

Why it evolved: The theory is that this form of openwork evolved because of the *purdah* (veil) system of Islâm. The sexes had to be segregated. And yet there were occasions when the women of the *zenana* needed to see what was going on in the men's section. For example, royal women wanted to see the proceedings of the court. On festive occasions middle-class women wanted to see the singing and dancing in the men's section. A screen that had little gaps, or interstices, between the artwork all over would separate the two sexes. Women could see through it without themselves being seen. At Islâmic shrines such ceiling-to-floor screens still surround the graves of saints inside. Women are not allowed inside, so they can look in through the interstices of the latticework. When you drive from the airport towards the city, then roughly 1.5 km. later, where the slope comes to an end, on the left you will see one such shrine.

Glass has been known to Islâmic lands almost since the advent of Islâm. In Kashmîr, too, there are references to glass in ancient literature. The 15th century Zaina Dab (see below) used glass panes as well as mirrors in its architecture. And yet one of the major uses of latticework was as a substitute for panes in windows. It filtered the rays of the sun: though in Kashmîr the only time when sun rays are unwelcome is July.

The craft came to Kashmîr along with Central Asian Islâmic architecture. Muslim craftsmen brought the art over. However, the Kashmîrî Pandits of Srînagar, Ânañtnâg and Bijbehara were among its biggest patrons.

In romantic poetry: There is a whole body of Urdu poetry from the rest of South Asia about spying the ladylove through the interstices of a *chilman* (screen). In Kashmîr, too, there are verses in which the beloved is asked to show her face through a *zâli pinjra* screen.

History: The existence of pinjra work on stone at Srînagar's 15th century Madni Sâheb mosque indicates that this craft was known during Zain-ul-Abedin's time. The Sultan's celebrated 12-storey palace, the Zaina Dab, was, however, the first building in Kashmîr to use windows made in this fashion. Thus, at least by the Sultan's time wood was being used for this craft. (See the chapter 'A History of Kashmîr' for more about the palace.)

Wood is a very Kashmîrî material. The Mughals alone made mosques of stone in Kashmîr. And yet *'pinjra-kâri'* started out during the era of Kashmîr's own Sultans, with local stone-workers carving flowers, plants and vines on stone. Standards were not as good as in other Islâmic lands. The art reached its peak in Kashmîr during the Mughal period, and on wood, not stone.

Zoona dab balconies

One of the most exciting forms of Kashmîrî architecture is the 'dab' (pron. the same as 'dub') balcony. These are wooden balconies that jut out of the outer wall, like cantilevers. Each balcony is big enough to seat eight or nine people, who sit on cushions, with their backs against the balcony's three wooden walls. There is plenty of space for several dishes between them. (The fourth side opens into the living room.)

Normally there are no brackets under the floors of these balconies, which are suspended in mid-air, often above River Jehlum. I have always admired the architect's confidence that his balconies won't collapse and fall into the river under the weight of the people and the food.

'Zoon' is the Kashmîrî word for 'moon.' A '*zoona dab*' is a balcony from which the moon can be seen. The windows of such balconies would normally have *'pinjra-kâri'* lattices instead of glass panes. Moonbeams would enter the living room through the spaces between the fancy pattern in wood. Sometimes glass panes of different colours would be fitted into the lattice. In such cases the moonbeams entering the room would be multi-coloured.

Some balconies of this kind have survived the arson of the 1990s and are to be found along the Jehlum riverfront in Srînagar. The riverfront near the Khânqâh-e-Mu'alla (Shah-e-Hamadân) and its opposite bank (the Patther Masjid side) is one such stretch.

Palanquins: Brides are no longer carried in 'palanquins'. They were till the first half of the 20th century. The sides of these 'palanquins' were made of *'pinjra-kâri'* latticework. If pieces of coloured glass were fitted in the interstices of a 'palanquin', it would be called an '*Aanâ Zânpânâ*' ('the palanquin with mirrors', even though it was glass and not mirrors that had been affixed).

Where to find pinjrâ-kârî *work:* i) Monuments and shrines: One of the finest examples of *'pinjra-kâri'* on stone is in the shrine of Thag (pron. like the central Indian *thug*) Bâbâ Sâheb in Srînagar. Limestone has been used on the windows and recesses of this shrine. Lattices have been created there using the grape-vine pattern. The shrine of Akbar Deen Sâheb at Dâdasar, near Trâl, is a first rate example of *'pinjra-kâri'* in wood. (See 'Pulwâmâ' district.) The Khânqâh-e-Faiz Panah shrine of Shah-e-Hamadân at Trâl used to be almost as good, but it got burnt in the 1990s. The shrine of Batamaloo Sâheb in Srînagar has some of the designs used at Dadasar.

The mausoleums of several Kashmîrî saints have 'lids' made of fine pinjra-kâri latticework. Examples are the shrine of Râh Bâb Sâheb in Srînagar, where the sun and the stars are included in the pattern. The shrine of Bâbâ Naseeb Sâheb is another example. Tsrar (Chrar)-e-Sharief used to be a third, till a Pakistani mercenary set it on fire in 1995.

ii) Private houses: Basheer Akhtar, writing in 1987, observed that 'Houses with '*zoona dabs*' were all the rage in [Srînagar] in the olden days. These days the few remaining examples of such houses are only to be found in such parts of Maisuma and Tashwân about which it is said that in those areas Hâfizas [female nautch girls] would once enliven gatherings with their song and dance. Pandit Billa Kak Dhar's house in Safa Kadal used to be an excellent example of *'pinjra-kâri'*. However, times have changed and all the latticework has been removed from the windows. Similarly, glass panes have replaced *'pinjra-kâri'* latticework in all the windows of the old Makhdoom Sâheb shrine.'

iii) Houseboats: Today this art is kept alive mainly in houseboats, some of which have railings in the *'pinjra-kâri'* style.

Other uses: Apart from screens and railings, *'pinjra-kâri'* is used in ventilators, ornamental room-partitions, windows and doors.

Houseboats and shikaras

A 19th century Englishman called Kennard is said to have built the first houseboat in Kashmîr. Entirely possible. However, all that he did was to build a houseboat in the European tradition. Kashmîr's own houseboats (*doongas*) have almost always existed. One of the earliest references to them (and a disparaging one at that) is in the 16th century *Ain-e-Akbari.*

Kennard's houseboat caught on. All modern Kashmîrî houseboats resemble their twins on the Seine in Paris-in concept, though not detail. Today there are more than 1,200 legal (and 700 illegal) 'modern' (i.e. not including traditional residential doongas) houseboats on the Dal Lake alone.

These are between 24 and 38 metres long, and 3 to 6 metres wide. Most of them are moored, almost permanently, to one of the shores of a lake (Dal or Nageen) or river (Jehlum or the tiny Tsont-e-Kol). If not a shore, then they'd be moored to an island. That's because they need permanent electricity lines and water connections. Some of them are connected to sewer lines, too.

Normally these boats are shifted only when they need repairs—or when they find a more profitable site. Otherwise they remain moored at that site, almost forever. Sometimes wealthy tourists want to travel on a lake or river in a houseboat. In that case tug-boats pull the houseboat to the destination.

A houseboat is a full-fledged house, with two to four bedrooms, bathrooms, kitchen, drawing and dining rooms, a little 'verandah' and a large deck above. It is made entirely of wood—walnut, normally—and is a boat that floats on a river or lake. All houseboats have flat bottoms. Except that the rooms and bathrooms are smaller, you can expect the same kind of facilities as in a hotel in that price range: televisions and refrigerators in the living room, attached bathrooms, running warm water, often a bathtub, western style toilets, clean linen and a shelf of books.

Typically, a *shikara* (boat) will ferry you from the road/ Boulevard to the houseboat. (This is not necessary if the boat is on the Jehlum. You can simply walk down from the Bund [embankment] to the boat.) Either way, the houseboat will be connected to firm land by a short plank. (The *shikara* ride to the nearest shore is normally free, if you've already checked into a houseboat or have a reservation. Obviously, it is free only on designated shikaras.)

You'll step onto a small 'verandah'. The first room that you will enter will be a living room, normally with a *khatam-band* ceiling and walls made of walnut. The carvings on these walls are generally a bit too rich by any standards, including Kashmîr's own. Coyingly rich. The next room usually is the dining room. Then comes a corridor, which leads to two or three (rarely four) bedrooms. It's uneconomical to have just one bedroom.

Bathrooms normally have western style toilets and can be quite modern. Almost all houseboats have a deck upstairs (often with garden umbrellas) where one can soak in the sun.

You can book the entire houseboat, or merely the rooms that you need. (Downmarket houseboats, popular only with young, foreign tourists, even let you hire just one bed in a dormitory.) Room charges normally include food. In case you don't want other people to stay in your houseboat, you can book the remaining rooms for half the advertised rent. Since tourists mostly come in the months when heating is not needed, heating is not included in the rent.

Sociologically, for some reason international tourists (who comprise just 9% of the total) prefer houseboats. This gets reflected in the choice of crockery, cutlery, furnishings, 'library' (one bookshelf, normally) and even cuisine. Tourists from the rest of India stay in hotels as well. Foreigners who choose to stay in one of the three luxury hotels in town often want a few nights in a houseboat as well. All luxury hotels arrange this as part of the package.

Tourists who like solitude opt for the Nageen Lake. The Dal Lake, however, is where the overwhelming majority of tourists stay, because it is better located.

To see what Kashmîr's own houseboats looked like before Mr. Kennard, all you have to do is to go to the Dal Gate and look at the downmarket boats parked on the still waters of the northern side (i.e. in the direction of the old Golf Course). These, too, have rooms but are not posh and are in the Kashmîrî style, i.e. people sit and sleep on the floor and not on chairs and beds.

These boats existed much before Akbar's time (he wrested Kashmîr in 1586). His court historians recorded that he did not like Kashmîrî houseboats. He preferred the two-storeyed version found in Bengal, which had elegant windows and of which he introduced a thousand into Kashmîr. Somehow two-storeyed houseboats never caught on in Kashmîr, partly because tall boats can't pass under bridges.

All Kashmîrî boatmen (except in Hindi-Urdu films) are Muslims, and belong to a community called *hernz* (silent 'r') in Kashmîrî and '*hân-ji*' in Hindi-Urdu. They all claim to be descendants of Noah. (see 'The people of Kashmir')

Through history the Kashmîrîs have travelled and carried grain, fruit and vegetables from one end of the Valley to the other in boats. Large transport boats are called the *bahach* and can carry up to 1,000 'maunds' of grain. The doonga has a sloping roof and sidewalls made of matting. The boatman and his family live in the rear, the passenger in the front. 'Doongas' carry up to 200 'maunds'.

Shikaras are scaled-down versions of the '*doonga*', meant entirely for ferrying passengers-from one bank of River Jehlum to the other if they are local passengers, and on pleasure cruises on lakes if tourists. Cloth awnings are used instead of matted roofs in '*shikaras*', which have low, cushioned seats for six to nine passengers. (Around four, in the case of pleasure cruises.)

While researching Kashmîrî art, I came upon a 15th century painting of what is now known as the Shankaracharya hill. It showed several '*shikaras*' floating on the Dal Lake. So, '*shikaras*' are at least that old.

18

Kashmîrî Shawls

History: Kashmîr is a cold place. Wool has always been plentiful. So it stands to reason that the Kashmîris have been making shawls for as long as there have been people in Kashmîr. The oldest extant reference to Kashmîri shawls is in Buddhist literature which dates to Emperor Ashok's age (c. 250 BC). The shawl industry of Kashmîr, according to one estimate, employed more than a lakh (a hundred thousand) workers at the beginning of the 21st century. This figure must surely be an exaggeration.

There are many references to Kashmîri shawls in ancient Hindu and Roman texts as well. Apparently, they "were worn by the proudest beauties at the court of the Cæsars". (Historian GMD Sufi has put this phrase in double-quotes but doesn't say where he got it from.)

The craft then went into a decline till the end of the 14th century AD. It was around AD 1378 that Shah-e-Hamadân, the much-loved saint from Iran, brought a new variant to Kashmîr. The then king of Kashmîr, Qutb-ud-Din, gave official patronage to the industry.

In the sixteenth century, Naghz Beigh, a craftsman from Khuqand (Central Asia), accompanied the Mughal governor, Mirza Haidar Dughlat, to Kashmîr. He brought with him some very refined techniques, mainly how to weave red and green spots in regular rows into the texture of the shawl.

The Mughals brought workers from Andijan [Turkestan] (see 'Carpets', above) to Kashmîr to upgrade the shawl industry here. They evolved the *jiugha* design. (The jiugha is an almond-shaped jewel worn on the turban.)

The Mughal Emperor Akbar (16th century) was a connoisseur of shawls. He would get four kinds of shawls made: a) Toos Asal. These shawls were very light, and yet warm and soft. The wool of the toos(h) goat would be used. The natural colour of these shawls is grey; b) Safed alich or 'tarahdar'. Their natural colour is either black or white; c) Zar doozi, Alich, Bandinun, Chheet, Gulibetun, Keshdeh, Kulya or Purzdar; and d) Jâmâs: These were longer shawls.

The 16th century Mughal historian, Abul Fazal wrote, 'In former times shawls were often brought from Kashmîr. People folded them up in four folds, and wore them for a very long time. Nowadays they are generally worn without folds, and merely thrown over the shoulder. His Majesty [Akbar] has commenced to wear them double, which looks very well. His Majesty encourages, in every possible way, the manufacture of shawls in Kashmîr. In Lahore also there are more than a thousand workshops...'

A Kashmîri journalist insists that Kashmîris ran these thousand-odd workshops of Lahore. Pakistani scholars Sherry Rehman and Naheed Jafri agree. Even Abul Fazal implies this. We thus have a very significant insight into how old the Kashmîri diasporâ in Lahore is.

Rehman and Jafri say that the Kashmîri shawl [or 'shal,' as they spell it] was a symbol of rank in Muslim courts all over the world and that it '[rose] to official recognition from the Mughal empire.' They attribute the excellence of these shawls to Kashmîr's 'unique access to the most unparalleled woolen yarn or raw material in the world through its location and trade routes through Kashmîr... Although the Kashmîri Shal's strength lies in the many forms and shapes it has assumed over the centuries, the peculiar weaving technique that it initially had became famous for the world over, the double-interlock twill tapestry method of handloom patterning and weaving is virtually extinct.'

In 1664, a visibly impressed Francois Bernier wrote, 'These shawls are about a yard and a half long and a yard broad, ornamental at both ends with a sort of embroidery, made in the loom, a foot in width.' (In the volume on 'Ladâkh' in the chapter on the history of Leh, there are several references to how this trade has affected the histories of Kashmîr and Leh.)

George Forester added in 1783, 'In Kashmîr are seen merchants and commercial agents of the principal cities of northern India and also of Tartary, Persia and Turkey who, at the same time, advance their fortunes and enjoy the fine climate.'

The priciest shawls are *toos(h), sozni* and *kâni*. Toos(h) shawls; referred to in the poetry of Habba Khatoon (late 16th century), are made of the wool of an animal of the same name and their natural colours are black, white and red.

Kashmîri weavers settled in Lahore and Amritsar in a big way, because of the demand there. The British built a bazar for Kashmîri weavers in Ludhiana to induce them to migrate there, to meet the demand for their shawls in England. Lahore was then ruled by the Sikhs. (In the chapter on the History of Leh we have more insights into why the British meddled with the shawl trade.) There was a major famine in Kashmîr in 1878 and 1879, the last straw that led to the exodus of even more Kashmîri craftsmen to Lahore, Amritsar and Ludhiana.

It was around then that the industry went into a decline in Kashmîr from which it never recovered. There were three main reasons: i) The loss of the

French market because of the Franco-Prussian war of 1870; ii) The loss of the upper end of the north Indian market because the Mahârâjâs and Nawabs were displaced by the British. Princely Awadh, which perhaps was the biggest single patron, was annexed by the British; and iii) The Industrial Revolution, which led to the manufacture of cheaper machine-made shawls. (The last two reasons are also responsible for the wiping out of several other arts and crafts of India such as Basohli and Kashmîri miniature paintings.) However, even in that period of decline, a shawl could cost £300 in Kashmîr itself, as Andrew Wilson recorded in 1875. (Before that the price of an expensive shawl could be over £1,000.) Rehman and Jafri add a fourth reason: 'the rapacity of the tax and duty regime.'

One market that has not changed over the last two centuries is that of Bengal. Because of their love of shawls, the Bengali elite would purchase Kashmîri shawls both from Kashmîr and Amritsar, in addition to sometimes employing Kashmîri weavers in Bengal itself. As in Awadh, a Kashmîri community settled in Bengal, because of the trade in and manufacture of shawls.

The Afghâns: The Afghâns were the other rulers who patronised this industry.

The craft attained its present sophistication during the 18th century. Âzâd Khân was one of the Afghân Governors in Kashmîr. (His period is variously given as 1783-92 and 1775-83.) It is said that during Âzâd's tenure an expert shawl maker called Ali Bâbâ saw an animal (perhaps a fowl) walk on a white sheet. Ali found the marks of the animal's claws etched on the sheet. The maestro decided to create shawls with similar etchings. He replicated the footprints in embroidery. Thus was born Kashmîr's first *sozan-kâri* shawl. (See 'Embroidery' above.) This soon became the dominant style in Kashmîr. Shawls of this kind used to be very inexpensive. (Ali Bâbâ used to live in Srînagar's Sokâli Pora neighbourhood. He was also known as Saeed Bâbâ and Ala Bâbâ. Some claim that he invented Amali or amilkar shawls.)

According to another tradition, Nadir Beigh, a master craftsman from Turkestan, came to Kashmîr in the sixteenth century. That's when Mirza Haider Dughlat ruled the Valley. Some say that it was Nadir who brought to Kashmîr the art of making shawls with colourful patterns.

In 1803, an Armenian trader called Khwaja Yusuf visited Kashmîr. Some say that it was the Khwaja who introduced in Kashmîr the art of making Amali shawls. Others say that Yusuf only brought new designs with him and thus infused new life into an older craft.

The manufacture of shawls flourished during the Sikh period (1819-1846). Some of the finest shawls were created during the reign of Mahârâjâ Ranjit Singh. The Mahârâjâ got a shawl made on which were embroidered all the achievements of his era. The shawl cost Rs. 5,000 to make.

'Double-sided' shawls, in which the embroidery on both sides looks the same, were first made in 1864, during the reign of the Dogrâ Mahârâjâ Gulab

Singh. (See 'Embroidery' above.) The first such shawl was created jointly by Mustafa Pandit and Aziz Pandit.

Exports to the West: Around 1796, Abdullah Khân, the Afghân governor of Kashmîr, gave Syed Yahya, a visitor from Baghdad, an orange-coloured shawl as a farewell gift. The Syed gifted that shawl to the Khedive of Egypt. The Khedive gave it to Napoleon Bonaparte, who passed it on to Josephine. And thus Paris acquired a taste for Kashmîri shawls. Or so the story goes.

Rival yarns would have it that the light veil on the back of Mona Lisa's head was a Kashmîri ring shawl, and that Europe knew of these shawls as early as in 1519 (not counting the ancient Romans, of course).

'Cashmere' (i.e. pashmina) was a household name in Europe by Balzac's time (late 19th century).

Forty thousand looms sprang up in Kashmîr by the early 19th century to meet the requirements of the European market. One to two thousand maunds of wool would be imported every year. As much as 80% of Kashmîr's shawl exports in the 19th century were to France; 10% to the USA; 5% to Italy and the remaining 5% to the rest of Europe.

French traders picked up two-thirds of these exports in Kashmîr itself. Kashmîri traders themselves exported the rest to London, where the shawls were sold at auctions. Even in London the purchasers were mostly French.

Moorcroft noted that shawls were exported not only to the rest of India but also to Russia and Central Asia. Sir Walter Lawrence gave a more precise estimate of this export trade. He said that between 1862 and 1870, the average annual export of shawls was 25 to 28 lakh (rupees or shawls is not clear). What is certain is that in the middle of the 19th century shawls worth £130,000 used to be exported every year from Kashmîr. Of this, shawls of a value of around £90,000 were sold to Europe alone, and the rest within Asia (mostly the rest of India).

In 1870, Prussia/ Germany started defeating the French in war. There would be widespread mourning in Kashmîr every time news of a fresh French reverse was received. An entire community of 90,000 weavers and traders stood to be wiped out. The Dogrâ Mahârâjâ stepped in and bought shawls worth several lakh rupees to prevent this.

In 1873, £2,500 worth of Amritsar's vastly inferior shawls were sold at the London sale, whereas 'nothing whatever... out of the £4,000 worth of Kashmîr shawls that were presented were sold'. (The quote is from an 1873 British report.) This was attributed by contemporâry British writers to Amritsar's more favourable location. The development greatly alarmed the Mahârâjâ who launched 'alleviation' measures, including employing some shawl-weavers in the government-run silk factory and in the carpet trade.

And then the European market began to vanish. Moorcroft had come to Kashmîr in 1820-22 and had studied the craft and its processes most thoroughly. He passed on the knowledge that he had gathered in Kashmîr to manufacturers back home in England. Thus were born the 'Paisley Shawls' of Scotland. They edged Kashmîri shawls out of Europe almost completely. High-quality imitations made in France cornered what was left of the market. Fashions changed in France and America, to deliver the final blow.

For over a century after that, Kashmîr's main market was the rest of India. Since the 1990s, however, there has been a great pashmina revival in New York in particular and the West in general.

The word 'shawl': It is said that the abovementioned Naghz Beigh once presented his master, Mirza Haider Dughlat, with a 1½-yard long sheet made of expensive pashmina. When asked what the raiment was called, Naghz replied that it was a 'shawl'. The name stuck. ('Shawl' is the word the people of Khuqand use to refer to blankets.)

Types of Shawls:

1) Classified According To Materials Used

Shawls are made of three kinds of material: wool, pashmina and shahtoosh.

i) *Woollen shawls:* The simplest kind of fabric woven in Kashmîr from pure wool is called 'ruffle/ raffal' or 'raffel'. (Sometimes cotton and/ or synthetic yarn is added to the wool.) This base is then embroidered upon.

The principal types of embroidery are:

a) Sozni or 'tamboured work': This is embroidery done in strips along the edges of the shawl. The colours used are few, never more than three, and sober. If done well, the embroidery does not result in a sketchy 'negative' on the reverse. Instead, the best sozni-work consists of motifs on both sides. The designs are either abstract or representations of flowers and leaves. Just the outline of the motifs is embroidered. 'Stem-stitching' is used. (See also 'Embroidery' above — 'do rukha'.)

b) Ari or hook embroidery: As in chain-stitching (see above), concentric circles are embroidered and atop them flowers and leaves.

c) The so-called papiér mâchè style: Motifs — flowers and petals once again — are as bright as in papiér mâchè and are woven into broad panels along the breadth of the shawl, on either side. Sometimes the entire shawl is embroidered upon. A black outline is drawn around each motif. 'Satin-stitching' is used.

d) Zari: Gold, silver or other metal thread is used in this kind of embroidery. Zari shawls are expensive and worn on formal occasions such as weddings. (See 'zar doozi' in the section on 'Embroidery' above.)

e) *chikin-doozi*

f) *jâlik-doozi* (see 'Embroidery'.)

Amali work is discussed later in this section.

European shawls were made on jacquards and drawlooms. Europeans were also fond of printed shawls.

Staple (ari-work) embroidery is done in Srînagar district.

ii) *Pashmina Shawls*: Pashmina is a soft yarn made of the hair of the Himâlayan ibex (*Capra sibirica),* a goat which lives in Ladâkh, around 4,500m./ 14,000' above the sea. The nomadic herdsmen of the Chang Thang plateau (Ladâkh) rear this goat. Every summer the herdsmen shear the thick growth on the goat's underbelly and sell it at a decent price. Some species of wild goat also yield wool that is almost as soft and fine. There are 19th century accounts that such goats—and undomesticated ibexes — were, sometimes trapped with snares or hunted for their wool. However, that is a thing of the past. Much of the pashmina used in the 20th and 21st centuries has come from goats domesticated by individuals and the government. Huge pashmina farms set up by the government ensure that the supply of the wool is plentiful, and reasonably priced.

Shawls made of pashmina are expensive and are woven in Kashmîr (the best and the most expensive), Basohli (medium quality and medium prices) and Kargil (cheapest and coarsest). They normally are white or the brownish colour of jute sacks (gunny bags). Their price comes down if the pashmina is blended with ordinary wool or rabbit's hair.

In the 19th century, Basohli, Bhaderwâh and Doda (all in Jammû) had sizeable shawl industries. *The Gazetteer* recorded in 1890 that these three 'enjoy great advantages, as they are free from many of the burdens and restrictions imposed upon their brethren in the valley of Kashmír. The shawls manufactured in these localities hold a middle place in the market; while greatly inferior to the veritable Kashmír shawl, they are of superior quality to shawls manufactured at Amritsár [sic] and other places in the Punjáb, which are largely adulterated with *wahabshahi*, an inferior wool produced at Kirmán.'

Most 18th and 19th century accounts speak of the relative inferiority of shawls made by ethnic Kashmîris at Lahore and Amritsar. And yet a fairly wide variety of shawls was made at these two cities of the Punjab. Soon the shawls of the Punjab took on an identity of their own. Because they were less expensive, they were more successful commercially.

'Half-pashmina' shawls normally contain no pashmina at all. They are made of some inferior material that feels and looks somewhat like pashmina.

Only Kashmîri pashmina shawls are embroidered, which adds considerably to their price. The very expensive *jâmâwâr* shawls are embroidered all over. (Jamawar literally means 'a gown-piece'.) Other pashmina shawls are embroidered to a lesser extent—normally just a thin strip along the edges.

The increasingly rare *chashm-e-bulbul* shawls are not embroidered upon at all, because the artistry lies in the weave itself, which consists of thousands of little 'lozenge-shaped squares'.

The history and politics of pashmina: Pashmina is expensive, though not half as fine or pricey as shahtoosh. However, the amount of pashmina wool gathered — and shawls made — is vastly greater. It has therefore loomed enormously large in the economics — and, thus, politics — of Kashmîr and Leh. So enormously large, that it was one of the major reasons why Punjab conquered Kashmîr and the Dogrâs Ladâkh. If since 1947 there has been a Kashmîri diasporâ in Pakistan's Punjab province, including some ranking politicians, pashmina is a factor.

Around 1680, the Dalai Lama's powerful Tibetan army allied with the Mongols. They attacked Deldan Namgyal, king of much of present-day Leh district. At his request, the Mughal army came to his rescue. The Mughals operated from their nearest provincial capital, Srînagar. In return, Deldan conceded to Kashmîr a monopoly on the purchase of pashmina wool.

In 1684, Leh and Tibet signed the Treaty of Tingmo(s) gang. The treaty gave Ladâkh a monopoly over the pashmina trade, including pashmina produced in western Tibet. Ladâkh operated its monopoly through Kashmîri traders, who were settled in Spituk (Leh) as part of this treaty. From Spituk the Kashmîris would buy up all the raw pashmina produced in Chang Thang as well as Rudok. They would then send the wool to Kashmîr, where it was woven into shawls.

That is why the Kashmîris are the only people in the world who really know how to work with pashmina. Even the weavers of Basohli are ethnic Kashmîris. The pashmina trade was so lucrative that both the British and Mahârâjâ Ranjit Singh's Punjab-based empire coveted it. It was also one of the reasons why the Mahârâjâ Ranjit Singh conquered Kashmîr. The rest of the story is best told in Janet Rizvi's words:

'The ensuing famine [drove] many Kashmîri shawl weavers to seek their livelihood on the plains [of the Punjab], particularly in the towns of Amritsar, Nurpur and Ludhiana. [There were several famines in Kashmîr in the first half of the 19th century. The one of 1833-34 is perhaps the best documented.—PD] In order to supply the growing demand from these places, a certain proportion of Western Tibet's pashmina had started being diverted down the Sutlej, through Spiti and Kinnaur [both in HP] to the plains, bypassing Kashmîr altogether and thus further impoverishing its traditional industry. The development of this trade in smuggled wool was encouraged by the British, through whose territory [in HP] it must pass. They repaired the tracks used by the traders in Kinnaur, and offered the nomadic goatherds of Western Tibet higher prices than those fixed by the Ladâkhi and Kashmîri monopolists.

'Both Ranjit Singh's own Government, and that of his most powerful vassal, the Dogrâ Gulab Singh, Raja of Jammû, were alive to the importance of this trade. The establishment of the shawl industry in Amritsar and Nurpur, both towns within the Sikh empire, was a development that suited Ranjit, who also undertook to rehabilitate the traditional industry in Kashmîr. Gulab Singh attempted to open a pashmina route to the plains via Kishtwâr, one of the hill districts he ruled over; this elicited complaints to Ranjit from the Sikh governor of Kashmîr.

'But Gulab Singh's ambitions went further than merely diversion of a part of this lucrative trade to his own territories. Ultimately he aimed at getting control over the entire pashmina producing area…'

It was thus that Amritsar came to be the place where pashmina shawls made in Basohli (and some in Kashmîr) are 'calendered'. This was also one of the reasons why a Kashmîri diasporâ developed in East as well as West Punjab, notably Lahore. Kashmîris based in Lahore were in the forefront of Kashmîr's freedom struggle against the Dogrâ Mahârâjâs, in the 1930s and 1940s. I suspect that in 1947, when Muslims migrated en masse from East Punjab, the Kashmîris living there did not return to Kashmîr. Instead, they went to West Punjab (Pakistan), along with their other Muslim neighbours.

iii) *Shahtoosh shawls*: 'Shah' means 'king' and this is the king of all shawls. By far the most expensive, too, mainly because its wool is so difficult to get.

The Tibetan antelope (*chiru* or Pantholops Hodgsoni) is only found at around 5,000 metres above the sea, where eastern Ladâkh meets the plateau of Tibet. In winter it grows a thick coat of 'under-wool' to protect itself from the extreme cold of the plateau. In summer, this very coat becomes an irritant. Besides, fleas tend to gather inside it, adding to the irritation. Whenever the chiru feels itchy it scratches its throat and body on thorny bushes. In the process it leaves behind a few strands of hair on the thorns. Shepherds and farmers collect these hairs tuft by tuft. Obviously it takes ages to collect enough hair to make a single shawl with. Which is why these shawls are so expensive.

(The Chinese have spread the canard that the antelope is being killed — on Chinese territory — for its wool. A spate of articles have appeared in support of this theory. All of them use the same photograph. So, obviously one or two such incidents might have taken place in Tibet. In Kashmîr no one is so foolish as to kill the antelope that, so to speak, lays the golden hair. Which is why Kashmîr had, till 2000, refused to ban trade in shahtoosh.

(More important, the hairs of the chiru start curling inwards as soon as it dies a natural or violent death. Such hairs yield inferior wool. Good shahtoosh can only be made from hairs left on thorny bushes by a living antelope.)

Pure shahtoosh yarn can be made to resemble silk yarn. Because shahtoosh shawls are woven loosely, it is very difficult to embroider pure shahtoosh. It is never dyed either: it would be foolish to tamper with the (brownish) colour of a material, the colour of which is an indicator of its snob value. These shawls are very light, soft and warm. Because they can pass through a ring, they are also called 'ring shawls'. Shahtoosh is sometimes blended with pashmina to make the shawl slightly more affordable.

Some 'ring shawls' are made of silk. This level of refinement was achieved during the Mughal era.

2) Classified According To Type Of Manufacture

There are another two kinds of shawls, distinguished by the type of their manufacture: kâni and amalikâr. *Kani* shawls are woven on looms.

Kânî shawls: One kind of *kani* shawl uses rafgar 'embroidery'. It is made by seamlessly joining together several little pieces of pashmina. If done well, it should not be possible to make out that the shawl consists of tiny shreds. In some ways, the kani variety of shawls represents shawl-making at its grandest. On the one hand, the technique is very intricate. On the other, it imposes limits on the ornamentation of the shawl. This kind of shawl was also made in Persia and parts of Central Asia.

Ghulâm Muhammad 'Kânihâmâ' was one private entrepreneur who tried to keep this tradition alive in the twentieth century. He died in 2001. The patronage of the Central and State governments helped. The Government of India commissioned him to make eight shawls for them, at prices ranging from one to two lakh rupees each. They are so expensive because it takes two artisans, working together, two and a half years each to make a single kani shawl. And it takes so long partly because no knitting needles are used, only wooden instruments.

These shawls can be the last word in sobriety, are extremely brightly coloured. Their colours range from sober greys and regal purples and violets to vibrant mustard yellows.

Amali/ amli/ amilkar/ amalikâr (paisley) shawls are made up of countless, almost invisible, little stitches that cover the entire area in a grand pattern. The amli shawl is really a 19th century variant of the kani shawl. Rehman and Jafri write, 'The Amli shal is important because it gave a new lease of life to the Kashmîri shal in a different form, which again remained inimitable to the late 20th century.'

The main difference between the two is that the amli shawl is embroidered. Patterns are woven into kâni shawls on the loom itself.

Rehman and Jafri mention a third category, the 'Combination Shal, which represents a 19th century transition between two defining techniques,' i.e. the kâni and the amli.

They also refer to another category, namely Dealer-Crafted Shawls, which were 'a twentieth century adaptation of antique shal fragments crafted onto new pieces enabling them to be worn as wearable stoles and shals.'

Sizes: There are two standard sizes, male (3 yards by 1.5 yards) and female (2 yards x 1 yard).

Embroidery: The amount of embroidery on a shawl can vary. 'Dor-dâr' shawls are embroidered at the two extreme ends only. These borders can be narrow or wide. The most commonly found motifs are almonds and Chinâr-leaves. In addition, sometimes thread is laid out on the four corners. 'Bootey wâla shawls' have flowers and saplings embroidered on them. These motifs are scattered all over the main body of the shawl, at regular intervals. These flowers and saplings can be small *(fali kâr)* or big.

If the amount of embroidery on a shawl is quite considerable, it is known as a *jâmâ* or *jâmâ-vâr* shawl. Within the jâmâ family, the ones with relatively little embroidery are known as *jâli wâlâ jâmâ.*

There are two kinds of embroidery: i) Shawls with perfunctory and scanty embroidery are known as *vatta chicken.* This kind of work is mostly done on shawls made of ruffle/ raffal, ii) If the embroidery is richly concentrated and the threads firmly embedded in the shawl, it is known as *reiz gâri.* ('Reiz' is like the English 'raise' or 'raze'.) This is the kind of work normally done on pashmina. The pattern is the same on both sides of the shawl: there is no 'negative' of the pattern on the reverse. Such shawls can be worn either way and are known as 'double sided shawls'. (See also 'Embroidery' above: *do-rukha.*)

Shawls are embroidered the sozni way in all six districts of the Valley, namely, Ânañtnâg, Bârâmullâ, Budgâm, Kupwârâ, Pulwâmâ and Srînagar.

Shawls, pashmina as well as ruffle, are made in the Mashadi Mohalla and Mughal Masjid areas of Srînagar city. They are sold everywhere in Kashmîr, Jammû and even Ladâkh. Shops in Jammû and Ladâkh often tend to stock Kashmîri shawls rather than the local variety.

19

The Wâzwân

The ceremony

The wedding guests sit cross-legged on spotless sheets spread on the ground. Men and women sit in separate tents. There are unlikely to be many children present.

A young man, a member of the family and not an employee, enters with a roll of white cloth which he starts unrolling expertly along the sides of the tent, in a rectangle. The guests start forming foursomes, seating themselves on either side of this white strip, which is about three feet (a metre) wide.

A few minutes later comes an attendant carrying an elaborate steel contraption, shaped somewhat like an hourglass, around two feet tall and and about fifteen inches wide. The top half would have been filled with lukewarm water. There is a little tap in the middle, and a receptacle in the lower half to receive the waste water. There is also a niche for soap. The attendant takes this *tasht-nâri* from guest to guest for them to wash their hands in. (Most tasht nâris since the 1990s have come in two pieces. The top, with the clean water, looks like a samovar. It is increasingly no longer attached to the ornamental base into which the dirty water flows.)

Now a silent procession begins to form outside the tent. These are male, able bodied relatives of the host, all normally dressed in white traditional dress. (The dress worn, increasingly since 1980, is the Punjabi shalwar-qameez. It was invented by the Sikhs and is now the national dress of Pakistan. It is, therefore, mistakenly identified with Islâm.) Each man holds at waist level a large and heavy copper plate, the *trâmi*, covered with an equally ornately patterned and heavy copper lid, the *sar-posh*. These men start moving wordlessly, in single file, towards the guests, depositing one trâmi between each foursome.

The tent, though filled with guests, is quite noiseless. Most people jokingly say that this is because everyone is so busy eating (and racing through that course before the next one arrives) that they have no time to talk. My theory is that it is because of the way the guests sit. They do talk to each other but only to the three persons in their group. There is no cross-talk over distances. As a result voices automatically drop to a level where only that foursome, and not the next foursome, can hear them.

When *all* the foursomes have been given their *trâmis* the silence is broken by one of the elders, who says 'Bismillah' (In the name of God) and lifts the *sarposh* (lid) of his *trâmi*. Under a tissue paper would have been placed a huge quantity of steaming hot rice with at least four mutton items and large pieces of chicken placed on it. These mutton items are four portions of *mayth-mâz* (chopped intestines), two large seekh ('sheesh') kababs, two strips of rib called *tabaq mâz*, and two gigantic pieces of chicken.

This 'Bismillah' is also a signal for the other guests to remove the lids (sar-poshes) of their *trâmis* and start eating. Thus begins the banquet called the *wazwan* (pron. wâz-wân). The *trâmi*, and therefore the bed of rice on it, can be up to three or four inches deep. This circular plate is almost 20 inches wide, to enable each of the four guests assigned to that *trâmî* to have an independent corner.

The custom of four people eating from the same plate is definitely Islâmic and Central and West Asian. It is the Sufis of Delhi, notably Hazrat Nizamuddin Auliya [d.1325], who introduced among Indian Muslims the practice of eating from separate plates. This made a Muslim prince from the Deccan wonder if Hazrat Nizamuddin was a Muslim at all. The Auliya explained that he had started the practice of one-man, one-plate because he had several Hindu disciples who could not get themselves to eat from the same plate as even fellow Hindus.

The Kashmîris, too, serve their non-Muslim guests in individual plates.

Very few of the dishes are served in four portions: *mayth mâz* and the *rista* are among these few. Most dishes are served in two portions (e.g. tabaq mâz, chicken and the seekh kabab). Just one (albeit huge) portion is served of some dishes (like the *goshtaba*). Therefore, these have to be broken into four portions by hand. Those portions are very large by any standards. All dishes in the *wazwan* are eaten by hand.

Barely would the guests have nibbled at the mutton preparations that came placed on the rice than an attendant (this time it won't be a member of the host's family) will arrive with a huge cauldron and pour out four portions of another mutton dish (normally the rista) on each *trâmi*.

And before this new dish can be eaten, yet another mutton preparation will arrive and be ladled onto your *trâmi*.

This process will go on till generous portions of around twenty-one different mutton dishes are put on your plate, whether you want them or not. Unlike in a buffet, where you take as much as you want, or even at a sit-down banquet where you can tell the server that you want no more, at a *wazwan* you have no choice. Once you sit before a *trâmi*, around two kilograms of mutton and chicken (not counting the rice, vegetables, salad and chutneys) will be put on your plate for each person, or 8 kg per *trami*. If you can't eat it all, just leave it behind.

(Or take it home in a doggy bag, as some women have always done. Since the 1980s, hosts have started handing out polythene bags in the women's tent because they know that few women can eat all that is served. The only choice that men have is to skip the lunch before and the breakfast after the *wazwan*.)

Till September 1989, the *wazwan* would be served around midnight (the lateness of the hour whets the appetite further). Kashmîr was uniquely free of crime. Female guests, loaded with gold jewellery, would leave wedding feasts around one or two a.m. and walk home in all-female groups without any fear.

Kashmîr ceased to be a paradise in the 1990s. Everyone wanted to be home by seven or eight in the evening. Therefore, *wazwans* were shifted to the afternoon. Conditions began to improve in the late 1990s. Once again *wazwans* started shifting back to dinner: to around eight or nine p.m. Midnight *wazwans* have not yet resumed, though

Cow slaughter is banned in all of Jammû and Kashmîr and the Kashmîris are not fond of goats' meat. Therefore, the *wazwan* is essentially a binge of sheep's mutton. The solitary chicken dish was introduced in the 1940s or '50s. Despite the abundance of trout and other excellent varieties of fish in the Valley, fish is not part of this lavish banquet. However, it includes half a dozen chutneys, lots of curds and maybe four vegetarian dishes, plus mineral water and, often, a cola.

Economic and social costs

Before 1947, the Valley of Kashmîr was a net exporter of meat: on hoof. Today it has the country's highest per capita consumption of mutton. Which is hardly surprising, considering that each guest at a *wazwan* eats six to eight times as much meat as Indians elsewhere consume at a feast.

In 1993, I did a little study of the mutton trade. Every day 10,000 sheep were transported to the Valley, mostly from Rajasthan (Alwar in particular). Entire sections of Delhi's Lajpat Nagar, Defence Colony and Khân Market are inhabited by those involved in this trade. In 1993, I estimated the value of the mutton trade at roughly Rs. 500 crore a year. In the year 2003, the figure would be around Rs. 2,000 crore a year. Not surprisingly, the trade used to wield considerable political clout in Kashmîr.

Till one man decided to take on the mutton lobby (the kothdârs), that is. Mohd. Shafi Pandit, a young IAS officer, then the Divisional Commissioner of Kashmîr, took the lobby on to control the price of mutton. He also helped launch the Samaj Sudhar (social reform) movement in 1986. Eminent doctors joined him and went on Doordarshan to explain the benefits of vegetarianism and the ill-effects of a non-vegetarian diet.

Indeed, all this mutton consumption comes with a huge price tag: in terms of health as well as social evils. Kashmîr tops national averages for several mutton-related diseases, including gout and forms of stomach cancer.

More important, even lower-middle class Kashmîris have since the 1950s felt obliged to host one or two *wazwans* during the course of a lifetime: especially on the occasion of a daughter's wedding. Well to do Kashmîris also look for other excuses to host wazwans, a son's wedding being the commonest of the lot. A favourite saint's annual day and thanksgiving for boons received from God are increasingly common reasons. Those who can afford to, host smaller *wazwans*, for twenty to thirty close friends and relatives, without having to look for justifications.

Till the 1990s the *wâza* (chef) would charge as his fee the price of one kilogram of meat for every kilo of meat that he would cook. Thus if you gave him 150 kg. of meat to cook (which is typical), his fee would be equal to the cost of 150 kg. of meat. However, by the year 2000 this had changed. Most *wâzas* now charge one and a half times the cost of the meat that they cook.

The main *wazwan* at a wedding costs at least seventy-five thousand rupees. Most middle-to upper-middle class weddings consist of a series of three to five *wazwans* (though not all of them for as many guests as at the main *wazwan*). The cost of the lot could be around two lakh rupees. Therefore, the whole thing can ruin the host economically.

A lot of the food goes waste. Most male guests eat around three-quarters of the meat and less than a quarter of the huge quantities of curds served. Since the 1990s one cola drink per guest and one 1.5 litre bottle of mineral water (with four plastic cups) per foursome has become the norm, adding to the expense-and wastage. Once someone somewhere in Srinagar introduces a new item into the *wazwan* (e.g. cola drinks and mineral water), everyone follows suit. No one wants to be considered a cheapskate.

The Samaj Sudhar movement helped restrict not only the number of guests that could be invited to a wedding feast to around a dozen, but also the number of mutton dishes that could be served. Anyone found violating this would be boycotted socially.

This sent a wave of relief among the middle classes of Kashmîr who, in the past, would not dare defy societal norms by serving fewer dishes or fewer guests than their neighbours or relatives had. (In a custom not unlike the Latin American pot lach, Kashmîris ensure that the drains outside their houses are choked with rice after the feast. Empty drains are taken to indicate that the host was a miser and there wasn't anything left over after the *wazwan*. Fortunately, this custom is dying out.)

For a couple of years Samaj Sudhar worked like a dream. The movement had not exactly sprung out of nowhere. In the mid-1970s the state government had issued a 'guest control' order, restricting the number of guests you could invite as well as the number of dishes that you could serve. At least on paper this still remains the law. It's a different thing that few Kashmîris are aware of its existence.

After all, Kashmîr is the land of the food snob: and thus of the celebrity chef. Gourmets would taste a single morsel and identify the *wâza* who had cooked it.

The Khosa family, the Bhandâris, Ahad Waza and Mom Waza are the chefs most sought after these days. A few months before the wedding season you will find elite fathers and brothers queuing up at the houses of these maestros in the Wâzpura area of Srinagar, to book them well in advance.

Parents are known to postpone marriages if their favourite *wâza* is not available on that day. Similarly, flying a favourite cook to Bangalore (which now has a substantial Kashmîri diasporâ) is hardly rare. Delhi, of course, has a resident *wâza*, who has acquired the sobriquet '*Dilli wâza*'.

In such an atmosphere can you seriously expect social reform to flourish? By 1989, the Sudhar movement had evaporâted. In 1990, several groups of militants introduced their own version of guest control. In that surcharged atmosphere it worked: till around 1993.

At each *wazwan* that I attend I find some 'new' dish or the other. Many of these are part of the original 105-course *wazwan*, which had been pruned to a 'mere' twenty or twenty-one mutton dishes till a few decades ago.

At the rate at which old dishes are being 'revived', it shouldn't be long before the entire 'original' *wazwan* is resurrected. And fathers bankrupted.

As with all revivalism, some of that which is sought to be revived probably never existed and, if it did, was restricted to royalty and, maybe, a handful of nobles. Mahârâjâ Hari Singh had a chef who wouldn't cook the same dessert twice in a year. (After Kashmîr acceded to India the chef joined the Raj Bhavan, where this author too has served.) Now, this does not mean that there were 365 (leave alone 730) desserts in Dogrâ cuisine or even that the other chefs of the state knew that many recipes. It only tells us about one single chef's repertoire. (In any case this chef came from Bengal, the capital of India's desserts.)

What we know for certain, from British records, is that even in the late 19th/ early 20th century the *wazas* could cook around fifty meat dishes, in addition to chutneys and vegetarian dishes. However, it is doubtful if all the fifty dishes were ever served together at a single meal even in that era. Not to mention the new dishes that *wazas* so proudly keep inventing to this day.

While the not-so-well off find themselves compelled to host at least middling *wazwans* (which, too, are very expensive), those with money to burn use *wazwans* as occasions to flaunt their money, sometimes offensively. Not content with all the innovations that they have introduced into the food, they sometimes place hard cash under the *trâmi*, for the guests to take home. (Rs. 400 per trâmi was the going rate in the year 2003.)

People all over India throw flowers on the bridegroom and his relatives, when they enter the bride's house. The Kashmîris shower their guests with dry fruits (and, increasingly, toffees) as well. At one *wazwan* I found ten rupee notes, folded into little fans, among the dry fruits that we had been showered with.

Origin and spread

Where did the *wazwan* originate? This is a question that continues to agitate all thinking Kashmîris. Everyone assumes that like so many other fine things (notably the khatamband ceiling, mosque architecture and carpets) gourmet cooking came to Kashmîr from Central Asia: from Uzbekistan, Kazakhstan or Iran. Perhaps it did. The *trâmi*, the *sar posh* and the *tasht nâri* belong to the same family of handicrafts as the Central Asian samovar. However, the problem is that none of these Central Asian countries has a banquet even remotely resembling the *wazwan*.

Of course, several Kashmîri dishes have a Central Asian equivalent. But that is also true of the Mughlai food of the Indian and Pakistani plains. On the other hand a large number of dishes served in the (Muslim) *wazwan* have a corresponding Kashmîri Pandit version, notably the *tabaq mâz/ qabergâh*, the *martsgand* and the *roghan josh*. Several dishes (e.g. *nadroo* and *hâk sâg*) are purely Kashmîri.

Therefore, it is tempting to conclude that the *wazwan* was invented by Kashmîri Muslims perhaps in the fifteenth or sixteenth centuries, borrowing a few dishes from Central Asia, Iran and the plains of India. That the feast has an Indian name, born of a Sanskrit prefix and a Kashmîri suffix, also indicates its likely origins. (See below.)

The community of *wâzas* is found only in Srinagar City. In the small towns and villages the local baker (*nânbâi*) doubles as chef at weddings. Since around 1950, almost all ethnic Kashmîris, rich and poor, have felt obliged to host *wazwans* at least as part of their daughters' wedding feasts.

However, perhaps this was not always so. Kashmîr was one of the poorest parts of India before 1947. Only well to do families of Srinagar City could host *wazwans*. Rural and small town elites had to import chefs from Srinagar City, which was not always easy. Kashmîr did not 'import' mutton from other parts of the country till the 1960s. The *wazwan* was thus not always as widespread as it has been since the 1950s.

In the 1970s, it spread to Jammû as well. Ethnic Kashmîris living in Jammû province were the first to take to it. By the late 1980s, even the Punjabi-speaking Muslims of Jammû had adopted the custom.

Individual dishes from the *wazwan* have been influencing the cuisine of neighbouring regions since at least the 19th century. The *yakhni* has at least since then been part of the everyday food of the Hindus of Jammû. The cuisine of the Muslims of the Punjab, Jammû and Ladâkh has drawn even more deeply from Kashmîr.

In the 1990s, Kashmîris, Hindus and Muslims alike, fled to Jammû and the Indian plains. With them went some wazas. In 1993, I launched an aggressive publicity campaign, through television and the press, as well as food festivals in Delhi and Bombay, to popularise the *wazwan* outside Kashmîr. I believe that I succeeded.

At least some rich Hindus of Delhi hosted *wazwans* at their children's weddings in the 1990s.

Scientific basis

Eating a *wazwan* in Delhi (or Jammû) is not the same as doing so in Kashmîr. It is so much more difficult to eat two kilos of meat in a single meal in the warmer plains, except perhaps in winter. Kashmîri water has a strong mineral content and helps digest all those mounds of food better.

Even within Kashmîr the same food, made by the same chef, doesn't taste the same if served in a buffet. That's because dishes of the *wazwan* are served in a particular order. This sequence is the result of several centuries of experience.

Let us assume that there are 21 meat dishes in the *wazwan* that you are eating. By the eighth or ninth dish your stomach will begin to complain and you will be filled with dread at the thought of the dishes that remain. Just then the chef will bring you a dish designed to soothe your stomach and prepare it for the rest of the feast. (Incidentally, all ice creams, especially the humble vanilla, do the same trick after a heavy meal.)

Another result of these centuries of experience is the system of washing the raw mutton with turmeric, which is an antiseptic and rids the mutton of several kinds of germs.

Shredded radish is invariably served at all *wazwans*. Radish rids the tongue of the flavour of the dish last eaten. Therefore, it is eaten between courses so that your palate can savour the taste of the next dish the better.

Also between courses one of the foursome will serve curds to the other three. He will serve the yoghurt with a spoon and the other three will receive it on their fingers. This is because curds dissolve the grease left behind on the fingers by the previous dish. Try it with food from any part of the world. Curds really clean up the fingers.

Sugar has traditionally been rare in Kashmîr (and in Ladâkh and Tibet). That's why there are no indigenous sweet dishes in these three regions. Their tea is mostly salt-flavoured. Habba Khatoon's 16th century poetry clearly states that sugar and sweets were the preserve of the rich in Kashmîr. Of the three regions mentioned, Kashmîr was the first to receive sugar in a big way. This was around the middle of the 19th century.

Phirni, a dessert favoured by the Muslims of the Indian plains, quickly became very popular, especially during the holy month of Ramzan, when fasts are broken by eating some *phirni*. Since Kashmîr has no sweets of its own, *phirni* has since the 19th century been the most popular dessert served after a *wazwan*. Because it is not part of the old tradition, since the 1990s it has often been replaced by slices of ice cream.

The Kashmîris' own way of completing the *wazwan* feast is with the *goshtaba*, a huge ball of pounded meat, cooked in yoghurt. It is sliced into four with a flat sharp bone that had emerged from one of the previous dishes, the Aab Gosh, after the meat had been removed.

The dishes

The word '*wâza*' is derived from the Sanskrit 'vâj' (cook). 'Wân' is the Kashmîri word for 'shop'. However, *wazwan* is no shop. It is, as we have seen, a feast, a banquet, prepared in the host's courtyard, where the 'wâza', specially hired to cook that meal, sets up shop, so to speak.

For various reasons the all-India trend of hosting wedding receptions at luxury hotels hasn't caught on in Kashmîr. For one, that would send costs, already very high, skyrocketing. Secondly, none of the luxury hotels in Kashmîr has a celebrity *waza* in its employ. Then the whole ceremony takes so long that the host would need to book the hotel for far longer than in the rest of India. Most important, at home the host can exercise a degree of control over the ceremony that is not possible in a hotel.

Today the word '*wazwan*' has come to describe the multi-course, sit-down Kashmîri banquet.

The twenty-odd mutton dishes of the average *wazwan* are served in a particular order: which has to do with the digestive process itself. Just when you feel that you can take no more, along comes a dish designed to soothe your innards, or another to rekindle your appetite.

Some dishes

Mayth Mâz: Finely chopped intestines of sheep, fried in oil with dried fenugreek (methi).

Kebab: Minced meat cooked on long skewers. Only the seekh (sheesh) kebab is supposed to be served at weddings. However, since the late 1990s, even shâmi (evening) kebabs have entered the menu, even if the wazwan is served at lunchtime. (In the Indian plains it is considered sacrilegious-and upstart behaviour-to serve shâmi kebabs before sunset.)

Tabaq mâz: Ribs of sheep cut into small rectangles and fried in ghee.

Rista: Brown meat ball. The mutton, instead of being minced with a metal knife, is pounded on a stone slab with a wooden mallet (hammer). Cooked with spices. Each meat ball serves one.

Goshtâbâ: Synonymous with the *wazwan*, and is its last dish. This, too, is a ball of meat, but is huge (serves four). Here, once again, a mallet is used to pound the meat, which is beaten till it turns white and is then cooked in boiling curds. Spices are not used. The ball is of a pistachio-grey colour.

Marts Vângan Qorma: Small pieces of mutton, cooked with red chillies and spices. Chilli-hot. Therefore, to be eaten with curds.

Dâna Val Qorma: Meat from the breast of the sheep. When ready, sweet curds and green coriander (dhaniya) are added to it before serving.

Roghan Josh: Large bones with flesh attached, cooked in ghee and reddened with saffron and other spices.

Aab Gosh: How good a chef is can be tested by how well he makes *Aab Gosh*. Cooked in milk, with cardamom and *dâr* (dâr, not dâl) *cheeni*, but without any *haldi* (turmeric). It is served at a stage when the guests are about to give up. Its soothing syrup perks them up and keeps them going for the remaining part of the feast.

Paneer: Large rectangles of cottage cheese, several times the size we'd serve in central India, cooked in tomato paste.

Hâk sâg: The Kashmîri lettuce, cooked, unfortunately, in far too much oil.

Nadru: Stem of the lotus. Increasingly disappearing from the menu.

Bam tsunt: The quince apple, cooked in a tangy, sweet and sour sauce.

20

Kashmîrî Painting

(First of all a disclaimer: I, the author, have had absolutely no formal training of any kind in art. Yet I have, since 1980, had an extremely deep involvement with one of India's best known schools of miniature painting. Upon joining the Indian Administrative Service, for my first posting I volunteered to serve in Basohli as the Sub Divisional Magistrate and Collector, with the express intention of reviving the Basohli school which became extinct in 1857. After a year of study, fieldwork and touring I was able to achieve my dream. On Dussehrâ day 1980, a hundred and twenty three years after his ancestors had left Basohli (for Amritsar, then Lahore and finally Rait (in Chambâ, HP) a scion of the Rainâ family of artists returned to Basohli. The school that I started in Basohli has flourished. Its alumni have since gone on to establish branches in places as far apart as Udhampur, Jammû and Kathuâ.

Personally, this has meant that for quite a few young scholars in this field my official residences in Srînagar and Jammû have become the first port of call. It was while helping out one such scholar from Harvard that I stumbled upon a series of illustrated manuscripts and stand-alone paintings in three different archives of Srînagar.)

Mridu Rai called me from New York to ask about Kashmîrî miniatures.[1]

There's no such thing as a Kashmîrî miniature, I told her.[2] Only Mughal and Persian miniatures painted in Kashmîr, and Perso-Mughal and Hindu-Buddhist paintings executed by Kashmîrîs outside Kashmîr (mainly in Ladâkh, Afghânistân and Delhi-Agra). Certainly no Kashmîrî school.

---

1 Dr. Rai is a Yale historian. She was then at Columbia University, working on a doctoral dissertation on 'Kashmîrî Identity and Notions of Sovereignty.' The eminent Pâkistâni scholar Ayesha Jalal was her guide.

2 And that is what I was told by every scholar that I met till then, in Kashmîr or elsewhere (with three exceptions, whom I met later).

Mridu said that she'd stumbled upon a reference to the effect that a school of miniature painting had briefly flourished in Kashmîr from 1810 to 1830. (In the history of Kashmîr this era is generally known as the Sikh period.)

Wait a minute, I told Mridu. I know what you are talking about and I know exactly how to find those miniatures.

In the weeks preceding that call from Mridu I had been working with a talented team of scholars from the Jammû and Kashmîr (J&K) Academy of Culture and Arts (aka the Cultural Academy). They were helping me look for damaged miniature paintings which a Harvard-returned Indian scholar had promised to restore.

Most of these miniatures were what you could call Kashmîr-Made Exotic[3] Miniatures: reproductions of Persian and Mughal miniatures done in Kashmîr by local artists. However, tucked away amidst them were paintings which clearly belonged to the Kashmîrî Qalam. To wit, they were Kashmîr-Made Kashmîrî Miniatures. (Qalam literally means `quill' or `pen'. In Indian art it refers to a school or style of art: e.g. the Basohli qalam, the Kâñgrâ qalam, and so on.)

Mridu's information made me sit up and wonder if Kashmîr might, after all, have had a qalam of its own.

Back I was at the Cultural Academy, from which I obtained a list of all the manuscripts that they had. After wading through their almost 900-page Urdu catalogue, I came upon references to six illustrated manuscripts penned in Kashmîr on Kashmîrî paper, even though some of these were copies of Persian or Mughal books. One of the illustrated manuscripts was painted as late as in the 1860s. So already we had managed to extend the known limits of this school by three decades.

In addition, the Academy had an album of more than 60 miniature paintings, all of them on Kashmîrî paper and, thus, certainly made locally.

What the catalogue did was to establish Mridu's (and Ayesha Jalal's) a priori contention — and take its boundaries further. The contention was that it was simply not possible for a people as incredibly talented as the Kashmîrîs to not have had their own school of painting. Their architecture and handicrafts have no equal in the sub-continent and their 21 to 50-course wedding feast is a major art form in itself. So why would they not have had their own school of painting?

Meanwhile, Mridu came upon a reference to a treasure-trove of Kashmîrî miniatures in Leningrad, which, in the 19th century, found its way to Russia, through Germany. She later sent me a photocopy of the 84-page text of a Russian book by A. Adamova and T. Greck, which has been translated as `Miniatures from Kashmîrîan Manuscripts.'

3 'Exotic' literally means of 'foreign origin'.

I started talking about these exciting findings. And information started pouring in. A senior police officer told me that someone had once come to him to discuss the legal aspects of a medieval copy that he possessed of the *Kathâ Sarit Sâgar*. I haven't yet laid my paws on a copy of this but its Persian version, '*Anwaar o Suheyli*,' is available in some Kashmîrî libraries and archives.

A Kashmîrî Pandit journalist told me of her family's old puja-(prayer) miniatures, which had decayed because of smoke from the puja diya (prayer lamp). I followed up this lead and found half a dozen mediæval Pandit puja miniatures.

The most important lead was to the 70-year old former `head moulvi' of Srînagar's Persian-language archives, a walking encyclopaedia called Moulvi Ghulam Rasool Bhatt, who gave me access to at least 900 purely Kashmîrî miniatures, and has helped me date them to the nearest century. (And what centuries!)

My other major research associate has been Mr. Ashraf, a young expert working for the J&K Cultural Academy, who has helped me date the miniatures in his office archives, and also to establish what is distinctly Kashmîrî about them.

The Six Periods

The following is an analysis of what I have been to find between these two archives and Srînagar's SPS Museum.

Kashmîr had a flourishing tradition of miniature painting that lasted till the early 20th century. This tradition has largely gone unrecognised. Only half a dozen archivists (e.g. Messrs. Ghulam Rasool Bhatt, Ashraf and Mir Jamshed Ahmed) are even aware of it. Next to no work had been done on this tradition till I announced my findings to the national press in October 1997. Around half a dozen scholars in India and abroad know of Perso-Mughal paintings done in Kashmîr. Only two papers that I had come across till then (Adamova-Greck and Karuna Goswamy) had even speculated about the possibility of a Kashmîr school. (Mrs. Goswamy's book was published in 1998.)

I have tentatively divided the evolution of this art into six periods, as follows:

i) *The ancient period* (from the beginning of human settlement in Kashmîr to, say, the thirteenth century AD): Illustrated Sañskrit-Shârdâ manuscripts as well as `stand alone' paintings were created during this period. There are several references (wonderful anecdotal evidence) in the *Kathâ Sarit Sâgar* and the *Nîlmat Purân* to portraits and other paintings. However, I have not yet come across a single extant portable painting from this period. Nor has any other researcher. Not yet. But I am still looking.

It is known in Kashmîr that during the pre-Islâmic period Kashmîrî artists went to Ladâkh and Afghânistân. There they created some brilliant works of Hindu-Buddhist art. The surviving miniatures are all painted on walls or doors. None of this art is on a portable substance like paper, parchment or cloth. Kashmîrî sculptors carved gigantic statues (mainly of the Buddhâ) on mountain sides. Again not portable.

Several scholars, mainly erudite Kashmîrî Pandits, have written books about the art of this period, based on works found in Ladâkh, Tibet and Afghânistân.

ii) *Kashmîr under its own Sultans* (1320-1586): This phase consisted of botanical and zoological paintings and, by the mid-1500s, human portraits. All these paintings are in colour. Mr. Ghulam Rasool Bhatt helped me gain access to a copy of a book that was begun in the 1370s. I have got photographed (by my colleague Shishu Pal) a better-preserved copy of the same book, which was copied in 1430.

The oldest 'portable' painting by a Kashmîrî that I have seen (and, I believe, the oldest extant Kashmîrî paper-painting), thus, dates to the 1370s.

With effort it should be possible to locate a copy of the *Kathâ Sarit Sâgar* copied during this pre-Mughal period. (The one that I have seen, *Anwaar Suheyli*, dates to the 18/19th century.)

In any case Mr. Ashraf helped me study some Hindu religious paintings (e.g. the Shankarachârya pantheon) which probably dates to the 15th century (and certainly not later than the 16th.)

Thus we now have evidence that painting flourished in Kashmîr well before the Mughals.

This is an extremely important point for those who believe that painting came to Kashmîr only along with the likes of Mohd Nadir of Samarqand (who perhaps belonged to the seventeenth century).

iii) *The Mughal period* (including the minor Mughal kings: 1586-1752): This period of painting in Kashmîr (often by Kashmîrîs) alone has been written about. However, even this period has not been adequately researched and very few scholars are familiar with it. During this period Kashmîr became one of the many provinces of the Mughals and its art became one of the many variants of the Mughal school.

Some very fine work was done in Kashmîr (by Kashmîrî as well as non-Kashmîrî artists) and by Kashmîrî artists in the Mughal court (e.g. the Némat Nâmâ during Akbar's time). However, the Mughal period smothered the indigenous identity of Kashmîr's paintings.

iv) *The post-Mughal period* (late 18th to mid 19th Century): This is the period when a distinctly Kashmîrî school began to flourish all over again. I don't think this period has been documented at all. The *Târîkh é Bîrbal Kâchrû* has a number of wholly Kashmîrî paintings: the themes, the locations, the paper, the artists — they were all Kashmîrî.

v) *The Kashmîr counterpart of the Company school* (Late 19th century): Either Englishmen, or Kashmîrîs influenced by the British, painted miniatures on Kashmîrî paper, using Kashmîrî themes, but stylistically very European. For instance, there would be sketches: in colour but with no backdrop at all or with a very sparse background. The genres included portraits and ethnographic pictures.

Neither the (East India) Company nor the Raj ever ruled the Valley of Kashmîr (or Jammû) directly. What the major part of the state instead had during the colonial era was a British Resident. So, perhaps, this sub-school should be called the Residency School.

vi) In the *19th century* there was a commingling of Dogrâ and Kashmîrî themes and styles. (I have all of one colour painting, but several b&w sketches to show for this period.)

What is uniquely Kashmîrî about these paintings?

1) *The paper:* This is a soft and slightly spongy white paper. (Basohli-Kâñgrâ paper, on the other hand, was made from the recycled sheets of bahîs [account books], and was very thick and stiff.)

Scholar Karuna Goswamy describes 'hand-made paper of the Kashmîrî kind' as `quite thin and bearing that distinctive glaze that comes from being made from rice husk in the Kashmîrî tradition'.

G. Forster, writing in 1798, noted that, `the Kashmîrîans (sic) fabricate the best writing paper in the East.'

This paper was made in the Kâgaz-gar mohallas of Naushera and Jama Masjid. (So if we are to revive Kashmîr's great miniature painting tradition, we should begin with reviving this paper's manufacture.) The paper is washable in water.

There are many legends from Budshah's time about this paper's unique qualities. Alterations (forgeries) made on documents written on it could be detected because scratch marks left on the paper by the nib of the pen would remain even after the ink had been washed off.

The outlines of figures were made on Kashmîrî paper with a brush dipped in plain water (yes, just water) which would leave a brush mark, into which colours were later filled.

Whenever during my researches a doubt arose about whether a manuscript or a painting available in Srînagar was a Persian original or a copy made in Kashmîr, Mr. Ghulam Rasool Bhatt, Mr. Ashraf and I would use a simple yardstick: is the paper Kashmîrî?

As we will see below, if a painting shows a person wearing a pheran or dajehroo (ear-chain), or sailing in a shikârâ, or sitting near a chinâr tree, then there can be no doubt that the painting is Kashmîrî.

But often the clothes or trees (or themes) shown in a painting have nothing to do with Kashmîr. In such cases we look for Kashmîrî borders and colours.

But again the borders varied over the centuries. The kind of colours used did not change to the same extent, but in some paintings they are too faded to tell us with certainty if the painting is indeed Kashmîrî.

Therefore the one clinching question that needs to be asked is: Is the paper used in the painting Kashmîrî?

2) *Borders:* Each `school' (qalam) of miniature painting has a distinct type of border around the main picture. Thus Basohli borders are almost an inch wide and `hot red.' Kâñgrâ borders are equally wide but softer pink. But then the Basohli qalam lasted only for around a century and only in the Basohli area. The Kâñgrâ qalam flourished for another hundred years or so.

The Kashmîrî paintings that I have studied cover almost six centuries and six fairly distinct phases. They include both `stand alone' miniatures as well as miniatures which are integrated into manuscripts. Hence it would be unfair to expect any one standard type of border to span all six centuries for which Kashmîrî miniatures are available.

Hindu themes, presumably painted by Hindu artists, are normally enclosed within a slim (1 cm. or so wide) black (or blue-black) border, within which floral motifs have been drawn throughout. These designs are similar to the ones Kashmîrî Pandit ladies make on festive occasions (mainly Shivrâtrî and weddings).

In manuscripts (and now we are talking of text pages, not paintings), Kashmîrî borders have a very different identity. Some manuscript borders are simply dazzling because of all the gold/ golden colour used. To begin with, there would be a border around the text itself. Then there would be one outer margin, golden or blue. This would be in three or even four strips, each of a different colour: blue (outermost strip), white, golden, and then blue again (innermost strip).

This is not so in the manuscripts of the other Indian schools. Some people mistake Kashmîrî borders for Persian ones: but the latter are quite different.

The columns of text in Kashmîrî manuscripts use a lot of golden colour, and even the arrangement of columns is distinct in Kashmîr. Manuscripts do not concern us as such but if a manuscript can be said to be definitely Kashmîrî, then it becomes easier to say that the paintings in that manuscript too are Kashmîrî. (Easier, not certain.)

There are other Kashmîrî borders, too. For instance, in painting no. 59 (in the album at the Cultural Academy), `Krishna dancing with Gopies,' there are three borders. The outer two are deep red and thick, the outermost (red) separated from the middle (also red) by two thin white lines. The innermost border is black with a floral motif of the Shivrâtrî/ Pandit-wedding type mentioned above.

Finally, some Kashmîrî miniatures have borders that the artist did not give them. That is because older paintings have been pasted on top of newer, coloured paper which is both bigger and stiffer. The painting is pasted skillfully (and seamlessly) in the exact centre of the larger sheet below.

Because the stiff sheet below the painting is much bigger, a portion of the lower, coloured (dull pink or dull blue) sheet remains uncovered by the painting. This uncovered portion becomes a kind of a two-inch (or wider) border on each of the four sides. Abstract little specks of gold-leaf, which have been ground into very thin pieces, have been stuck on this 'border' at several dozen places.

(The painting is pasted so smoothly on this stiffer sheet that you have to run the tip of your finger along the outer edges of the painting to determine whether it has been pasted or painted on the lower sheet.)

3) *Colours:* Basohli colours are what art historians call 'extremely hot' (i.e. deep and bright). Kâñgrâ colours are softer. Neither goes in much for shades or gradation of colour.

Kashmîrî colours are soft, subtle, diverse, many, and, because of their variety, as close to Western colours as any that I have seen in the Perso Indian tradition.

Kashmîrî paintings — especially portraits — also happen to be among the most realistic in the East (a hemisphere from Egypt to China where realism has never been much prized in the plastic arts). The subtlety and diversity of Kashmîrî colours has helped achieved this realism.

The yellow used is made of `haldi' (turmeric). The red skirt of Goddess Durga (painting no. 65, Cultural Academy) is made of sindoor powder. In many of the early 19th century paintings (e.g. *Târîkh é Bîrbal Kâchrû*) and even in older miniatures available with the Academy, a very deep `lapis' blue is used, especially to depict the skies. Gold is another colour used aplenty in Kashmîrî miniatures. Yellow-green grass is also a typical feature of many Kashmîrî paintings, especially those in the Bîrbal Kâchrû manuscript.

Then there are some conventions: Lord Shiva, whose skin is blue in most of India, is white-skinned (yes, I mean white, and not `fair' or `pink') in Kashmîrî miniatures. (Some sects in Karnataka, too, depict Lord Shiva as white-skinned. Supports my theory that some people from Karnataka and coastal Mahârâshtra are of Kashmîrî origin.)

The Dal Lake in the 'Shankar Âchârya' painting (no. 26, Cultural Academy) is absolutely green, rather than blue. (Who knows, perhaps the weed problem was even worse then than it is now. But water-bodies such as lakes are painted a deep green in most Kashmîrî miniatures.)

4) *Clothes and ornaments:* Just as there is a Shankarachârya hill (and temple of the same name) in no other part of the world, shikârâs (rowboats with canopy), pherans (gowns) and dajehroos (ear ornaments), too, are unique to Kashmîr.

Therefore, if for no other reason, the world will have to accept that these paintings are distinctly Kashmîrî because of the depiction of that hill and those artefacts in several Kashmîrî paintings created over the centuries.

The *nath* (nose ring) and *orhni* (cotton stole) worn by many women in these miniatures, too, are typically Kashmîrî. The headgear of the menfolk in many Hindu religious paintings is normally of the kind that Kashmîrî Pandits would wear. The *orhnis* normally have typically Kashmîrî (Muslim) patterns on them.

In 'no. 65/ Durga,' on the left is a Pandit woman in a calf-length pheran, belt and kasava. On the right is a bearded Pandit, also in a calf-length pheran and Mughal-style turban. Both pherans have, near the bottom, a fold (laad), which is normally sewn in to cater for later shrinkage.

In '62/ Krishna with gopies' the gopies wear saris the way Pandit women started doing in the late 19th and early 20th centuries.

In '26/ Shankar Âchârya ' the Kashmîrî Pandit men are shown wearing turbans typically worn by the community.

That said, it must be pointed out that in a very large number of Kashmîrî paintings, perhaps in the majority, the clothes worn are not Kashmîrî. The reason is obvious: the themes are Persian, or concern the Hinduism or Islâm of the Indian plains, so it would not be correct for the artist to give them Kashmîrî clothes.

5) *Human artefacts:* Some typically Kashmîrî artefacts shown in Kashmîrî miniatures include:

i) *Boats:* Dugouts and Shikârâs. The shikârâ is to be found nowhere but in Kashmîr.

ii) The carpet designs shown in many paintings are distinctly Kashmîrî.

iii) Among the Shaivite images in some pictures are the wooden spoon (used in Shiv temples to dispense holy water with) and a rectangular object of the same colour, perhaps a book. (I assume that it is a book because in one picture a similarly shaped and coloured object in the hands of a deity is a book.)

6) *Vegetation and flowers:*

i) The Kashmîrî lotus occurs frequently in the hands of Lord Vishnû, or as the throne of a deity, or just as a flower. The tradition in Kashmîrî paintings is for the outer edges of each petal to be a deep pink and the inner blade of the petals to be white or a pink so pale that it is almost white.

ii) *Trees:* Pines and chinârs occur off and on. So do cherry blossoms. The baid (willow?) is shown in '26/ Shankar Âchârya.' At the bottom of this painting, in the centre, is a row of chinâr trees.

iii) Yellow-green grass is a standard feature of a very large number of Kashmîrî miniatures.

Equally, quite often the vegetation shown has nothing to do with Kashmîr, or even with reality. It is so even in Basohli and other Indian qalams, where the trees shown are normally products of the artist's imagination.

7) *Facial features:* Basohli paintings show people with the huge, beautiful, fish-like eyes of Braj, Avadhi and even Urdu poetry. `Perhaps the people of Basohli have eyes and features like those,' a Delhi-based art critic (who has never been to Basohli) once argued. Having spent two and a quarter years in Basohli I know better.

Eastern miniature painting, from Egypt to China and Japan, via India and Persia, is often not too concerned about realism in the depiction of facial features. (Equally, of course, there are many Mughal—and Kashmîrî—paintings where the faces have been drawn quite realistically. Central Asian-as well as Japanese-miniatures might have faces drawn without too many details, but you can always tell that the people shown are of the Mongoloid race, and not `Aryans'.)

Therefore, not too much should be made of facial features in a painting as a means of identifying the place where it had been painted.

Besides, I do not believe that all the people of Kashmîr belong to the same sub-racial group. There has been a fair amount of migration from the Middle East and West Asia. Besides, within the Caucasoid race at least two groups are represented substantially in Kashmîr: the light-skinned Indo-Aryan as well as the darker Mediterranean.

Those notes of caution having been sounded, we can say that almost all the Kashmîrî paintings studied show people who have features traditionally associated with Kashmîr: high noses and foreheads, and `Aryan' eyes.

7b) *Hair:* From one particular painting we can tell that the person who has been shown meditating is obviously a Hindu and a Shaivite. Hindu saints (and many traditional Japanese men) normally knot their hair into a bun on top of the head. In this painting there is a small human figure, the size of a saint's top-knot, where the bun would have been. On his stomach is the blue figure of Lord Krishn.

8) *Animals:* Horses in Kashmîrî paintings are invariably Kashmîrî, even if the theme depicted is Persian. Deer and antlers have been shown in some paintings. In one painting Lord Narsimha looks like a cross between the Kashmîrî snow leopard and the Kashmîrî brown bear. In '65/ Durga on Tiger,' too, the tiger looks more like its Kashmîrî counterpart.

9) The topography, too, is almost always Kashmîrî. Mountains, big or small, always tend to creep into the landscape. Therefore, as the received wisdom goes, these paintings are definitely Kashmîrî.

I wouldn't like to make too much of this tendency, because after all there are hills and mountains in Persian paintings, too. Besides, the mountains shown in many of the paintings that I have studied are hardly realistic. They often look more like lumps of barren rock heaped one atop the other. '26/ Shankar

Âchârya ' certainly looks like that. Today that hill is so full of trees. Other hills shown seem to be `karewa' plateaux, which are unique to Kashmîr.

10) *Architecture:* In the Academy's painting no. 62 'Krishna dancing with Gopies' there are two houses in the background, both with slanting roofs. This indicates that the houses belong to the `snow zone' and not to Srî Krishn's native plains.

In '23/ Nayika at her toilet alongwith (sic) attends (sic)' there are wooden steps leading to a lower level. There is a low, pink, wooden wall below. This use of wood, too, is Kashmîrî.

In the *Târîkh é Bîrbal Kâchrû* manuscript some fine Kashmîrî tents and palaces have been shown. They normally jut into one corner of the painting, as is the Indian (Mughal as well as Rajpût) tradition.

Typically Kashmîrî architecture occurs in a few Kashmîrî paintings. These examples, though few, indicate that even in this regard Kashmîrî paintings were sometimes rooted in the local reality.

Most of the time, the architecture shown in Kashmîrî paintings was the same as in Basohli, Kâñgrâ and Mughal paintings. A terrace with a low wall (parapet) runs from left to right. In a corner of the painting we see the edges of a balcony, with a portion of its sloping roof.

11) *Dances:* In `59/ Krishna dancing with Gopies' we see the `hikkat' dance: in which two partners, each holding both hands of the other, together twirl around an axis,

12) *The contents of the manuscript:* All the numbered examples given above are of stand-alone paintings. However, the majority of Kashmîrî paintings are manuscript illustrations. If the manuscript contains Kashmîrî folktales (e.g. *Kathâ Sarit Sâgar/Anwaar o Suheyli*) then the paintings that illustrate it are likely to be Kashmîrî.

12b) *The contents of the paintings*: Some paintings tell a story (as the ones in the *Târîkh é Bîrbal Kâchrû* do). The story that they tell is so obviously rooted in the culture (in this case, history) of Kashmîr that there can be little doubt about the painting's provenance.

The Themes

Kashmîrî miniatures were used to illustrate the following kinds of books:

1) Scientific literature:
   - i) Botany
   - ii) Zoology
   - iii) Anatomy: The human body (organs as well as bones) is the subject of many sketches and paintings. Works copied from Emperor Budshah's 15th century medical books reflect the local or Unani (Greek) tradition. Those of the 19th century reveal a very European realism.

iv) Freaks of nature and the wonders of the world.

v) The manufacture of guns.

2) Famous works of Persian literature.
3) Persian histories.
4) Kashmîr's own folk tales.
5) Kashmîr's own histories.
6) Romantic scenes: One bathing scene, which shows a woman in the nude, and one painting of a couple making love, their upper bodies clothed but lower parts naked, are among the paintings that I discovered.
7) Scenes depicting the history of the Sikh period.
8) Hunting scenes: These are the staple of Central Asian miniatures but, mercifully, there few such paintings in Kashmîr.

Then there were themes that were found in stand-alone miniatures as well as in manuscript illustrations:

9) The Auliya (Muslim saints) of Kashmîr, as well as non-Kashmîrî auliya.
10) Hindu religious themes.
11) `Charts' (with animals in the borders).
12) Secular Persian themes, e.g. Omar Khayyam.
13) Kashmîrî Pandit saints.
14) Life in rural Kashmîr: These include pictures of a ceremony at Lall-trâg- the spring of Lal Ded; and a depiction of the sati ceremony — yes, there were cases of sati even in Kashmîr.
15) Scenes from the Mughal court.

Ancient Kashmîrî Sculpture

In 2001, the Taliban government of Afghânistân destroyed gigantic sculptures of the Buddha. These had been carved into the mountainside at Bamiyan. At the time several people claimed that the sculptures were the creations of Kashmîrî sculptors. Now, these sculptures belonged to the Gândhâr School, which had extended into Kashmîr as well.

Kashmîr and its neighbouring areas have influenced each other's cultural traditions. Sculpture is one of them. Thus, while it is not certain that Kashmîrîs had sculpted the Bamiyan Buddhas, the point is well taken: from Kashmîr to Kabul it is one continuum as far as ancient sculpture is concerned.

Later that year I took a large media team to various parts of Kargil (Ladâkh), notably Kartse Khar. The idea was to show them similar sculptures, also carved into the mountainside. The local people and some scholars have always known about these sculptures (especially the one at Mulbek, on the Leh-Kargil highway). However, this was the first time that the Kartse Khar Buddha was brought to public notice. This was also the first time that someone had grouped five such Buddhas, located in different parts of Ladâkh, into one school: the

Gândhâr. (The other three sculptures are in Sani/ Kargil-Zâñskâr, Apati/ Leh and Durbuk/ Leh.)

Twelve to fourteen centuries later it is impossible to say if Kashmîrî sculptors had gone over to Afghânistân to do the Bamiyan statues, or sculptors from Gândhâr had come over to sculpt the ones in Leh and Kargil. It is sufficient that they all belong to the same school. However, it is generally believed that Kashmîrî artists did these sculptures, as well as the paintings at Alchi (also in Leh).

Within Kashmîr Valley, apart from the SPS Museum, the best place to find such sculptures are temples like the ones at Mârtañd and Awantipora.

Brahmâ images: In Kashmîr, J.L. Bhan writes, Lord Brahmâ is depicted 'either in association with Siva [Lord Shiv] or Vishnû or he is depicted in the Shesheaski theme.' After the sixth century AD the worship of Lord Brahmâ seems to have become more popular than before. Several images of Lord Brahmâ, all by himself, have been found dating to after then.

Bhan has discovered images of Lord Brahmâ at Dhumatbal, Verinag, Nadihal, Awantiporâ and Devsar.

The Buddha in Kashmîrî art: Buddhist images sculpted in Kashmîr after the 8th century AD have a unique feature. A flower emerges from behind the shoulder of the deity. Later it merges with the crown. This motif has possibly been inspired by the flowers that grow behind each of Lord Brahmâ's ears in sculpture — to show where one of his four heads ends and the next one begins.

21

Kashmîrî Music

Traditional Kashmîrî music, like music almost everywhere, is either classical or folk. Kashmîrî classical music is called Sufiana, or the music of the Sufi saints. Folk forms include Chhakri, Roef/Rauf, and Wanawon[i].

King Yusuf Shah Chak (16th century) is said to be the father of Kashmîrî classical music. He patterned the Kashmîrî system directly on its Persian counterpart, rather than on the Hindustani system of Central India (which, too, has some Persian influences). Following an internal coup he fled to Emperor Akbar's court in Agra. There, according to Kashmîrî sources[1], he met an Italian (yes, Italian) called Tona Santa, better known in India as Tansen, and on at least two occasions corrected the latter's technique. He authored the *Râst Kashmîrî*, a group of notes which correspond to Persia's *Râst Farsi*. Kashmîrî music has since taken on several Hindustani influences, too.

Just as Hindustani classical music has *râgs*, Kashmîrî music has *muqâms* (modes).

Kashmîrî muqâms based on Hindustani râgs include:

Lalit	Multani
Bageshwari	Jaijaiwanti
Bahar	Koshi (Paharhi)
Basant Bihag	Bhairavi
Kalyan	

Kashmîrî muqâms taken from Persian râsts include:

Araq	Hussaini
Navroz e Subah	Rehavi
Isphahân	Râst Farsi
Dugah	Panjgah
Sehgah	

1 *Bahâristân-é-Shâhî,* a 16th-17th century history by an anonymous Kashmiri noble.

Yusuf was hardly the only, or even the first, Kashmîrî king to be expert at music. Zain-ul-Abedin was an accomplished classical singer. Sultan Hassan Shah (1472-84) invited Carnatic musicians to Kashmîr. They left behind their influence on Kashmîrî music.

Hindustani percussion instruments are struck according to *tâls*. So are Kashmîrî drums. However, the tâls of the two regions are quite dissimilar.

Sufiana Mauseeqi (music)

(Pron: soo-fee-â-nâ) This used to be an elitist form of music played by quartets only at royal courts and gatherings of the rich. The lyrics, mostly in Kashmîrî, are sometimes in Persian, too. These quartets, one of whose members, the ustad (maestro), acts as the leader, play on the santoor, the Kashmîrî sitar (different from its Hindustani cousin), the *sâz* and the *dhukra* (a drum, like the tabla). They sing, together and in harmony, verses called the *baeth* which are either romantic or mystic. These songs could as well be about nature as about the saints of Islâm (especially Kashmîrî rishis), including Prophet Muhammad (PBUH).

Baeth songs sometimes are ballads about Heemâl and Nâgrâi, legendary Kashmîrî lovers, or about Solomon and Sheba.

Muqâms are the basis of melody. They are to Kashmîrî music what râgs are to Hindustani: a group of notes, the order of which, or emphasis on, can not be changed while going up (or coming down) the scale. Classical songs (and instrumental compositions) use one muqâm or another as their base. There are 54 *muqâms* in all.

As we have seen, some *muqâms* are based on Hindustani *râgs*, e.g. *Asawari*, *Poorabi* and *Khamaj*. Others, as we saw, were based on Persian *muqâms*. The basic notes, however, are and have always been Hindustani.

Like the alâp of Hindustani music, the first movement, called the *shakal*, is slow and introduces the theme. However, unlike the *alap*, the *shakal* is an instrumental rendition of the base (or structure) of the muqâm. The shakal is followed by the *muqâm* itself: where verses and couplets are *sung*.

The popular *tâls* (beats) are *sehtal* (teen tâl), *nimdur*, *dur-e-khafit* and *Turki zarb*. *Talana* is a rhythm popular in Sufiana. (It is also found in some South Indian dances and could be one of the influences of Carnatic music.)

Unlike Hindustani music, Sufiana is always sung in chorus. Secondly, musicians who are *both* vocalists and instrumentalists perform it. In the past, singing would be accompanied by Hafiz Naghma, a dance in which the meaning of the song is expressed by physical movements. A female dancer, called the Hafeeza, would sing and dance with Sufiana.

Instruments: In Sufiana music, the *sâz* is the only instrument played with a bow. All the other stringed instruments are struck with a plectrum, the miz-rabor, and a pair of wooden sticks, the qalams.

The santoor (lit.: one hundred strings) actually has only 96 strings, stretched over a hollow wooden frame made of the wood of the mulberry tree. It is the principal instrument in Kashmîrî music, its strings being struck with two elegantly carved, curved sticks, made of wood or, increasingly, plastic. It came to Kashmîr during Budshah's era and has been thoroughly indigenised. (Its Persian counterpart is quite different. In most respects the Kashmîrî santoor is closer to the hundred-stringed, ancient Indian *shadtantra veena*.)

Folk Music

Folk music is of many kinds, depending on the occasion:

***Wanawun* (marriage songs):** The songs sung at Muslim weddings are quite different from those sung at Hindu weddings.

Muslim wedding songs generally cover the first few years of married life: beginning with the nuptials and the bride's departure from her parents' home, to the circumcision (*khatna*) of the couple's son and the son's *haqeeq mundan* (ceremonial shaving of the head). The *wanawun baeths* of Abdul Ahad Nadim of Bandiporâ are particularly popular.

The songs sung at Hindu weddings, on the other hand, are Vedic chants, steeped in classical Hinduism.

As at weddings elsewhere in India, percussion instruments are employed to provide the beat (*tâl*). These are the *tumbakhnari* and the *noet*. The *tumbakhnari* is derived from the Persian tumbak. It is a hollow clay pot with animal skin tautly stretched over its open end at the top. The difference between this and western drums is that the *tumbakhnari* is struck with the tips of fingers. The noet, too, is a clay pot but with an open mouth. This open end and the sides are struck while playing.

Roef: Like the wanawun, the roef has traditionally been sung only by women. (Only since the late 1940s, with the return of political power to the Kashmîrîs after almost 360 years, have experiments taken place, most of them in the portals of the government-run Radio Kashmîr and, later, television. The roef is now also sung by men—but in conjunction with the chhakri.) This form—a group dance accompanied by a song—is performed at festivals like Eid, but also at weddings.

Chhakri: This is rural music performed by at least four musicians at a time. It was brought to the towns by the *rababis* (rabab players) of Kreer, Kawdara and Akingam. Qaiser Qalander notes, 'During the Afghân period a male dancer, Bacha, became associated with it, adding [Kathak] to Chhakri.' Generally, four instruments are played along with the singing: the *sarang* and the Persian *rabab* (both stringed instruments, for the melody) and the *tumbakhnari* and the *noet* (for the beat). The *noet* is also called the *ghara*. In the 1950s the harmonium was added.

Chhakri, the music most favoured by the peasants, owes its origins to Lal (pron. like the English 'lull') Vâkh, the poetry of Lal Ded. Since then it has been augmented by the religious poetry of a host of luminaries including Rasool Mîr and Mehmood Gâmi.

Laddi Shah is a kind of folk-music that is very popular in the rural areas, partly because of the satire, sarcasm and humour contained in its lyrics.

The *bachcha naghma* is one of the few forms of singing and dancing performed by just one person. (The others are all group forms and choruses.) However, even here the audience can join the soloist.

Folk Dances of Kashmîr

There are no mixed, coed, folk dances in Kashmîr. Many Kashmîrî dances are performed along with song. Therefore, they have already been mentioned in the section on 'Music' in this chapter.

Hafiza dances: This was one dance that was liked by the rich and the poor alike. The rich would finance such dances on their own; the poor would take out subscriptions. Women alone performed this dance. The clothes that they wore were similar to those worn in Kathak: tight bodices and cummerbunds. The Sikhs' governors of Kashmîr (early 19th century) were great patrons, as were the early Dogras (mid-19th century). The Sikhs' governors even maintained Hafiza troupes in their courts to perform for their guests, and for themselves. For various reasons the later Dogras started shying away from maintaining such troupes. Deprived of royal patronage this art withered away.

Wattal Dambal: The Wattals are one of the most deprived communities of Kashmîr: they are 'scavengers' (charpersons; sweepers) and shoemakers. Other subaltern classes also join them in this dance. This is a vigorous, joyous group dance of thirty to forty men who move to the beat of a *dool* (drum). The men sit in a circle and chant hymns and prayers in their own dialect. As the beat quickens the movements get more athletic and the dancers jump about skillfully and entertainingly.

Patthar: (pron.: per-therr) Traditional folk theatre is called *patther*. It literally means 'to act', 'to imitate' or 'to pretend'. It is performed by the *Bhâñds*. This form of theatre is satirical. It occupies a position similar to that of the art of the court jester: Through it the players were able to criticise the rulers without giving obvious offence.

The **Bhands** are a community, a 'tribe', of folk artistes, not only in Kashmîr but all over North India and Pakistan. They hold a subaltern position in the social hierarchy.

Reference

i. From *Music of Kashmîr* by Qaisar Qalander, *Kashmîr Today*, June 1976

22

The Festivals of Kashmîr

Festivals unique to Kashmîr

The four seasons are called *sonth* (spring), *har* (summer), *harduh* (autumn) and *wandh* (winter). The seventy-day winter is divided into three parts, *chill-e-kalân* (the first forty days), *chill-e-khurd* (the next twenty days) and *chill-e-bachh* (the last ten days).

The end of winter is formally celebrated by Tel Ashthami. In the evening of that day, children take old, discarded baskets, especially those that were used to cover kangris (see 'Handicrafts') to the steps by the banks of River Jehlum and set them on fire.

Sonth is the season welcomed the most. Almonds break into a blossom in March and the Kashmîris make a beeline for almond orchards (Badamwaris), especially the one near Hari Parbat in Srînagar. M. Amin Pandit says that this is 'a month-long fair'. I hope to revive this tradition someday.

The Baisakhi Mela of the Mughal Garden at Nishat (Srînagar) comes next. (Baisakhi is on April 13 or 14.) This is an institution that I revived in 2002. I extended the celebrations to other venues in Srînagar and the rest of Kashmîr, as well.

The Kashmîri New Year is called *Nau Reh* (or Nau Verih) and usually occurs in March or April. The Hindus seek the blessings of God for a prosperous year for their family. They do so by getting one of the young girls of the family to decorate a large metal dish with rice, sugar, fruit and dry fruits and a sheet of paper about the new year. The girl takes this plate to each member of the family. On this day, both Hindus and Muslims go to the Hari Parbat of Srînagar with samovars to make tea and sit in the spring sun.

One of the finest spring festivals is the Yâsmîn (jasmine) festival held at the shrine of Hyder Sâheb, in a jasmine grove in Hyderpora (near the airport).

Aish Muqâm's 'Zool' festival (Ânañtnâg, April)

Such festivals are a good time to hear the chhakri sung in its original habitat (vs. on television). Rural people from the three valleys around the hilltop shrine—*Doru-Shahbad, Lidder* and *Trâl*—come to pay homage, beginning their journey in the early morning. Torches are lit in each of the three valleys when the festival begins. *Bhâñds*, who are traditional folk singers, mimics, satirists and actors, arrive with their instruments, the sarang and noot. So do magicians. In the evening drums begin to beat and people start chanting religious hymns as they dance around the shrine. A torchlight procession begins, signifying the victory of good over evil. The next day farmers go from the shrine to their fields to begin the process of ploughing the earth and sowing.

The other end of the agricultural season is when the crop has been harvested. Now autumn festivals are held, the best known being those at Bijbehara, Ânañtnâg proper and Achâbal, when the peasants get a respite from work on the fields. At Bijbehara festivities last three days. Apparently at all three places there are 'mock' wedding processions, complete with a faux bridegroom who is dressed and rides a horse like one. Drum beaters and *shehnai* players lead the people of that and nearby villages in a joyous procession, everyone infected with the hilarity of it all.

Other harvest festivals are at Akingam, Bring and Kulgam (all in the chapter on 'Ânañtnâg') and at Budgâm town ('Budgâm'). In Ganderbal, a suburb of Srînagar, this coincides with the *urs* of Qamar Sâheb, where most devotees come by bus, but some still do it the traditional way, by slow moving boats. They 'indulge in fun and frolic' and 'take time off for a week-long vacation and stay in boats near the (Chinâr) groves of Beehama near Ganderbal,' says Mr. Pandit.

To get back to summer, the Jeshth and Har Ashthamis are important to the Hindus.

On the occasion of Raksha Bandhan (August), the Pandits of Srînagar climb the hill now known as the Shankaracharya hill. Some Pandits, and over a hundred thousand Hindus from all over, try to spend a few days during the preceding month at the holy cave of Sri Amar Nath ji (see 'Amar Nath Yatra').

On the fourteenth day of *Sawan* (July/August) a fair (mela) is held at a Hindu temple atop a hillock in Khrew, 22 km. from Srînagar.

Har (pron.: herr) means 'bird' in Kashmîri—in particular, *Shârikâ*, the bird-goddess. The 'herr' of the Hari Parbat is named after *Shârikâ ji*. (See the book 'A History of Kashmîr') The ninth day of the Kashmîri month of Har (June/July) is celebrated as *Har Navmi*, when the Pandits go to the temple of *Shârikâ Mata* on the Hari Parbat in tens of thousands. (I am not using the past tense for any of the Pandit festivals, despite the migration of most of them to the plains outside Kashmîr. This is partly because even at the turn of the millennium these festivals are being celebrated, though on a lower key: the Kheer Bhawânî fair and Amar Nath Yatra are, in fact, more crowded than ever before. And partly because I fondly hope things will be as before again.)

Festivals popular in Kashmîr

Without doubt the two Eids (the dates of which change every year) are the most popular festivals in Kashmîr. Since sweets ('sweetmeats') are not really part of the Kashmîri tradition, it's the bakers' shops that everyone throngs to pick up cakes and pastries for friends. Some quintessentially Kashmîri traditions have evolved on this front. One is the cake baked to look like a log with a little fork. It's a hot favourite at Eid. Maybe because this is the kind of log they all wish they had in their fireplaces but, because of modern gadgets, no longer do. The other is the 'White Forest cake', the Kashmîri confectioner's answer to the 'Black Forest cake'.)

Ramzan is the month of fasting and prayer. In many Muslim-majority areas the whole town comes alive at night during this month: shopping, socialising, and, for the children, putting on new clothes and attending religious sessions even at night. Not so in Kashmîr. Perhaps the cold did not allow such a tradition to develop. But even here some modern traditions have grown.

I used to be a neighbour of the Khanyaris, among the richest families in Kashmîr. They would give away raw meat to the poor every morning during this holy month. So, enormous queues would form, and well before the hour appointed by the Khanyaris. Because it would take almost an hour (if not longer) to serve the last person in the queue, that's how long the crowd would stay there. A whole cottage industry of hawkers would materialise to service the other needs of the people in this queue. That always struck me as ironic, because they were supposed to be poor, seeking alms, not consumers buying the wares of these hawkers.

During the holy month some families get the Quran Sharief recited all day. Others go to the neighbourhood after the pre-dawn breakfast to listen to the holy word.

The *Shiva Ratri* (February; on the 14th Phalgun) might be an all-India festival but most Kashmîri Pandits genuinely believe that it is uniquely theirs. And in some ways it is. No other part of India gives this auspicious day the importance that Kashmîr does.

Festivals celebrated all over Kashmîr

Ashoora

Ashoora (lit.: 'the tenth') is the tenth day of the Islâmic month of Muharram. This is when Imam Hussain was killed at Karbala (Iraq). The Imam was the grandson of Prophet Muhammad, peace be upon him. He died fighting the army of Yazeed, who wanted to be the caliph of Arabia. The two main Shia organisations of Srînagar City take turns to lead a large procession of mourners to commemorate the Imam's martyrdom. This procession goes through much of the city and ends at the Imâmbârâs (Shiite places of worship) of Hassanabad and Jadibal (misspelt Zadibal). The procession consists of several thousand Shia men. They recite elegies, beat their breasts and, if young, flagellate themselves till they bleed. The wounds heal miraculously fast, leaving no scars. A fine horse is included in every such procession. It reprsents Zuljinah, the horse Imam Hussain rode on the battlefield of Karbala. There are processions in Budgâm, Pattan, Gom Ahmed Pora and other places as well.

Baisakhi (Kashmîr)

This major Hindu-Sikh festival falls on the first day Baisakh (normally, the 13th April). It is a spring festival that celebrates the new Bikrami year. The Hindus of Kashmîr would gather at Ishber (about a kilometre above the Nishat gardens). They would then bathe in the holy Guptganga spring and perform some prayers. After that tens of thousands of Kashmîri Hindus (and countless Muslims) would go to the Nishat gardens, where scores of temporary stalls would be set up. The better off Kashmîri Pandits would hire a *doonga* (large boat) on the day before the festival, where they would lay out a feast for their extended family and friends.

First Navaratra (Chaitra) (Srînagar and other parts of Kashmîr)

This is the New Year's Day of the Kashmîri Pandits. It is the first day of the *Laukik* or Sapt Rishi calendar. It falls on the first day of the bright half of the luni-solar month of Chaitra. Because the month is partly lunar, this event does not occur on the same Gregorian date every year. But because it is partly solar, the *Laukik* date varies by only a few days each time.

The Kashmîri Pandits would visit their second most important temple, that of Sharika Devi, on this occasion. Almost all the Pandits of Srînagar would be there at some stage during the day. Those who lived in distant villages and towns would go to the nearest important temple.

This is a spring festival. Almond flowers are all a-blossom at that time of the year. The finest almond orchards of Srînagar are located on the Hari Parbat hill near the temple of Sharika ji. After paying homage to the bird-goddess, the Pandits would go over to the almond groves to picnic with their families. The whole hill would come alive with colour and merrymaking: and these are not my own words. All Kashmîris recall this with nostalgia.

At the bottom of the hill where the temple is, there is a flat, open area called the Devi Âñgan (lit. 'the courtyard of the goddess'). Hundreds of shops would spring up on the day of the fair.

LADÂKH

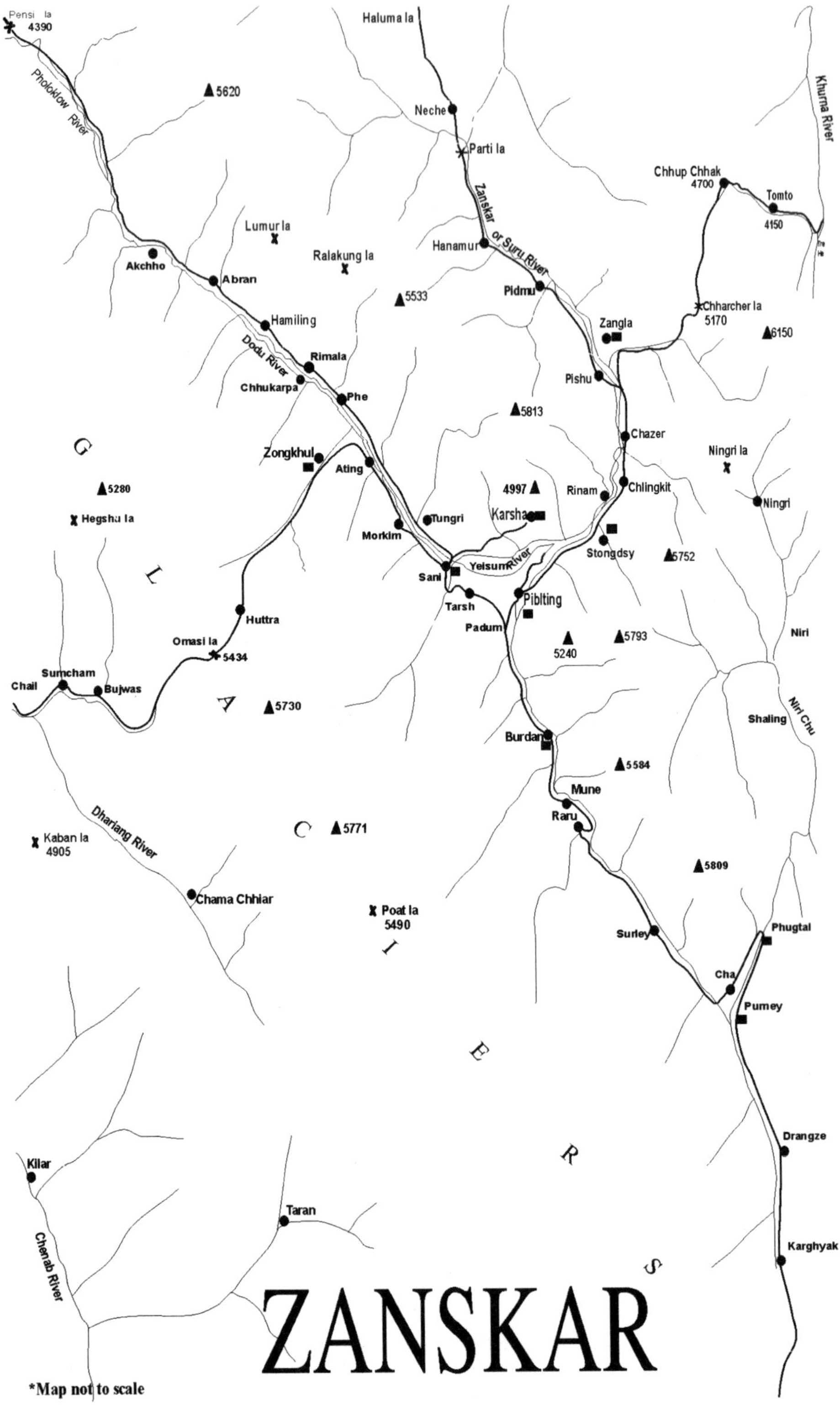

Pensi la
4390
Pholoklow River
5620
Haluma la
Neche
Parti la
Zanskar or Suru River
Khurna River
Chhup Chhak
4700
Tomto
4150
Lumur la
Ralakung la
Hanamur
Akchho
Abran
5533
Pidmu
Chharcher la
5170
Hamiling
Zangla
6150
Dodu River
Rimala
Chhukarpa
Phe
Pishu
5813
Chazer
G
Zongkhul
Ating
Ningri la
5280
4997
Rinam
Chlingkit
Ningri
Hegsha la
Karsha
Tungri
Morkim
Stongdsy
5752
L
Yelsum River
Sani
Tarsh
Piblting
Huttra
Padum
Niri
Omasi la
5434
5240
5793
Sumcham
Chail
Bujwas
A
5730
Shaling
Niri Chu
Burdan
5584
Mune
Raru
Dhariang River
Kaban la
4905
C
5771
5809
Chama Chhiar
Poat la
5490
I
Surley
Phugtal
Cha
Pumey
E
Drangze
Kilar
R
Taran
Karghyak
Chenab River
S
ZANSKAR
*Map not to scale

23

Ladâkh: Rapid Rise in Population

In 1911, the population of Ladâkh as a whole was 67,994. This went up in the next decade to 68,886, an increase of 1.3%. Even in 1931, the population was only 72,181, which meant that it had gone up by 4.8% in *ten* years. Higher than before, but still very low by international (leave alone South Asian) standards. In the next census (1941) the population was 76,030 and the increase 5.3%. The graph was rising. In 1951, it had risen to 82,340 and 8.29%, a huge increase by Ladâkh's own standards, but low in absolute terms.

From well-below to way above the national average

Leh is one of India's smallest districts in terms of population. It also has one of the lowest population densities in the world—with around two people to a square kilometre. All right, 2.44 people. Over the centuries the population of the district did not grow much, because of a series of social arrangements that ensured this. They had to, because this arctic desert has very little cultivable land. The system under which one of the sons would become a *lâmâ* (monk) – and sometimes one of the daughters a *chomo* (nun) – was part of these arrangements. So was polyandry.

Between 1951 and 1961, the population of Leh (then a tehsil of Ladâkh district) grew by a mere 9.2 percent, from 39,947 to 43,585. Its population thus grow at a rate that was less than *half* the national average. In 1971, the population was 51,891, i.e. an increase of 19%: dangerously close to, but still less than, the all - India growth rate. Modernisation and the breakdown of the old social arrangements had clearly swung into action.

The 1981 figures were even more dramatic: the population was 68,380, which meant an increase of 31.7% over the previous decade or almost *one and a half times* the national average. In 1991, it jumped further to an estimated 92,000—a leap of 34.6%, a little less than twice the national average and way ahead even of the increase in neighbouring Muslim-majority Kargil. By 2001, it had increased to 1,07,777, an increase of 17.14%. (Or between 1981 and 2001 the population had increased by 57.61%.)

By way of comparison, in the decade between 1971 and 1981, India's population grew at 2.2% a year. The nation's growth rate fell to 2.1% a year in the decade between 1981 and 1991. There are indications that in the 1990s it fell further to 1.9% a year.

The situation in Leh is not alarming. Ladâkh is still the country's—perhaps the world's—most sparsely populated region. However, in recent decades, because of social change Leh is being transformed, and more rapidly than elsewhere. Leh has perhaps just 4,393 hectares of 'cultivable vast land' where grains, vegetables or trees have been planted. It has another 25,274 hectares of 'barren cultivable land'.

Improved technology can accommodate growing populations. Since the 1970s Leh has been going through an economic boom, what with all the money provided in by the government (the highest in per capita terms for any region in India), tourism and the army. Affluence has percolated to the bottom. You have to pay unskilled labour much higher than the wage laid down by the Government of India for the nation. (In 1982, the minimum wage in Ladâkh was three times the national average.) The labour that constructs roads in Ladâkh comes from Central India. The Ladâkhis are, thanks to this boom, too well off to work as unskilled labour.

However, the wisdom received through the ages in Ladâkh has been that the land can only support so many people and no more.

(Population figures for the undivided Ladâkh district: In 1951, the population was 82,340; in 1961, it was 88,651. This meant that Kargil- which is perhaps 88% Muslim- grew at a mere 6.3% in a decade when Leh's population increased by 9.2%. In 1971, the population of Ladâkh as a whole was 105,201.)

***Kargil* district:** Compared to Leh, Kargil is overcrowded. It has all of nine people per square kilometre.

In 1951, the population of the areas now in Kargil district was 42,393. By 1961, this increased by 6.3% to 45,066. This growth was lower than that in Leh by a third, and way below the all India average. However, during the next decade there was an 18.3% jump to a 1971 population of 53,310.

Clearly something, some custom or control, which had kept the population in check over the centuries, had suddenly disappeared. However, the growth rate was still well below the national average, and marginally less than that in Leh. In 1981, the population grew to 65,992: this time there was an even steeper increase of 23.8%. Now arid Kargil's growth was dangerously close to India's shameful average, but way below Leh's 31.7%.

It is *estimated* that in 1991 Kargil's population was 81,067, an increase of 22.84% in a decade, close to the national level, much below Leh's 34.6%, but still too high by any standards, especially Ladâkh's own tradition. By 2001, Kargil's population had swelled to 1,14,821—an alarming 41.63% increase. (All right, the 1991 figure is only an estimate. So the increase in 1991 might have been higher than 22.84% and therefore the increase in 2001, was less than 41.63%. Still, between 1981 and 2001, the increase was an extremely worrisome 73.99%.)

Urbanisation

One significant change that has taken place is that the rural: urban ratio suddenly changed in the 1971 and 1981 censuses. Let's leave the 1911 and 1921 censuses, because all over India they showed atypical results. Between 1931 and 1961, just under 96% of all Ladâkhis were rural and the ratio 22:1. In 1971, the figures changed to 92% and 12:1. By 1981, the urban population had risen to 9.11% of the total and the ratio had fallen to 10:1, which was less than half the traditional figure.

Permanently Single

Almost half of all Ladâkhis (51.7% in 1981) had 'never married'. Or so the census revealed. The figure is higher in predominantly Buddhist Leh (53.38%), understandable because of the system of monks and nuns. However, even in mostly Muslim Kargil the percentage is as high as 48.86%, which really needs to be investigated.

And investigate I did, though with a small sample. I studied Ladâkh as a whole, and used 1981 figures. Firstly, the census department seems to have included children in these obviously ridiculous figures. Happily, none of the children in the 0-9 age group was married. Between 10 and 14 years about 0.76% of the boys and around 0.88% of the girls were. Since the figures indicated that it was not unusual for Ladâkhis to marry even in their late thirties, I took two samples—the 40-44 age group and those between 45 and 49 years old. In the first group 9.7% of the men and 6.24% of the women had 'never married'. The figures for the second group were 10.24% and 5.6% respectively. Now, that is closer to the truth than saying that more than half of all Ladâkhis had never married.

In both districts the proportion of permanently single men is slightly higher than of similarly placed women. The reason is obvious: in both districts, as in all of India except Kerala and except among the Christians, men outnumber women. Again, as the South Asian trend has led us to expect, the position is bad in Buddhist-majority Leh (870 women for every 1000 men) but in Muslim-majority Kargil it is worse (853: 1000).

Divorce

Divorce is low but it exists. Interestingly, in Buddhist-majority Leh 0.69%

of the population (which includes, I am convinced, children of age five) is divorced or separated. In Muslim-majority Kargil the figure is *lower*, even if marginally (0.63%). Among the Buddhists divorce used to be (and in the rural areas, unofficially, still is) granted by a council of village elders (and officially by the civil courts). Among the Muslims of Zâñskâr there are some cases of 'trial marriage'. If the marriage doesn't work out, the child born during the 'trial' will be assumed to be the child of whoever its mother finally marries. Divorce among Muslims follows the same procedures as elsewhere in India.

However, in Zâñskâr even women (Muslim) can divorce their husbands under the *khola* system. (Islam allows women to *seek* a divorce, called khola, for one of a few specified reasons such as adultery by the husband or his impotence. In Zâñskâr Muslim women divorce their husbands under customary law much in the same manner as Muslim men do elsewhere in South Asia.)

Linguistic groups

Some 56% of the people of Ladâkh speak Ladâkhi, including the Sham, Leh and Rong dialects, and 37% speak Balti, which isn't all that different, and is spoken in most of Kargil. ('Dragon', for instance, is druk in Leh, Bruk in Kargil and duk in Zâñskâr.) Another 4% speak Tibetan and 'Buddhi' (Bodhi?) and 1% Brokpâ and Kashmîri.

Low death rate

Leh has one of the lowest death rates in the country—1.5 for every 1,000 persons, vs. a national average of 6.1 per 1000, both in the year 2001. (*Kashmîr Times,* 11 July 2004.)

24

Sports, Pastimes and Festivity

Archery

Archery is a living tradition in all of Ladâkh. It is taken quite seriously in the relatively sombre Kargil. Contests are held in the villages of Kargil when the snow begins to melt in early spring.

In Leh, writes Janet Rizvi, 'archery festivals seem to be little more than excuses for a summer party' with dancing and *chhang* (the local beer). Mrs. Rizvi adds that 'as with dance, a strict etiquette prevails. Each competing teams must be captained by someone from an aristocratic family, preferably the senior member present.' Targets are really a heap of mud not more than two or three feet high, placed at ground level. At least in Leh and Zâñskâr there's a lot of ribaldry attached. For instance, if an archer's arrow hits a particular spot on the target he'll be appreciatively ribbed by his friends that he will get a virgin as girlfriend.

Only particular families make the Scythian bow. The central shaft is made of mulberry wood. Slivers from the horns of the ibex goat are pasted on this shaft. This gives them great tensile strength. The craftsmen of Trespon village in Kargil sell these bows to almost all of Ladâkh.

Related festivities: On the last day of the tournament a sheep or a goat is slaughtered and chopped into pieces. Its various parts are placed at the same level as the target. If an archer hits one of these pieces he gets to keep that portion and also scores a few points.

There is a mock battle of the sexes in the finale. It consists of hitting a melong, which is made of brass. Before glass reached Ladâkh the melong was used as a mirror. Therefore, it is supposed to represent the fairer sex. The first challenge for the archers is to secretly persuade a newly married bride to give them her melong. Women in the audience feign disappointment if one of their ranks betrays them thus to the men.

The melong is then placed on the target. If the archers manage to hit, indeed smash, the melong, it is considered a victory for the men. Therefore, when archers aim at the target the women kick up a ruckus to distract them, so that their arrows miss the melong. If an archer hits the melong, he has to slaughter a sheep or goat and distribute its parts (or money, in lieu) among the other archers. This is a kind of prize-in-reverse. Instead of receiving a prize, the best archer celebrates his triumph by treating his colleagues.

When the players and audience leave the stadium, some of them shoot a few arrows in the direction of the edge of the village. They cry out, 'The arrows have gone to the land of the arrows' and 'The feathers have gone to the land of the feathers.' They also pray for the well being of everyone.

In some areas such as Shakar-Chiktan, archery is an excuse for several days of feasting. Groups, each consisting of three archers, organise and pay for these feasts. Villages elsewhere frown on feasting during the tournament. These include Sot-Pashkum, Suru-Karchey and Mulbek-Wakha. These villages have a feast at the end of the tournament.

In much of Leh district colourful tents are put up at the 'stadium' by the youths of the village. Archers who hit certain parts of the target are garlanded with white scarves made of silk (khataks). They also have to dance at the 'stadium' between rounds of archery. The local elders and notables are invited and given seats of honour.

In most parts of Ladâkh, there is feasting after the tournament is over. Everyone participates in these feasts, regardless of class or religion. Apart from dancing, short plays are staged on such occasions.

During the 20th century, song and dance gradually diappeared from the Shia Muslim areas and got replaced by devotional chants.

Hunting

Hunting in art and history: Rock carvings found all over Ladâkh indicate an almost obsession with hunting. Most of them show hunters with bows and arrows chasing an ibex or two. Therefore, when historians say that the Ladâkhis have been hunters since pre-historic times, they are stating more than just the obvious. (There is an entire chapter on 'Rock engravings...' in this book. For details of the villages where these ancient and mediæval engravings can be found please use the index.)

The code of the hunter: The ancients hunted with enormous politically-correct self-restraint. They followed three basic rules: i) Animals were to be hunted strictly on a need-to-kill basis, and not for pleasure or sport. ii) Animals of certain species were not to be killed at all. (To this day the Buddhists consider it a sin to kill or eat fish. Most Ladâkhis do not kill marmots either.) iii) Young ibexes were not to be killed either.

Each tribe had its own hunting-grounds. It was against the rules to hunt in another tribe's beat. Some wealthy families had private hunting grounds till as recently as the 19th century.

Methods: Some early hunters would trap their prey with nets. Tourists with an interest in pre-historic archæology might like to visit the Mangshûn hunting grounds of Purîg (Kargil), where evidence of this kind of hunting is available.

Later, bows and arrows appeared. Falcons and hunting dogs were used, especially to pin down the ibex. This kind of hunting has been copiusly recorded in the rock — art of Ladâkh.

Kachu Sikander Khan says that guns appeared as early as during the Mughal-era (the 17th century, in this case). He adds that remnants of old guns and cannon can be found at places like Chiktan Khar, Sot Khar and Khar Purchey. Rifles were the last in this succession of hunting-weapons. However, soon after their appearance also came various bans and restrictions on hunting.

The hunt: All able-bodied men from a group of villages would together surround the grounds where the prey was. They would raise a din. Some of them would occupy the heights and roll down boulders from there. The idea was to scare the quarry into coming out of hiding. The animal would start running helter-skelter in panic.

The hunters would then bring out their bows (and, in later times, guns) and kill the prey.

Favoured game: The other sought after game were wild sheep such as the shâpû, the ranâ and the sanyân, and birds like the chakor, the Râm chakor and the water-fowl. The king and nobles of Skardu famously liked to hunt the chakor.

Polo

Polo, which was popular throughout Kashmir and Ladâkh in mediæval times, survives as a living tradition in Ladâkh. The Drâss polo team is the best in all of Kargil, probably because Drâss has for centuries been the polo capital of Kargil. The Baltis of Chushot (a village between Stok and Stakna in Leh district) and the people of Chiktan are the other champions.

Popular in Leh and Kargil and among the Muslims and Buddhists alike, polo probably came to Ladâkh from Baltistân. One theory is that King Jamyang Namgyâl brought it to Leh in the fifteenth century. His wife was a Balti princess. The Baltis indeed are very good at polo.

However, this theory does not take into account that polo is very popular in Kargil, which is closer to Baltistân. It was the game of kings in mediæval Kashmir as well. Therefore, polo is more likely to have come from Kargil, and maybe even from Kashmir.

There are six players in a team, each player atop a horse. The game lasts an hour, with an intermission of ten minutes. Every time a team scores a goal, musicians stationed nearby break into a loud musical cheer. The two teams exchange goalposts after each goal.

Where was the game invented? The game is so old that it is difficult to say when it came to Leh and Kargil, and from where. A good guess is that it came from Baltistân, which is a part of undivided Ladâkh. It has been in Ladâkh at least since the first millennium AD.

Frederic Drew says that the game was invented in Anatolia (Rome). If he is right then the Baltis/ Dards must have gotten the game from there. What is certain is that the Aryan or Scythian Dards brought the game to Leh and Kargil.

In the Ladâkhi language (including its Balti variant), the word 'polo' means 'ball.' It is almost certain that the name of this game is of Ladâkhi origin. Therefore, there is every reason to suspect that the people of Ladâkh probably invented the game itself. Within Ladâkh there is unanimity that the Baltis were the first.

From Baltistân the game spread northwards into Central Asia, and south into Kashmir. Ali Shah Chak, the Sultan of Kashmir (1570-79) died while playing the game at Srinagar's Idgah. When he bent down to hit the ball, a sharp part of his saddle pierced his stomach. This shows how well established this game was in Kashmir by the 16th century. The Chaks were ethnic Dards. They, thus, belonged to the same stock as the people of Drâss and Dâ-Hânu. Dardistân is close to Baltistân. Many Dards have settled in Baltistân. Therefore, it is understandable that these Dardic rulers of Kashmir were fond of polo.

The folksongs of ancient Tibet have much to say about horse racing, but do not mention polo. The later folksongs of Guge (the part of Tibet that borders Ladâkh) and Leh even tell us of the general principles according to which the game is played.

Pologrounds: The game was at its peak when Leh was ruled by the gyâlpos (kings). Pologrounds, called shagharan in Ladâkhi, sprang up in many villages during that era. The most famous traditional shagharans of Ladâkh are at Chiktan, Sot and Lambtas (all in Kargil), Skardu, Chhorbat and Khapalu (in Baltistân) and Leh town and Chushot (in Leh). A British writer has described Rondu and Gilgit, especially the former, as 'polo-mad.' After 1947, illegal squatters encroached upon the shagharan of Chiktan.

Ceremonies before the game: A few hours before all major matches Mon singers would collect at a designated spot near the royal palace, if it was in a capital city. (In the villages they would gather near the house of whoever was most powerful. This would be a Kalon, a lungpo, a vazîr-goyâ or a trâng-po. These, incidentally, are the titles of Ladâkhi nobility.) The percussion and woodwind ensemble would then start playing Lhârnâ ('music for the gods'). This was the musicians' salute to the king/ village chief. It would also convey to the other people of the village that there would be a polo match later that day.

The players: Every able-bodied adult in the village who has a horse and knows how to play polo can join the team. This is possible because there are no limits on the size of the team.

'Rules': There are no rules in Ladâkhi polo. That's what endears it to the boisterous audience. There are no chukkers and if the ball drops into the audience, the spectators can throw the ball back in, and thus temporarily be part of the game. A player, too, can pick up the ball and carry it with him to the goal. But the rival team can retrieve the ball from him through all means short of murder. Ends are changed after each goal. The game is played in two parts. A part is completed when one of the teams has scored nine goals.

In the 1980s the Kargil polo team started playing against the Army's team. The Army has the finest horses, and some of the finest riders and polo players, in India. India, in turn, has sometimes been the world champion in polo. The Army plays according to international rules. The Kargilis found that too staid and boring for their liking. Therefore, the Kargilis went back to playing only with fellow Ladâkhis.

Horses—in commerce, songs and superstition: Horses are expensive everywhere, polo horses more so. The outside world invaded Ladâkh in the 1960s with automobiles and other expensive consumer goods. Before that a horse would be a household's costliest possession.

No wonder horses loom large in the songs and literature of Ladâkh. Poets would go into raptures while talking about their favourite horses. 'That horse is as strong as a lion, as swift as a shâpû [wild sheep], swims like a fish...' Each limb and muscle of the horse would be eulogised. So would his fancy saddles and bridles. (There are several songs about great riders, too: 'Fearless, with the right riding posture...')

The people of Ladâkh prefer horses with manes that are blue, black, pale yellow and 'the colour of the nightingale.' Like the Tibetans (and central Indians) they consider some horses lucky, some jinxed and others in between. They believe that you can tell from the colour of a horse's mane and according to the colour of its body whether or not it will prove lucky for its owner.

An ancient Tibetan king wrote a very well informed book about horses, their types and how to purchase a good horse. The ancient Ladâkhis lapped up this book and have used it over the centuries with great profit.

The game: The game is played in the late afternoon. The Mons are the first to reach the pologround. Their music announces to the whole village that the game is about to begin.

The ball is made of the wood of the willow.

Ree-sair: ritual trekking, mountain climbing and nature-worship

Ree-sair means 'a stroll in the hills.' A Kargili teenager described this festival, which takes place during the spring, as a picnic. I see it as 'ritual trekking,' 'ritual mountain-climbing' and 'ritual worship of nature.' The Ladâkhis probably invented this festival to make sure that their youths got to climb at least one mountain every year. The idea is also to get used to living at high altitudes, even higher than the villages people live in. This is also a means to make people aware of the beauty of the nature around them—the hills, the streams, the waterfalls, the flowers...

Ladâkh has no grass, flowers, waterfalls or streams during its dry, six-month winter. Therefore, in spring the people of Ladâkh need rituals like this and festivals like Snolâ—to savour the few blades of grass that grow in that desert, and the few streams that flow through it.

Men, women, young girls and young boys form separate groups. Each group goes up to a peak of its choice and camps in that area for several days. They are lost to the world for that period. *Ree-sair* is also designed to give people a break from the stresses of everyday life.

In most parts of Ladâkh these groups are arranged according to gender and age alone. In ancient times groups were mixed. Today co-ed groups are to be found only among the Dards of Darchiks and Garkun. Nowhere are the groups organised by religion, race or class. Thus, barriers are consciously broken down.

In the old days Mon musicians would acompany the groups. There would, thus, be singing and dancing at camps in the Buddhist areas. Shiite Muslims avoid light-hearted songs. Instead, they recite religious poetry, sing of Muslim saints and chant verses about Karbala (Iraq) and its martyrs.

Snolâ/ Minduk stanmo: The festival of flowers

Snolâ (pron. snow-laa) is the spring-festival of Ladâkh. People travel great distances, often on foot, to be with their families, friends and relatives during this festival.

Origin: This is almost certainly a Dard festival, brought to Ladâkh by the earliest Dard settlers. It used to be celebrated by all communities. Now it is mainly celebrated in Buddhist villages. Different communities celebrate it differently. In Kargil they call it Minduk Stanmo.

Kachu Sikander Khan writes that Snola resembles the Sheenu-Bozânoo spring festival of Gilgit. In Gilgit, apart from merrymaking, people use the occasion to pray for a good crop.

The day before the festival: The youths of the village, girls as well as boys, go to nearby hills to collect flowers (minduk) on sticks. They spend the night in the hills, feasting and celebrating.

Day one: The 'flower people' come down from the hills early the next morning. They sing and dance on the way. Their staffs, now laden with flowers, are called chhâk ching. There would be flowers in their hats, too. Whenever they pass through a field, they crush the crop with their shod feet. The Ladâkhis believe that crops that have been trampled upon in springtime are more bounteous.

The people of the village, and their guests, gather in the village playground (changrâh) to receive the 'flower people.' After they reach the village, the 'flower people' sing songs that celebrate the spring, while the others provide the beat.

Typically, the songs go thus, 'The festival of flowers is so exciting, ah, the festival of flowers! Flowers are a-blossom in the meadows, ah, the festival of flowers! We've just crushed the crop in the field outside my uncle's house, ah, the festival of flowers!'

Day two: The Buddhists take the flower-sticks to the temple of the local god or goddess. A goat is slaughtered to please the deity. These customs are later, Buddhist or Mon, additions to the festival.

The highlight of the second day is a fair at which there is singing, dancing and, sometimes, polo.

Strublâ

Strublâ or Stroblâ means 'festival' or even 'fair.' All festivals are called Strublâ. However, the word also refers to a particular festival, which is held in September or October, when the crops have ripened. The festivity is spread over three or four days. Strublâ is the descendant of a Dard festival of Gilgit. It was originally called Gânoni.

The first place in present Ladâkh to adopt the festival was Darchiks-Garkun. From there the custom spread to other Dard areas such as Sot and Shakar-Chiktan (in Purîg/ Kargil) and Khaltse (in Leh).

The celebration of Strublâ was at its peak during the era of the Gyâpos (Buddhist kings), i.e. till the mid-nineteenth century. The rich and the poor alike got new clothes stitched for the occasion. The people celebrated the festival with enthusiasm because they believed that it brought peace and prosperity wherever it was observed. Despite having got itself a new name in Ladâkh, the festival is still celebrated in some of the areas mentioned. Bereft of royal patronage it has lost much of the pomp described in this section.

Before the festival is formally inaugurated, a group of teenaged girls go up to the Head (or Chief Guest) of the Festival and give him some flowers. At the conclusion of the festival, people give him butter. In the days when the local king was invariably the Head of the Festival, he would, in turn, host a feast for the people after the festival was over.

The festival began with polo, as it still does. However, till the twentieth century, every evening, after the day's polo was over, one of the participating villages would—in its turn—play host and invite the men and women of the neighbouring villages. The guests would assemble at the pologround to sing and dance.

Co-ed processions would saunter at a leisurely pace between the village, the *shagran* and back. Local music would be played on drums and woodwinds. Every day the Mons would go from house to house playing the *lhârnâ*, before and after the festivity. (This custom is similar to the *dhambâlî* festival of Kashmîr's Bîjbehârâ town.) Every householder would give the Mon minstrels some money, uncooked foodstuffs or other useful gifts.

People would host feasts at their homes and groups of people would do so at the venue of the festival. They would serve snacks, rather than complete meals. This particular tradition (like the music) continues to this day. The foods served include tea, local cheese, local bread, butter and foods made of barley.

Strublâ in its entire, pristine form, like many of the pastimes mentioned in this chapter, has started disappearing from Purîg (Kargil), the population of which is almost entirely Muslim. However, it has survived to an extent in Buddhist-majority villages like Mulbék, Wâkhâ and Darchiks-Garkun.

Sham is perhaps the only part of Ladâkh where Strublâ is still celebrated substantially in its original form.

Sâkâ

Sâkâ is a festival which is celebrated when the Rabi crop is sown, normally on the 21st February. This, too, was a Dard festival that later became popular all over Ladâkh. Ethnic Tibetans (which term includes Balti Muslims as well as the Buddhists of Leh) gave it a whole new twist and soaked it in their very own style of singing and dancing.

In Purîg there is a special song that is sung mainly during the Sâkâ festival. It talks about the migration of the ancient Dards to what is now Purîg/ Kargil. It also informs us that the Dards of present day Ladâkh had migrated from that part of Dardistân which is now known as Bunji. The song also consists of questions and answers and traces the history of the Dard race right back to the creation of the world and mankind.

The song begins with the question, 'O daughter, in the beginning what was the World of Humans [i.e. Planet Earth] established on?' The worldview of the Dards and Purgîs is spelt out in these songs.

These views were modified somewhat after Islâm came to the region.

Mâni or Mamâni

This Dard festival occurs on the 21st January and marks the end of the worst part of winter. Officially it is the anniversary of the founding of the Bâniyân tribe. However, over the years all of Ladâkh has come to adopt the festival. People spend the evening feasting with family and friends.

In Shakar-Chiktan boys and girls skate and play games on ice, wearing indigenous 'skates.' That girls in a predominantly Muslim area should take part (or would, till the mid-20th century, take part) in co-ed sports is significant.

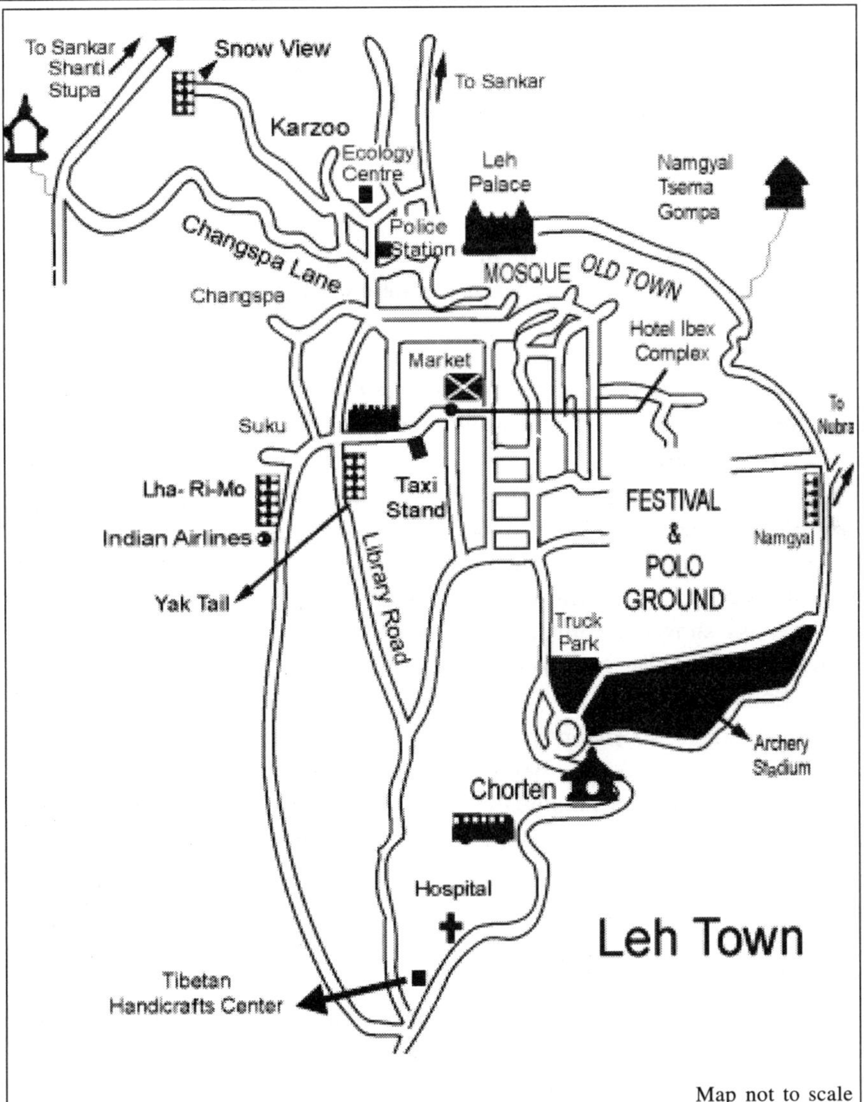

Map not to scale

25

Rock-engravings and Carvings

All over Ladakh there are boulders with ancient or mediæval figures engraved on them. You will find these in the Drâss area, in the Suru valley, in Zâñskâr, on and near the Leh-Kargil National Highway, in the Dâ-Hânu area, in south-eastern Ladakh, in Nubra and even in Baltistan and other areas under Pakistani occupation. Ladakh is a huge region, bigger than many countries. And yet the themes depicted are normally the same: ibexes, goats, hunters with bows and arows, horse-riders, deer... Even the style varies only slightly.

However, within this narrow range of themes there is some variety. The horns of goats and the necks of ibexes vary. Some regions (especially Batâlik, Dâ, etc.) have line drawings of groups of people dancing arm in arm. One engraving (at Skinbrisa) shows a man with a long sword (lance?). Another (at Nor Nis) shows a camel, which is essentially an animal unknown in Ladakh. Nor Nis also has sketches of conical huts, again unusual for flat-roofed Ladakh.

Why are there so many ibexes in Ladakhi rock engravings? AH Dani writes that the local people believe that if a male ibex is drawn on a rock, this act leads to human pregnancy. Dr Dani is a Pakistani archæologist who has worked in neighbouring Baltistan. He notes that ibex hunting is called *thuma saling* in much of this region. The hunt, too, gets refelcted in many of these rock-engravings.

Please consult the index for the precise places where such engraved rocks can be found.

How old are these engravings? Unless I have specified otherwise in a particular entry, the non- Buddhist engravings (i.e. ibexes and hunters) date to the Dard era, i.e. between pre-history and the eighth century AD. There is a possibility that the engravings at Nyurla might even be neolithic. If that is true, then there is the possibility that some of the other rock engravings, too, are as old as that. The rest could date to between the neolithic age and the early centuries of the Christian era. It is because of their antiquity that I have devoted considerable space in this book to rock engravings.

We also find Buddhist themes in rock-engravings. The oldest such engravings are of non-Tibetan origin: therefore, they must be Kashmiri or Gândhâr art. Finally, (e.g. near the Saspol bridge) there are Tibetan- Buddhist engravings.

Carving on stone is an art that survives to this day (see the entry on 'Stone work...' in chapter 27, 'Handicrafts of Ladakh').

26

The Language and Literature of Ladâkh

The language: Ladâkh does not have much of a high literature.[1] That, Kachu Sikander feels, is partly because Ladâkhi is essentially a regional language derived from the Tibetan language, with inputs from the languages of the Dards, Mongols and Mons. However, Ladâkh has two great epics[2] and a very sophisticated treasury of folksongs. Ladâkhi is an Aryo-Tibetan language, which has been influenced somewhat by the Kashmîrî and Sheena languages. In turn it has influenced the languages of Kashmir and Kishtwâr[3].

The base of the language, its sentence structure and the bulk of its vocabulary are Tibetan. Pronunciation, accent and even folksongs, on the other hand, are Indo-Aryan.

Script: The Ladâkhi-Tibetan (Bodhi) script is very close to Devanagri (the script of North India and Nepal) and Bengali. The alphabet uses a grid identical to the *varg* system of Devanagri (*k, ch, t, T* and *p*). The letters look similar to their Hindi, Bengali and Assamese counterparts.

Of all the languages available to the Ladâkhis, Tibetan alone had all the sounds used by them. Therefore, the Tibetan script was adopted. For the same reason, the Tibetan system of education became the Ladâkhi system. It suited local needs the best.

---

1. For that matter nor did most Indian languages till the 19th century (apart from the epics), even though these languages are spoken by several times as many people.
2. '*Gyâlam Késar*' and '*Norbu Zâñgpo*' (The latter has been translated into English by Parvez Diwan).
3. For instance, the people of Kishtwâr use the word 'zampa' for a particular kind of bridge. This is a Ladakhi word.

Tibetophilia: This Aryo-Tibetan fusion enabled the Dards and Mons to adopt the language, and even the cultural heritage, of the Tibetans. A cultural interchange took place and a composite culture evolved.

Every generation of the Buddhists of Ladâkh needs to learn the Tibetan language afresh in order to be able to read their common scriptures. In the process they had developed a taste for Tibetan literature, too. This continued till the 14th or 15th century, when Islam became an important religion in Ladâkh.

The influence of Islam: Purig, Baltistan and parts of Leh converted to Islam. They turned their attention from Tibet to Iran and the Arab world. Now the epics, poetry, names, customs, beliefs, folk heroes and saints of the Middle East became those of the newly Islamised areas. Happily, though, they adopted Middle Eastern heroes (say, Yusuf- Zuleikha) without giving up Tibetan ones (e.g. Gyalam Kesar, Darpon and Api-so).

Balti poets began to write *hamds* (poems in praise of God), *naats* (songs in praise of Prophet Muhammad, peace be upon him) and *sanaas*, all mostly in the Persian style. However, the language that they wrote in was Balti, a Tibetan language.

27

The Handicrafts of Ladâkh

Leh and Zâñskâr

The Ladâkhis make crafts for themselves, and not to sell in the marketplace. So, many of the handicrafts mentioned below are not easily found in shops. Leh town is different, though. It has got used to tourists. Therefore, some shops try to stock the local crafts.

On the other hand, some crafts, such as dragon carpets and thankhas, are made by Tibetan refugees specifically to sell in the market.

Baskets

Baskets made from the *chipkiang* reed are used by rural folk. This reed grows along the Indus.

Carpets, dragon

The Ladâkhis, like most South Asians, sit on the floor while dining or simply relaxing in the living room. In much of North India and Pakistan these floors are carpeted. In Ladâkh, as in Tibet, the carpets are small (around 3' x 6', just big enough for a medium sized man to lie on), made of pure wool and have brightly coloured pictures of dragons woven on them. Several such carpets are placed on the floor along the walls of the room, i.e. in a rectangle, for people to sit on. (The centre of the room is either left bare or will have an inexpensive rug, normally non-Ladâkhi.)

The Tibetan refugees of Choglamsar make the best dragon carpets in Ladâkh.

Other designs: Buddhist deities, the snow-lion, chrysanthemums and lotuses are the other figures depicted in Ladâkhi carpets. Often there are geometrical patterns on the borders.

Other kinds of floor coverings: The Tsukdan is a speciality of Chang Thâñg. Such carpets are made of the hair of yâks.

Copper and brass

Copper and brass are the metals most commonly used in Ladâkhi handicrafts. Zâñskâr possibly derives its name from these metals. The word probably means 'white copper' or brass. Therefore, fittingly, Ladâkh's best metalwork is done in Zâñskâr, in Chiling village in particular.

Objects used in worship, as well as fancy kettles and pots, are made of these two metals. Often medallions made of silver are affixed on them. Equally often, the main body of the craft might be made of copper or brass, but a few parts would be of silver. Pots in which *chhang* (beer) is served, as well as the cups that *chhang* is drunk from, bowls, ladles and teapots are among the metal utensils made in Ladâkh.

Goncha

All Ladâkhis and Tibetans, young or old, male or female, wear a double-breasted, calf-length gown throughout the year. A wide cloth belt ensures that the gown is tightly wrapped around the body. Brass buttons on the right side fasten the front flap on the fold beneath it. Traditionally the Buddhists used to wear a burnt red gown made of strips of local, home-made tweed, and the Shia Muslims of Kargil black. Since the 1980s things have been changing. The thick and rough local tweed has given way to 'finer' cloth made by mills in the Indian plains. Materials used range from worsted to synthetic fabrics. Women's gowns in fashion-conscious Leh have since come in all possible colours. Summer gowns have become lighter than the *gonchas* worn in winter. Rich women wear gowns made of velvet on formal occasions. Women's gowns sometimes have a hoop below the belt.

The position of the belt varies from region to region. It is worn above the waist in Chiktan. The people of Leh tie it around the waist. In Sham/Khaltse they wear it below the waist.

Jewellery

The perak is, of course, Ladâkh's best known ornament. This is the elaborate, gem-studded hat-cum-cape worn by Ladâkhi women. Not only are crude, uncut, precious stones affixed to the leather base, often so are beautifully designed little silver boxes. That apart Leh and Zâñskâr have little jewellery of their own. The little that there is is made and sold in the side-lanes that branch off the main market of Leh town.

Metalwork

Items made of iron might not appeal to the casual tourist, but they are much valued by Ladâkhis. The locks and keys of Leh and Kargil are masterpieces of engineering, as well as being very good to look at. Neither looks or works anything like the conventional locks of the rest of India.

Instead, the keys have holes and slots that open different levers. Together the lock and key are called *kulik.*

Iron stoves, too, can be very elegant, with artistic designs. Blacksmiths are called *gaaraa*s in Ladâkhi. They also make conch-bangles and tools for agriculture.

Papiér Mâchè

The Ladâkhis use papiér mâchè masks during religious celebrations at *gompas* (monasteries). These masks have the faces of demons as well as benign deities, and are used to portray particular characters in the dance-dramas performed at monastic festivals. The masks are made of mashed paper and come in bright colours. However, in terms of style and artistry, they are nothing like the delicately decorated, understated papiér mâchè of Kashmir.

Pappu shoes

(Also spelt and pronounced 'pabbu.') Local shoes are woven from a fibre and are not made of leather. They wear hard and offer protection from Ladâkh's extreme cold and the snows of Zâñskâr. Kalpana Manglik points out that they are 'made out of hessian cloth, used wool felt, coarse hair of the yâk and goat, woollen tweed and leather for the sole.' Normally these shoes are made by members of the family for their own use and that of other members. They are normally not sold in shops.

Perâk

Pron. peraak. This is not a handicraft that you can purchase either. It is the head-dress of well to do women. The base is made of a tough, thick, long strip of leather dyed blue, wide and long enough to cover the hair, including the long plait. There are flaps to protect the ears from the cold. Over the generations, one by one, precious stones and silver jewellery are affixed on this blue base. Some gold, too, is used.

Peraks are, thus, not made in a week or a month. Each perak continues to grow over the decades—indeed, centuries, if any space is left on the leather base for even more gems.

Women wear them on festive occasions. By the time most women get to inherit their mother/ grandmother's peraak they would be middle aged or older. In rich families even young women have peraaks all to themselves. The average peraak costs Rs.1,00,000 (at 2004 prices, when turquoise prices were lower than in preceding years).

To untrained eyes all peraaks look similar. However, they change with the region. For instance, in Mulbek (Kargil) they have a small pill- box hat at the top. Most peraaks are long strips. However, some are shorter. Some have caps affixed atop the head. In other peraaks the cap is above the back of the head. Yet others have no cap at all. Some peraaks have cobra hoods. Others have wing-like flaps behind the ears.

Male head-dresses, too, vary from region to region. In fact, throughout the Ladâkh-Balawaristan region you can easily tell where a man is from by his hat.

Pottery

Earthenware made in Ladâkh includes bowls, braziers, jugs, kettles and the *zoma* (the vessel in which *chhang* is stored). Water and curds are stored in clay pots. Some people still cook food in earthen pots. Likir is one village where pottery is made.

Stone-work and sculpture

Everywhere that you travel in the Buddhist parts of Ladâkh (Leh, Zâñskâr and some other villages of east Kargil) you will find *maaney* walls. These are made up of slabs of stone on which the words 'Om maaney Padmey hum' have been carved, in intaglio, in elegant Bodhi letters. Such elegant calligraphy-on-stone is normally done on order. At least one calligrapher is normally attached to every major gompa, especially to gompas near villages with a large Buddhist population.

Lâmâ Stag tsang ras chen is said to have invented the mâné (maaney) wall. At the very least he brought this concept to Ladâkh. Stag tsang ras chen was one of the most eminent monks and authors of his time.[1] King Señggé Namgyâl (16th/17th century) had invited him to Ladâkh, presumably from Tibet. Francke wrote in 1907 that he had not seen a single mâné wall that dated to before Señggé's time.

Precious stones, turquoise in particular, are needed for the *perak* head-dress. They are also carved into cups and curios.

Thukmus, a village near Siksa in Nubra, specialises in making chhang pots, frying pans, griddles and lamps out of stone. As the Dastakari Haat Samiti points out, 'Cooking at extremely high altitudes is a lengthy process.' For instance, *rajma,* the red bean so popular in Jammu, takes almost two and a half hours to cook in a pressure cooker in Zâñskâr, and much longer in a normal pot. (In Jammu, on the other hand, it takes just around thirty minutes in a pressure cooker.) In at least one case in the 1970s, during the long process of cooking the pressure inside the cooker became so intense that its lid blew off and sliced away the head of the person for whom the food was being cooked. The cooking pots of Thukmus have heavy stone lids that do not fly off. These lids also exert the necessary pressure on the food to compensate for the low atmospheric pressure outside.

---

1. A famous travelogue, *A Journey to Shamba La,* is attributed to him.

Tables, low and carved

(*Choktse* or *chogtse*) Most Asians sit cross-legged on the floor during meals. When food is served in most parts of South Asia, dishes and utensils are placed on a carpet, sheet or banana leaf spread on the floor. In Ladâkh and Tibet (and parts of East Asia) dishes are placed on low wooden tables. Often there are dragons carved on the sides and top of these rectangular tables. These tables are placed on the above mentioned dragon carpets, one carpet and one table per person. During the rest of the day these brilliantly coloured tables double as desks and books and pens are placed on them. These tables are about two or two and a half feet long and about 15 inches high.

Than(g)kha

(Also spelt thankha, tangkha, tankha and tanka.) These are mostly cloth—normally silk or brocade—scrolls with Buddhist religious paintings on them. Sometimes thankhas are made of paper. The household thankha is usually a long rectangle the size of a large rock-star poster or small window. There could be wooden or brass rollers at the top and bottom, especially if the thankha is made of cloth.

You can get domestic thankhas on Delhi's Janpath and Srinagar's Boulevard. Other thankhas are big enough to cover the façade of a three-storey building. The bigger thankhas are the property of the major gompas (monasteries). The Hemis gompâ displays its famous thankha only once in twelve years.

Both kinds of thankhas have very colourful Buddhist religious pictures painted and/ or embroidered on them. Thankhas often depict tantric themes, Lord Buddha, his disciples, animals and 'the elements' (e.g. water, fire). As elsewhere in India, the colours used are extracted from minerals and plants.

Thankhas are painted (and sold) at various places in the district. Choglamsar has a major training centre for would-be artists.

Tweed

Till the 1960s, *all* families, rich as well as poor, would have a loom at home on which they would weave thick, rough tweed (*pattoo*) for the family. Each household wove its own tweed and made pappu shoes, there being no shops which (or craftsmen who) sold anything. The tweed is later dyed red.

So, every household had to be self-sufficient in everything. They had to make their own milk and butter, bricks if they wanted to add or repair a room, clothes, shoes, everything. The only things that craftsmen made for others were goods made of metal and wood. And music. Families were not expected to make their own music. These artisans belonged to the *lak-shes* (lak= hand; shes= worker) caste which, unfortunately, as in the rest of India, is placed at the bottom of society.

In places like Zâñskâr and the remoter villages of Leh, people still make their own tweed. The women spin the yarn while men weave the cloth. The middle-classes of Leh and Kargil towns have taken to purchasing cloth made by the mills of Mahârashtra and Gujarat, not just woollen cloth but also (blasphemy) synthetics.

Woodwork

The Ladâkhis also make items of furniture other than the '*Choktse* tables' mentioned above. These items are based on principles similar to the *choktse* tables. The wood is painted in bright colours, mainly yellow, red, blue and green. Sometimes patterns are carved on the wood, in relief (i.e. raised figures). Dragons and demon-faces are popular motifs.

Colourful cupboards made in this manner, often with glass panes, are a traditional item, though the panes are a 20th century addition. Larger tables and bowls, too, are made of wood. Almost all gompas, and some private residences, have traditional bookshelves, with a separate shelf for each wood-bound book. These shelves could be made to order, though their design would need to be modified if modern, Western-style books are to be kept in them.

Kargil

Jewellery

Balti women wear jewellery that is heavy and complex. Silver is predominantly used. Elsewhere in the district, especially in Suru Valley, jewellery is very cheerful, Central Asian and subtle. Materials used include agate, corals, carnelians, pearls and turquoise.

Amulets and charm boxes with intricate patterns are some of the other specialities of Kargil's jewellers. Women often make crude necklaces at home.

Shawls, pashmina

There is a government-run handicrafts centre where inexpensive pashmina shawls are made, and sold. They are not as fine as their Kashmiri (or even Basohli) counterparts. But they are also the least expensive of the three varieties.

Rugs

The Tsuk tul can also be used as a rug or blanket. Therefore, it is made of soft wool. Like gonchas (see above), which are made of strips of tweed sewn together, Tsuk tuls are made of a number of 9" strips. These strips are placed side by side, lengthways, each stitched to the next one.

Wickerwork and willow-basketry

Willow (*malchang*) is one of the few trees that grow naturally in Ladâkh. Willow baskets are inexpensive, made at several places in Ladâkh and commonly used.

28

The important gompâs of Ladâkh

A gompâ is a Buddhist monastery. Buddhist nunneries are called chomo gompâs. 'Chomo' means 'nun' and 'lâmâ' means 'monk.'

There are gompas in Leh as well as Kargil. Within Kargil they are either on the National Highway between Leh and Kargil, or in Zâñskâr,

Leh district

(All distances are from Leh town. Please allow for an error of up to +2 km. because it all depends on where you are counting from.)

Alchi: 70km. from Leh. 5km. from Saspol village.

It is generally believed that the great scholar Lotsâvâ Rinchen (b) Zâñgpo (born AD 985) founded the monastery. However, he did not introduce a monastic community here. Instead he nominated four families as the caretakers of the Chos Khor. This made a take-over by another monastery inevitable. Since the 15th century the management of the Likir monastery has been looking after Alchi as well.

This 11th century gompa is arguably the oldest extant monastery in all Ladâkh—perhaps even the region's oldest extant building of any kind.

Basgo: 39-42km. from Leh. There are three shrines at Basgo, all dedicated to the Maitreya. King Senggé Namgyâl got most of them constructed. They belong to the red hat sect. Snellgrove and Skorupski write that 'this is probably the only temple in Ladâkh to have survived with some of its murals intact from the 16th century.'

The Maitreya Buddha: The management of the Maitreya temples at Basgo claims that these temples are 'a world heritage site' and one of the '100 most endangered' sites in the world. Actually UNESCO has included the 75-foot, copper-coated Maitreya (future) Buddha in the latter category. It sits atop a cliff, 300 metres above the village. King Senggé Namgyâl got it constructed to honour the memory of his father, King Jamyang Namgyâl.

Chemray: 45km. (11,800'). The great King Senggé Namgyâl died in 1645. This monastery was built as part of the funeral rites, to confer merit on the dead king.

Gongo Kargyat: There are eight places in Nubra where naturally formed Buddhist Arhats are found. Gongo Kargyat is the collective name of these eight places.

Deskit: Lama Shesrab Zangpo of Stod founded this monastery when Dragspâ Bum Lde (1400-40) was the king of Ladâkh.

Hemis: 49km. Hemis was probably built in 1630 at the behest of King Senggé Namgyâl. It is the best known—and thus the wealthiest—gompa in Ladâkh. Its fame owes to the fact that it is the headquarters of the red-hat Drukpa sect and, for that reason, Ladâkh's biggest gompa.

Lâmâ Yûrû: (2,957m.) 127km. west of Leh. Lâmâ Yûrû is the oldest monastery still in use. It possibly became a Buddhist gompa in the 10th century AD, apparently at the behest of Lama Mahâsiddh Nâropâ.

Leh: See 'Namgyâl...' below.

Likir: 61km. to the west. The earliest that the frescoes of Likir can be dated to is the 11th century. Lama Duwang Chosje established a monastery at this spot around AD 1065.

Matho: 27km. southeast. Lama Tungpâ Dorjay built the gompa in the early 16th century. It was named Thupstan-Sharling Choskor. The then king granted the monastery a large estate in the surrounding villages.

Mangyu(r): It is believed that Lotsâvâ Rinchen Zâñgpo, the great translator, built three monasteries in the 11th century, including Mangyu. Alchi and Sumdah are the other two.

Namgyâl Tsemo Monastery, Leh : This used to one of the royal monasteries of Ladâkh. It is located in the palace complex. King Dragspâ Bum Lde built it around AD 1430.

Phyâng. 17km. to the west. The Zagâñg Snon Krâshish Chhos Rizong monastery: Around fifty monks live in this monastery, which was built in the 15th or 16th century.

Rizong: 74km. west of Leh. Rizong is the most inaccessible monastery in all Ladâkh. In its strict adherence to principles, and in its seclusion, Rizong is unique in all Ladâkh.

Sankar: 3km. This is said to be the only monastery built on flat land, in the 'plains', so to speak. (But so are Mangyu and even Alchi.) Sankar is the seat of the Yellow Hat sect and, thus, linked to Spituk.

Spituk: 9km. to the southwest. The present Spituk gompa was built in the 15th century.

Stak(h)na: 26km. from Leh or a few kilometres upstream from Thiksey. This is one of the older monasteries in Ladâkh. The Drukpa monastery itself was built around 1580 by Chosje Jamyang Palkhar, a saint.

Stok: 17km. to the south-east/ a one-hour drive from Leh. In the 1830s the Dogrâs annexed Ladâkh to the kingdom of Jammu and Kashmîr. The Ladâkhi royal family then shifted to Stok and the palace at Stok was probably built then. The Gurphuk monastery is at a short distance from the palace. It is a branch of the Spituk monastery.

Sumdo: (Roughly 65km. southwest of Leh town.) There are three temples in the complex.

Taktak: 46km. east of Leh; a few kilometres from Chemray; right above village Sâkti. This monastery is the only one in Ladâkh that belongs to Nying ma pa, the oldest Tibetan sect of monks.

Thiksey: 20km. to the south. Sherab Zâñgpo built a monastery at Stakmo. His nephew, Paldan Sherab, shifted it to Thiksey. The gompâ is said to date to the 11th century, maybe the 12th.

Nyarmâ: Close to Thiksey are the ruins of Nyarma, a monastery and seminary founded by the great 10th century scholar Rinchen (b)Zâñgpo.

Urgyan Rizong: This is a 'meditational retreat' in a little valley.

Kargil district

On or near the Leh-Kargil Highway

Mulbek(h) (3,230m.) is 45km. before and east of Kargil. It is 190km. from Leh.

Right next to the road there is a nine metre deep relief idol of the Maitreya Buddha, carved out of a rock. This is the future Buddha.

Wâkhâ (Rgyâl) has a nunnery called the Jangchup Chosling monastery, very close to the highway.

Shargol(e) is another ten kilometres ahead of Mulbek, or 35km. before Kargil. Its small but old Ge Lugs pâ Buddhist monastery has few but interesting frescoes.

There is a tiny Buddhist nunnery nearby.

Phokar (also Fokar) is 4km. ahead of the Shargol monastery. A tall hill rises from the Phokar plain. You will have to climb it to get to the Phokar Rizong/ Urgyan Dzong.

In Suru Valley

Rangdum (3,657 metres; 130km. from Kargil town, 65km. from Pânikhar, on the road to Zâñskâr.) Around forty monks live in this 18th century gompa.

In Zâñskâr sub-division

Sani: (8km. from Padam.) Emperor Kanishka (aka Kanika) had got 108 chortens constructed in the first century. One of these 'Kanika chortens' is in Sani. Two 9th or 10th century stone slabs flank the entrance to the main hall.

Padam (240km. from Kargil town) has a monastery, but it is not one of the ranking gompas of Ladâkh. There are gompas in Pipiting and Stagrimo, both near Padam.

Karshâ (4-6km. from Padam): Around 150 monks live here, not in the gompa itself, but in houses scattered all over the town. Phagspâ Sherab (Zâñskâr Lotsâvâ) founded the gompa, perhaps in the eleventh century.

Stongdey: (20km. north of Padam on the way to Zangla.) The highlight of the Marpaling monastery is its gon khong (temple of guardian deities). Marpa, the saint, founded it.

Phugtâl/ Phuktâl is a stunning monastic village built inside a huge cave. Csoma Körös, the 18th century Hungarian mystic-scholar, wrote the *Zâñskâr Chronicles* here.

Zongkhul: The Zongkhul gompa is said to have been founded by Mahâsiddh Nâropâ. This legendary 10th century monk from Kashmîr had taught at the universities of Vikramshila and Nalanda.

29

A Calendar of Buddhist Festivals

For the convenience of tourists the Department of Tourism, Jammu and Kashmir sought the services of Ladâkhi astrologers, especially Mr Thupstan Shanfan, who drew up the following schedule of festivals till the year 2009. The schedules of past years have been listed for reference.

Monastery/ Festival	**2000**	**2001**	**2002**	**2003**	**2004**
Stongde (in Zâñskâr)/ Gustor	Jan 4-5	Jan 22-23	Jan 11-12	Jan 30-31	Jan 19-20
Spituk/ Gustor	Jan 4-5	Jan 22-23	Jan 11-12	Jan 30-31	Jan 19-20
Deskit/ Dosmochey	Feb 3-4	Feb 21-22	Feb 10-11	Feb 28-Mar	1 Feb 18-19
Leh/ Dosmochey	Feb 3-4	Feb 21-22	Feb 10-11	Feb 28-Mar	1 Feb 18-19
Likir/ Dosmochey	Feb 3-4	Feb 21-22	Feb 10-11	Feb 28-Mar	1 Feb 18-19
Yarma-Gonbo/ Ltung-Shaks		not	available		
Stok/ Guru Tse Chu	Mar 14-15	Mar 4-5	Feb 21-22	Mar 12-13	Feb 29-Mar 1
Matho/Nagrang	Mar 20-21	Mar 9-10	Feb 26-27	Mar 17-18	Mar 5-6
Buddha Purnima	June 16	June 6	May 26	June 14	June 3
Hemis/ Tse Chu	July 11-12	June 30-Jul 1	June 20-21	July 9-10	June 27-28

Monastery/ Festival	**2000**	**2001**	**2002**	**2003**	**2004**
LamaYuru/ Kabgyat	July 18-19	July 7-8	June 26-27	July 15-16	July 4-5
Karshâ/Gustor	July 28-29	July 17-18	July 7-8	July 26-27	July 14-15
Phyâng/Tsedup	Aug 1-2	July 22-23	July 12-13	July 31-Aug	1 July 19-20
Korzok/Gustor	Aug 2-3	July 23-24	July 13-14	Aug 1-2	July 20-21
Dakthok/ Tse Chu	Aug 9-10	July 29-30	July 19-20	Aug 7-8	July 27-28
Sani/ Naro Nasjal	Aug 14-15	Aug 3-4	July 23-24	Aug 11-12	July 30-31
Shachukul/ Gustor	Aug 20-21	Aug 16-17	Aug 5-6	Aug 24-25	Aug 12-13
Thiksey/ Gustor	Nov 14-15	Nov 4-5	Oct 24-25	Nov 12-13	Oct31-Nov1
Chamday/ Angchok	Nov 23-24	Nov 13-14	Nov 2-3	Nov 21-22	Nov 10-11
Galdan Namchot	Dec 20	Dec 9	Dec 29	Dec 18	Dec 7
Losar	Dec 26	Dec 15	Jan 3, 2003	Dec 24	Dec 12

Monastery/ Festival	**2005**	**2006**	**2007**	**2008**	**2009**
Stongde (in Zâñskâr)/ Spituk Gustor	Jan 8-9	Jan 27-28	Jan 17-18	Jan 6-7	Jan 23-24
Deskit/ Dosmochey	Feb 6-7	Feb 26-27	Feb 15-16	Feb 4-5	Feb 22-23
Leh/ Dosmochey	Feb 6-7	Feb 26-27	Feb 15-16	Feb 4-5	Feb 22-23
Likir/ Dosmochey	Feb 6-7	Feb 26-27	Feb 15-16	Feb 4-5	Feb 22-23
Yarma-Gonbo/ Ltung-Shaks	Feb 12	Mar 3	Feb 21	Feb 10	Feb 28
Stok/ Guru Tse Chu	Feb 17-18	Mar 8-9	Feb 25-26	Feb 15-16	Mar 5-6
Matho/Nagrang	Feb 22-23	Mar 14-15	Mar 3-4	Feb 20-21	Mar 10-11
Buddha Purnima	May 23	June 11	May 31	June 18	June 6
Hemis/ Tse Chu	June 17-18	July 6-7	June 25-26	July 12-13	July 1-2
LamaYuru/ Kabgyat	June 23-24	July 12-13	July 2-3	July 20-21	July 8-9
Karshâ/Gustor	July 3-4	July 22-23	July 11-12	July 29-30	July 18-19
Phyâng/Tsedup	Aug 7-8	July 27-28	July 16-17	Aug 3-4	July 22-23
Korzok/Gustor	Aug 8-9	July 28-29	July 17-18	Aug 4-5	July 23-24
Dakthok/Tse Chu	Aug 15-16	Aug 4-5	July 24-25	Aug 11-12	July 30-31

Monastery/ Festival	**2005**	**2006**	**2007**	**2008**	**2009**
Sani/ Naro Nasjal	Aug 18-19	Aug 8-9	July 29-30	Aug 15-16	Aug 3-4
Shachukul/ Gustor	Aug 31-Sep.1	Aug 20-21	Aug 10-11	Aug 27-28	Aug 16-17
Thiksey/ Gustor	Nov 18-19	Nov 8-9	Oct 28-29	Nov 15-16	Nov 4-5
Chamday/ Angchok	Nov 29-30	Nov 18-19	Nov 7-8	Nov 25-26	Nov 13-14
Galdan Namchot	Dec 26	Dec 15	Dec 4	Dec 21	Dec 10
Losar	Jan 1,2006	Dec 21	Dec 10	Dec 28	Dec 16

30

Islâm in Leh and Zâñskâr

Muslims live in Leh town and in twenty-five other villages of Leh district.[1] Before 1947, the Muslim population was greater. In the 1950s some Muslims[2] migrated to the areas occupied by Pâkistân. In Zâñskâr the Muslims live in Padum (the 'capital') and Pipiting.

The first Muslims—and mosques

The advent of Islâm: Hussain Mansûr Hallaj of Baghdad was among the first known Muslims to have travelled through Ladakh. This was in the 10th century. Historian Abdul Ghani Sheikh[i] asserts that 'the first Muslim set foot in the area as early as in the 7th or 8th century.'

By way of proof he mentions a group of boulders near Tangchey (Tângtsé?) on which a verse from the Holy Qurân and the names of some Arabs have been engraved in Arabic. These Arabs include Nâsir ibn Sâleh Abu Mansûr, Abul Âyat and Zakâriâ ibn Qâsim. On cross checking with Central Asian records, Sheikh found that these were Arab army commanders and administrators of the 7th/8th century. That, incidentally, was the first century of Islâm, internationally.

However, it was Amîr Kabîr Mîr Syed Ali Hamadâni who first propagated Islâm in Ladâkh. This great 14th century saint spent some time in Ladâkh while travelling between Kashmîr and Kâshghar (Chinese Turkestân).

The first mosques: Amîr Kabîr Mîr Syed Ali Hamadâni built the first mosque in Ladakh. He did so in Shey, perhaps in 1381. The mosques at Tiyaqshi and Padum are among the many said to have been built by him in Leh and Zâñskâr.[3] He also got several mosques constructed in Baltistân.

---

1 The district has 112 villages in all.

2. The entire Muslim populations of Sespol, Khâltsé and Nemo, and many from Bazgo left for the occupied territory.

3. According to most historians the first Muslims went to Zâñskâr with Day-tsok (some time between 1570 and 1642). Therefore, would the Shah é Hamadân have built a mosque there in 1381-82?

Chhushat Yoqmâ has an extremely old mosque and an almost equally old Imâmbârâ (Shiite place of worship). No one knows when either was built.

The Jâmia Masjid, Leh: For some reason most histories put the construction of the first mosque in Ladakh at more than two—even three—centuries after 1381. An official publication of the state government puts the date of the first mosque as 'later' than the '15th century'. Many books seem to indicate that Leh's Jâmia Masjid, built in 1594 or 1666, was the first mosque in Leh district.

However, evidence of the Shah é Hamadân's 1381 visit to Shey is overwhelming. Equally certainly it was he who got the first mosque (perhaps, mosques) built in Leh district.

Trying to put a date on when the Jâmia Masjid of Leh town was built has been an interesting exercise for this author. A publication of the J&K Tourism Department says that 'built in 1594 by Senggé Namgyâl [as] a tribute to his Muslim mother, the Leh mosque, an exquisite work of Turko-Iranian architecture, stands majestically in the main bazar.'

This belief is based on a folksong, which tells us that Senggé had donated land for the mosque.

The grand mosque that we see today is mainly in the Indo-Islâmic style. There is a smaller and older mosque close to it.

Now we know that Prince Nawâñg Namgyâl, too, had a Muslim mother, Queen Tsering rGyâlmo. The mother and son were definitely alive in 1594. Senggé probably wasn't even born then. So Nawâñg could have got the mosque built. He was one of the sons of King Jamyâñg. But he never got to be king. Nor is there a belief in Leh that it was Nawâñg who built the mosque for his mother.

Ali Shér Khân Añchan, the Emperor of Skardu, defeated Jamyâñg around 1600, imprisoned him and ransacked and briefly ruled over Leh. Jamyâñg married Ali's daughter, Gyâl Kâtûn. Jamyâñg died around 1616. His son Senggé was a minor then. Therefore, his Muslim mother Gyâl Kâtûn ruled as the regent for a while. According to many historians, all that she got built was one room in the Bazgo palace. (However, Sheikh says that she got mosques constructed at Hunder, Leh and Bazgo.)

Obviously the minor Senggé could not have built the mosque in 1594. On the other hand Ali Sher could, and there is some weak evidence that he might have. At one stage, his name, or that of his grandson, Shâh Murâd, had been inscribed on the mosque. But why would Ali Sher, a Shia, have got a Sunni mosque built? Even Nawâñg's mother was a Shiite.

However, Jamyâñg could have built the mosque for either or both of his Muslim wives. No one says that he did. Therefore, we have to accept the theory that the Jamia Masjid was built in 1666. This followed the 1663 agreement between the Sunni Mughal Emperor Aurangzeb and Gyâlpo Deldan

Namgyâl of Leh. But then the question arises as to why the names of Ali Sher and/ or Shâh Murâd got to be written on a Sunni mosque.

Other sects: The Muslim world is not divided neatly into Shîãs and Sunnîs, as simplistic accounts would have us believe. As I have shown in the volume on Kashmîr, there are sects that have tried to bridge this divide. The Nûr Bakhshîs are one such sect. (There is a major Nûr Bakhshî population in Turtuk which, since 1971, has been on the Indian side of the Line of Control in Leh district. For the almost two and a half decades before that it had been under Pâkistâni occupation.)

The Kelumcheh, a clan from Purîg (Kargil), which went over to Baltistân around 1730, were neither Shia nor Sunni. Like the Shîãs they did not accept the first three Righteous Caliphs of Islâm. However, they gave an extremely high place to Hazrat Abu Bâkr's daughter, Âyéshâ, and Hazrat Usmân's daughter, Hafzâ. (Both noble ladies were the wives of Hazrat Muhammad, peace be upon him, the prophet of Islâm.)

Apparently, there was a Muslim saint in Kashmîr who put his interpretation of Islâm down in a book. He probably migrated to Baltistân in the late seventeenth century. The Kelumcheh follow his principles.

Later mosques: In the 19th century, an Imâmiâ (Shiite) mosque was built in Leh.

Conversion and Migration

Conversions: The defeated Deldan, and his son, went through the motions of converting to Islâm. They went back to Buddhism immediately thereafter. No other conversions from Buddhism to Islâm took place in that era, certainly not in significant numbers. And yet almost 16% of the population of Leh (and 4.76% of Zâñskâr) is Muslim. How come?

Migrations: Since mediæval times Ladakh had extensive trading links with the neighbouring Muslim-majority Yârqañd. This came to an end in 1949. Over the centuries, some Yârqañdi traders settled in Leh and married local Buddhist women. Their descendants form a community that is now called Argon. Most Argons are Sunnis and follow the Hanafiâ school.

Muslims from Yârqañd (and Tibet) continued to trickle into Leh (and Kashmir) even after 1949, like their Tibetan Buddhist counterparts. The head of one such Muslim family reached Leh through Darjeeling (where he married a Tibetan Buddhist). Another Yârqañdi family, including the women and children, did the difficult journey over the Kârâkorams on foot and horseback. Muslim or Buddhist, post-1949 immigrants have been very few.

Till the late 1970s there were almost two dozen Yârqañdi families in Leh. Many went over to Kashmir and settled there. One such family migrated to Kargil instead. Then the Government of Turkey invited all ethnic Turkestanis to return to Turkey. Almost all Yârqañdis living in Kashmir accepted the offer.

By the 21st century there were just two Yârqañdi families left in Leh.

However, the Argons as a whole make up only around a third of the Muslims of Leh district. The rest are Shia or, as in Turtuk, Nûr Bakhshî.

In 'A history of Leh' we saw how the pashmînâ trade of Ladâkh was controlled by Kashmîrî Muslims. This was commented upon by visiting Europeans as early as in 1715. That tells us why there is a small Kashmîrî population, dependent on the wool trade, in Leh district.

Today the Dogrâ contingent of the Sikh army that conquered Gilgit-Ladâkh for the Punjâb (and, thus, India) is sought to be painted as a Hiñdu (all right, Hiñdu-Sikh) force. However, as I have pointed out in 'A history of Balâwaristân,' it had a very substantial number of Muslim officers and soldiers. Some of them settled in Ladâkh.

Each of the Muslim queens mentioned earlier brought a small retinue of maids and musicians with her. These would be Muslims from her land.

A village of Balti Muslims was set up in Chushot, perhaps in the sixteenth century. Shiites from neighbouring Purig (Kargil), too, sometimes settled in Leh district: often to escape some natural calamity back home.

Migration by invitation: The Buddhist kings of Leh and Zâñskâr often invited talented Muslims to come and settle in their land. (King Ranjit Dev of Jammu would later follow their example.) Some, like the Zargars of Kashmîr, were brought in to mint coins for the Government of Ladâkh.[4]

The Persian language skills of yet others, notably the elite Khowjas of Leh, were in great demand in Ladâkh. In the 17th and 18th centuries the Lo Pchak religious and trade missions to Tibet were managed by Ladakhi Muslims. The Khowjas were often the Muslim family that controlled these missions.

King Jamyâñg Namgyal's favourite traders were a group of seven Kashmîrî Muslims. He gave them land to settle on, in and around Leh town. Each of them went on to found an important clan.

All over India, except in Sikh and Christian areas, butchers almost always are Muslims. The majority of Buddhists in Leh and Zâñskâr eat meat but do not kill animals themselves. So, Muslim butchers were requested to come to Leh.

Emigration: Over the same centuries Kashmîrî and Ladâkhi Muslims too went to Yârqañd and Tibet to trade. To this day there is a small community of two thousand Kashmîrî-Ladâkhi Muslims in Tibet.

A growing population: On the whole the population of Muslims in Leh has been rising consistently. PH Francky'[ii] wrote in the early 20th century, 'The Arghon population of Ladâkh (Leh in particular) is increasing more rapidly than the Buddhist population.'

---

4. Ladâkh has a very old tradition of its kings inviting talented Kashmîrîs to settle in Ladâkh. Rinchen bZangpo, for instance, brought a hundred artists from Kashmîr to Ladâkh in the 11th century AD. Of course, they were all Hiñdu-Buddhists.

This was at a time when Ladâkh (and the state) was supposedly ruled by Dogrâ Hiñdus.

The Argons

Most Argons are well educated. Some of them have risen to senior positions in the government and academics, though the odds are stacked against them.

Exclusion from affirmative action: In the 1980s the Government of India determined that all the people of Leh and Kargil, including the Gyâpo princes, the Lungpo nobility and the Kargil aristocracy, were tribals. All the people were tribals, except the Sunnis of Leh and Kargil. Tribals are entitled, by law, to several kinds of affirmative action, including a certain number of jobs at every level in the government.

The Argons have always distinguished themselves through hard work and high standards of honesty. They now have to redouble their efforts just to stay where they are.

The title: The Argons mainly live in and around Leh town. Till the 1980s 'Argon' was a very exalted title. Only the wealthiest Sunni Muslim businessmen, who traded goods in Lhâsa, Yârqañd and Kâshghar, were called Argons.

It's the politics of 'reservation' (affirmative action) that welded the Sunnis together. Till then they were known as Yârqañdis or Puriks (Purgis), depending on where their male ancestors had migrated from. Now that they alone had been excluded from the benefits of 'reservation,' they had a common goal, and identity. They needed a name to call themselves, and the word 'Argon' came in handy. The entire community started using a title thitherto confined to the elite.

The Shias

As in Kargil, the Shias account for the majority of Muslims in Leh district. They live in the villages where the two districts meet, as well as in Bogdang, Nubra, Pheyang, Thiksey and Chechot.

References

i Sheikh, Abdul Ghani, 'Muslims in Ladâkh and Sufi Traditions', *New Hope*, vol.4, no.1, January-February, 2003.

ii Quoted by Sheikh, op. cit., p. 36.

31

The annual cycle of life, the privations of winter

Should Ladâkh become a museum piece?

A European Union diplomat had lately returned from a memorable vacation in Ladâkh. (But then all visits to that unique land are unforgettable. No one can ever erase from the mind the rugged weeks spent in Ladâkh, even after memories of international casinos, shopping malls, luxury hotels and pleasure spots become a blur and merge into each other.)

My friend pleaded with me not to let Ladâkh be 'spoiled' by television and other mod cons, and to let it remain pure, 'Like Bhutân has done,' his wife added.

It is an old debate, at least in India. Modern tribal leaders, most of them with advanced educational degrees acquired in Delhi and other Indian metropolises, often resent being 'preserved as museum pieces.'

On the other hand, romantics like that EU diplomat (and, secretly, even I) trot out one hundred reasons — some of them extremely sophisticated —why the 'pristine' state of tribal areas like Ladâkh should be 'retained.' (In the companion volume 'Ladâkh' I have referred to my work with nomadic Gujjar cowherds, whose life expectancy and health standards, including average height, drop sharply whenever they give up their traditional ways. At Cambridge, not just at the Green Party's bland vegan lunches but also in the classroom, we would discuss studies about how 'development' had destroyed tribal societies.)

The diplomat was saying things that I have never had the courage to, outside my own thoughts. So I felt that it was my duty to take the line that many Indian tribal leaders have since the 1960s: "It is unfair to deny the people of places like Ladâkh things that the people of the plains consider good enough for themselves—roads, allopathic medicine, electricity, telephones and, yes, television. It is like the nuclear powers preaching to India.'

Over the years I have devised a formula, a method, that balances 'development' with the romantic/ Green approach to the world: Let the tribal people decide what is good for them and what is not. Outsiders have no business to either impose 'development' on Ladâkh or keep it backward in the name of pristine purity.

I believe that the Ladâkh Festival is the best example of this approach. The publicity that it generates brings in tourists, and thus money, throughout the year. However, it is also one of the reasons why the Ladâkhis have started taking greater pride in their traditional clothes, architecture, culture and frescoes.

A place where real people live

Ladâkh is a great place for an adventurous summer vacation. But it is also a place where real people spend the entire year. While this book is meant for the visitor, it is about the real Ladâkh—where people with a rich history and even richer culture live. Even in the choice of trekking routes, I have included all the tracks that the Ladâkhi people themselves travel on, not for exercise but to actually get somewhere.

I hope that this has been a cheerful, optimistic, positive book. If 'yes' then perhaps I am entitled to give you some tragic relief. Let me tell you why it is positively sinful to deprive Ladâkh of the things that we in the plains take for granted.

So let me tell you about Queen It Thoq Lhâmo[1] of the epics-and about the first year that I spent in Zâñskâr, a place that, even by Ladâkh's own very daunting standards, is extremely remote.

How snow on the passes destroys hope

It Thoq, a beautiful angel, once came down from heaven to see Planet Earth. Here she fell in love with Norbu Zâñgpo, who was the king of Tibet-Ladâkh. They got married, but not everyone was pleased. The Bad People manoeuvred to get King Norbu Zâñgpo to leave Ladâkh in late autumn.

The king crossed the passes and went to the world beyond. In that age it took two weeks of travelling on horseback or foot just to reach the outermost passes of Ladâkh. In many parts of Ladâkh, especially Zâñskâr, it takes as long even today.

A few weeks later, in November, snow began to fall on the passes. It Thoq was crushed. She knew that now her husband would not be able to return to

1. Lhâmo means 'female deity.' It is the exact equivalent of the Hiñdî-Sañskrit word 'dévî.'

Ladâkh for another seven months, because the snow on the passes would melt only in May (or June). And for those seven months not only would she be alone on Earth, she would also be at the mercy of the Bad People.

A moving—and very long—passage in the Ladâkhi epic "The Story of Norbu, the King, and It Thoq, the Angel[2]" describes the sadness that gripped the angel-queen. Of course, it is possible that I found that passage needlessly poignant.

I was posted to Zâñskâr as the head of its administration in late October. The rules require all postings to Ladâkh to be effected by June, so that the officer has time to acclimatise himself and also study the land while it is still possible to move about. Being a non-smoker and an exercise buff, I had absolutely no complaints about the lack of oxygen. (Many people who fly into Leh—instead of driving up from Kashmîr—tend to have breathing and other medical difficulties on the first day.) That I am from warm Delhi and night temperatures in Zâñskâr by then were somewhat below zero—the freezing point—was also not the issue because, as I just said, I am a fitness freak.

But reaching Zâñskâr on a 29th October brought with it problems of many other kinds. The biggest of these was leaving the place in December, when all the roads and passes were blocked by snow. My brother, Prasun, then a graduate student at the University of Wisconsin, Madison, had been saving for years to make his first trip home after he left India. We had planned to meet in Delhi in December, when my annual vacation was due. However, my senior was desperate to find a fall guy who would not resist a posting in Zâñskâr.[3] So he told me sweet lies about sending a helicopter to fetch me from there in December.

A shopless, self-sufficient economy

And then there was the issue of supplies. Not only does Ladâkh not make any consumer goods, in the 1980s Zâñskâr had no shops either.[4] That's right, like some other inaccessible parts of Ladâkh-Balâwaristân, it did not have a market economy. The remoter parts of Kashmîr, Jammu and neighbouring Himâchal Pradésh at least had a barter system. In Zâñskâr (and parts of Baltistân-Hunzâ) every family had to make everything that it needed, including tweed and shoes and bricks and houses.

As part of my iron-pumping regime I drink huge quantities of milk and eat (all right, ate) lots of animal flesh. I mean, have a heart. I was freshly out of college—and a mountain climbing guy in his early twenties needs lots of milk and meat.

---

2. Translated into English by Parvéz Dewân.
3. This was in the 1980s. Since then only two other officers of the national civil service, the IAS, have held office in Zâñskâr. I was the first IAS officer to be posted there.
4. A few shops would spring up in summer to cater to tourists.

But in Zâñskâr there was no way that I could purchase milk. Things were simply not sold. Yes, I could get milk, free of charge, from the people who came to my office for work related to the government. In most of Jammu and Kashmîr, including Gilgit-Baltistân-Hunzâ-Chitrâl, there is no private sector worth talking about. So, everyone depends on the government. Therefore, I could get all the free milk that I needed.

'No, it won't be a bribe,' I was assured. But that's the way I saw it.[5] Besides, it was extremely humiliating to have to depend on a new person every day for the day's requirements of milk.

Absolutely no vegetables grow in that desert in winter. Indeed, several kinds of summer vegetables were introduced into Leh as recently as in the 1970s, and had not then reached Zâñskâr. So, people would place the few summer vegetables that grew in their kitchen gardens out to dry ('dehydrate') on their flat rooftops. In winter they would boil ('rehydrate') the dried vegetables and then cook them as normal. (Because there was no electricity then—and only for a few hours a day now—there was no question of refrigeration. Not that any was needed in winter. Thanks to sub-zero temperatures throughout the day, that huge valley becomes one big deep freeze in winter.)

Now, on the 29th October, I could hardly start drying vegetables to last me seven and a half months. 'No problem,' my senior, the Liar, said. 'Take over your new assignment. Assume charge and go to Kargil or Srînagar to purchase winter supplies for yourself.' He assured me that I had all of November (and maybe the first week of December) before snow blocked the passes.

But I had an even more important thing to do before snow fell—I had to tour the area of which I was now the SDM or Sub-divisional Magistrate. (A good district officer should visit every village in his jurisdiction at least once a year. I was able to this in the valley of Kashmîr and in Jammu district, both of which are huge. In Basohli [Jammu] I tried to go to each village twice a year, or more.)

So, on reaching Padum, the headquarters of Zâñskâr, I dumped my bags in the incomplete (but smart, clean and spacious) house (made of mud-masonry) that was to be my official residence for the next one year. Two days later I headed off for the one part of Zâñskâr that was impossible to tour after snowfall—the Châr Nâllâh (gorge).

When I awoke on the morning of the 1st November, my fourth day in Zâñskâr, I saw nice, clean snowflakes descend to the earth. Pretty sight, I thought. I was lodged in a large, comfortable house in a village called Châ. However, soon it began to dawn on me that this was no mere snowfall. It

5. Levels of corruption in Ladâkh (again including Gilgit-Baltistân-Hunzâ-Chitrâl) are among the lowest in the sub-continent. Government officials normally don't expect bribes, and the people don't like offering any either.

was the big one, which blocked the passes and covered the roads and made them impossible to drive (or even walk) on. (For that reason the government did not allot me a jeep—making me the only officer of my rank in all of India who had to trek—or hire a pony—if I wanted to tour my area. Needless to say, there were no buses or taxis in all of Zâñskâr, leave alone privately owned vehicles. And no petrol pump either.)

There, I realised, went my plans of meeting my brother after several years. There was no saying when he would be able to save enough from his student grant to travel to India again. There, also, went my hope of purchasing dried vegetables and other supplies from Kargil or Srînagar.

My favourite uncle, then a bachelor in his forties, had finally decided to get married that winter. Now there was no way that I could attend the wedding, which we had been looking forward to for years.

Besides, I had won—through a draw of lots—the right to purchase a flat in an upmarket part of New Delhi. This had been a huge stroke of luck, because most people had to wait for a decade or more before they were allotted such a flat. I had to go to Delhi to sign a set of agreements with the public sector agency that built these flats—and this normally took at least a week. Besides, I had to raise money to pay the first two instalments, and getting a housing loan was a nightmare in India till the beginning of the 21st century.

I now saw all hopes of getting that flat vanish.[6]

Which is why I knew exactly how the angel It Thoq felt as she watched the first snowflakes of November waft down towards the passes. She was devastated—as, several centuries later, was I.

Winter festivity

Hey, cheer up! Only people who have loved ones outside Ladâkh have to go through this. For most local people winters are a time for lots of fun.

Winters are when all but a few monasteries have their colourful annual fair. Monks put on exotic masks and act out religious plays and dance-dramas. Winters are also a time for feasting. Till the 1960s and early 1970s, wealthy people would host dinners for a couple of consecutive days. If there was no rich patron around, the women would pool money together and organise a hen party, as they still do. Or young men of a particular age group would throw a 'peer group' party.

In all three cases, the guests would eat noiselessly, because the host would have paid a professional 'remembrancer'[7] to recite, in daily instalments,

6. In the event, my no-longer-young parents in Delhi bailed me out by going through the nerve-wracking process of signing the agreement. They paid the instalments from their own savings.

7. I have borrowed this term from an English-language translation of the word *hifz*. This is the Islâmic (and also Hiñdu -Buddhist) tradition of learning entire holy texts and epics by heart—memorised accurately to the last comma.

either of the two ancient epics dear to Buddhists and Muslims, Ladâkhis and Baltis, alike: "The Story of King [Gyâlam] Késar" and "The story of Norbu, the King, and It Thoq, the Angel." Most remembrancers would complete the recitation of an epic over four or five dinners.

By the time I was posted in Ladâkh—the 1980s—the tradition of remembrancers was dying out. With growing affluence it was no longer worth the while for the Mon community to memorise bulky epics, when the government paid so handsomely to join even its juniormost ranks. (Some Mons are Muslims while others are Buddhist.) Besides, in some parts of Ladâkh it was the women who did this. There were just two or three teenaged girls in the area that I was in who were keeping this tradition alive when I was there. Conservatism comes with material well-being. The people were no longer willing to let their women recite stories at dinners where men would be among the guests.

On the other hand, some housewives discover that after several years of listening to Mon storytellers, they have managed to memorise the entire text of one or both of the epics. The skills of such women are in great demand within the extended family. They recite either of the epics for the benefit of a family audience, over a series of winter dinners.

Winters are the only time of the year when tradition permits grandmothers (and others) to tell stories to the children. The superstition is that if anyone in Ladâkh recounts stories before the first major snowfall of the season—the one that blocks the passes—this act will cause a wayfarer somewhere in Ladâkh to lose his way.

There is an almost identical superstition in the plains of North India. The difference is that out there people are not allowed to tell tales before sunset—for if they do a traveller somewhere will inadvertently take the wrong road. My mother and grandmother believe that this superstition was invented so that people could work all day and get down to telling and listening to stories only after it was dark. That way they could utilise the hours of precious sunlight tilling the fields and doing useful things, and not waste them on talk.

The Ladâkhis do not want to fritter away the precious months of summer, spring and autumn. But once there's enough snow to block the passes, there's nothing to be done in the fields, again due to the snow. And, because very few villages have electricity even as in the year 2004, there's little to be done elsewhere either.

Winter privations

With no electricity anywhere in Zâñskâr, we had to read by the light of 'petromaxes'—lamps filled with kerosene. I had brought just two books with me. So I decided to ravish the little library that my predecessor had built up. While it had an Emile Zola and the *Shâhnâmâ*, a Persian classic (both of which I quickly devoured), it mostly consisted of, um, middle-brow stuff like Dale Carnegie. They would had ostracised me at Delhi's St. Stephen's had they caught me reading *How to win friends...* But I read Mr. C all the same, and with great benefit.

I was so desperate for reading material that I would have been grateful even for railway timetables. Naturally, no newspapers or magazines were published in or imported into Zâñskâr (not even in summer). And no bookshop, either. Someone had one copy of the *National Geographic.* I read it over and over again.

The reason why there's no electricity in most parts of Ladâkh is that the rivers are mostly too shallow, especially in winter, to generate hydro-electricity. While I am one of the pioneers of solar and wind energy in Zâñskâr—and one of the first in India—the problem with the sun, as someone put it, is that it doesn't come out at night when we need it the most. And storing solar and wind electricity is a major problem to this day.

The reason why winters in Ladâkh are so difficult is only in part because of the incredible cold of the region.[8]

Ladâkh is a series of valleys surrounded by some of the highest mountains in the world. Only two roads link it with the rest of India—the Srînagar road, through the dZoji Lâ pass and the Manâli road, through the Bârâ Lachâ Lâ and Rohtang passes. There are several feet of snow on both sets of passes between November-December and May-June. India does not have the wherewithal to clear this snow, I wonder if any country in the world does. Similarly, it is impossible to travel northwards to Yârqañd in winter.

Zâñskâr is cut off even from the rest of Ladâkh in winter because of snow on the Penzi Lâ.

Therefore, the Ladâkhis spend all of October in Kashmîr, Jammu and Delhi purchasing seven months' worth of petrol, kerosene, pencils, battery cells, paper, spare parts for everything, biscuits, canned food, medicines—in short, all kinds of manufactured goods, plus rice, wheat and lentils.

That entire winter all that I ate was chapatis smeared with pasteurised butter (of which supplies were fairly adequate in the government-run cooperative store, because the local people preferred homemade butter) and a huge bowl of lentils. That's what I ate for lunch and dinner, day after day, from late-October to mid-June.

I bought huge polythene bags filled with some awful tasting milk powder. The boy who cooked my food—my nono (lit. 'younger brother')—did not know how to convert it into milk. So, twice a day I would chew the required number of spoonfuls to make a kilogram of milk a day, and wash it down

8. Drâss, a village in Ladâkh—yes, the one on the highway from Kashmîr, is the world's second coldest inhabited place after Siberia. As a whole, Ladâkh is one of the coldest places in the world.

with boiled water. That was my breakfast and evening 'tea' for the entire year—a few spoons of milk powder and boiled water.

A seasonal local shop that catered to tourists had one can of curried chicken left. I promptly purchased it, as well as the six or seven bottles of jam that hadn't been sold. I also discovered two little cans of condensed milk in that shop. Its keeper was delighted to get rid of all the leftovers, and begin the new tourist season with a zero inventory. For me it was like finding a hoard of caviar—even though back home my family would have dismissed all these as junk food.

At home, as a teenager (which hadn't been very long before) I would avoid all vegetables, except perhaps peas and ladies' fingers. That's because I had a choice. In Zâñskâr, being forced to live without meat and vegetables, I was constantly wracked by visions of Christopher Columbus (or was it HMS Bounty?) and his sailors dying of scurvy, and boiling their shoes to eat the leather.

My father in Delhi panicked when he learnt about the lack of vegetables. He wrote (and I received his letter seven months later, in May) asking me to boil grass and eat it rather than risk scurvy. I was about to eat any grass that I could spot (and by May a few tufts of grass can be found near human habitations) when a local officer told me how to identify edible grass.[9]

As a sporty young man with high levels of testosterone, and with lots of time on my hands, I would naturally spend all my spare time fantasising about young ladies. And in every single romantic fantasy of mine during that year I would take those beauties to my favourite gourmet eatery in Delhi, and then gorge on delicately cooked meat.

There were no butchers' shops in Zâñskâr. So a colleague and I would try to purchase one sheep a month and share it half and half. Because there wasn't any grass around in winter, the sheep would be emaciated and would yield only around four kilos of mutton. My colleague and I would each get two kilograms, which had to last a month, or an average of less than seventy grams a day. During the entire winter we were able to purchase sheep only twice, from someone who had use for paper currency. And both these occasions were towards the end of the winter, in May and June.

That June I weighed myself as soon as I reached Srînagar (on a week's visit, to get my housing loan sanctioned). I had lost twenty-two pounds, on an already slim frame.

For the eight previous months the entire world around me had been a six-foot thick cushion of snow. During the drive from Zâñskâr to Srînagar, I got to see the first flowers and trees and leaves—and streams—since October. This was in Kargil's Suru valley, which I am strongly attached to for that reason.

9. In that desert, tufts of grass grow—for some five months a year—wherever humans and other animals have been urinating and defecating. That's a nice thought to keep in the mind while eating that grass.

At Srînagar's Lal Chowk I also saw something that I hadn't in ages—human crowds. What a treat it was for the eye. (Zâñskâr has a population density of roughly one and a half person for every square kilometre.)

But let us return to winter life in Ladâkh.

If there wasn't any electricity in Zâñskâr, there was naturally no television either, not that I watch much television when in the plains. In the days before I went to Zâñskâr I would spend an hour or two every day listening to the radio—Radio Australia, Netherlands, VOA's Now Music and the BBC. But I had taken no battery cells with me to Zâñskâr, apart from the six inside my powerful, battery-guzzling FM radio. I had to make these six cells last all of seven months. So I cut down my radio-listening very drastically. All battery cells lose their effectiveness because of the sub-zero cold. So, I would remove the batteries from the transistor radio and put them in the sun every morning, to heat and rejuvenate them.

Water was another issue. Needless to say, there was no running water even in the house of the SDM. My nono would go down to the frozen river every morning, cut some ice with a pick, crush it and stuff it into a 'gerrycan' and bring it up to my hut. There he would boil enough water for me to drink all day.

Why did we need to boil the water? After all there was no industrial waste to pollute it in those pristine mountains.

In Ladâkh all human and cattle urine freezes into icicles in winter. When it melts it necessarily flows down to the river. For that reason, at least half a dozen people died because of gastric problems that winter. (In summer, on the other hand, urine might get absorbed by the earth.)

The rest of the water in the gerrycan was for washing and cleaning. I was one of the handful of people who would wash every day and bathe once a week. I taught myself how to clean every pore with exactly one bucket of water. (I can do it with even less now. The trick is to stand absolutely straight, pour water slowly on the head and let it flow down to the feet. Keep varying the spot on the head where you pour the water. You can wet every millimetre of your body this way. Only the arms have to be washed separately.)

Sometimes when I switched on my FM radio during the day, I would hear the telephone ring—and one end of the conversation. Some lucky person in Leh town, who had access to a telephone, would be talking to his relatives in the rest of India. Naturally, there were no telephones in Zâñskâr, a region spread over five thousand square kilometres, and bigger than many city-states.

Because the roads were all blocked and there were no air services, there was no post office either. In June, when the passes opened, I found three wedding invitations lying for me in the Kargil post office. Apart from the favourite uncle, two of my dearest first cousins had got married. People commented on my absence at these weddings. They asked my parents, 'Have you had a fight with your elder son? If your son who is a student in the USA can be in Delhi, why not your older son who lives in India and is in the "all powerful" IAS?'

To this day people in the plains can't understand that there are places in Ladâkh if you enter which in November, you can't get out of till June.

If you live in India you simply cannot help reading vicious stories, planted by FLs (frustrated losers), about how privileged the Indian Administrative Service (IAS) is.

No 'gazetted' (covenanted) officer of the national police service (the IPS), the Indian Army or any national para-military force has ever been posted to Zâñskâr. Doctors, who had been given much-coveted seats in medical colleges on the Ladâkh quota, refused to serve in Zâñskâr, preferring to fly off to Libya instead. Engineers posted to Zâñskâr spent the winter in Kargil. The highest-ranking para-military force officials in Zâñskâr those days were two sub-inspectors of the Indo-Tibetan Border Force. And they were sent vegetables, fresh and canned fruit, medicines, meat-on-hoof (live sheep), newspapers, battery cells, a wireless set that received messages in Morse-code, magazines, condensed milk... You see, they did not belong to the pampered IAS.

Of course, we in the IAS are spoilt silly. After not getting to see a blade of grass for seven months, we could, in the summer, choose between eating edible grass and non-edible grass.

Ladâkh and the perfect balance

So, is this the paradise which should be spared the 'scars of development' so that we can maintain its 'purity'? Today there are telephones in Zâñskâr and, in the summer, running water in bathrooms.[10] Thank heavens for that.

I am an inveterate traveller. I love Indian Ocean lagoons like the one in Minicoy which have been left untouched by oil spills. Since my childhood I have had Gauguin-inspired dreams of idyllic islands in the Pacific where people still live as they did a thousand years ago. James Hilton made me fantasise about Shâñgri Lâs in the Himâlayas.

However, surely it isn't fair to make the local people live in hell so that we vacationers can spend a few weeks in an unspoilt paradise.

---

10. Ah, but I haven't even told you about Ladâkhi toilets. Except for luxury hotels everywhere in Ladâkh, and the homes of the well-to-do in Leh town and Kargil town, they are exactly as they have been for centuries.

    Michel Peissel, the French writer, went into raptures about the 'royal' loo at Zânglâ's mud palace. It was like other Ladâkhi loos, except that there was synthetic linoleum on the floor, instead of loose mud (to be thrown into the pit after the act). But it was such a change from what he had been seing (and smelling) that it merited a mention in his book.

    Let me not nauseate you with the details. You will see those toilets for yourself when you go to the various tourist attractions. And you will drive past them all the time.

32

Dâ-Hânu : The 'Purest' Aryans

Dâ-Hânu and the 'Aryan' Drokpâs

This is a substantial region that is partly in Leh and partly in Kargil. It lies between Hanu and Batâlik and is spread over 180 kilometres. Some Ladâkhi writers call the area 'Brok-land'. It consists of four major villages, and some hamlets. It is as scenic as you would expect of a region of Ladâkh be that is two thousand feet lower (and thus more green, less cold and less dry) than Leh or Zâñskâr. However, the tourists' main interest in Dâ-Hânu is cultural and anthropological.

The region is located in a narrow gorge of River Indus. The sun is so intense here that it is possible to grow two crops a year. Along with Nubra, Dâ-Hânu is one of the few places in Ladâkh where this can be done.

The Brokpas/ Drokpâs

(Also spelt 'Dokpa' in Leh. In Kargil the name is spelt and pronounced 'Brokpa'. In this chapter, the names of the ethnic group, Dard, sub-group, Drokpâ, and region, Dâ-Hânu, have been used interchangeably.)

Brok/ Drok/ Dok mean 'the highlands.' Pâ means 'of' (or 'the people of'). The Drokpâs, thus, are 'the people of the highland [pastures]'. The women are called Drokmos or Brokmos. These, incidentally, are the names that other Ladâkhis call the Dards of Dâ-Hânu by.

The Drokpâs almost certainly migrated here from Dardistan (POK). One of their songs talks about their migration from Gilgit (POK), led by Gil Sengge (the Lion of Gilgit). A set of eighteen songs, sung at the Bono-na festival, contains the history and value system of this tribe. Many of the songs are between sixty and ninety minutes long, each. Considering how detailed and encyclopædic they are, their length is not surprising.

According to these songs, several centuries ago the Drokpâs migrated from Gilgit to mountain pastures (called *drok*). Some scholars believe their original home was in the Bagrot valley of Gilgit. Their Lhâs (deities), too, migrated with them. For the Drokpâs dancing was something to be done only once in a while, during pauses in the real business of life- farming and hunting. The Lhâs were lotus-eaters who spent all their waking hours dancing. This began to tell on the pastures, which they (the deities) wore out by their constant dancing. To this day grass does not grow on the Mal Mal Khatu pasture at the place where the Lhâs would dance.

What is worse, the Lhâs wanted the Drokpâs to dance with them. For a while the Drokpâs went along with the Lhâs' demands. But soon this got to be a bit too much. Work began to suffer. And the Drokpâs could hardly refuse to obey the Lhâs. So they began to look for ways to get rid of their unwelcome celestial guests.

One of the Drokpâs had an idea. So, the next time that the gods and goddesses forced the Drokpâs to dance with them, the Drokpâs began to kiss them all, and kept at it. Now, the Lhâs were a bashful lot. They drew the line at being kissed by humans- en masse at that. They decided to pack up and leave. The Drokpâs cheered the Lhâs and even gave them a prolonged farewell.

Nice story. Might even be true. In any case, it has given every generation of Drokpâs an excuse to enact that last fateful dance, especially the ritual public kissing part. (Around the 1980s, the new generation of Drokpas started getting uncomfortable with outsiders' voyeuristic obsession with the mass kissing bit.)

The other songs

Not all Drokpâ songs are so dismissive of their divine guests. One of the songs describes the exodus of the Drokpas' ancestors from Gilgit to Dâ-Hânu, complete with details of the route. It expresses gratitude to the Lhâs for having conducted their ancestors safely across the mountains.

Another song is about pastoral duties. It talks about the life and duties of goat-herds, from tending the flock and feeding goats in the mountain pastures to the things that you can get from a goat i.e. milk, wool, horns and, above all, fine mutton.

A third song is about an ibex hunt. It describes in detail how the hunter scales the mountains, stalks his quarry, zeroes in on the prey and, the deities be praised, succeeds in killing the ibex. The Lhâs are thanked for their help. (See also the chapter on 'sports, pastimes and festivals.')

Racial 'purity'

The Drokpâs, who are supposed to be the purest 'Aryans' in the world, live in Dâ-Hânu. This author, like many others, believes that the Aryans are a linguistic group, not a race. Hence the quotes around the word Aryan.

Of course, racially the Drokpâs are totally different from the Mongoloid people of Leh. They number around three or four thousand. Their culture, religion and language, too, are very different from the rest of Leh.

This racial purity thing is getting diluted in Da and Hanu. The tract between these two villages is mainly in Leh district. In this region some 'Aryan' Drokpâs have intermarried with the Mongoloids.

The neighbouring tract, that between Garkun and Darchiks, is entirely in Kargil district. Drokpâs live there as well. They have guarded the 'purity' of their race more zealously there.

Inter-racial marriages: And yet, even Garkun can't claim absolute 'purity.' One of its families gave a daughter in marriage to a man from neighbouring Da (c.1960). Nothing unusual about that. Except that around 1930 his mother had come from as far away as Khardung. Thus, while the 'dilution' first came to Da, a generation later the 'dilution' travelled to Garkun. Da society had not held the mother's Khardung background against her. Nor did Garkun complain about the son being of mixed blood. Apparently, we outsiders are more concerned about 'racial purity' than at least these particular families.

Some of this 'dilution' was part of a conscious policy of the Gyâlpos (kings) of Leh. At some stage they sent three or four non-Dard families over to settle in Garkun. The Dards are Caucasoid/ Aryans, whereas the settlers were Mongoloid. This happened at some stage between the 10th and 18th centuries. While dealing with historical events in Ladâkh we should be prepared to be off the mark by a couple of centuries this way or that. Also, when we talk of people in Ladâkh the numbers are so small that the migration of four families in a span of eight hundred years is historically significant. Especially when the community that they migrated to (and married into), and which this chapter is all about, numbers just around 3000.

Theories about the Drokpâs' origin

Some Drokpâs have blond hair and blue eyes. They are tall and fair. Therefore, some scholars have suggested that the Drokpâs might be the descendants of the army of Alexander, who is (incorrectly) believed to have gone to Gilgit/ Dardistan. Others feel that the Drokpâs might be the people who, according to Ptolemy and Megasthenes, possessed ants that dug up gold.

The Dards also live in Baltistan, Gilgit and Kalash, all in the 'Northern Areas' of Pakistan Occupied Kashmir. Their traditions and customs are, but for minor variations, the same as those in Dâ-Hânu.

Religion and customs

In Leh-Kargil, the Dards settled in two broad areas, Drâss (where they are entirely Muslim) and Dâ-Hânu. The people of Dâ-Hânu are mostly Buddhist by religion. They retain a way of life and culture that is totally different from that of the Buddhists of Leh or the Muslim Dards of Drâss. Their language is similar to that of the Muslim Dards of Drâss and Gilgit (POK), though. Their Buddhism, on the other hand, is nothing like that of the Buddhists of the rest of Ladâkh. In fact many local people say that they are neither Buddhist nor Muslim.

In any case, they converted to Buddhism only around the 1820s or '30s, because of the efforts of Lâmâ Samphel of nearby Lâmâ Yûrû. Before that the Drokpâs belonged to a religion called Bon-chos and worshipped animals, nature and ancestors. They still retain many Bon-chos rituals, including the great harvest festival, Bono-na or Chopo Srubla. Their shamanism, their songs and their cosmic system, too, are Bon-chos. ('Chos' means 'religion.' 'Bon' means 'animism' and includes the worship of fire and nature.)

Islam and the Drokpâs: The Brokpas of Chuli Chan and Da Da Do have converted to Islam. However, they live outside the areas covered in this chapter. They do not practice the customs described here. However, they speak the same language and often come over to watch the festivals of their Buddhist and animist cousins. The Dards of Drâss cannot be called Drokpâ or Brokpa. However, even they sometimes participate in Bono-Na as spectators.

Eggs and dairy products are taboo: The Drokpâs abhor the cow as well as all dairy and other products obtained from it. This, as J&K Tourism's website notes, is 'most baffling for a people believed to be of Aryan descent.' On the other hand, they consider the ibex sacred and sing songs about ibex hunts. They worship the goat and consider it a symbol of fertility and prosperity.

The website adds that the goat is the Drokpâs' cult animal and is the 'preferred animal for offering as sacrifice [at the altar of Shringman Lhâmo, the Goddess of Wealth, on important occasions such as] Bono-na, held alternately in Garkun and [Da] villages, with a one-year break in between.' The sacrifice is conducted by the Lhâbdag-pa, 'who is the traditional officiant for this deity'. Indeed, the number of goats and sheep a family owns is a measure of its wealth. Many families have hundreds of each.

Regarding the cow, the website explans that it is only the Indian and Iranian Aryans who worship the cow. German Aryans, for instance, don't. E. Joldan has a better theory. Cattle are clumsy animals. The narrow and precipitous terrain of Dâ-Hânu is much too dangerous for them, for they routinely slip off and die. Besides, feeding them in winter is expensive and difficult. Goats, on the other hand, are sure-footed.

Eggs and fowls, too, are taboo. But men, being men, are bound to ignore taboos when away from the watchful eyes of women and elders. When visiting Kargil or Skardu they often eat eggs as well as dairy products. However, even they maintain the sanctity of their land. There is an auspicious Kagaaney Maaney three kilometres west of Da. The men eat up all the eggs and dairy products that they might have bought in Kargil before they reach this maaney, so that the area beyond it is undefiled by eggs, milk or butter.

The Zo (or dZo) is what is born when a cow mates with a yâk. It is the only cattle that the Drokpâs put up with, though quite unwillingly. They need this tough animal to plough their fields. As soon as ploughing is over, they drive the dZos away to the mountains above. They don't even use dZo dung as manure in their fields. (The dZo is male. The female is called Zomo or dZomo. The dZo is sterile, but the dZomo is not. In this respect they differ from that other crossbreed, the mule, both genders of which are sterile.)

Things are changing, at least in Hanu, where some families took to rearing cows in the 1980s.

Traditional dress: The easiest way to tell if someone is a Drokpâ is from the bunch of colourful flowers (increasingly made of paper or plastic) on top of that person's bonnet or hat. The said website says that the Drokpâs' dress consists of 'tight trousers made from the local coarse woollen tweed worn under a short upper tunic of the same cloth, both of which are richly decorated with geometric designs along the borders and seams. This colourful ensemble is topped off with a bonnet heavily bedecked with a variety of trinkets, beads, ribbons and rows... of needles, strings of cowry shells etc.' Most Drokpâ ornaments are beaded.

Astronomy: The Drokpâs have a rudimentary knowledge of astronomy. But they are fairly accurate at whatever little use they make of it. From the movements of the sun they can predict when the solstices and equinoxes will take place, dates that the rest of us take as a given.

Disputes: Like many other tribals (especially the Gujjars), the Drokpâs try to settle their disputes themselves, rather than in courts of law. (The same is true of most of Zâñskâr and much of rural Leh.) If neither party in a dispute can prove its case conclusively, both parties are taken to the village monastery (gompa). Both are asked to swear that they are telling the truth. Such is the fear of God that the liar rarely agrees to swear. He looks for excuses to wriggle out. The party that takes the oath wins.

The two are then kept away from each other on festive occasions, so that they don't start fighting again. A year later, by when the dispute would have been forgotten, the two are made to sit together and patch up.

Are the Drokpâs insular? In theory, yes. For centuries they tried to keep away from the other people of Leh and Kargil. And yet there is so much of Leh in their lives. In turn they have influenced the culture of Leh. Most importantly, they became Buddhists even if their practices are quite distinctive. Like other Buddhists they call their gods and goddesses Lhâ and Lhâmo, even if their main Lhâmo is entirely their own, as are several other deities. Their new year, too, is called Losar, though on a different day. They have a gompa, even if tiny and with just two or three lâmâs. They, too, have maaneys.

On the other hand, other Ladâkhi Buddhists have adopted Drokpâ customs like throwing lit torches at a designated spot during Losar celebrations. Joldan argues that perhaps 'the Ladâkhi custom[s] of making wild sheep from dough and decorating their kitchen walls with crescent and other designs, at Losar, have their origins in Brokpâ traditions. Tibetans don't do such things.' He adds that the bass drum (Dang Dang) of the Drokpâs was once part of Ladâkh's royal orchestras. The Namgyâl Tsemo in Leh has a wall painting in which musicians play on such a drum for the king. Joldan also points out that 'the fashion among [other] Ladâkhi ladies of wearing goat skin having long white hair, to cover their back comes from Brok-land [i.e. Dâ-Hânu].'

The people of Dâ-Hânu must surely have had some contacts with the Kashmiris, too. Several Drokpâ families possess elegant brass pitchers and other handicrafts of Kashmiri origin.

Language: The Drokpâs' language is very similar to Sheena, which, in turn, is much like Hindi-Urdu and, sometimes, English. ('Two' is 'du' and 'three' is 'tera/ tre.') I haven't rubbed in the Drokpâs' 'Aryanness' in this chapter thus far. Maybe it is time to do so, and remind the reader that this is their USP. Yes, their language is very Indo-Aryan. Actually, it is eerily close to Sanskrit. For instance, they call the sun 'suri' (from the Sanskrit 'surya'). Their word for 'hand' is 'hath.' However, over the years thousands of Ladâkhi words have entered their vocabulary, perhaps a result of their 19th century conversion to Buddhism.

Joldan says that some of the Drokpâs' Ladâkhification was because of pressure from a particular Ladâkhi king. He adds that while the Dards of Hanu started speaking some Ladâkhi, the women did not. 'If the idea was integration with the [other] Ladâkhis...,' he writes, 'that did not happen.'

Funerals: The Drokpâs cremate their dead on pyres, on the banks of a river. This is very Hindu, and quite different from the anaerobic cremation of other Ladâkhi Buddhists.

Flora: As mentioned, Dâ-Hânu, along with Nubra, is one of the few places in Ladâkh where two crops can be grown in a year. Farmers grow apricots and grapes to sell in Leh and Kargil. They also grow flowers, especially their beloved Skalzâñg flower. The flower that they wear in their caps is called Shoklo and often grows on its own.

Washing/ bathing: Mrs. Janet Rizvi says that 'among the most striking of [the Drokpâs'] customs is a dread, and almost complete avoidance, of washing. For ceremonial purification they burn the fragrant twigs of the pencil cedar.'

As far as washing is concerned Mrs. Rizvi has been unfair to the Drokpâs because, this is true of many others in Ladâkh as well. In fact, Mrs. Rizvi herself quotes Drew as saying, 'All [Ladâkhis] have a rooted objection to washing. I was told that there was a custom of bathing once a year...'

It is true that even elite Ladâkhis argue that there is no need for them to bathe frequently in winter because i) in winter they don't get dirty anyway, and ii) each time that you bathe a layer of your skin flows down with the water. Argument ii) above is true: but those are dead cells and get replaced immediately. The first assertion is totally incorrect. There's plenty of dust in the air even in regions like Zâñskâr, which are entirely covered with snow.

And yet this author would disagree with Drew and Rizvi. The Ladâkhis bathe quite regularly in the summer and once a month or so in winter. Even Europeans wouldn't traditionally bathe more often than that in winter. At Cambridge there were no baths in the halls of residence at the University till the 19th century. The dons argued that baths weren't needed because students were never at the University for more than eight weeks at a time.

Besides, we should show more understanding of the Ladâkhis' problems. Few parts of the world are as cold in the winter. Water is in short supply. It has to be heated with scarce wood. Even a health freak like this author would bathe only once a week (but wash twice a day) during his winter in Zâñskâr.

But I digress.

The Great Harvest Festival—Chopo Srupla

Shringman Lhâmo is the Drokpâs' Goddess of Wealth and Fertility. (Lhâ is exactly the same as the Hindu 'devata' or deity. Lhâmo in turn is the precise translation of 'Devi' or goddess.) The Lhâbdag-pâ or Lapdraks has been variously defined as 'the caretaker of the gods' and 'the traditional officiant for [the Lhâmo alone]'. Da and Garkun have one Lapdrak each.

The Drokpâs' Great Harvest Festival is called Chopo Srubla as well as Bono-na. It is held at Da and Garkun in alternate years. There is no festival in the third year[1]. In the fourth year, the three-year cycle begins all over again. The festival lasts four or five days. It is normally held in October, in the first or second week. Apart from the religious rites performed at this festival, what strikes most outsiders (including people from the rest of Ladâkh) is the ritual public kissing that takes place.

The dancing ground at Da is much bigger than the one at Garkun. Two large walnut trees, and some willows, grow over it. In both villages this is a largeish, circular patch of land in the open, and has been designated specially for this purpose. (The details given below are mainly about the festival when held at Da. The one at Garkun is almost identical.)

Warming up for the festival: At most Buddhist, and some Hindu festivals, stories taken from religious lore are acted out in the form of plays or operas. The actors as well as the audience take these plays most seriously.

1. Because, as I discovered by accident, in the third year it is held in a village in the 'Northern Areas' of occupied Kashmir.

At Basohli (Kathua district, Jammu province), for instance, actors who are supposed to play the deities lead a life of abstinence and purity for several weeks before the actual show.

In Da-Hanu, little boy is chosen to play the Lhâ. He has to be between eight and ten years old. There is a rock near Da. It has a designated section on which the boy lives for many days before the festival.

On the evening before the festival, 'warming up' exercises begin. The sweet smelling wood of the pencil cedar wood is burnt, a bass drum is played near the Da fort and a young goat is sacrificed, all to please the gods. Men gather in a room near the gompa and silently drink *chhang* as they listen to the music. (The *chhang* is sometimes served in elegant Kashmiri pitchers made of brass and designed in the Central Asian style.)

The procession: In the early afternoon of the first day, some meat from the sacrificed goats is given to each of the families assembled near the designated rock. The top people of the village, including the Lapdrak, then dance up to the rock, where the boy who plays the Lhâ (god) awaits them in 'divine clothes'. They bring him down, after which he leads a slow procession. They first go to a field, where they dance. The procession ends at the village square. After that the Lapdrak takes over.

On that and subsequent evenings, the Lapdrak sings the famous epic songs mentioned above. The men, and later the women, start dancing.

The dancing: Ladâkhi dances must surely be the slowest in the world. My theory is that they take half an hour to do a pirouette, though on occasion it's known to have been done in as few as twenty-nine minutes. No, seriously, they take forever. Their own explanation is that because oxygen is in short supply at those incredibly high altitudes they have to move very slowly. I suppose they are right. But the fact also is that before the advent of electricity they used to have so much time on their hands in winter that they had to look for things to do. (For that reason, Ladâkhi adults work all summer and don't tell their children fairy-, folk- or religious stories till after the first major snowfall.)

And yet other Ladâkhis consider the Drokpâs' dances much too slow even by their standards. Dâ-Hânu is almost two thousand feet lower than the areas around Leh town, with far more oxygen all around. Therefore, they should have been dancing faster if the altitude/ oxygen theory was the right explanation.

The other difference is that in the rest of Leh the sexes intermingle while dancing—every other dancer will, for instance, be a woman. (Most Ladâkhis, enter the dance floor in a single file. After that they generally form a wide circle. The circle goes around the dance-ground several times.) The Drokpâs, too, enter in a single file. However, the men come first and then do the women. Thirdly, most Ladâkhi dances have three sections. The Drokpâs' dances have only two. Finally, unlike other Ladâkhis, Drokpâ dancers cut an anti-clockwise circle when they go around the ground.

Mentog Stanmo— the flower dance: This joyous dance is popular in Darchiks (Dartsiks) and Garkun (both villages are in the Dâ-Hânu region). It is also the main dance of other places in Kargil and Leh, which are as far apart as Mulbek, Wâkhâ, Purîg and the Nubra valley.

Men and women hold bunches of flowers as they dance. Flowers cheer up people everywhere. They do the same here—the audience as well as the dancers.

The musicians: In most of Buddhist Ladâkh (i.e. Leh and Zâñskâr) musicians form two specific castes, the Mons and the Bedas, which are considered socially inferior. In Dâ-Hânu any talented person can perform professionally in public on festive occasions, something that doesn't happen in most of rural, feudal South Asia. (Classical music is the preserve of the Brahmins and Khans of India, and traditionally they did not perform before the masses. Folk-artistes are given the same low status among pan-Indian—the Hindus and Muslims as among the Buddhists of Ladâkh.)

E. Joldan says that the respect that is accorded to musicians is unique to the Buddhist Dards. Even the Muslims Dards of Gilgit (POK) have a separate, and socially inferior, caste of musicians, the Doms. My theory is that there's so few of them that the Buddhist Dards can't afford the luxury of having a separate caste of musicians.

But then having specialised castes of musicians has its advantages. The Mons and Bedas know as many as 350 different tunes. The music of Dâ-Hânu is quite basic in comparison.

Ritual public kissing: After it gets dark, the dancing picks up. The men are quite high by now. They start kissing their lady friends/ wives (Or they used to till recently). Joldan calls this 'mass kissing.' However, it is no orgy. The men normally kiss only their own beaux. Maybe I am making it sound a bit antiseptic. Oh, no. They all get their kicks, as in the rest of the world. They then go home for dinner, after which they come back for another round of dancing. (And yet they complain that the Lhâs were overly fond of dancing.)

Note: Educated Drokpas are embarrassed by all mention of this (mass kissing) custom. They even deny that it ever existed. This is an all India trend. Several Himalayan people will lynch you (or at least ban your book) if you remind them that their people practised polyandry till the 1990s and that some of them still do.

Other festivals

The Drokpâs have the same word for the New Year as other Buddhists—Losar. However, the date is not the same. The Drokpâs celebrate it shortly after the winter solstice. From Gilgit they brought the custom of lighting many wooden torches and collectively throwing them all at a designated place in the village. The custom was later adopted in Zâñskâr and the rest of Leh. ('Lo' means 'year'.)

The Drokpâs' calendar, like that of the Chinese, Tibetans and other Ladâkhis, follows a twelve-year cycle. Each year is named after an animal. Lo-dron is the festival of completing a twelve-year cycle. Instead of celebrating birthdays every year, people do so after every twelve years. A feast is laid out on the occasion of Lo-dron. (The Lo-dron is often celebrated on the occasion of the Great Harvest Festival, and not on the precise date of birth.)

When girls complete their first 12-year cycle (i.e. turn thirteen), they normally attain puberty. During Losar all girls who celebrate their first Lo-dron that year have to perform a group dance.

Like the baker's dozen, the Drokpâs are deliberately inexact about the completion of the sixth Lo-dron cycle, except that they err on the other side. People are deemed to have completed six Lo-drons a year in advance, i.e. when they complete 71 years. This, too, calls for a major celebration.

The ban and its partial lifting

Around 1975, some neo-Nazi German women came over to Dâ-Hânu to collect the seed of these 'pure Aryans'. At the very least the women were Aryan-supermacists. Some killjoy government official in Delhi reacted by banning the entry of foreigners to this region. Venus envy.

This author got the ban removed in 1993—Well, substantially. Tourists have since been allowed to visit Da(h) and Biama. This region begins near Khaltse and is close to Likir-Alchi-Lâmâ Yûrû. Much of it is on the banks on the Indus.

Already tourism has caused ecological damage to some of the thitherto banned (or 'restricted') places that I had got "opened up". I would request tourists to stay away from the ritual public kissing, even if invited to by a section of the people, because other sections might be annoyed by this and might lobby to get the ban imposed all over again.

Index